International Economics

Global Market Competition

5th Edition

International Economics

Global Market Competition

5th Edition

Henry Thompson

Auburn University, USA

NEW JERSEY · LONDON · SINGAPORE · BEIJING · SHANGHAI · HONG KONG · TAIPEI · CHENNAI · TOKYO

Published by

World Scientific Publishing Co. Pte. Ltd.

5 Toh Tuck Link, Singapore 596224

USA office: 27 Warren Street, Suite 401-402, Hackensack, NJ 07601

UK office: 57 Shelton Street, Covent Garden, London WC2H 9HE

Library of Congress Cataloging-in-Publication Data
Names: Thompson, Henry, 1947–   author.
Title: International economics : global market competition / Henry Thompson, Auburn University, USA.
Description: 5th edition. | New Jersy : World Scientific Publishing Co. Pte. Ltd., [2024] |
    Revised edition of the author's International economics, [2017] |
    Includes bibliographical references and index.
Identifiers: LCCN 2023057806 | ISBN 9789811279348 (hardcover) | ISBN 9789811280252 (paperback) |
    ISBN 9789811279355 (ebook)
Subjects: LCSH: International trade. | Competition, International. | Globalization.
Classification: LCC HF1379 .T49 2024
LC record available at https://lccn.loc.gov/2023057806

British Library Cataloguing-in-Publication Data
A catalogue record for this book is available from the British Library.

For any available supplementary material, please visit
https://www.worldscientific.com/worldscibooks/10.1142/13499#t=suppl

Desk Editor: Catherine Domingo Ong

Typeset by Stallion Press
Email: enquiries@stallionpress.com

Preface for Students

International economics is gaining more attention due to increasing trade, foreign investment, and migration as improved transportation and communication bring countries closer together. Firms and industries thrive or collapse through the international market competition that provides the wide array of products available for consumers.

This text develops the theory of market competition with supply and demand determining what is produced and consumed. Countries as a collection of markets have links to other countries. Competition increases economic efficiency.

Trade policy of the government redistributes income toward favored industries and labor groups. Import tariffs taxes on products cross the border to protect favored domestic industries from competition and hurt the rest of the economy. Industry and labor groups lobby paying politicians to pass protective tariffs.

Export subsidies for favored industries cost taxpayers and waste resources. Restrictive policy on international investment diminishes competition and lowers efficiency and economic growth. Immigration policy influences the labor force and future generations.

Exchange rate policy set by government central banks aims to control or influence the largest market in the world. Fixed exchange rates diminish the effects of fiscal and monetary policies and impede international trade and investment.

This text relies on diagrams to present international trade theory and open economy macroeconomics. The problems will help you absorb the theory with hints at the back of the book. The boxed examples illustrate the importance of theory. Visit my website *www.auburn.eduy~thomph1*.

Preface for Instructors

International Economics: Global Market Competition is a unique textbook:

- a one term text with transition from trade theory to open economy macro
- intermediate theory not required in the diagrammatic approach
- gains from international competition and limits of trade policy stressed
- numerous boxed examples illustrating the relevance of theory
- problems in each section solidify learning

This text develops trade theory leading into open economy macroeconomics with foreign exchange rates and the balance of payments. The theory presented in diagrams based on numerical examples backs up classroom presentation with familiar algebra. Numerous boxed examples illustrate the theory.

The text moves from neoclassical economics through general equilibrium trade theory to industrial organization. Foreign exchange rates illustrate balance of payments theory leading into open economy macroeconomics with micro foundations of neoclassical production and overlapping generations. A seamless transition builds consistently through the text.

The problems in each chapter were developed for classroom presentation. Hints for even numbered problems are in the Appendix. You will be surprised at how much your students can absorb with this text.

Students and colleagues provided numerous suggestions and comments. The staff at World Scientific Publishing has been consistently excellent. My webpage is *auburn.edu/~thomph1* and email *henry.thompson@auburn.edu*.

Contents

TRADE AND PROTECTIONISM

Markets and Comparative Advantage

Preview

This introductory chapter covers some fundamentals of international economics:

- Export and import markets in small countries
- Excess supply and demand in markets between large countries
- The balance of trade (BOT)
- Comparative advantage and trade

INTRODUCTION

The most important concept in economics is the market. Supply and demand determine the prices and quantities of goods and services in markets from the corner grocery to the global financial market. Money changes hands between buyers and sellers in market transactions. Transactions in international markets cross borders involving different currencies traded in the foreign exchange market.

International borders influence market transactions. Governments discourage imports with tariffs and encourage exports with subsidies. Governments tax exports as well except in the US where it is unconstitutional. Labor mobility is restricted across national borders. International investment is a challenge crossing borders and legal systems.

The balance of trade (BOT) reports export revenue minus import spending on merchandise. A BOT deficit means import spending is greater than export revenue, and a trade surplus the opposite. A deficit in the BOT plays into the hands of industries wanting protection from imports and politicians wanting their support.

Comparative advantage refers to the relative efficiency of a country in different products leading to trade. Competition ensures countries tend to export the products they can produce with relative efficiently. Exporting products based on comparative advantage leads to gains from trade for all countries.

A. INTERNATIONAL MARKETS

Everyone is involved every day in international trade as almost every product we buy has foreign content. Almost every job contributes to exports and uses imported products directly or indirectly. International markets are essential for everyday life.

Demand

The law of demand states that the quantity demanded of a good moves in the opposite direction to price. As examples, car dealers and oil refineries offer discounts when their inventories are too high.

Figure 1.1 includes the domestic demand D for manufactures. This demand curve represents the quantity demanded at various prices by domestic consumers. At $15 the quantity demanded is 100 units per month. Demand curves slope downward due to

- substitution effect — an increased price induces consumers to find substitutes
- income effect — an increased price lowers real income.

Some goods have readily available substitutes. If the price of Japanese cars rises with a voluntary export restraint, consumers switch to European cars. If the price of Dutch cheese rises with a tariff, consumers switch to Wisconsin cheese.

Embargoes of the Organization of Petroleum Exporting Countries (OPEC) during the 1970s tripled the price of crude oil. Consumers began to substitute away from gasoline by relocating residence closer to work. Real incomes fell as the higher relative price of gas lowered the purchasing power of income.

Demand curves slope downward due to substitution and income effects.

Various market influences shift demand curves:

- consumer tastes
- number of consumers
- price expectations
- income
- prices of related products

If tastes for a product increase, the demand curve shifts right. Consumers demand more at any price. An example is that US consumers had little taste for foreign cars or imported beer a few decades ago.

When a country opens to trade, the number of consumers for its exports increase. If Europe opens its protected agricultural industry to trade, the demand for US agricultural exports will increase.

Expected higher prices induce consumers to buy now to avoid higher prices later. With predictions that the Ukrainian wheat harvest will be poor, demand increases right away to avoid the higher price later.

Higher income raises demand for normal goods and lowers demand for inferior goods. As incomes rise in newly industrialized countries, their demand for US steak exports rises while demand for red beans falls.

Demand for a good is positively related to the price of its substitutes. In the early 1970s when the international coffee cartel restricted output, demand for tea rose. Another example is an OPEC embargo reducing the demand for large cars.

Demand curves increase shifting to the right or decrease shifting to the left due to nonprice influences.

EXAMPLE 1.1   *Growth in International Trade*

Since World War II, international trade has grown faster and more steadily than global output. Firms in the US continue becoming more involved in trade. Consumers take products from around the world for granted.

Domestic Supply

Supply curves are the marginal cost of producing output. Marginal cost slopes upward for two reasons:

- Marginal productivity of an input diminishes with more of that input
- Increasing the output bids up input prices

Diminishing marginal productivity implies that the additional output declines as the input increases. In a factory, the marginal product of additional labor declines beyond a certain point due to the limited availability of machinery.

A higher price increases the quantity supplied. Figure 1.1 includes the upward sloping domestic supply of manufactures. Supply curves shift due to:

- technology
- the number of firms
- prices of inputs
- price expectations

Improved technology allows firms to produce more output with the same inputs. More efficient jet engines lower the cost of international air travel shifting supply to the right.

An increase in the number of firms increases supply. The original personal computers were made by only a few firms, although others soon shifted supply to the right.

Lower input prices increase supply. Immigration increases the supply of agricultural goods and construction.

Price expectations shift supply. If firms expect lower prices, they sell inventory before the price falls. An OPEC agreement to restrict output decreases supply of other producers who wait for prices to rise.

Supply curves slope upward, reflecting higher marginal cost associated with higher output. Supply curves shift due to nonprice influences.

Shifts in supply and demand are different from movements along the curves. A change in price causes a change in the quantity supplied or demanded along the curves. A change in a nonprice influence shifts the curves.

EXAMPLE 1.2   *A Relatively Closed Giant*

Relative to other countries, the US is a closed giant economy. The US produces about 1/6 of the world's output. Although the US leads all countries in its share of world trade, total trade is a small share of US output. The ratio $(X + M)$/GDP of exports plus imports to output has grown to about 30% in the US. The ratio is similar for Japan but over 50% for countries in the EU. For many countries this openness index is much higher.

Markets and Market Clearing

The domestic market for manufactures is shown in Figure 1.1. The domestic price of $10 is determined where the quantity that domestic buyers are willing to consume equals the quantity domestic suppliers are willing to produce at 200.

At any other price, quantities supplied and demanded are not equal. At a price of $15, production is 300 and consumption 100. Suppliers would lower the price to keep their inventories from accumulating. At $5, consumption at 300 would be greater than production at 100 and the price is bid up.

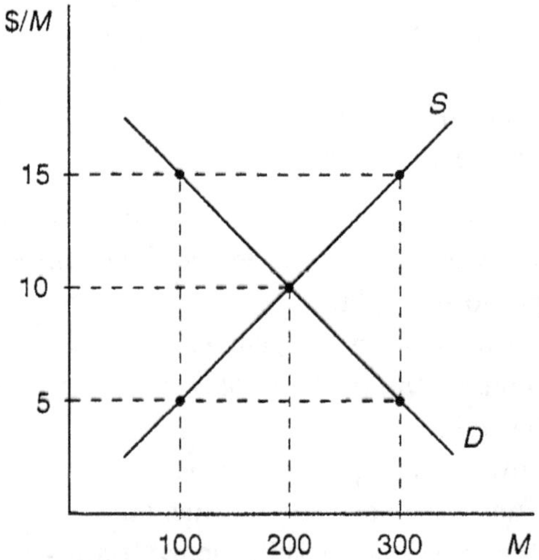

Figure 1.1
The Domestic Market for Manufactures M
Domestic supply S and demand D interact to determine the domestic equilibrium price $10 and the domestic equilibrium quantity 200. The equilibrium price equates quantity supplied and quantity demanded.

Market clearing explains why government policymakers cannot simply set prices. A politician thinking a $5 price would be popular might set a price ceiling. Buyers want 300 but suppliers produce only 100.

At the other extreme, a $15 price floor would benefit producers that would make political contributions. Firms would produce 300 but consumers would purchase 100. The government could buy the surplus as happens with agricultural support programs.

Markets clear at equilibrium prices that equate quantity demanded and supplied.

EXAMPLE 1.3   *Ports for US Exports*

Ports in California, Texas, and New York account for about 1/3 of US exports. California and Washington are located on the Pacific Rim and trade heavily with Asia. Texas and Louisiana trade heavily with Latin America. New York and Philadelphia on the Atlantic, trade with the EU. Michigan and Illinois have ports on the Great Lakes for trade with Canada.

Markets for Traded Goods

Producers and customers in different countries are involved in international markets. Figure 1.2 shows home and foreign markets for manufactures M. Asterisks indicate the foreign country. The equilibrium price in the home market is $10 and in the foreign market 250 yen.

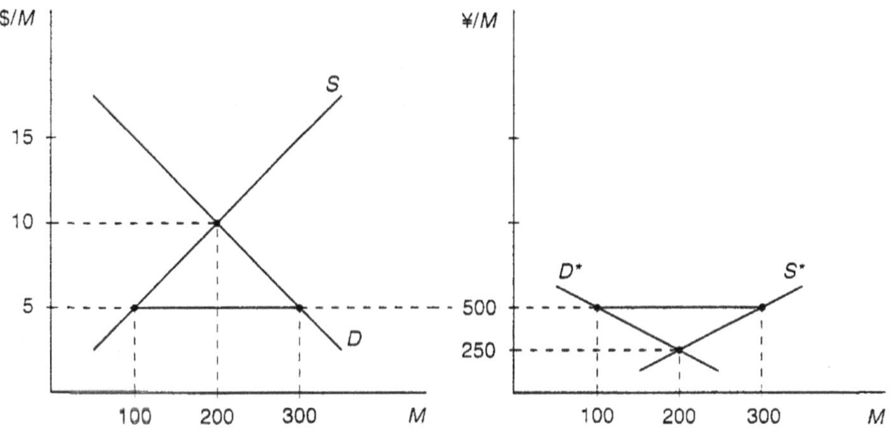

Figure 1.2
The International Market for Manufactures (M)
Free trade takes place at $5 where foreign country exports of 200 M equal home country imports.

When comparing prices, traders convert currencies. The exchange rate is the dollar prize of the yen or $/yen. In Figure 1.2, the exchange rate is $/yen = 0.01 with each yen worth 1 cent.

This international market offers an opportunity for arbitrage. Traders buy the good in the foreign country at 250 yen or $2.50 = 250 × 0.01 or less than the $10 domestic price. Arbitrage profit is the foundation of international trade.

A price of $5 clears this international market. The home country imports 200 = 300 = 100 units at a price of $5. Domestic production falls from 200 to 100. Domestic consumers enjoy the lower price and increase the quantity demanded from 200 to 300. On the foreign side, production rises from 200 to 300 with the increase in price from 250 to 500 yen. Foreign consumers suffer higher prices, cutting their consumption from 200 to 100.

International trade takes place at a price where excess demand from one country equals excess supply from the other.

International trade creates winners and losers. In an export market, firms are better off but consumers suffer due to trade. In an import market, producers suffer due to trade while consumers benefit.

International markets arise when prices vary across countries. International market prices equate excess demand with excess supply.

In practice, traders are concerned with transport costs that include costs of shipping, storage, insurance, and delivery. If each unit of M in Figure 1.2 cost $6 to transport, imported goods would cost $5 + $6 = $11 leading to no trade.

EXAMPLE 1.4   *Trade in Services*

World trade in services amounts to about a quarter of merchandise trade. The US is a major exporter of business services including engineering, construction, banking, mineral exploration, insurance, and shipping. Tourism and education are also US exports. Increasing specialization in services can be expected in the future as the US reveals its comparative advantage.

Section A Problems

A1. Draw the shift in demand for manufactures if the quantity demanded at every price in Figure 1.1 increases by 200. Find the new market equilibrium.

A2. Predict what happens to the international price and quantity traded in Figure 1.2 with improved technology in the home country.

A3. If the home wage rises, show what happens in the international market in Figure 1.2.

A4. Create a diagram such as Figure 1.2 with home exports due to differences in supply.

EXAMPLE 1.5   *Trade Index*

The openness index of export revenue X plus import spending M relative to output $(X + M)$/GDP is a gauge of the importance of trade to an economy. The top three and bottom three listed are major US trading partners. Singapore, Hong Kong, and Luxembourg are city trade centers. The US index of 30% is about equal to Mexico.

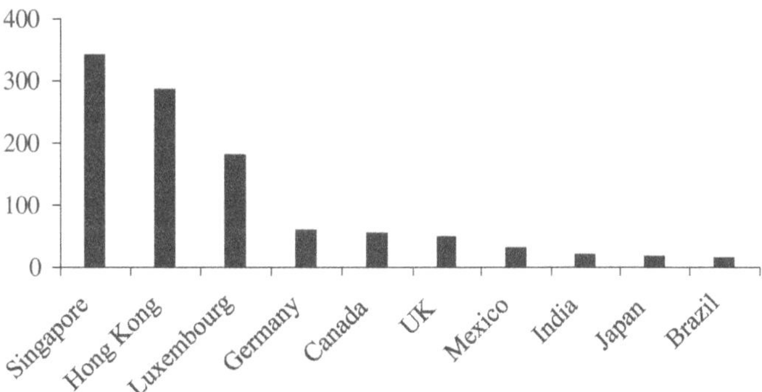

B. EXCESS SUPPLY AND DEMAND

Excess supply (*XS*) and excess demand (*XD*) simplify the analysis of international markets. The difference between quantity demanded and quantity supplied is excess demand. The difference between quantity supplied and quantity demanded is excess supply. The international market is reduced to a simpler excess supply and demand diagram.

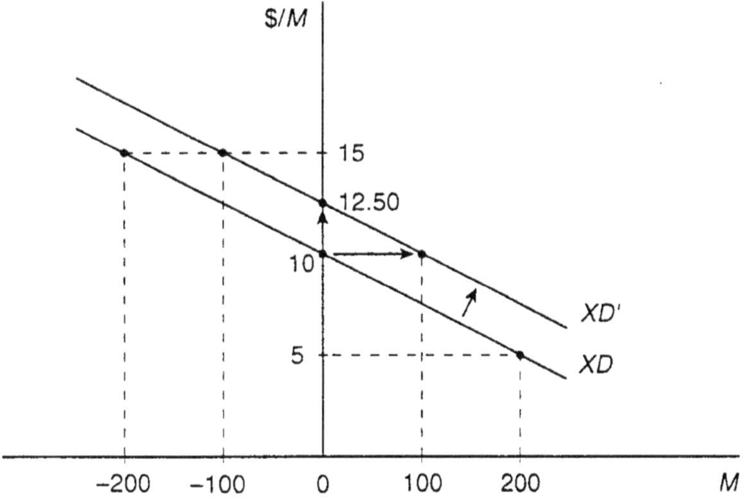

Figure 1.3
Home Excess Demand
Excess demand XD is inversely related to price. Increased demand in the home country shifts XD to the right. Decreased supply of manufactures has the same effect.

Excess Demand

The excess demand XD in Figure 1.4 is derived from the home market in Figure 1.1. At the domestic $10 equilibrium price XD is zero. At $5, XD is 200 with home firms supplying 100 and home consumers demanding 300.

A shift in supply or demand shifts the XD curve. If an increased demand or a decreased supply drives the domestic price up to $12.50, the excess demand shifts to the right.

Excess demand shows the quantity a country wants to import at every price. Excess demand shifts due to its underlying supply or demand.

EXAMPLE 1.6   *Trade between DCs, LDCs, and NICs*

Most exports come from developed countries (DCs) and most of that is exported to other DCs. Less developed countries (LDCs), accounting for about a quarter of the world exports, ship mostly to DCs. Newly industrial countries (NICs) such as India and Brazil are increasing their shares of world trade.

Excess Supply

Foreign excess supply in Figure 1.2 is derived from the foreign demand and supply curves in Figure 1.2. Foreign excess supply XS^* is zero at the foreign market price of 250 yen. At 500 yen XS^* is 200. Changes in foreign supply and demand shift foreign excess supply.

Excess supply shows the quantity a country is willing to export as a function of price. Excess supply shifts with its underlying supply or demand.

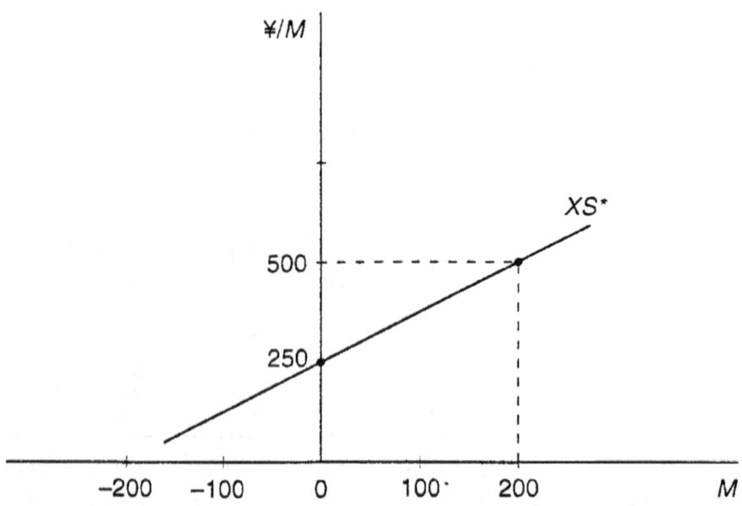

Figure 1.4
The Foreign Excess Supply of Manufactures
Excess supply XS is positively related to price. As price rises, quantity supplied by the foreign country rises and quantity demanded falls.

EXAMPLE 1.7   *Largest US Ports — Millions of Short Tons*

Houston	497
New Orleans	430
Los Angeles	138
New York	124
Mobile	53
Savannah	43

International Markets

International excess supply and demand determine the quantity traded and the international equilibrium price. Figure 1.5 shows the international price of the manufactured good at $5 where foreign excess supply is matched by home excess demand. The two large countries determine the international price.

For any price below $5, there would be an international shortage. Foreign exporters would raise the price to ration their supply. Any price above $5, would be reduced to eliminate the resulting surplus.

International markets clear at the price where excess demand from importers equals excess supply from exporters.

Transport costs can be crucial to trade. Gravel and cement are too heavy relative to the value and are not shipped very far. At the other extreme, the ratio of weight to value is low for electronic components, drugs, and jewelry, making them heavily traded.

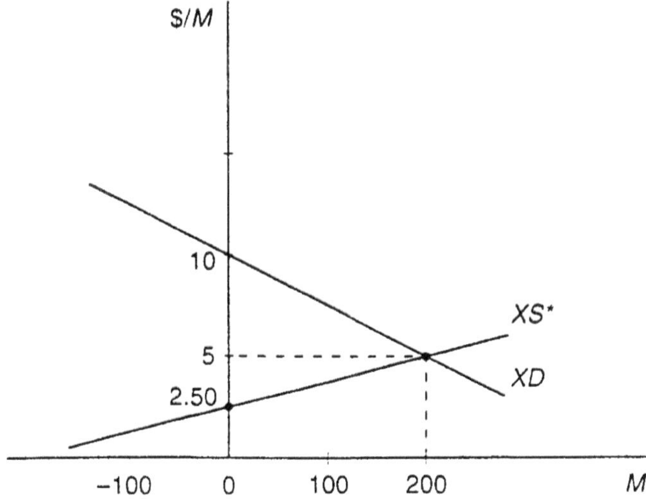

Figure 1.5
Large Economy International Market
In this international market for manufactures, the foreign country exports 200 units of *M* to the home country. The international equilibrium price of $5 equates to *XD* with excess supply *XS**.

National borders impose costs of customs procedures and paperwork. Foreign exchange transactions, cross-border insurance, and border delays raise costs. Charles Engel and John Rogers (1994) estimate the border between the US and Canadian cities effectively adds the equivalent of 2500 miles transport.

EXAMPLE 1.8   *US Agriculture Trade*

The US has a trade surplus in agriculture. The major categories in US agricultural trade are as follows:

Exports	Imports
Animal products	Animal products
Oil seeds	Fruits and vegetables
Grains	Coffee

Shifts in Excess Supply and Demand

The exchange rate influences international prices and trade levels. The exchange rate of \$/yen = 0.01 leads to the international price of \$5 and trade level of 200 in Figure 1.5. If the dollar depreciates, the foreign country supplies less at every dollar price reducing XS^*. The dollar price rises and the volume of trade falls.

Figure 1.6 shows a decrease in XS^* due to an increase in foreign demand D^* or decrease in foreign supply S^*. Turning to domestic excess demand, any shift in domestic demand D or supply S would shift XD.

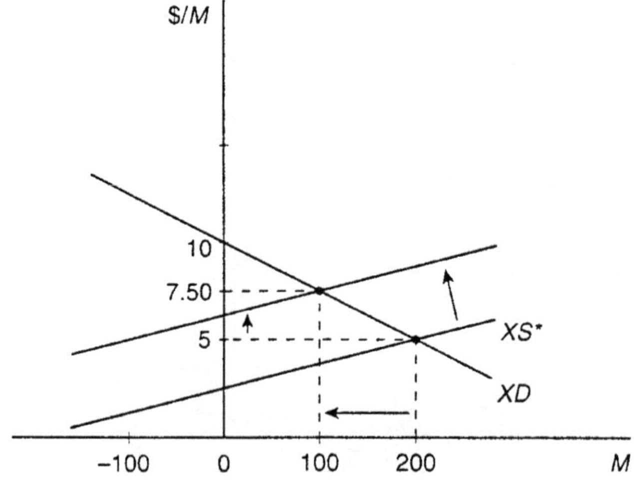

Figure 1.6
A Decrease in Foreign Excess Supply
Declining foreign excess supply could be due to higher income raising the demand D^* or higher input prices reducing the supply S^*. The result is a higher international price and lower trade level.

Anything that shifts supply or demand in a country shifts its excess supply or excess demand affecting the international price and quantity traded.

EXAMPLE 1.9   *Trade and War*

Countries that trade tend not to go to war with each other. Solomon Polachek (1997) examines the history of wars from 1800 to 1986 finding that while democracy has no effect, higher levels of trade reduce wars. Countries do not want to attack their suppliers or their customers.

Section B Problems

B1. Show what happens to the international market for manufactures in Figure 1.7 if (a) foreign income falls; (b) home tastes for imported manufactures falls; and (c) home production technology improves.

B2. Illustrate the effects on excess demand XD of a simultaneous decrease in domestic demand D and supply S. Predict what will happen to the international price and import level.

B3. Suppose Japan imports wood. Japanese supply rises when a forest matures. Show the effect on the international market for lumber assuming excess supply from North America.

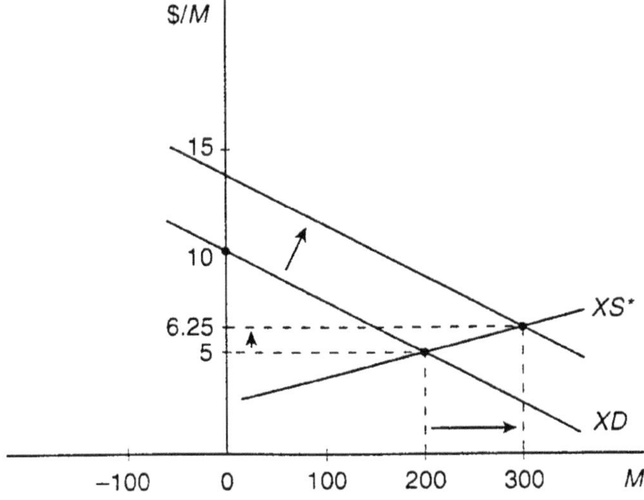

Figure 1.7
An Increase in Home Excess Demand
Rising excess demand XD from the home country increases the international price of manufactures and raises the level of trade.

EXAMPLE 1.10   *How to Trade*

The Department of Commerce has a Trade Promotion Association with practical information on international trade. The Small Business Administration has an Office of International Trade offering training conferences and counseling. The Service Corps of Retired Executives provides free advice to those interested in international trade.

C. THE BALANCE OF TRADE

Imports are products a country consumes without having to produce. Exports are goods a country produces but does not consume. Importing consumers pay firms in the foreign country for the imports. Millions of products are traded internationally among hundreds of nations. The BOT reports the net trade flow.

International Transactions

A country pays for imports and creates revenue with exports in transactions involving banks and foreign exchange. The BOT is estimated and updated regularly based on surveys.

EXAMPLE 1.11   *The US BOT*

The US has BOT deficits with Mexico, Japan, and the EU but surpluses with many small countries. BOT deficits in goods are offset somewhat by surpluses in trade in services (TS). The two are added together in the balance on goods and services (BGS).

Calculating the BOT

The BOT in goods equals the difference between export revenue X and import expenditure M,

$$BOT = X - M = (P_{exp} \times Q_{exp}) - (P_{imp} \times Q_{imp})$$

The BOT regularly makes the news — a deficit when negative and a surplus when positive.

The balance of trade reports the difference between revenue from exports and spending on imports.

Figure 1.8 shows the international market for agricultural goods with domestic excess supply and foreign excess demand. The exchange rate is yen/\$ = 100. In the foreign country, the autarky price is 1500 yen = \$15.

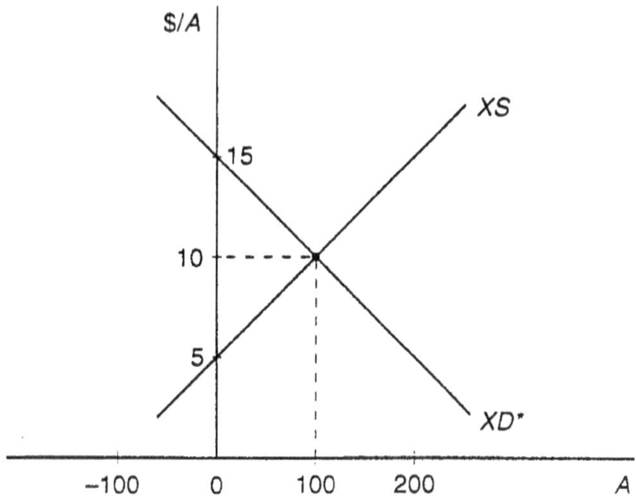

Figure 1.8
The International Market for Agricultural Goods
XS from the home country and *XD** from the foreign country meet at the international price $10 with 100 units exported from the home country.

EXAMPLE 1.12   *US Merchandise Exports by State*

The top four merchandise-exporting states in the US are listed below. California and Texas are the largest exporters. Washington is the most involved in export production, primarily aerospace.

	% Total
Texas	21
California	10
New York	5
Louisiana	4

Excess supply comes from the home country where the autarky price is $5. The international market clears at $10 = 1000 yen with 100 units of agricultural goods traded. Export revenue X is $10 × 100 = $1000. If import spending on manufactures is also $1000, as in Figure 1.5, then the trade is balanced at BOT = 0.

Balanced trade with BOT = 0 almost never occurs, given the thousands of international markets for different goods and services. Suppose a bumper crop of agricultural goods is enjoyed in an importing country. Supply increases, lowering excess demand and import spending M, creating a trade surplus. Export revenue X^* for the other country falls creating a BOT deficit.

> *A deficit in the BOT occurs when the country spends more on imports than it receives from exports, X < M. A trade surplus means X > M.*

Manufacturing firms in the US like to suggest that the trade deficit is an economic problem. Both exports and imports are growing as the US economy becomes more open. The BOT deficit is overstated as export revenue is underestimated due to the lack of mandatory reporting and taxes on exports. There are forces that would move an economy toward balanced trade.

EXAMPLE 1.13   *The Big 3*

North America, the EU, and Japan account for about half of world output and over half of the world trade. The big three currencies are the dollar, euro, and yen. China, India, and Brazil are emerging as major economies.

Trade Deficits

If a country spends more on imports than it makes from exports, the opposite must be true for another country. A country with a trade deficit must either:

- Borrow and go into debt
- Spend its wealth

Deficits and debt are different but related. Debt is essential for economic growth and higher income. Firms borrow to invest in capital equipment to increase production. Consumers borrow to buy a house or go to college. Governments also borrow to support spending on infrastructure to raise income.

Mercantilism is the mistaken belief that a trade surplus is a sign of wealth. Adam Smith wrote over 200 years ago in *The Wealth of Nations* that wealth is not measured by the amount of money or gold a country amasses. The true gauge of wealth is productivity that leads to higher income. BOT deficits are not necessarily a bad sign for a country.

Another reason not to worry much over BOT deficits is that the estimates are not very reliable. Reported data are accumulated through surveys by the Department of Commerce that are more reliable for imports because of import tariffs and quotas. The US underestimates its merchandise exports. Comparing US export data with Canadian data on imports from the US, it is not clear that the US has trade deficits. The sum of trade balances for all nations should be zero but it is negative implying exports are underestimated.

Another mistake to avoid is to concentrate on bilateral trade. The US has BOT deficits with Japan. Figure 1.9 includes trade with the rest of the world (ROW). The US has a trade deficit with Japan. Japan has a deficit with the ROW. The ROW has a deficit with the US. Bilateral deficits can be offset by other bilateral surpluses.

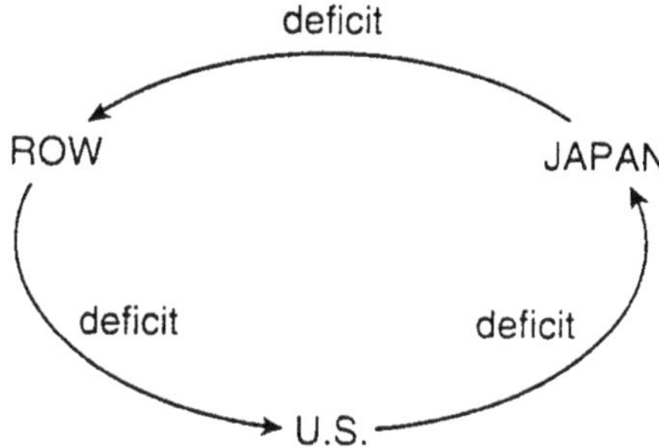

Figure 1.9
Multilateral Trade Balance
Imbalanced bilateral trade can be balanced for each country.

Automatic adjustment processes lead to balanced trade. A trade deficit leads to currency depreciation making imports become more expensive. Money leaves the economy with a trade deficit, lowering the purchasing power of consumers.

EXAMPLE 1.14   *Confusing News*

Trade regularly makes the news. The story below is edited from *USA Today* in November 1999. Deficits are depicted as bad news. One mistake is to focus on any bilateral deficit. The "world currency crisis" refers to the exchange rate depreciation. China had joined the World Trade Organization (WTO) at the time after decades of inefficient command and control.

* * * * *

WASHINGTON (edited from AP): The US trade deficit widened to $24 billion in September even though beleaguered American farmers saw their exports climb to the highest level in 19 months. America's deficits with China and Japan rose with China setting an all-time high. The latest deterioration in trade left the overall deficit running at an annual rate 56% above last year's record. Exports edged back reflecting declines in exports of airliners and autos. Imports hit a new high as the price of foreign crude oil shot up to the highest level in 31 months. American manufacturers have lost a half million jobs since early 1998 as the world currency crisis has cut sharply into exports and contributed to a flood of cheap imports. The US deficit with OPEC set a record as the foreign oil bill climbed reflecting higher volume and price.

US Exports and Imports

The largest categories of US exports are machinery, agricultural products, aircraft, chemicals, and metal products. The largest categories of imports are capital goods, consumer goods, vehicles, oil, steel, and food.

Table 1.1 US Trade Partners

NAFTA
EU
NICs
Japan
Americas
ROW

Table 1.2 US Manufacturing Trade

Product	% X	% M
Vehicles	8	13
Electrical machinery	11	9
Office equipment	7	8
Misc manufacturing	5	5
Telecommunication equip	4	5
Transport equip	8	4
Industrial machines	5	3
Power generation equip	4	3
Machinery	4	3
Apparel	0	4
Nonmetallic mineral mfg	0	2
Scientific instruments	4	0

Table 1.1 shows the largest buyers of US exports and suppliers of US imports. Canada and Mexico are the largest trading partners with about 1/3 of export revenue and import expenditure. The EU is next, accounting for about 1/5 of each. North America is growing in importance as a US trading partner while Japan and the EU are declining. NICs supply about 1/5 of imports. Both X and M are increasing as the US economy becomes more open.

Table 1.2 shows the largest categories of US manufacturing trade. The top imports are typically consumer goods manufactured on assembly lines with low-wage labor.

There is good reason to focus on business services such as banking and finance, engineering, construction, architecture, telecommunications, transportation, and insurance. These services represent about 3/4 of US jobs and 1/3 of US export revenue. Trade in services accounts for about one quarter of world trade. The US is the world's leader in service exports. Japan and Germany are net service importers.

In the early 1900s, most workers in the US were in agriculture. The service sector has grown to 75% of the labor force while agriculture shrunk to 2%. Manufacturing has consistently accounted for about 30% of all jobs.

EXAMPLE 1.15   *US BGS*

> The BOT was positive through the 1960s and 1970s but turned negative in the 1980s with imports of oil and labor-intensive manufactures. TS has been positive and growing but smaller in magnitude offsetting about a quarter of the BOT deficit.

Section C Problems

C1. Find import spending with the decrease in foreign excess supply for manufactures in Figure 1.6. Find the resulting BOT with the export revenue in Figure 1.8.

C2. Predict what will happen to the BOT if excess supply of agricultural goods in Figure 1.8 increases due to improved home technology.

EXAMPLE 1.16   *The Battle in Seattle*

> WTO countries held a meeting in Seattle during December 1999. Major issues were protection and subsidies in the EU and Japan, labor issues in the LDCs, global environmental regulations, and export dumping into the US. The colorful protests in Seattle included anti-globalists, protectionist reactionaries, US steelworkers, French farmers, clergy demonstrating for third-world debt relief, radical political groups, Industrial Workers of the World, forest activists, and environmentalists.

D. COMPARATIVE ADVANTAGE AND TRADE

International trade theory stresses the gains from specialization and trade. The opposition to international trade comes from industries that have to compete with imports. This section introduces comparative advantage as the underlying reason for the gains from specialization and trade.

EXAMPLE 1.17   *Trade Openness in the US*

> The US economy has become steadily more open to international trade since World War II due to falling tariffs, more efficient transport, and improved telecommunication. The openness index $(X + M)/\text{GDP}$ gauges trade relative to national income. The US has become much more involved in trade with the index rising from 8% in 1950 to about 30%.

Absolute versus Comparative Advantage

Absolute advantage in a good means it requires less input per unit of output in a country compared to other countries. A country with more capital input and more highly trained labor would have absolute advantages in both manufactures and services. The question becomes whether it should trade or be self-sufficient, consuming only its own products.

EXAMPLE 1.18   *Regional Trade*

Most trade occurs between countries located close together. Only about 10% of world trade occurs between the Americas, Japan, the EU, and Africa. The rest is mostly between neighboring countries based on low transport costs, cultural ties, and regional trade agreements.

Comparative Advantage

Comparative advantage based on a lower opportunity cost for a product amounts to relative efficiency. Suppose the inputs it takes to produce the same amount of manufactures (M) or services (S) in the US and Mexico are as follows:

	US	MX
S	2	3
M	3	4

The US has an absolute advantage in both products but is relatively more efficient in S. With the inputs to produce one S, 2/3 of an M could be produced. In Mexico, 3/4 of M could be produced with the inputs that produce one S. The US gives up less M to produce S, giving it the comparative advantage in S.

Competition leads nations toward producing products that have comparative advantage. Global resources are used more efficiently leading to increased world output.

Comparative advantage abstracts markets predicting all countries can consume more of all products with specialization and trade according to comparative advantage.

The original example of comparative advantage by David Ricardo involves labor required to produce wine W and cloth C in Portugal and England,

	PORT	ENG
W	80	120
C	90	100

Portugal has absolute advantages in both goods. With the inputs to produce W, the 8/9 C produced in Portugal is less than the 6/5 C produced in England. The opportunity cost of wine is less in Portugal giving it comparative advantage in wine. England has the comparative advantage in cloth.

No matter how inefficient a country might be in an absolute sense, it has comparative advantage in some products. Comparative advantage applies to trade between nations, regions, states, cities, neighborhoods, and individual people as well.

EXAMPLE 1.19   *Infrastructure and Trade*

Infrastructure includes roads, bridges, utilities, telecommunication, airports, ports, water, and sewage. Infrastructure facilitates international trade. Spiros Bougheas, Panicos Demetriades, and Edgar Morgenroth (1999) uncover evidence that better infrastructure lowers transport costs and increases trade levels inside the EU.

Section D Problems

D1. You are a whiz and can clean the bathroom in 15 minutes and the kitchen in 30 minutes, while your roommate takes 20 and 45 minutes for the two tasks. Explain who has the absolute and comparative advantages.

D2. Determine the absolute and comparative advantages in this example between the US and Canada.

	US	CN
S	2	3
M	3	2

EXAMPLE 1.20   *LDCs and Trade*

The US and the EU account for a large share of world output and exports although Asia is growing. LDCs have almost 80% of the world's population but produce 40% of world output and only 2% of world exports.

EXAMPLE 1.21   *Fresh Tomato Imports*

The quantity of fresh tomatoes consumed in the US has risen over recent decades. Domestic quantity supplied kept up pace with quantity demanded until the North American Free Trade Agreement (NAFTA) in the early 1990s when imports from Mexico began to rise. Most US tomatoes grown in California, Florida, and Texas involve immigrant workers.

CONCLUSION

International markets adjust to determine trade levels and prices of traded goods. Market fundamentals are critical to anticipate how trade will adjust to underlying changes in market conditions. Consumers around the world are enjoying increasing trade goods and services. Firms actively import intermediate products, export, and adjust to import competition.

Terms

Absolute advantage	Import spending
Arbitrage	International price
Autarky price	Mercantilism
Balance of trade (BOT)	Normal and inferior goods
Comparative advantage	Opportunity cost
Excess supply	Specialization
Exchange rates	Substitution and income effects
Export revenue	Transport costs
Expected price	

MAIN POINTS

- Small countries face world prices.
- Large countries determine price where excess supply equals excess demand.
- Shift in demand or supply affects trade levels and prices.
- The balance of trade equals export revenue minus import spending.
- Comparative advantage is a low opportunity cost of production.

REVIEW PROBLEMS

1. Diagram what will happen to the price and quantity of oil traded when OPEC restricts supply in a diagram like Figure 1.3.

2. By tradition, Japanese businesses deal only with Japanese banks. As Japanese businesses begin dealing more with foreign banks, show what will happen in the international market for banking services.

3. Illustrate what will happen in the international car market as income rises in China.

4. Russia imports wheat. Diagram what will happen in the market for wheat between the US and Russia when Russia has a poor harvest.

5. Show and explain what happens if the Buy American campaign aimed at US consumers decreases domestic tastes for imported apparel.

6. Show and explain what will happen in the international market for business services if foreign nations lower their protection from US exports of business services.

7. Diagram what will happen in the international market for cars if the US announces a lower tariff on imports that will take effect after one year.

8. Show what will happen in the international car market if the technology for auto production improves in the importing countries.

9. Illustrate what will happen in the international market for gold if news of war causes buyers and sellers to expect higher gold prices.

10. Suppose US and Venezuelan demands for steel are approximately the same. The domestic and foreign autarky prices are $500 and 18,000 bolivars. The exchange rate is bol/$ = 45.

    Determine the exporter. Show the excess supply and demand when the international price is $475, the volume of trade 100, US production 100, and production in Venezuela 300. Find consumption in each nation.

11. In Problem 10, find US import spending on steel. How many bushels of wheat would the US have to export at $2.50/bu to balance trade? At $2/bu?

12. Explain whether you think a BOT surplus or deficit should be preferred. Should governmental policy help attain this goal?

13. Consider the following pattern of inputs between the US and the EU. Who has the absolute and comparative advantage in each product? Predict the trade pattern.

	US	EU
S	2	3
M	3	4.5

14. Justify your opinion about which products on this list the US has a comparative advantage: oil, insurance, new cars, thread, accounting, textiles, engineering, clothing, olive oil, economic forecasting, chemicals, wheat, telecommunications, warm winter vacations, cool summer vacations, citrus fruits, fast food, architectural design, education, internet service.

READINGS

John Adams (1979) *International Economics: A Self-Teaching Introduction to the Basic Concepts,* Wellesley Hills: Riverdale. Drills on international economics.

Lynden Moore (1985) *The Growth and Structure of International Trade since the Second World War,* Sussex: Wheatsheaf Books. Descriptive study.

Kenneth Pomeranz and Steven Topik (1995) *The World That Trade Created: Society, Culture, and the World Economy, 1400 — the Present,* New York: M.E. Sharpe. Lively history.

MATHEMATICAL APPENDIX

The analysis of international markets begins with the supply and demand functions of a country. Demand functions are based on constrained utility maximization. Consider the Lagrangian function for consumer choice between manufactures M and services S spending income Y on the optimal c_j for good j = M, S to maximize utility u facing prices p_j,

$$\Lambda = u(c_j) + \lambda(Y - \Sigma p_j c_j).$$

The first-order condition (FOC) for c_j is $\partial \Lambda / \partial c_j = u_j - \lambda p_j = 0$ implying equal marginal utilities, $\lambda = u_j/p_j$. The Lagrangian multiplier λ is the marginal utility of income $\partial \Lambda / \partial Y = \lambda$ with its FOC $\partial \Lambda / \partial \lambda = 0$ imposing the budget constraint. The absolute value of the slope dc_M/dc_S of the budget line equals the relative price p_S/p_M and the marginal rate of substitution on the indifference curve, MRS = u_S/u_M. Consumer optimization implies equal slopes $-p_S/p_M$ of the budget line and $-u_S/u_M$ of the indifference curve.

For given income, the relative price p_M/p_S determines the consumption c_j. An increase in p_M/p_S reduces c_M and increases c_S for the two substitutes. With three or more goods, complements are possible with consumption adjusting in the same direction.

The qualitative demand function D_j is downward sloping in its price p_j,

$$\overset{- \;\; + \;\; + \;\; - \;\; +}{D_j = D_j(p_j, \; Y, \; p_s, \; p_c, \; Ep_j).}$$

Income Y has a positive effect on demand D_j. The price of related goods alters the slope of the budget line with a positive effect of the price p_s of a substitute and a negative effect for the price p_c of a complement. An increase in the expected price Ep_j induces consumers to buy before the price increase, raising price. A decrease in Ep_j induces consumers to wait until the price decreases, lowering price.

Trade theory begins with the exogenous international price ep_j^* for a small open economy where e is its exchange rate $e = \$/\yen$ and $p^* = \yen/$good is the foreign currency $\yen$ price. Changes in ep_j^* occur on the international market with consumers adjusting quantity demanded D_j in $D_j = D_j(ep_j^*, Y)$.

Supply functions are based on the constrained cost minimization of firms producing profit maximizing output q_j facing prices r and w. Firms choose levels of inputs capital K_j and labor L_j g in the constrained Lagrangian optimization,

$$\Gamma_j = rK_j + wL_j + \gamma_j(q_j - q_j(K_j, \; L_j)).$$

The FOC for the constrained optimization are $\partial \Gamma / \partial K_j = r - \gamma q_{jK}$ and $\partial \Gamma / \partial L_j = w - \gamma q_{jL}$, where q_{ji} is the marginal product $MP_i = \partial q_j / \partial v_i$ for i = K, L. Cost minimization implies the multiplier γ_j is marginal cost $\gamma_j = \partial \Gamma_j / \partial q_j$ equal to the returns from marginal spending on each input, $\gamma_j = r/q_K = w/q_L$. An increase in price p_j raises marginal cost $\gamma_j = d\Gamma_j/dq_j$ and output q_j.

Cost minimization implies the slope w/r of the unit isocost line $1 = c_j = rK_j + wL_j$ equals the slope x_L/x_K of the unit isoquant $1 = q_j(K_j, L_j)$ leading to $dK_j/dL_j = w/r = q_L/q_K$. An increase in an input price requires an increase in its marginal product with a reduction in its level and substitution toward the other input. A third input such as skilled labor, natural resources, or energy introduces potential complements in production as input levels move in the same direction.

The qualitative supply function is written as

$$\overset{+ \;\;\; - \;\; - \;\; + \;\; + \;\;\; -}{S_j = S_j(ep_j^*, \; w, \; r, \; t, \; n, \; Ep).}$$

A higher input price w or r reduces S_j. Improved technology t increases S_j. Higher expected profit would raise the number of firms n and S_j. An increase in expected price Ep lowers supply as firms hold inventory until the price increases. A decrease in Ep raises supply as firms want to sell before the price falls. A change in price $p_j = ep_j^*$ affects quantity supplied S_j.

Without international trade, the domestic market equilibrium price p_j equates quantity demanded D_j and quantity supplied S_j in $D(p_j, Y) = S(p_j, w, r)$. The market clears at the equilibrium price p_j and quantity $q_j = D_j = S_j$. While this is the concept of market equilibrium, very few markets have no international trade.

Trade implies the international price for a small country, $ep_j^* = p_j = \$/good$. A small country cannot affect the world price p_j^* although it can change its exchange rate e. If $ep_j^* < p_j$ the good is imported in quantity $q_{jM} = D_j - S_j$. If $ep_j^* > p_j$ the good is exported in quantity $q_{jX} = S_j - D_j$. Comparative static market analysis involves adjustments in exports q_{jX} or imports q_{ijM} to changes in e and p^*. This international market model is more appropriate than the domestic model with endogenous p_j for many goods and services.

Trade between two large countries involves adjustments in the equilibrium international price $p_j = ep_j^*$ that clears the markets in both countries. For a home import, excess demand $XD_j = D_j - S_j$ equals foreign excess supply $XS_j^* = S_j^* - D_j^*$. The international market for a home import determines the endogenous price $p_{jM} = ep_{jX}^*$ with import quantity q_{jM} equal to foreign export q_{jX}^*. In a home export market, $XS_j = XD_j^*$ determines price $p_{jX} = ep_{jM}^*$ and quantity $q_{jX} = q_{jM}^*$.

Comparative static analysis involves adjustments in export or import quantities as well as the equilibrium price $p_j = ep_j^*$. Trade among many countries follows the same principle with the markets clearing across all countries.

The BOT is export revenue X minus import spending M, $BOT = X - M$. For the home country, export revenue is $X = \Sigma_j p_j q_{Xj}$ and import spending $M \equiv \Sigma_j p_j q_{Mj}$. Balanced trade means $BOT = 0$. There is a trade surplus if $BOT = X - M > 0$, or a trade deficit if $BOT < 0$. A trade deficit implies the country is borrowing or spending wealth, and a trade surplus lending or accumulating wealth. Trade is balanced across countries as $\Sigma BOT = 0$. Bilateral trade balances are not relevant in a world with many countries.

Comparative advantage is relative efficiency of production. Consider production requiring input a_j per unit of good j output. Comparing two countries producing manufactures M and services S suppose $a_S < a_S^*$ and $a_M > a_M^*$. This efficiency of the home country H in S and the foreign country F in M are called absolute advantages. If input costs are similar in the two countries, H would export S in exchange for M from F.

The weaker relative efficiency of comparative advantage $a_S/a_M < a_S^*/a_M^*$ is sufficient to determine trade. The lower opportunity costs make it efficient for

H and F to specialize with each gaining from imports at a low relative price. Even if $a_S < a_S^*$ and $a_M < a_M^*$ with absolute advantages for H in both goods, trade according to comparative advantage leads to gains. The unit inputs a_j can be thought of as prices p_j implying relative prices $p_S/p_M < p_S^*/p_M^*$ are sufficient for home country exports of S.

CHAPTER 2

The Gains from Trade

Preview

The gains from trade relate to:

- The production possibility frontier (PPF)
- Increased levels of utility and real income due to trade
- Increased economic growth due to trade
- Industrial trade policy that aims to increase the gains from trade

---

INTRODUCTION

Firms and industries are constrained by the capital, labor, and natural resources available for production. These factors of production play a critical role determining the pattern of production and trade across countries. Capital equipment and infrastructure vary widely. Labor comes in a wide variety of skills. Natural resources inputs include the high variation in land, climate, minerals, and energy. The technology combining these inputs into goods and services is continuously evolving.

When prices of products change inside a country due to trade, inputs move between industries. The potential production in an economy is described by the production possibilities frontier (PPF). The output of one industry increases by attracting limited inputs from the rest of the economy.

Consumers make choices between available products based on prices and income. The utility function describes how consumers value different products. Consumers maximize utility from consumption subject to their income. If the price of a good increases, consumers substitute toward other goods.

The products that a country produces more efficiently are exported to gain from trade. A measure of the gains from trade is the potential to increase consumption of all products beyond the PPF. Trade raises income increasing the level of utility.

The increased income or utility from trade requires adjustments in the economy. Production expands in some industries but falls in others. Some industries may disappear. Business is a risky business, even more so due to international competition. Workers retrain and relocate along the PPF.

Trade plays a vital role as an engine of economic growth. Early US history provides a prime example with exports of inexpensive agricultural products to Europe based on abundant natural resources. Tariffs on manufactured imports provided the main source of early government revenue. Large tariff increases led to recessions and wars throughout US economic history.

One open question in economics is the potential of industrial trade policy to increase the gains from trade. Should import-competing industry be protected by tariffs until they grow enough to compete with the rest of the world? Should export industries be subsidized by taxpayers to help them compete? Should the government subsidize research and development (R&D) into new products? These are the questions facing industrial trade policy.

A. THE PRODUCTION FRONTIER AND REAL INCOME

The PPF shows the potential of an economy to produce all goods and services. This section develops the PPF with increasing costs. Consumption and production are gauged by prices along the PPF.

Production in an Economy

Prices and quantities of products are determined in markets. Prices and quantities of productive inputs including labor, capital, and natural resources are determined in factor markets. Firms sell their outputs to consumers who have earned income by supplying their factors of production. Both product markets and factor markets are influenced by international trade and investment.

Figure 2.1 shows the total economic activity. Solid arrows show the flow of goods and services, and dotted arrows show flows of factor inputs. Payments flow in opposite directions. Some firms sell intermediate products to produce other products indicated by the circular flow. The government hires factors and provides services collecting revenue through taxes.

The flow includes exchange across the border for an open economy studied in international economics. Domestic firms sell to foreign firms, consumers, and government, and buy intermediate inputs from foreign firms. Foreign firms make similar international transactions. Factor owners can supply capital and natural resources to foreign firms or governments, and also their labor to some extent.

EXAMPLE 2.1   *Expanding Services Sector*

Investment in the US since the 1950s has tended toward services rather than manufactures. Over 50% of investment during the 1960s went to services, and over 90% during the 1980s. About 80% of the present stock of capital is in services. Services are now about 2/3 of total output in developed countries.

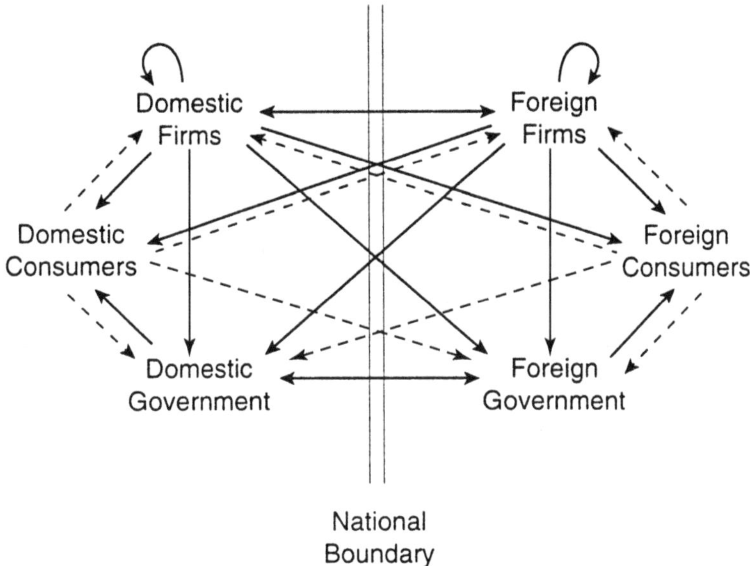

Figure 2.1
Circular Flow of Economic Activity
International economics studies the transactions that cross the national boundary.

Increasing Opportunity Costs

Figure 2.2 shows a hypothetical PPF. The economy at point C would produce 300 units of manufactures M and zero services S. All resources would be involved in producing manufactures with complete specialization in the economy. As the economy moves along the PPF toward B, resources are bid away from manufactures with higher payments in services. Firms in services want to hire inputs that are more productive.

The economy reaches B with service output of 50 while output of M drops to 275. The *opportunity cost* of the first 50 S is the lost 25 M. From point C to B with 1/2 M is given up for every S.

The slope of the PPF is an estimate of the opportunity cost of S in terms of M. The tangent at point B estimates how much M an extra unit of S would cost. The slope of the PPF is called the marginal rate of transformation (MRT).

The PPF shows the potential of the economy to produce with full employment and efficient production. The slope of the PPF is the MRT.

If the relative price of S increases, more resources will be attracted to services. The economy moves toward point A where another 50 units of S are produced and output of M drops to 200. The opportunity cost of the added 50 units of S is $275 - 200 = 75$ M or 1.5 units of M for every unit of S. The MRT increases moving down the PPF.

Increasing opportunity costs imply a concave PPF. Theory and empirical evidence suggest these increasing costs due to diminishing marginal productivity.

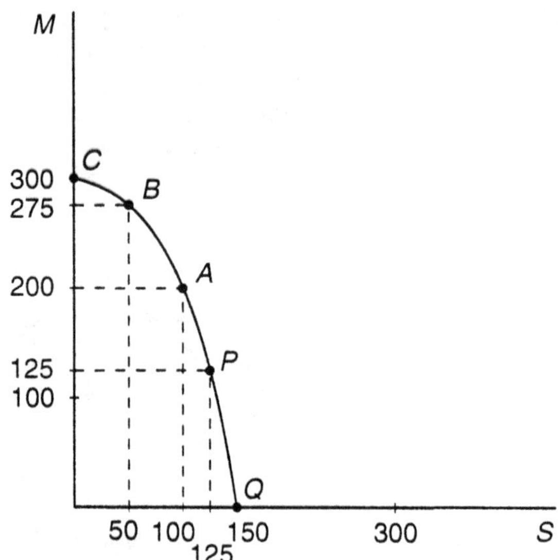

Figure 2.2
Production Frontier with Increasing Cost
Increasing opportunity costs of production imply a concave PPF. The opportunity cost
of additional production of S rises from 0.5 between C and B to 5 between P and Q.

The marginal product of an extra unit of input diminishes as more of the input
enters production.

> *Increasing costs of production and a concave PPF are based on the principle*
> *of diminishing marginal productivity.*

Consumers in autarky would choose a point on the PPF according to demand
for the two goods. The interaction of consumer and producer choice determines
the relative price of the two products. Factor markets in the background determine
prices of labor, capital, and natural resources. All markets in the economy are
linked in this general equilibrium.

EXAMPLE **2.2**   *Who is Growing?*

Yearly growth rates in income per capita vary over time and by location.
The fastest growing region in the world has been the Pacific Rim due to its
free trade. The slowest growing region has been Africa largely due to corrupt
governments. North America and the EU have steadily grown. Latin America
suffered declines during the 1980s but rebounded over the following 30 years
with mixed performance since.

Consumer Choice

Consumers' choice is based on utility and indifference curves. Consumers equally
value combinations of M and S along the indifference curve I in Figure 2.3.

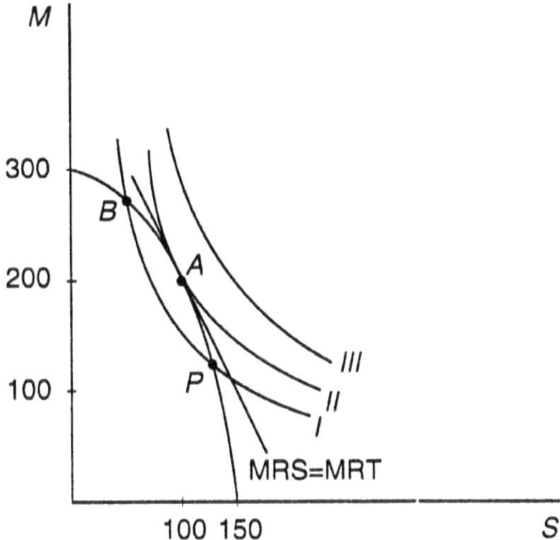

Figure 2.3
Maximizing Utility
Indifference curve I represents a low level of utility, II a higher level, and III the highest. In autarky, consumers maximize utility subject to the PPF. Point A represents the optimal consumer equilibrium where MRS = MRT.

Consumers value points along the indifference curve II preferring any point on II to any point on I. Indifference curve III represents a higher level of utility.

In autarky, consumers must choose a point on the PPF. Bundles B or P on indifference curve I would be inferior to point A on II. Consumers would like to be on indifference curve III but it is beyond the PPF. The optimal choice is point A with utility maximized subject to the PPF.

The slope of an indifference curve is the marginal rate of substitution (MRS). The MRS indicates how many units of one good consumers would sacrifice for an extra unit of the other. At the consumer optimum, the MRS is equal to the MRT. Consumers value an extra unit of S exactly the same as its opportunity cost of production at point A.

At point B, MRS > MRT. Consumers value an extra unit of S more than its opportunity cost in production. At point P, consumers value an extra unit of M more than its opportunity cost in production.

In equilibrium, the MRS equals the MRT. Markets lead the economy in autarky to this general equilibrium.

EXAMPLE **2.3**   *Investment and Growth*

Investing more leads to higher income in the future. Investment relative to output varies around the world. Higher growth can be anticipated from the higher percentages of income invested in these examples.

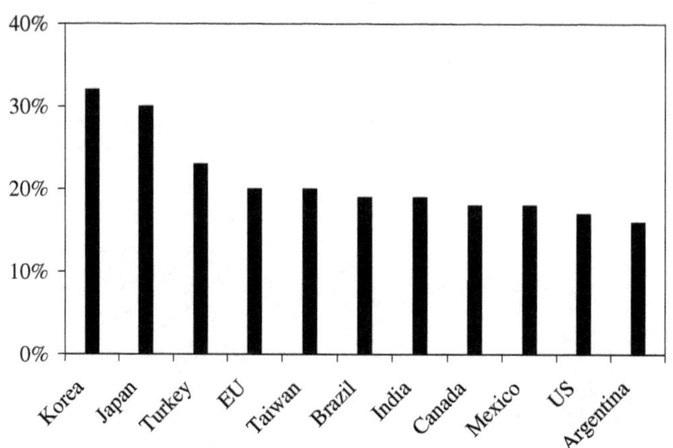

Real Income

In Figure 2.4, the slope at point A is equal to the rise over run, $-400/200 = -2$. The negative sign indicates that 2 units of M are given up for the extra unit of S at point A. The endpoints of this domestic price line are real income.

The value of national income at point A is 400 M. Consumption is 200 M and 100 S. Each unit of S is valued at 2 M so the 100 S are worth $2 \times 100 = 200$ M. Real income is $200 M + (2 \times 100 S) = 400 M$ equal to 200 S.

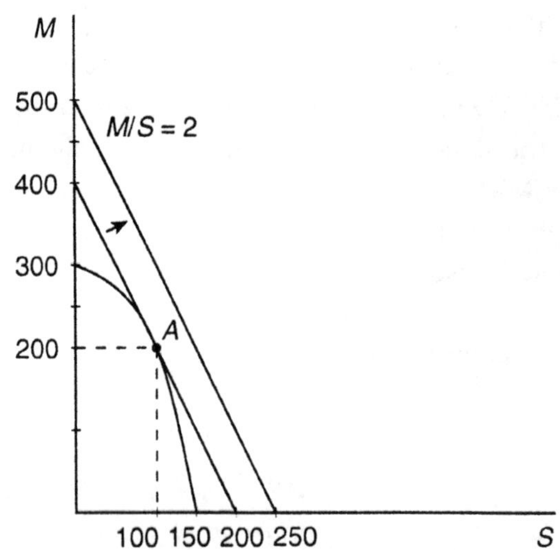

Figure 2.4
Relative Price Lines and Real Income
Production and consumption take place in autarky at point A. The line tangent to the PPF is the relative price line. National income is 400 M = 200 S. The parallel shift in the price line shows the increase in national income.

Real income is stated in terms of goods. At the same relative price, a price line farther from the origin implies higher income. The price line at 500 M in Figure 2.4 illustrates higher income. National income is 25% higher at 500 M or 250 S.

One way to measure the gains from trade is real income at autarky prices. Trade produces gains if consumers end up with a bundle of goods valued higher at autarky prices. The gains from trade could also be indicated by the higher level of utility.

EXAMPLE **2.4**   *Expanding PPF and Specialization*

The US production frontier has expanded as production shifts toward services due to specialization. Patricia Beeson and Michael Bryan (1986) estimate the ratio of services to manufacturing output rose from 2.8 to 3.5 between 1950 and 1985. Output in services rose 252% while manufacturing output rose 178%. The relative price of services rose 26% according to Lynn Brown (1986). Developed countries (DCs) are specializing in the production of services as less developed countries (LDCs) with lower wages specialize in manufacturing.

Section A Problems

A1. Diagram a PPF with points $(M, S) = (100, 0)$, $(90, 25)$, $(70, 50)$, $(40, 75)$, and $(0, 100)$. Show the increasing opportunity costs.

A2. From the diagram of A1, *estimate* the MRT when consumption is $(M, S) = (90, 25)$. What is the value of consumption in terms of S?

A3. *Estimate* the change in relative price in the shift from $(90, 25)$ to $(40, 75)$ along the PPF in Problem A1.

B. SPECIALIZATION AND THE GAINS FROM TRADE

A trading economy opening to international prices rearranges its production and increases income. Production of exports expands while import-competing industries shrink. There are net gains and higher utility but losers as well as winners. The two ways to increase income and consumption are economic growth or international trade.

International Prices

The supply side of an economy is pictured by its production frontier with efficiency and full employment. The demand side is pictured by indifference curves. The interaction of supply and demand determines prices, production, consumption, and national income.

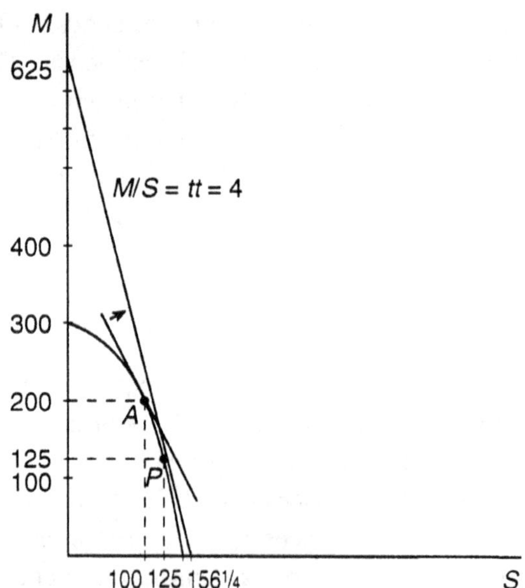

Figure 2.5
International Prices and Specialization
The line $tt = 4$ is the international price of services, higher than the domestic relative price. The open economy specializes moving from A to P.

Figure 2.5 shows an economy with autarky relative price of services $M/S = 2$ at point A in autarky. The economy produces and consumes 200 M and 100 S in autarky.

On the international market, one unit of services is worth 4 M. If the economy opens to trade, the higher price leads to services export. Figure 2.5 shows the international price $M/S = 4$ with the small economy taking the international price.

The industry responds to the higher price of services with specialization. The increased factor prices move capital, labor, and natural resources into services with output rising to 125 at point P. Manufactures output drops to 125.

EXAMPLE **2.5**   *The Nirvana Economy*

With the North American Free Trade Agreement (NAFTA) and the World Trade Organization (WTO) introduced during the 1990s protectionists warned a giant sucking sound would drain jobs from the US. Instead, the economy transformed. The Associated Press ran a series of articles called "The Nirvana Economy?" during October 1999. One article "Transforming Middletown USA and the Nation" focuses on Muncie, Indiana. Blue collar workers became programmers and switched from making jet parts to semiconductor equipment and software. Jobs in the industrial rust belt switched from manufacturing to services and wages rose.

Real Gains from Trade

Figure 2.6 shows the economy taking the terms of trade (*tt*) and adjusting production to point P and trading to the optimal point T based on utility and demand. Consumer choice finds T on the highest indifference curve along *tt*. At T, the marginal rate of substitution along indifference curve III equals the terms of trade. Consumption at T has higher utility than at autarky A.

With trade consumption takes place where the MRS equals to the tt.

Trade leads to 205 M and 105 S consumed. Production takes place at P where $(M, S) = (125, 125)$. Exports of services are $125 - 105 = 20$ S. Imports of manufactures are $205 - 125 = 80$ M. This trade reflects the terms of trade at $tt = 80/20 = 4$ M/S.

The shaded triangle in Figure 2.6 is called the trade triangle. Point T is northeast of point A. Consumers can consume more of every good moving from autarky to free trade.

International prices determine the pattern of production and trade for a small open economy.

The *real gains from trade* are found valuing consumption at autarky prices. The autarky relative price of M is 2 from Figure 2.4. Each unit of M consumed is valued at the domestic autarky price $1/2$ S. With trade in Figure 2.6, the value

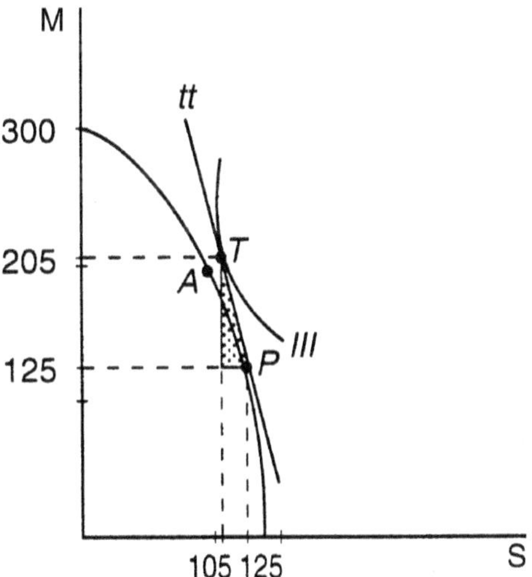

Figure 2.6
Production and Consumption with Trade
With international specialization at P, consumers at T move to a higher utility level than in autarky at A.

of consumption in terms of services is 105 S + (205 M × 1/2) = 207.5 S. The gains from trade are 7.5 S. Gains can be also calculated in terms of M.

The real gains from trade in a commodity show the increased value of consumption.

EXAMPLE **2.6**   *Moving from Autarky to Trade in Japan*

Before 1858, Japan was an isolated feudal society without trade when a fleet of US warships arrived to pry it open. Over the next 30 years, the level of trade in Japan increased 70 times as estimated by Richard Huber (1971). Japan exported silk, tea, copper, dried fish, and coal. Prices of these exports rose by 1/3. Japan imported sugar, cotton, and metals with these prices falling 40%. World prices for these commodities were not affected by Japan. Huber estimates national income rose by over 1/2 due to free trade. Daniel Bernhofen and John Brown (2005) estimate a smaller gain in income.

Production Adjustment

Domestic import-competing firms face competition when the economy opens to free trade. Foreign firms have an advantage in the products that a country imports. An economy opening to trade adjusts along its PPF toward products with higher international prices. The economy in the example exports its higher priced services in exchange for less expensive manufactures.

Some firms in manufactures go out of business and some workers must retrain and relocate. Stockholders in manufactures lose. Only the more efficient firms survive. Adjustment costs are outweighed, however, by the efficiency gains from free trade.

The friction of adjustment can push the economy below its PPF as pictured in Figure 2.7. Resources in manufacturing may not readily transform into services. Labor with specialized skills and manufacturing equipment may not be suitable for production in services. Some resources may have to relocate. The costs of retraining, retooling, and relocating must be paid. Policy by the government has the potential to lower these adjustment costs.

As firms in an economy open to competition, they adjust to world market conditions. The gains from free trade may involve transition costs.

The shape and curvature of the PPF determines how much outputs and factor prices adjust. Jon Ford and Henry Thompson (1997) find the PPF would be relatively flat implying price changes have large effects on output. Complete specialization and industrial shutdowns are the likely outcomes of trade. While input prices undergo adjustments, outputs adjust more.

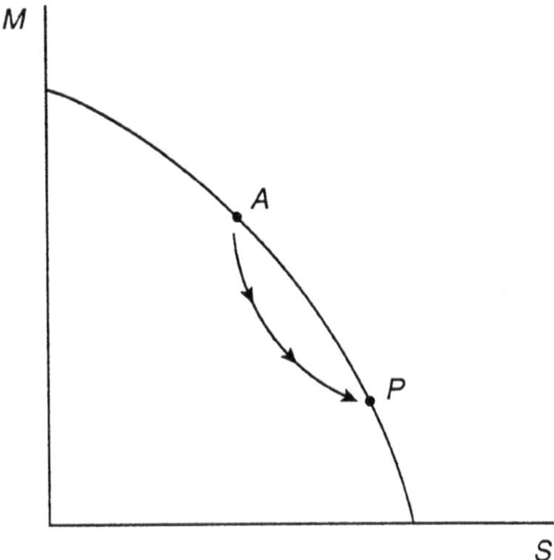

Figure 2.7
Adjustment Frictions
Production may be forced to a path below the PPF in adjustment. These adjustment costs push the economy below its long-run potential.

EXAMPLE **2.7**   *Free Trade Fallacy?*

The NAFTA debate brought free trade into the headlines. Ravi Batra (1992) and Batra and Daniel Slottje (1993) present evidence that free trade was a fallacy causing a decline in US wages since the 1970s. Declining wages were due in part to increased import competition. Sugata Marjit (1994), Farhad Rassekh (1994), and Channing Arndt and Thomas Hertel (1997) disagree. Free trade may cause wages to fall in high-wage countries but investment and training can lead to gains even for losers.

Section B Problems

B1. Find the real gains from trade in terms of manufactured goods in Figures 2.4 and 2.6.

B2. Starting with Figure 2.4, show the specialization if the tt are 0.9 M for every S.

B3. At $tt = M/S = 0.9$ suppose production moves to point B in Figure 2.2. Diagram the trade triangle if 72 units of M are exported. Find consumption with trade.

B4. In Figure 2.2, if the domestic autarky price at A is equal to 2, find the real gains from trade in terms of S.

EXAMPLE **2.8**   *Compact Pickup Tariffs*

Compact pickup trucks were first imported to the US from Japan during the late 1960s. Protectionist tariffs increased from 4% to 25% in a panicked response jammed through Congress by the Big 3 automakers. The imports proved reliable and import levels increased regardless. Robert Feenstra (1988) estimates the consumer gains from imported trucks were about 20% of the price. The tariff reduced consumer gains by 2/3, lowered the quality of trucks produced in the US, and raised the price of pickups for US consumers. Protectionist tariffs are a fool's game.

C. TRADE AND ECONOMIC GROWTH

International trade makes a country more competitive and raises income. Trade leads to economic growth defined by increasing income per capita.

Trade Policy and Economic Growth

Economies grow by increasing their level of capital input. Capital equipment and machinery are accumulated with investment spending. The typical LDC has little capital and unskilled labor. Human capital improves the labor force through education and training. Economic growth is a gradual process with no shortcuts.

Economic growth is pictured by an expanding PPF with the growing economy able to produce more of every product.

Trade plays a role in economic growth. As an economy specializes, workers train by competing in international markets. Export-led growth occurs when growth is biased toward producing exports. Export promotion policy aims to lead the economy toward specialization with tax cuts or subsidies.

Governments of LDCs often turn to import substitution policy aiming to produce domestically rather than import. Tariffs and other restrictions promote domestic industry with the idea it can mature and compete.

The US imposed high infant industry tariffs following the Great Tariff Debate of 1888. Democratic Republican Benjamin Harrison favored tariffs to protect US manufacturing in the North. Grover Cleveland opposed tariffs with agriculture favoring free trade with Europe. Cleveland won the popular vote, but Harrison the electoral vote. The resulting high tariffs in the 1890s followed. Douglas Irwin (1998) makes the point that the tariffs on iron slowed US industrialization when global steel and iron prices were falling.

Figure 2.8 illustrates the losses due to import substitution. Suppose the economy is operating with free trade at production point P, specializing and exporting agricultural goods A. Import substitution policy moves the economy

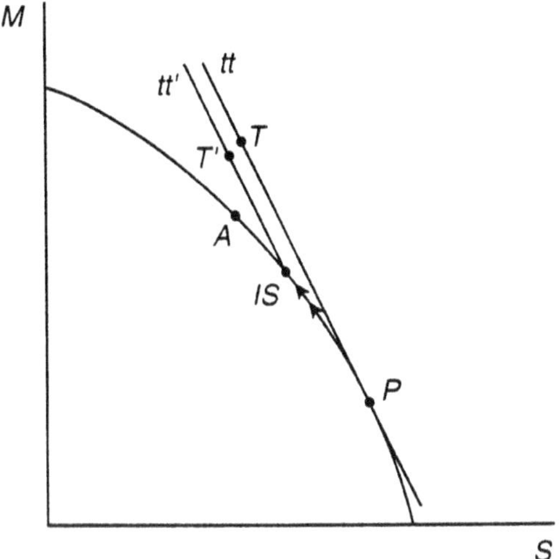

Figure 2.8
Import Substitution
Import substitution encourages the economy to shift from point P to point IS. Trade occurs along the terms of trade line *tt'*. Consumption point T' is below T with consumers losing utility.

to point IS. The economy trades at the international terms of trade along line *tt'* parallel to *tt*.

Consumption with import substitution T' is below consumption T with free trade. Consumers are forced to lower utility and lower real income by import substitution.

The direction of economic growth is determined by the availability of capital, labor, and natural resources. Mineral deposits, fertile land, and climate are critical natural resource inputs. Labor includes management and entrepreneurship. Capital includes infrastructure of roads, telecommunication, police, public health, airports, and seaports provided by government.

EXAMPLE **2.9**   *Evidence on Trade and Growth*

Countries that specialize and trade grow faster. Zhenhui Xu (1996) presents evidence that increased exports stimulated output in 17 of 32 LDCs between 1960 and 1990. Wenshwo Fang, Wenrong Liu, and Henry Thompson (2000) examine evidence for fast growing Taiwan between 1971 and 1995 finding imports as well as exports stimulated economic growth.

Export-Led Growth

Figure 2.9 shows economic growth led by manufactures export. The production frontier expands favoring the manufactures sector. The *tt* determine production for the open economy.

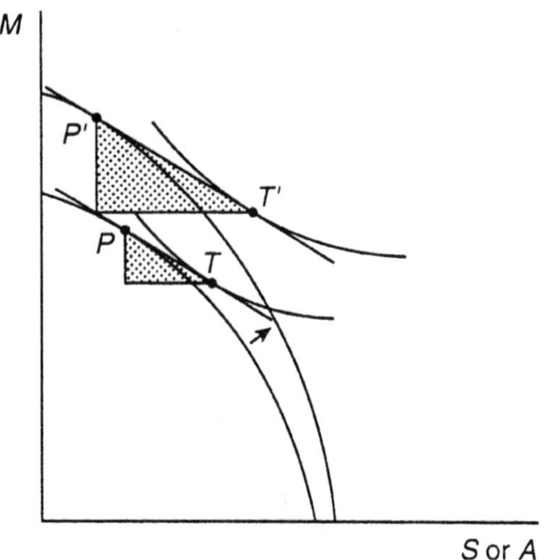

Figure 2.9
Export-Led Growth
Concentrating on export production of manufactures can lead to increased potential
illustrated by a PPF that expands favoring the export.

The economy starts at point P and trades to point T. As the economy grows,
its potential to produce manufactures grows more rapidly than its potential to
produce agriculture A. This bias can be due to international investment, acquired
labor skills, or improving technology.

With economic growth, the economy produces at point P′ and trades to
point T′. Consumers enjoy a higher level of utility and higher real income.
Production frontiers expand faster with export-led growth. When an LDC trades
freely, there is increased incentive and opportunity to expand.

*The developmental gains from trade are the enhanced growth in the PPF
due to specialization in export industries.*

The US provides an example of export-led growth as agricultural exports
to Europe dominated US export revenue during the 1800s. Technology was
developing to replace labor with machinery and equipment.

Growth biased toward export has the potential to lower the price of the
exported good when the economy is a major supplier on the international
market. Examples are Chile — copper, Bolivia — tin, Saudi Arabia — oil,
South Africa — diamonds, and Colombia — coffee. If the *tt* fall enough the
exporter may end up worse off due to immiserizing growth.

Figure 2.10 pictures immiserizing growth. Before growth, production is at
point P and consumption point C. With increasing exports, the terms of trade
fall to *tt′*. The terms of trade fall to *tt′* with production ending up at P′ and
consumption at C′ below C.

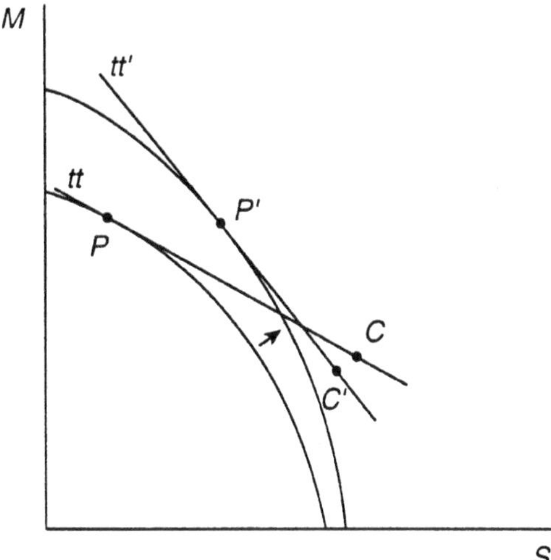

Figure 2.10
Immiserizing Growth
Increased export can lead to a fall in the terms of trade if the economy is a major supplier on the world market. The fall in the terms of trade to *tt'* forces the economy to an inferior bundle at C'.

Foreign Investment and Growth

The potential to specialize is an incentive for investing in exports. LDCs typically depend on DCs for initial investment. For instance, rapid development in the US began with British and European investment in railroads during the early 1800s. Many countries limit foreign ownership, curtailing international investment and slowing economic growth. Foreign investment expands export industries and raises economic growth.

Robert Lucas (1993) examines the importance of human capital and learning on the job. Workers in fast-growing economies quickly learn how to produce more sophisticated products.

Less Developed Countries and Newly Industrializing Countries

LDCs are typically agricultural economies with subsistence farming. Newly industrializing countries (NICs) develop to rely on manufactured exports. A large share of assembly line production takes place in NICs. DCs have high wages and cannot compete with the lower manufacturing wages in the NICs. The LDCs would like to become NICs but are often stuck with import substitution policy. The infrastructure in NICs is generally better than in LDCs.

The DCs protect their manufacturing industries. For the LDCs and NICs, this protectionism is a hindrance to export and growth. Tariffs can keep LDCs from selling in the large DC markets. Protection of basic industries including textiles, apparel, and footwear remains high in the DCs. Protection is high for the products that would be exported by LDCs and NICs.

EXAMPLE **2.10**   *Rice and Fertilizer Trade in Vietnam*

Vietnam has a large agricultural sector with poor households. Vietnam liberalized trade in rice and fertilizer during the 1990s period of reforming from socialism toward a market economy. The poverty rate fell by half. Ganesh Seshan (2005) finds that trade in rice and fertilizer accounts for about half this reduction in poverty.

EXAMPLE **2.11**   *LDCs, NICs, and DCs*

LDCs have much lower income per capita and the highest labor growth. DCs specialize in service production. Investment is risky but returns are higher in the LDCs. The DCs use energy intensively. NICs turn to manufactures for export as when Brazil switched from exporting agricultural products during the 1970s. South Korea was an agricultural economy up to the 1960s but now earns almost all export revenue from manufactures. Mexico emerged as a supplier of manufactures and now earns about half its export revenue from manufactures. The NICs have moderate wages, good infrastructure, and foreign investment.

Section C Problems

C1. Brazil grows trees and exports plywood. Illustrate export-led growth with a PPF.

C2. With growth biased toward manufactures, explain what happens to the opportunity cost of a unit of manufactures when the ratio of outputs is constant. How does this changing opportunity cost reflect biased growth?

C3. Growth can be unbiased across sectors. Illustrate unbiased growth showing what happens to the level of trade when there is unbiased growth.

EXAMPLE **2.12**   *Capital Production and Growth*

Capital machinery and equipment are essential for growth. Countries with abundant productive capital grow faster as Bradford DeLong and Larry Summers (1990) show in a study of 61 countries. Japan invested 12% of its income in new capital between 1965 and 1980 leading to a yearly output growth of 5%. At the other extreme, Argentina invested only 2% of its income and grew at a 1% rate. Protection of machinery and equipment industries slows economic growth.

D. INDUSTRIAL TRADE POLICY

Industrial trade policy aims to support export- and import-competing industries favored by politicians and government. Exports are encouraged with subsidies. Free trade zones (FTZs) and free enterprise zones (FEZs) eliminate tariffs inside the zones. The costs of industrial trade policies should be considered as well as the benefits.

Export Promotion

Governments devise industrial trade policy to promote exports of favored industries. These programs are often the result of contributions of the industries to politicians.

An export subsidy lowers the cost or increases the revenue for an exporting firm. The simplest export subsidy is a direct payment per unit exported. Other subsidies include wage subsidies, waivers on tariffs of imported intermediate products, and lower taxes. Government-sponsored R&D can lower cost and improve technology in export industries. Foreign aid can be given to poor countries tied to their import of domestically produced products. The US military aid tied to the purchase of US weapons amounts to subsidies for the producing firms. The low interest loans of the Export-Import Bank of the US Department of Commerce to exporting firms amount to a subsidy.

Cost-reducing subsidies enable exporting firms to sell at lower prices on international markets. Foreign firms in the competing markets view subsidies as unfair.

Export subsidies involve spending tax revenue to make goods cheaper for foreign consumers. Export subsidies tax domestic consumers effectively subsidizing foreign consumers.

Export subsidies aim to make exports cheaper and the exporting firms more competitive in global industry.

EXAMPLE **2.13**   *Production Subsidies*

Politicians support their favored industries with subsidies, direct payments, subsidized loans, and R&D support. The industries return the favor with political contributions. The Organisation for Economic Co-operation and Development (OECD) estimates the level of subsidies as a percentage of income in these DCs:

Italy	3%
France, Canada, UK	2.5%
Germany, Japan	1.5%
US	0.5%

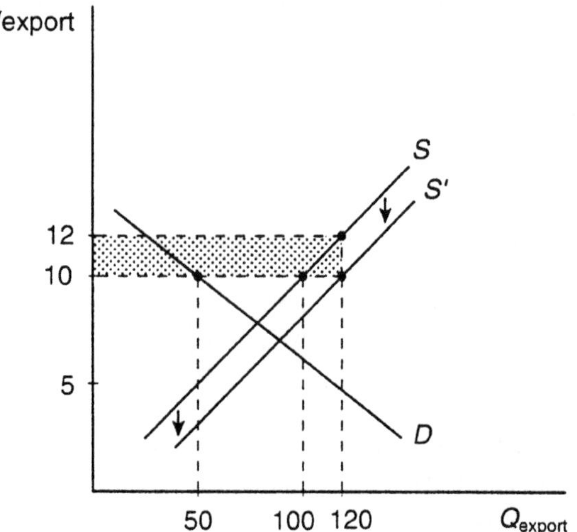

Figure 2.11
Subsidy Burden
A subsidy of $2 per unit increases domestic supply from S to S'. At an international price of $10, production increases from 100 to 120, and exports from 50 to 70. The subsidy costs domestic taxpayers $2 \times 120 = $240 in the shaded rectangle.

Costs of Export Subsidies

An export subsidy lowers the cost of production. In Figure 2.11, the domestic supply of exports increases from S to S' due to an export subsidy. At the international price of $10, the output increases from 100 to 120. Domestic quantity demanded remains at 50. The level of excess supply increases from 50 to 70, and export revenue from $500 to $700.

While the suppliers benefit from the subsidy in Figure 2.11, it does not come from thin air. Taxes are levied to pay the subsidy. The subsidy of $2 per unit is the distance between S and S'. The cost to taxpayers is $2 for every unit sold. The tax burden of the subsidy is $240 in the shaded rectangle.

The costs as well as the benefits of a subsidy should be considered. The tax burden may outweigh gains to producers.

A subsidy can lead to long-run gains if it biases growth toward an industry with rising prices on international markets. Subsidies generally have not been successful in identifying and targeting growth industries. As a rule, subsidies are based on the political support given from the benefiting firms to the politicians awarding the subsidies.

EXAMPLE 2.14   *Wartime Industrial Policy*

During World War II, economic policy funneling resources toward wartime production disrupted markets. *Business Week* (October 23, 1943) reported the price ceilings on corn caused shortages of animal feed. Imports of Canadian wheat substituted for corn but displaced iron ore shipping on the Great Lakes. The wheat had been used to produce alcohol and synthetic rubber. To replace the lost wheat, alcohol producers substituted molasses imported from the Caribbean. Those diverted freighters had been carrying petroleum products from the Gulf Coast leading to petroleum shortages. Meanwhile, hog farmers substituted skim milk for feed leading to a shortage of adhesives as casein from skim milk is used in adhesives. Casein had to be imported from Argentina. Arbitrary trade policy always has unintended market consequences.

Free Trade Zones and Free Enterprise Zones

FTZs are areas inside a country exempt from tariffs and taxes on foreign investment. FTZs encourage foreign multinational firms for export production. FTZs increase trade by skirting protectionist policy.

FTZs are close to ports and airports. Goods are brought for storage, reshipping, and manufacturing. Costly customs procedures are avoided. US manufacturers began using FTZs during the 1970s. Jafar Alavi and Henry Thompson (1988) report that 3% of US production occurs inside FTZs. Industries in the US enjoy inverted tariff structures that protect production of intermediate goods.

Production inside an FTZ avoids the inverted tariff since intermediate goods are imported without duty, assembled, and shipped into the country at the lower tariff rate for finished goods. The first automobile firm to become an FTZ in the US was Honda. All auto plants are now FTZs. Almost all the goods shipped from FTZs remain inside the US.

A FEZ is an area where consumers can shop with no import tariffs. Goods and services are traded without tariffs, quotas, or customs hassle inside the FEZ. Airports have FEZs where imported products are duty-free. The whole of Singapore is an FEZ.

Laws controlling FTZs and FEZs are handled at the state level but have to be approved through Congress.

The Pros and Cons of Industrial Trade Policy

Debate in economics continues over export subsidies, import substitution, and other measures for the government to actively manage trade. The imperfect competition in "new trade theory" opens the door to policymakers aided by economists to outguess the foreign competition.

This political economy argument is familiar in the debate over tariffs that gave rise to the theory of comparative advantage and the gains from trade. Taxpayers must support subsidies to industries favored by industrial trade policy.

Industrial trade policy should have to pass the economic test of costs versus benefits.

EXAMPLE **2.15**   *Deadly Industrial Trade Policy*

> Two instances of industrial trade policy led to deadly consequences. In 1985, US pharmaceutical firms developed a test for HIV and a method to decontaminate blood for transfusions. French health officials would not import the products and waited for their Pasteur Institute to develop its own test and method. As a result, 1,200 hemophiliacs received tainted blood and over 250 died. Another deadly example was Japanese officials not allowing import of a highly reliable vaccine for measles, mumps, and rubella from a US drug company as Japanese companies developed their own vaccine. Cases of meningitis, encephalitis, paralysis, brain damage, and death were the result.

Section D Problems

D1. How is currency devaluation like an export subsidy? How is it different?

D2. As a consumer, would you prefer to live inside an FTZ or an FEZ? As a firm, in which would you prefer to locate?

D3. Predict the effects of a subsidy for an import-competing industry in a small open economy.

D4. If two trading economies both subsidize their export industries, analyze the possible outcomes.

EXAMPLE **2.16**   *Productivity and Exporting*

> Exporting firms perform better than non-exporting firms in productivity. Good firms may become exporters, or export competition may make firms better. Andrew Bernard and Bradford Jensen (1998) uncover evidence favoring the hypothesis that good firms become exporters.

EXAMPLE **2.17**   *Gains from Used Car Trade*

> In 1993, Cyprus began to allow the import of Japanese used cars more than two years old. Japan has an excess supply of three-year-old cars due to a warranty renewal system. Steering wheels are on the right in both countries. Sofronis Clerides (2005) finds consumers in Cyprus substituted toward the higher quality used car imports realizing gains of a few hundred dollars per consumer.

CONCLUSION

International trade leads to overall gains. Regardless, every nation hinders trade with tariffs, quotas, foreign exchange controls, subsidies, and other trade policy. Protectionism is the oldest topic in economics and remains an issue. Protectionist policy persists because some groups gain at the expense of others.

Terms

Developmental gains from trade	Indifference curves and utility
Diminishing marginal returns	Industrial trade policy
Domestic relative prices	LDCs, DCs, NICs
Export promotion	Marginal productivity
FTZs and FEZs	Marginal rate of substitution
Gains from trade	Marginal rate of transformation
Human capital	Production possibility frontier
Immiserizing growth	Subsidies
Import substitution	Terms of trade
Increasing opportunity cost	Trade triangle

MAIN POINTS

- The PPF illustrates limited resources and increasing opportunity costs. Relative prices determine outputs.
- Specialization and trade allow a country to increase utility and enjoy gains from trade.
- Economic growth means higher per capita income base on an expanding production frontier. Export-led growth focuses on free trade policy.
- Industrial trade policy of export promotion and import substitution is not successful in practice.

REVIEW PROBLEMS

1. If income rises to 220 S in Figure 2.4 with the same relative price of S, find real income in terms of M.
2. From Example 2.1, sketch the PPFs comparing 1950 and 1986. Discuss the underlying rise in the relative price of services.
3. Sketch a PPF with constant costs of production and maximum manufacturing output of 200. What is the relative price of M on the PPF?
4. Sketch a PPF with increasing costs of production and M outputs of 200, 150, 100, 50, and 0. Show the opportunity costs. What determines where production takes place?
5. Suppose the domestic autarky relative price $M/S = 1$ with autarky consumption at $(M, S) = (100, 100)$. Production with free trade takes place at $(M, S) = (50, 160)$ with 50 exported and 60 imported. Find the consumption bundle (M, S). Sketch the trade triangle. What are the terms of trade?
6. In Problem 5, find the gains from trade in terms of M and as a percentage.
7. Illustrate consumer choice and the welfare gains in Problem 6 with indifference curves.
8. Comparing unbiased with biased growth, which leads to higher gains from trade? Which leads to higher national income?
9. Distinguish between the gains from trade and the developmental gains from trade.
10. There is a large FTZ in McAllen, Texas, on the border with Mexico. Workers pass freely in both directions. If you were organizing a

firm, what would you consider when deciding whether to operate inside the FTZ or across the border in Mexico?

11. What would be the effects of Texas declaring itself an FEZ? What would be the effects on the rest of the US?

12. The most heavily subsidized industry in developed countries is agriculture. What would happen to the pattern of trade if these agricultural subsidies were eliminated?

READINGS

Robert Barro and Xavier Sala-i-Martin (1999) *Economic Growth*, Cambridge: The MIT Press. Excellent textbook.

Douglas Irwin (1996) *Against the Tide: An Intellectual History of Free Trade*, Princeton: Princeton University Press. The free trade argument through history.

David Landes (1999) *The Wealth and Poverty of Nations*, New York: Norton. A big picture of history and economics.

Robert Lawrence (1983) *Can America Compete?* Washington: Brookings Institution. Changing structure of US industry.

Peter Morici (1995) Export our way to prosperity, *Foreign Policy*, Winter. How the US has gained from trade.

Robert Solow (2000) *Growth Theory: An Exposition*, Oxford: Oxford University Press. A concise presentation.

MATHEMATICAL APPENDIX

Trade leads to gains that can be measured by utility or real income. Country k produces each good j fully employed factors of production v_k in the production function $x_j(v_{kj})$. Each factor is fully employed, $v_k = \Sigma_j v_{kj}$. With two goods, producing more S implies producing less M along the production possibility frontier (PPF) that plot the output combinations the economy can produce. The slope $dx_M/dx_S < 0$ of the PPF is the marginal rate of transformation (MRT) reflecting the M lost as the opportunity cost of an increase in S. The downward sloping PPF is concave with increasing opportunity cost of S production, given diminishing marginal productivity of inputs.

The fundamental measure of the gains from trade is the increase in utility moving to a higher indifference curve for consumption with trade compared to consumption on the PPF. Along an indifference curve, there is no change in utility, $du = \Sigma_i u_i dc_i = 0$. The slope of an indifference curve is the ratio of marginal utilities, $dc_M/dc_S = -u_M/u_S < 0$. This marginal rate of substitution (MRS) shows how much M consumers would be willing to give up for an extra unit of S and remain at the same level of utility u.

A country in autarky maximizes utility $u(c_j)$ at the optimal bundle $x = c$ on the PPF where the slope of the optimal indifference curve MRS $= -u_M/u_S$ equals the slope of the PPF as the marginal rate of transformation (MRT) = $-dx_M/dx_S$. The relative price of the two goods is p_M/p_S = MRS = MRT in autarky.

Trade increases utility by separating consumption from production. A small economy faces terms of trade tt = ep_X*/ep_M* = p_X*/p_M*, where ep_X* is the international price of its export and ep_M* its import. A small economy specializes to the point on its PPF where MRT = tt and trades to the indifference curve where MRS = tt. Utility increases in the move from autarky to trade for any tt = p_X*/p_M* ≠ p_M/p_S.

The gains from trade can also be measured in real terms by the increased income measured at autarky prices p_M and p_S. Autarky income is Y = $p_M q_M$ + $p_S q_S$ = $p_M c_M$ + $p_S c_S$. Real income in terms of S is Y/p_S = $(p_M/p_S)c_M$ + c_S. Trade raises real income to Y'/p_S = $(p_M/p_S)c_M'$ + c_S' at the consumption bundle (c_M', c_S') with trade. Consumers reveal their preference for the trade bundle (c_M', c_S') with the potential that $c_M' > c_M$ and $c_S' > c_S$.

While trade raises aggregate utility or real income, not everyone benefits. Import-competing industries suffer as a country moves along its PPF to specialize and increase exports. Income is also redistributed among the factors of production including labor, capital, and natural resources. Incomes of some households fall while incomes of other households rise. Trade raises but also redistributes income in the economy and can lead to losers as well as winners.

Trade policy refers primarily to taxes or subsidies on imports or exports. Trade policy designed to help one industry must hurt others. Taxes on imports or exports lower the gains from trade but help targeted groups. An import tariff raises the price for the import-competing industry raising its output but reducing other output along the PPF. The economy trades on a lower tt line reducing utility u(c) and real income. An export subsidy increases export production lowering output in other industries along the PPF moving the economy to a lower tt line with reduced utility u(c) or real income.

Import tariffs are one of the oldest issues in political economy. The losses due to tariffs persist due to the lobby spending by the winning industries in payments to politicians to pass laws that hurt the rest of the economy and lower the gains from trade. The government collects tariff revenue. Consumers lose due to the higher price. There are net losses in the economy.

CHAPTER 3

Tariffs and Protectionism

Preview

The politics of protecting import-competing industries with tariffs is a classic issue that remains intensely debated today. This chapter covers:

* Deadweight loss due to import tariffs
* Import quotas and other nontariff barriers
* Losses due to tariffs in general equilibrium
* Political economy of tariffs and protectionism

INTRODUCTION

Government policy can protect domestic industry from foreign competition with tariffs and other forms of protectionism. The debate over protectionism some 200 years ago gave rise to the discipline of economics. Almost all economists favor international competition with minimal, if any, tariffs and very limited restrictions on trade.

Protectionism creates gains for a few with large losses spread across the economy. The owners and workers in the protected industry are organized and lobby by paying politicians for protectionist policies. The rest of the economy and consumers may not realize the extent of their losses.

A. IMPORT TARIFFS

A tariff is a tax on a good when it enters the country at a border, port, or airport. As with any tax, the consumer pays the increased price of the good. Tariffs are easy to collect and have been popular with governments throughout history as an easy way to collect taxes. Tariffs benefit the industry producing the good inside the country, setting up an alliance between the government and industry wanting protection from foreign competition. Tariffs are easy to conceal as consumers are generally not aware of how much tariffs raise prices.

The fledgling US government earned more than half of its revenue from tariffs for almost a century until 1870, and more than a quarter until the income tax was made constitutional in 1913. Governments in less developed countries (LDCs) rely on import tariff revenue as income and sales taxes are a challenge to collect.

The average US tariff jumped from 4% to 12% in 2018 after the gradual reduction from the 1950s due to a treaty called the General Agreement on Tariffs and Trade (GATT). The treaty enforced by the World Trade Organization (WTO) was an agreement for all nations to lower their tariffs and other protectionism.

GATT sprung from the desire to restore international trade following World War II. The world average tariff fell from 40% to below 10% under GATT. Countries also lowered a variety of nontariff barriers (NTBs) designed primarily to protect import-competing industries.

The Escape Clause allows the US Congress to enact temporary tariffs for an industry that can prove to the International Trade Commission (ITC) that it has been damaged by import competition. The President can also impose temporary tariffs based on national defense, unreasonable business practice, and damage from import competition. These vague legal criteria encourage lobbying by industry and tariff protection in the US.

EXAMPLE **3.1**   *US Tariff History*

The chart below shows the average US tariff on all imports since 1830. High tariffs on manufactures in the 1800s hurt the southern states contributing to the Civil War. Tariffs provided over a quarter of government revenue until income taxes were made constitutional in the 1920s. The high Smoot–Hawley tariffs in 1930 slowed trade, deepening the Great Depression as discussed by Alfred Eckels (1998). In 1934, the Reciprocal Trade Agreements Act allowed the President to negotiate tariff reductions. The GATT at the end of World War II and North American trade agreements from the 1970s led to the downward trend until the increase in 2018 although the average remains low at 3%.

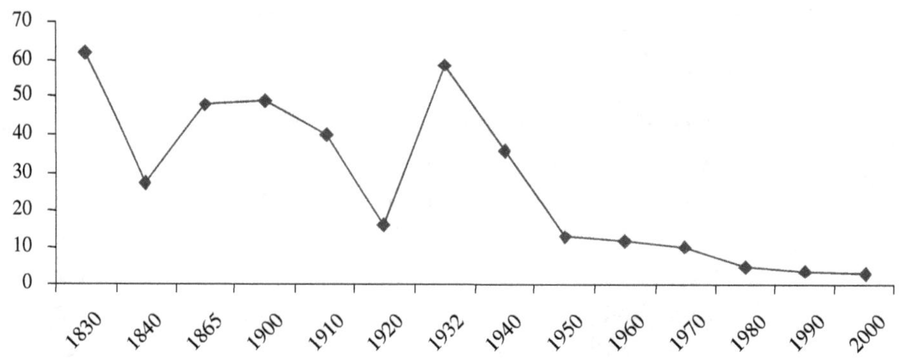

The Costs of Import Tariffs

The rough effects of tariffs on prices of familiar products in Table 3.1 are based on Murray Weidenbaum and Michael Munger (1983). The higher domestic price due to a tariff benefits import-competing industry. The government benefits as well with tariff revenue. Consumers including firms buying input in production are the losers.

Table 3.1 Estimated Price Effects of Tariffs

	Free Trade	**Protectionism**
Cars	$22,500	$30,000
Box of candy	$6	$15
Blue jeans	$45	$54

Tariffs can be levied on finished products such as cars or they can be hidden in intermediate goods such as electronic components. The imported intermediate products are included in goods labeled "Made in the USA" even if very little value is added to the finished product inside the country.

The effective rate of protection (ERP) includes tariffs on intermediate inputs as well as quotas and other NTBs. Quotas are quantitative restrictions on imports. NTBs include voluntary export restraints and regulations designed to limit imports. Effective protection is resulting total increase in the price compared to the share of price accounted for by domestic inputs.

Where t is the tariff rate, the price ep^* of a good increases to $(1 + t)ep^*$ inside the country. Suppose the price of an imported shirt is $20, but a 10% import tariff raises the domestic price to $22. A domestic firm can import material worth $8 but pays $12 due to the 50% tariff on material. The shirtmaker adds domestic value of $10 and sells the $22 shirt. The tariffs protect domestic value added by $6/$10 = 60%.

Estimates of ERP in Table 3.2 from Alan Deardorff and Robert Stern (1984) compare the US, Japan, and EU. The ERP is higher than the average tariff. Howard Wall (1999) estimates US imports were 26% lower in 1996 than they would have been without protection.

Table 3.2 Effective Rates of Protection

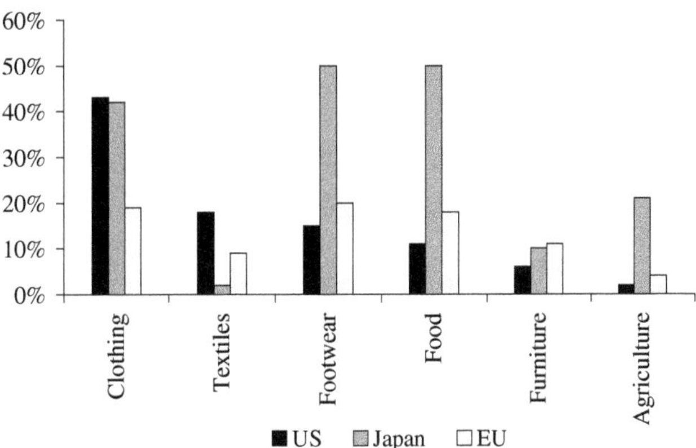

Protectionism costs consumers in the higher prices of finished goods.

EXAMPLE **3.2**   *Tariff Duties Per Capita*

The percentage of tariff-free goods has slowly increased. In the US, over half of all imported goods are duty-free. There has been little decline, however, in average duties paid per capita over recent decades.

Market Analysis of a Tariff

Figure 3.1 shows the effects of a tariff on the market for a manufactured good M with the international price $ep^* = \$5$ given the exchange rate e and foreign currency price p^*. The economy is a price taker in the international market. At $5, the difference between quantity demanded $Q_D = 300$ and quantity supplied $Q_S = 100$ is imports $Q_{imp} = 100$.

A 20% tariff $t = 0.2$ increases the domestic price to $1.2 \times \$5 = \$6$. Consumers reduce quantity demanded to 270. Domestic producers increase the quantity supplied to 120. Imports drop to $150 = 270 - 120$.

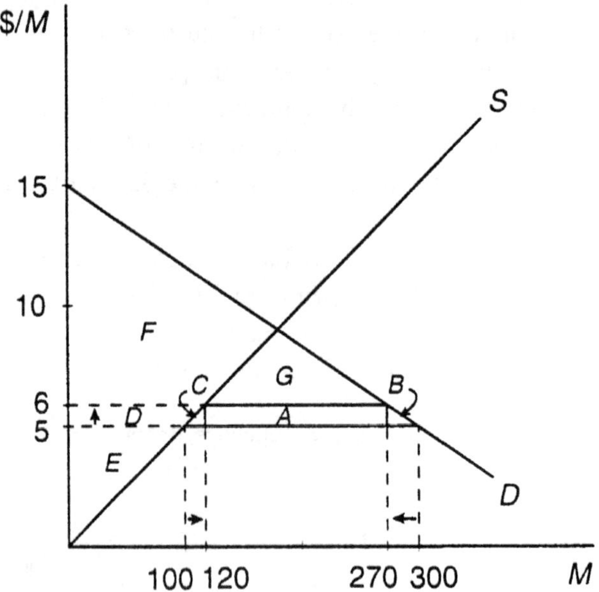

Figure 3.1
Market Effects of a Tariff
A 20% tariff raises the domestic price from $5 to $6. Imports drop from 200 to 150. The government collects $150 tariff revenue A. Domestic firms enjoy increased producer surplus of $110 in D. Consumer surplus falls by $285 in ABCD. The deadweight loss of the tariff is $25 = B + C = \$15 + \$10$.

Tariff revenue for the government is tariff per unit $1 = 0.2ep^*$ times the quantity of imports 150. Tariff revenue of \$150 is rectangle A.

When the price is \$5, the quantity demanded is 300. The consumers up along the demand curve would pay more than \$5, some willing to pay close to \$15. The large triangle composed of the areas ABCDFG provides a measure of the gains to consumers. This area below the demand curve and above price is consumer surplus, $CS = 1/2[(\$15 - \$5) \times 300] = \$1500$.

Consumers lose ABCD due to the tariff. Some are squeezed out of the market and those remaining must pay the higher price. The tariff lowers CS to the area FG $= 1/2[(\$15 - \$6) \times 270] = \$1215$. The lost consumer surplus due to the tariff is \$285.

The area above the supply curve and below the price measures producer surplus PS. Producers gain D selling more at a higher price as firms expand output and enter the industry. Firms along the supply curve sell at a price above what they would be willing to accept. At the \$5 price, $PS =$ E $= 1/2(\$5 \times 100) = \$250$. When the price rises to \$6 due to the tariff, $PS =$ ED $= 1/2(\$6 \times 120) = \$360$. The gain in producer surplus in area D is \$110.

Triangles B and C are the deadweight loss (DWL) of the tariff, lost consumer surplus not offset by transfers of A to the government and D firms in the industry. The losses B = \$15 and C = \$10 total to DWL = \$25. Table 3.3 summarizes the income redistribution due to the tariff.

Tariffs redistribute income away from consumers and cause DWL.

Tariffs increase the value of stocks of firms in protected industries as found by Gene Grossman and Jim Levinsohn (1989). Shareholders have an interest in keeping their industry protected. There is ample empirical evidence that protection supports wages in protected industries at least for some time. The winners from tariffs spend money lobbying for protection. Government officials are happy to accept the lobby support. The politics of protection in various forms of payoffs explain the persistence of import tariffs even though consumers pay the DWLs.

Table 3.3   Income Redistribution from the Tariff in Figure 3.1

Consumer Loss	Producer Gain	Government Revenue	Deadweight Loss
A + B + C + D	D	A	B + C
\$285	\$110	\$15	\$15 + \$10 = \$25

EXAMPLE **3.3**   *The Costs of Saving Jobs*

The following partial list of protected US industries from Gary Hufbauer, Diane Berliner, and Kimberly Elliott (1986) rank industries by yearly cost per job saved. The date of the law, the primary region of the world hurt, the percentage price increase, and the cost per job saved are listed. The costs include DWLs and damage to other industries. The US would be better off paying the workers not to work and eliminating the protectionism.

Cost/Job	Year	Industry	Region	Price Increase
$750,000	1969	Steel	Argentina, Brazil	30%
$270,000	1789	Shipping	Global	60%
$220,000	1953	Dairy	Global	80%
$200,000	1922	Glassware	Europe	19%
$135,000	1930	Ceramic tiles	Brazil, Italy	21%
$100,000	1891	Books	Asia	40%
$60,000	1934	Sugar	Global	30%

Protection Versus Free Trade

The DWLs due to tariffs can be estimated. Inefficient production results from tariffs wasting valuable labor, capital, and natural resources. The economy could be producing higher valued exports. Murray Weidenbaum and Tracy Munger (1983) estimate protectionism leads to annual losses of about $4000 per capita.

Lobbying efforts of industry and labor groups also lead to losses. Protected industries employ lobbyists who give money and favors to politicians. It would be better to face international competition rather than settle for the inefficient quick political fix of protectionism.

Tariffs are inefficient but persistent. Protection is for sale by politicians.

Developed countries have witnessed declines during recent decades in manufacturing industries such as iron and steel, footwear, nonferrous metal, and apparel. These industries have faced increasing competition from newly industrialized countries (NICs) and LDCs where wages are much lower.

Since the 1950s, manufacturing employment has dropped from over 1/3 of the US labor force to less than 1/5 while employment in services has risen from 1/2 to 3/4. This trend reflects the comparative advantage of the US with increasing specialization and trade. Tariff protection of manufacturing has not been effective.

Manufactures have shifted toward skilled labor in developed countries (DCs). Falling unskilled wages have increased the incentive for education and training. Politicians gain by passing tariff laws. The oldest issue in economics promises not to go away soon.

Section A Problems

A1. Show the gains from trade in an import market with total surplus.
A2. Show the gains from trade in an export market.
A3. Suppose a 40% tariff is levied on imported manufactures in Figure 3.1. Find imports, tariff revenue, changes in producer surplus and consumer surplus, and DWL.
A4. Why is steel protected in the US while toys and games are not?
A5. Explain the negative effective rate of protection on cars.
A6. Explain how producer and consumers surplus would differ if demand is less elastic and supply more elastic than in Figure 3.1.

EXAMPLE **3.4**   *Transport Costs*

Transportation costs partly determine trade. Donald Rousslang and Theodore To (1993) find total transport costs are about as large as tariffs for US imports. For imported consumer products tariff rates are 6%, the international freight rate 3%, and wholesale costs 9% of the final price.

EXAMPLE **3.5**   *North American Trade*

The North American Free Trade Agreement (NAFTA) eliminated import protection between Canada, Mexico, and the US in 1994. Mexican tariffs on US products had dropped from 10% to 2% as US tariffs on Mexican products dropped from 4% to 0.5%. Mexican exports are generally labor intensive but some trade is based on natural resources. Incomes per capita and manufacturing wages are shown below.

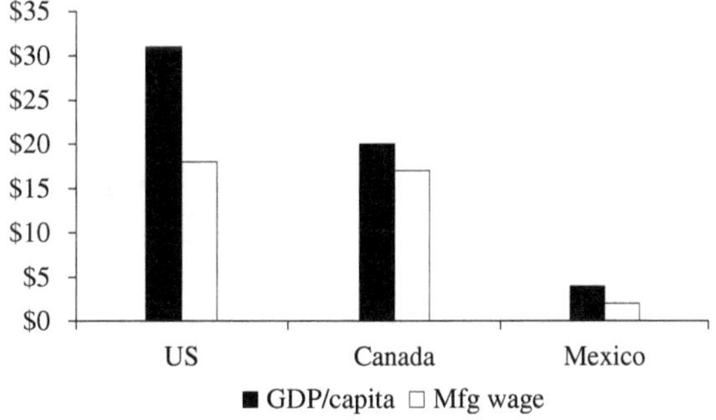

B. QUOTAS AND NONTARIFF BARRIERS

A quota is a quantitative restriction on the level of imports, so many tons of steel or sugar as examples. A disadvantage of quotas for consumers is that adjustments are forced onto the price. Other NTBs such as health restrictions and electrical certificates may sound reasonable but are subject to abuse.

Market Analysis of a Quota

Figure 3.2 illustrates a quota of 150 units at the international price $ep^* = \$5$. Without a quota, 200 units of M would be imported. The quota pushes the domestic price to the point where quantity demanded minus supplied equals 150. The domestic price is pushed above the international price by a binding quota.

The quota lowers consumer surplus by the area ABCD. Producer surplus increases by D. The area ABC is the DWL from the quota. With the equivalent tariff, government revenue would be A.

With the quota, foreign exporting firms sell at the higher $6 price. Before the quota, foreign export revenue was $5 × 200 = $1000. The quota lowers foreign export revenue to $6 × 150 = $900 in this example.

The DWL from the quota is $175. Quotas are more costly than equivalent tariffs because of the larger DWL. This quota costs the economy $150 compared to the equivalent tariff that costs the economy $25 with the government collecting tariff revenue.

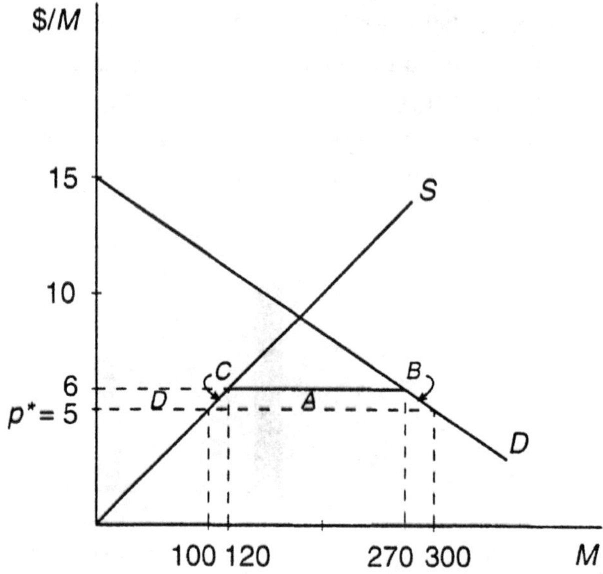

Figure 3.2
Import Quota
A quota of 150 pushes the domestic price up 20% from the world price of $5. The 20% tariff would raise the tariff revenue. The DWL is ABC = $175 compared to BC = $25 for a tariff.

Governments may raise revenue-auctioning quotas to firms selling at the artificially high domestic price. If foreign firms were forced to bid for the right to export, the government could appropriate A.

EXAMPLE **3.6**   *Costly Quotas*

David Tarr and Morris Morkre (1987) estimate DWLs due to various US quotas are equivalent to a 19% tariff. The average cost-to-benefit ratio of all quotas is hardly a bargain at 35 to 1.

Market Adjustments with a Quota

Market adjustments is forced entirely onto price in an import market with a quota. Consider the increased domestic demand in Figure 3.3. With a quota of 150, the increased demand forces the price to rise to $7. The level of imports remains at 15. Domestic production increases to 14. Consumers are worse off with the quota than with an equivalent tariff.

Quotas force market adjustment onto price hurting consumers more than tariffs.

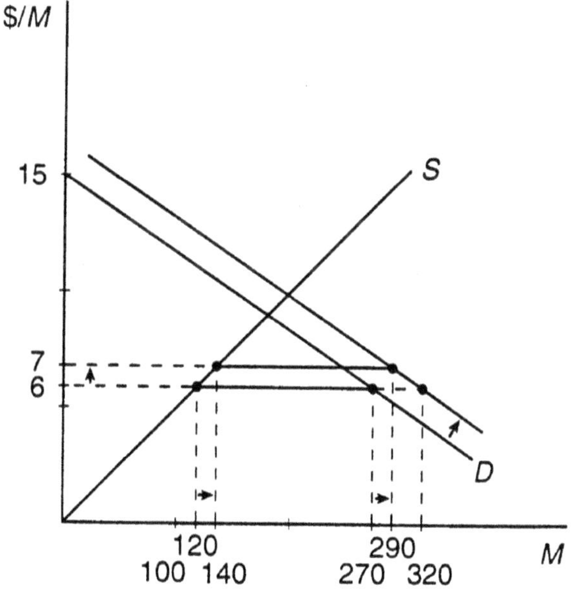

Figure 3.3
Market Adjustment with a Quota
With a quota of 150 an increase in demand forces adjustment onto price. Only 150 units of *M* can be imported. Price rises from $6 to $7.

Protected industries prefer quotas when the international price is falling, when domestic demand is rising, or when domestic supply is falling. In these circumstances, the domestic industry maintains output.

Protected industries would favor tariffs over quotas when the international price rises, domestic demand falls, or domestic supply is increasing. In these circumstances a quota would be nonbinding. These circumstances are impossible to predict in advance.

Quotas can lower the quality of domestic output. George Sweeney, Randy Beard, and Henry Thompson (1997) show a quota lowers domestic quality when there are high-quality imports. Domestic firms relax when imports fall competing less with quality. Foreign quality rises, another reason to avoid quotas.

EXAMPLE **3.7**   *The Customary Hassle*

The American Association of Exporters and Importers (AAEI) was founded in 1921 to lobby for free trade and offer technical assistance to those involved in trade. The AAEI publishes *US Customs House Guide*, a tour-de-force of the US trade policy. As an example, dolls representing only human beings and their parts have one rate, while dolls whether dressed or not another rate. All dolls dressed or stuffed must be imported in two parts.

Other Nontariff Barriers

DCs are committed to lower tariffs under GATT and the WTO. Regional free trade agreements lower tariffs. Quotas and other NTBs have become popular because they skirt these arrangements to liberalize trade. Governments under pressure devise various protectionist methods.

A popular NTB is the voluntary export restraint (VER). Japanese car exporters "voluntarily" limit exports to the US. The threat is tougher US protectionist measures against Japanese exports. The US auto industry puts pressure on the US government, which puts pressure on the Japanese government, which puts pressure on Japanese automakers.

A VER has the same basic effects as a quota but targets an exporter. European auto producers benefit from the Japanese VER because they are not subject to such quantity restrictions. The result of the VER is higher prices inside the US.

VERs create a cartel for exporters. Japanese automakers restrict competition among themselves in the US market. The VER gives market power to the foreign industry.

Import quality upgrading also occurs due to a VER or quota. If Japanese automakers agree to export a limited number of cars, they also aim to sell higher quality cars.

Japan has a voluntary import expansion (VIE) program for US goods. Computer chips, coal, beef, and construction industries in the US have benefited. Such VIE programs discriminate against other countries.

Legal trade restrictions favor domestic firms. Lawyers, doctors, and other professionals restrict practice across borders. Telecommunications and electric utility industries are government franchises protected from foreign competition.

Health laws are selectively applied to foreign goods to protect domestic producers. Fruits from South America were banned when a test showed evidence of insecticides. Later it appeared contaminated fruits had been placed in samples. Another example was banned imports of British beef during the "mad cow" pandemic. Also the EU bans imports of genetically engineered crops.

Licensing also restricts competition. Constant monitoring is necessary to ensure fair application of product standards. International law handling claims of unfair trade practice is a growing legal field.

Another sort of NTB is the transportation industry in Japan not delivering imported goods. The "Buy American" campaign sponsored by US producers aims to be an NTB.

Quotas and other NTBs are protectionist.

Jong-Wha Lee and Phillip Swagel (1994) examine the causes of NTBs for 41 countries. They find governments tend to protect large declining industries facing import competition. Governments use a combination of NTBs along with the usual tariffs as well as restrictions on exchange rate transactions.

EXAMPLE **3.8**   *Lobby Spending*

The US steel industry has a long history of protection. In 1998, it began an active effort to buy protection. Four years later the steel tariffs were invoked. Douglas Brook (2005) documents the large sums the steel industry spent on Congress and government regulators.

EXAMPLE **3.9**   *Quota Losses*

Japan's VER on car exports to the US raises the price of cars and benefits exporters in other countries. Car firms in Europe enjoy higher export prices. Elias Dinopoulos and Mordechai Kreinin (1988) estimate the average price of a European car sold in the US to be 53% higher due to the Japanese VER with the 22,000 jobs saved in the US each costing over $300,000. Bee Yan Aw and Mark Roberts (1986) examine US shoe imports and find the quota agreement with Korea and Taiwan resulted in a 12% increase in the price of shoes. Korea and Taiwan shifted to exporting higher quality shoes with more profit per pair.

Section B Problems

B1. Calculate the DWL from the quota after the demand increase in Figure 3.3.
B2. Compare market adjustment with a quota versus a tariff when domestic supply decreases due to a higher wage in a new labor contract.

B3. Compare adjustment with a quota versus a tariff when there is decreased demand.

EXAMPLE **3.10**   *Winners and Losers with Protection*

The effects of protection vary across industries and regions. Linda Hunter (1990) finds the largest industrial winners in the US during the 1980s were textiles, autos, steel, chemicals, mining, plastics, and utilities. The largest losers were furniture, fixtures, and construction. Regions winning with protection are the Southeast and East with losses spread across the Midwest and West.

C. PROTECTION AND PRODUCTION

Losses from protection include the inefficiency in specialization on the production frontier and the reduced consumer choice on the indifference curves.

Tariffs and the Production Frontier

Along the production possibilities frontier (PPF) in Figure 3.4, there is full employment of all resources. The slope of the PPF is the marginal rate of

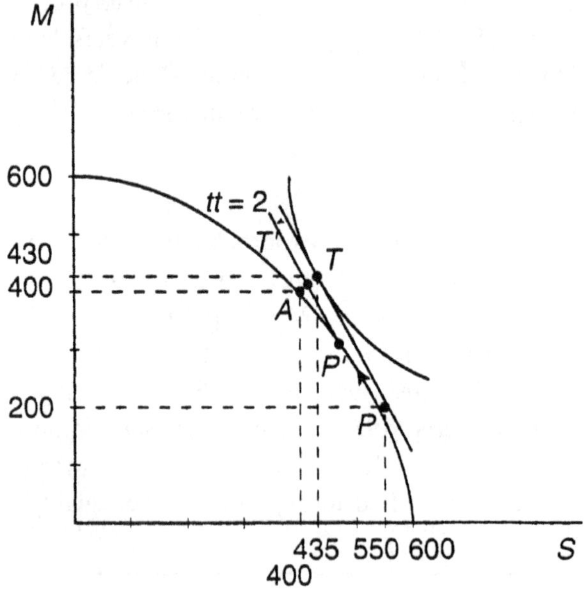

Figure 3.4
Tariffs and Economy-Wide Consumption
The economy trades at *tt* = 2 producing at P with consumers choosing T to maximize utility. Exports of 115 are traded for imports of 230 *M*. A tariff pushes the economy to produce at P'. Consumers are forced to the lower *tt* reducing the consumption to T'.

transformation (MRT) that shows how many units of manufactures M are given up for an additional unit of services S. A higher relative price of services M/S moves the economy toward producing S.

Without trade, consumers pick the point they most prefer on the PPF indicated at the autarky point A. Consumers maximize utility subject to the PPF. In autarky, 400 units of both goods are produced and consumed.

If the relative price of services is higher on the international market, the economy opens to trade by specializing and moving from point A to P. Resources shift from producing M to S. At point P, the MRT is equal to the terms of trade, $tt = M/S = 2$.

From P, the economy trades at the world prices, importing 2 M for every exported S. Consumers maximize utility subject to the terms of trade tt choosing point T tangent to the optimal indifference curve. The slope of the indifference curve is the marginal rate of substitution (MRS). Production is at P where $tt =$ MRT and consumption at T where $tt =$ MRS.

More of both goods are consumed with trade at T than in autarky at A. Consumers are better off with higher utility due to trade. The indifference curve tangent to T lies above the autarky utility at A.

A tariff lowers the relative price of services moving production to P'. From P', the economy trades along the lower terms of trade line. The tt line from point P' lies below the tt line from P. Consumption falls to T'. The indifference curve tangent to tt' at T' lies below the one tangent at T. The tariff reduces consumer utility. Resources are wasted in the protected sector M.

Tariffs reduce specialization and trade with inefficient production, reducing consumption and lowering utility.

EXAMPLE 3.11   *Smuggling*

Smuggling is illegal trade aimed at avoiding protection or prohibition. Smuggling totals about 10% of international trade. A smuggler considers benefits as well as costs including the probability of being caught and penalized. Smuggling increases international specialization and trade but uses more resources than free trade because the goods are more costly to transport.

Section C Problems

C1. Explain the relative price of S with autarky and trade for the open economy of Figure 3.4. Illustrate the effects of a tariff.

C2. What would happen if the relative price of S in the world exactly equals the autarky price in Figure 3.4? What would be the effect of a tariff in that situation?

EXAMPLE **3.12**   *Tariffs as Tax Surcharges*

Tariffs are regressive as lower income groups pay a higher percentage of their income due to the higher prices with protection. Basic items such as food, clothing, autos, and shoes have higher prices due to protection. Susan Hickok (1985) estimates the tax burden of tariffs as a percentage of income finding low-income groups pay up to 40% while high-income groups pay less than 10%.

D. POLITICAL ECONOMY OF PROTECTION

Economics presents the argument against tariffs based on their inefficient allocation of resources and losses for consumers. Economists have been making these points for over 200 years. Commerce has pursued the gains from trade since the dawn of history. The section addresses how protectionism persists.

EXAMPLE **3.13**   *Who Is WTO?*

GATT is an international treaty that succeeded in lowering tariffs on manufactures since the end of World War II. The WTO began in 1993 as its judicial branch awarding damages from complaints about treaty violations. Services were added to the treaty in 1994 as countries maintain protection of monopolies in telecommunications, utilities, and postal service. Banking and finance remain highly protected as well.

Rent Seeking Protection

Import-competing industries and the labor in those industries are willing to pay for tariff protection. The payments are made to politicians in charge of setting tariffs and NTBs. Political contributions go to the representatives as lobby support and business arrangements.

Industries hire lobbyists to organize payments to politicians. Union labor groups lobby for protection on their industries. This rent seeking adds to the wasted resources due to protectionism. Politicians trade votes logrolling to gain signatures for tariffs protecting their districts. Politicians are local protectionists for the industries in the areas they represent.

Industries and labor groups lobby to buy tariff protection. Consumers suffer from tariffs but are disorganized and unable to affect the politics of protectionism.

Figure 3.5 illustrates the optimal amount of lobby spending by an industry or labor group. The marginal benefit (MB) of lobbying shows positive diminishing benefits. Marginal cost (MC) shows the increasing cost of effective lobbying. The optimal amount of lobbying occurs where MC = MB.

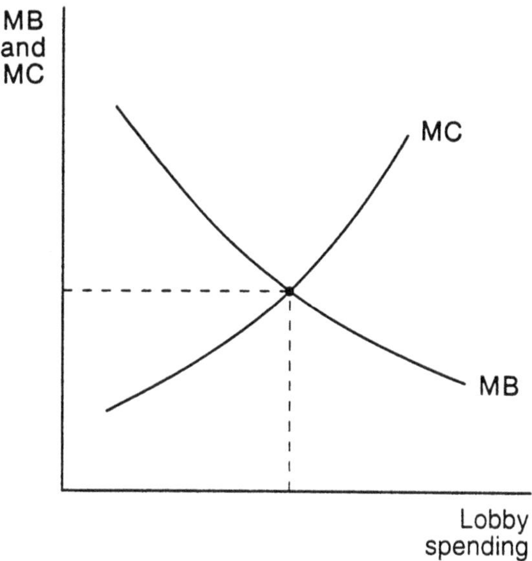

Figure 3.5
Optimal Lobby Spending
The MB of lobbying is the higher tariffs and prices for the industry. The MC determines
the optimal lobby spending where MC = MB.

Figure 3.6 shows the decision facing politicians setting tariffs. Political parties
gain the support of some voters with tariffs. Workers in a protected industry
support political candidates delivering tariff protection. Stockholders and local
business interests want protection for their investments. These marginal benefits
diminish as the tariff increases.

Tariffs also create losses as exporting firms are disrupted, prices increase,
and national income falls. These MCs increase with higher tariffs. These costs
and benefits are considered by politicians who pass the 10% tariff in to gain
200,000 votes.

*Industries lobby and politicians set tariffs each according to their costs and
benefits in the political economy of protectionism.*

EXAMPLE **3.14**   *An Appeal for Protection*

This speech might be heard in Congress one day this week:

*Our domestic industry faces unfair foreign competition. They flood the
domestic market and steal our customers, killing an important branch of
industry. We cannot win this contest. Our workers need tariff protection.*

In fact, this is satire written in the early 1800s by Frederic Bastiat pretending to
favor a prohibitive tariff to shut all "windows, openings, and fissures" to protect
the domestic candle industry . . . from the sun!

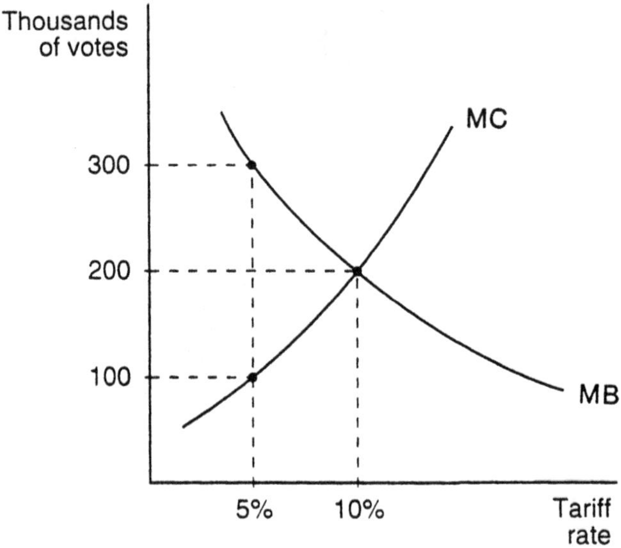

Figure 3.6
Optimizing Votes with a Tariff
A tariff gains votes from those who benefit but loses votes of those who suffer. If the tariff is 5%, a small tariff increases costs 100,000 lost voters but attracts 300,000 others. These incentives result in 10% tariff.

EXAMPLE **3.15**   *Quotas, Export Taxes, Good-Bye*

When apparel manufacturers in China recently faced quotas on their exports to the EU, China retaliated with taxes on their exports to the EU. The apparel manufacturers soon left China for other countries.

Dumping as Unfair Competition

Industries in the US can file claims of unfair trade practices with the ITC. Dumping is selling below the cost temporarily to drive out the competition. The ITC regularly hears complaints of dumping by foreign exporters. Subsidies by foreign governments to their export industries are also considered unfair business practice.

The President can award dumping damages with restrictive quotas. The number of claims and value of awards has steadily increased from the 1990s. Dumping typically cannot be proven but awards are regularly handed out.

EXAMPLE **3.16**   *Dumping the International Trade Commission*

Labor unions pursue trade policy goals. The AFL-CIO publishes *The Pocketbook Issues* aimed at increasing protection. Its recommendations include policy to:

- Reduce bilateral trade deficits
- Eliminate unfair trade practice

- Require domestic content in production
- Require raw products to be processed before export
- Require a larger share of cargo on US merchant ships

EXAMPLE 3.17   *Buy American Regardless*

The Crafted with Pride in the USA Council promotes domestic products. One large retailer conducted an experiment with identical jeans sold side by side, one "Made in USA" and the other with foreign labels. More of the domestic jeans sold. Surveys have shown that consumers consider country of origin. In the long run, quality and price must be critical.

EXAMPLE 3.18   *Shrimp Dumping and Soybeans*

Shrimp is a leading seafood in the US due to efficient farming techniques and global competition. US shrimpers won a dumping case with the ITC in 2004 and were awarded tariffs of 100% on imports. There was no evidence of predatory pricing by exporting Asian countries. The money to pay for the ITC filing came from disaster relief for shrimpers. Congress also awarded the shrimping industry the tariff revenue in violation of WTO rules. The US exports soybeans to Asia for shrimp food. Soybean farmers lobbied to repeal the shrimp tariffs. The only sure winners are lawyers and government officials receiving lobby payoffs.

Section D Problems

D1. Why are larger firms and industries more protected than smaller ones?

D2. Why might senators favor protectionism less than representatives in Congress? Presidents less than senators?

D3. Some industries claim they must be protected because their products are essential for national defense. Which products would you recommend for national defense tariffs?

CONCLUSION

Protection is one of the oldest issues in economics and remains important. Protectionism will continue if the benefits to the protected industries outweigh their lobbying costs. Politicians are happy to supply protection in return for lobby spending. Chapter 4 shows tariffs have the potential to improve the *tt* for a large country.

Terms

Anti-protectionism	Production distortion
Deadweight losses	Protectionism
Dumping	Quality upgrading
Effective protection	Quota licensing
Import tariffs	Quotas
ITC	Rent seeking
Logrolling	Import tariffs
Nontariff barrier (NTB)	Voluntary export restraint (VER)

MAIN POINTS

- Tariffs impose DWLs that benefit the protected industry and create revenue for the government at the expense of the economy.
- Quotas and other NTBs have become popular due to treaty agreements to lower tariffs.
- Protectionism shifts production away from export industries lowering income in the economy.
- Tariffs are enacted by politicians when the benefits for the protected industry outweigh their cost of lobbying. Consumers would benefit from free trade. Anti-protectionism comes from industries that export or buy imported intermediate products.

REVIEW PROBLEMS

1. Problems 1 through 9 are based on domestic demand $D = 100 - P$ and supply $S = -10 + P$ for sports shoes. Diagram the domestic market. Find the level of imports if the world price is $30.

2. Suppose a 50% tariff is put on imported shoes. Find and diagram the change in imports.

3. Find the tariff revenue and the DWL with the 50% tariff.

4. Diagram and find the prohibitive tariff rate.

5. With an international price of $30, suppose a quota of 10 is imposed on the market. Find the domestic price with this quota.

6. Find the total DWL due to the quota of 10.

7. Find the producer surplus of domestic shoe producers when the quota is 10. Compare it to free trade.

8. Suppose foreign shoe producers voluntarily agree to limit their exports to 30. Find the domestic price with this VER. Compare the total losses to those when the quota is 10.

9. With free trade, suppose all shoe imports come from countries A and B each supplying half of imports. Under political pressure, A agrees to a VER of 15 and country B agrees not to increase export. Find the price, imports, and the change in export revenue for A and B.

10. Diagram the PPF of a closed economy where the relative price of manufactures is higher on the international market than at home. In which direction will the economy specialize if it moves to free trade? Describe the direction of trade. Illustrate the effects of a tariff on production.

11. Consider an economy producing services, manufactures, and agricultural goods. Describe its PPF. What determines which goods are imported or exported? What are the output effects of tariffs on manufactures?

12. If all congressional representatives were elected at the state level rather than in districts, predict whether there would be higher or lower tariffs.

READINGS

Jagdish Bhagwati (1988) *Protectionism* Cambridge: MIT Press. A lively look at the oldest issue in political economy.

Forrest Capie (1994) *Tariffs and Growth*, Manchester: Manchester University. The history of tariffs from 1850 to 1940.

William R. Cline, ed. (1983) *Trade Policy in the 1980s*, Washington: Institute for International Economics. Applied studies of trade policy.

I.M. Destler (1986) *American Trade Politics: System Under Stress*, Washington: Institute for International Economics. Analysis of the domestic politics of US trade policy.

Gary Clyde Hufbauer and Howard Rosen (1986) *Trade Policy for Troubled Industries*, Washington: Institute for International Economics. Potential of policy for US industry facing foreign competition.

Ron Jones and Anne Krueger, eds. (1990) *The Political Economy of International Trade*, London: Blackwell. Readings on the economics of protection.

Stephen P. Magee, William A. Brock, and Leslie Young (1989) *Black Hole Tariffs and Endogenous Policy Theory*, Cambridge: Cambridge University Press. Political theory of protection.

Dominick Salvatore, ed. (1987) *The New Protectionist Threat to World Welfare*, Amsterdam: North-Holland. Studies on policy issues.

Martin Wolf (2005) *Why Globalization Works*, Cambridge: Yale University Press. Excellent survey.

MATHEMATICAL APPENDIX

Tariffs protect import-competing industries by reducing imports and raising price inside the country with a deadweight loss in the market and reduced gains from trade. A tariff is a tax t on imports that raises the international price $p = ep^*_{imp}$ inside a small country to $(1 + t)ep^*_{imp}$. The level of import $q_{imp} = q_D - q_S$ falls as q_D decreases and q_S increases due to the increase in p_t. Tariff revenue for the government is $TR = tep^* \times q_{imp}$.

A quota is similar to restricting imports to q_q and raising the domestic price to $p_q = (1 + t_q)ep_M^*$ where t_q represents the increase in price due to the quota. A quota has an equivalent tariff that would result in the same import level and price but provide tariff revenue (TR). A quota is also less efficient than a tariff as imports cannot adjust to changes in demand D_M, supply S_M, or world price ep_M^*.

The market loss due to a tariff or quota is the decrease in total surplus (TS). Consumer surplus (CS) is due to consumers paying less than they would be willing to pay. CS is the area under the demand curve D above price p. Let L be the limit price where quantity demanded drops to zero. CS is the area $CS = \int_0^{qD} Dn(q)dq$ under the inverse demand function Dn as p ranges from L to p.

Producer surplus (PS) represents the additional revenue of firms able to sell at market price p for more than they would be willing to accept according to marginal cost along supply curve S. Let $p0$ be the price at which output in the market disappears. PS is the area $PS = \int_0^{qS} Sn(q)dq$ above the inverse supply function Sn from 0 where $p = p0$ up to the market price p.

Total surplus is the sum $TS = CS + PS$. A tariff hurts consumers raising price $p = ep^*$ by tep^* and lowering consumption from q_D to $q_D{}'$ with CS falling by $dCS = -\int_{q_D{}'}^{qD} Dn(q)dq$. On the supply side, a tariff benefits firms with the price increase raising quantity supplied from q_S to $q_S{}'$ with PS rising by $dPS = \int_{q_S}^{q_S{}'} S(q) dq$. Producers gain less than consumers lose as $dPS < -dCS$ with some of the lost CS going into PS. The government gains some of the lost CS in tariff revenue $TR = tep^*q_M$. The difference between lost CS and the gains in PS and TR is the deadweight loss $DWL = dTS = dCS + dPS + TR < 0$. The equivalent quota that raises price to the same level has a larger DWL as $TR = 0$.

In the general equilibrium, a tariff lowers utility $u(c)$. A tariff increases output of the import-competing good and lowers output of the exported good along the PPF. The PPF between goods M and S can be written $x_M(x_S)$. A tariff implies lower gains from trade as utility is maximized subject to the lower terms of trade tt leading to the first-order condition (FOC), $MRS = u_M/u_S = p_M/p_S = tt = MRT$ on a lower indifference curve. An equivalent quota has the lowering of utility in the general equilibrium.

Tariffs and quotas persist despite these losses as firms share some of their PS with politicians who pass the tariff and quota laws. Anti-protectionist lobby spending by exporters favoring free trade is less successful. Consumers only have the power to vote for politicians favoring increased CS. Politicians weigh lobby spending from protectionists versus anti-protectionists and the consumers they represent when writing detailed trade laws. Consumers are generally unaware of their losses due to tariffs and quotas. Consumers working in an import-competing industry would vote for politicians providing import protection. The original US Constitution allowed only a minimum uniform import tariff to keep ports operating and pay the navy to keep shipping lines open.

CHAPTER 4

Terms of Trade

Preview

The terms of trade (*tt*) refer to the price of exports relative to the price of imports, the price of what a country sells relative to what it buys. A higher relative price of exports is better *tt*. For a small country, the *tt* are given by international markets. In contrast, a large country lowering aggregate demand for its import improves its *tt*. This chapter covers:

- Offer curves and the *tt*
- The optimal tariff for a large country
- Strategic tariff games between large
- The *tt* with a nonrenewable resource

INTRODUCTION

Some countries are large enough for exporters to have market power over the price of their exports. Examples are the US in aircraft, Saudi Arabia in oil, Germany in machinery, and Greece in tourism. Large countries that buy enough imports can lower those international prices with tariffs. Examples are the US in petroleum, Japan in food, Latin America in machinery, and China in textiles.

Interaction between the production frontiers and consumption preferences of large countries determine their *tt* and levels of trade. Offer curves picture this international trade equilibrium in a simple diagram. A large country has an optimal tariff that will maximize income unless its trading partners impose tariffs.

Large countries can select tariffs opposing each other in a "tariff game" with the outcome depending on their strategies. Game theory provides a structure to analyze tariff games between large countries.

The *tt* for nonrenewable resources such as oil and minerals are critical to the world economy. Optimal depletion leads to a predictable rising trend in price to ration consumption. Offer curves provide a framework for the analysis of international resource trade.

A. OFFER CURVES

Offer curves show how the tt and level of trade are determined. Gains from trade occur when two economies differ in their production potentials or consumer preferences.

Trade Triangles and Offer Curves

Figure 4.1 shows an economy with its production frontier and consumer preferences leading to 100 units of M and S in autarky at point A. Consumer utility is maximized on the highest attainable indifference curve I tangent to the production possibility frontier (PPF). The autarky relative price at A is equal to the marginal rate of transformation (MRT) on the PPF and the marginal rate of substitution (MRS) on indifference curve I.

If the international relative price of services is higher than the domestic MRT, production shifts toward S. At the relative price $M/S = 2$ the economy produces at point P where $(M, S) = (50, 135)$. The economy trades along the tt line to the higher indifference curve II at point T where consumption is $(M, S) = (110, 105)$. The shaded trade triangle shows exports of 30 S and imports of 60 M.

Figure 4.2 shows improved terms of trade at $tt = 3$ with the economy increasing its specialization. Production moves to P′ where $(M, S) = (25, 145)$. Exports of 35 S are traded for 105 M. More is exported in exchange for the increased imports at the better terms of trade.

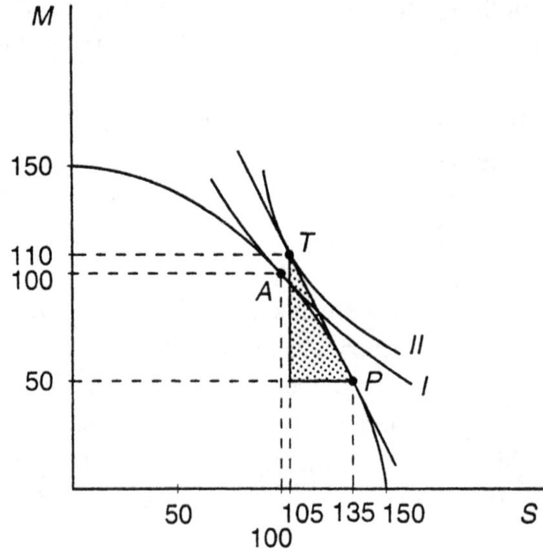

Figure 4.1
International Specialization
When $tt = 2$ the economy exports services and consumes at T. The level of trade grows from zero in autarky A to the trade triangle. Utility increases from I to II.

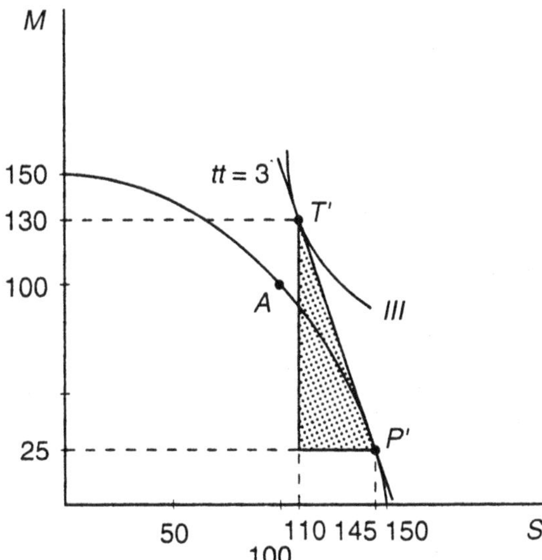

Figure 4.2
Increased International Specialization
If *tt* rises to 3 the economy exports more services consuming at T'. The level of trade grows with the larger trade triangle as utility increases from II in Figure 4.1 to III.

Figure 4.3 summarizes the response to these different *tt* plotting the imports of M and exports of S on the axes. The ray from the origin represents the *tt* as the number of imports received per unit of export. The trade triangles in Figures 4.1 and 4.2 correspond to the imports of M and exports of S on offer curve H.

Every point on offer curve H represents a potential international equilibrium. Improving *tt* creates larger gains from trade and expands the volume of trade along the offer curve.

An offer curve shows the increasing exports of a country with better terms of trade. Consumers enjoy gains from trade moving out the offer curve.

Figure 4.4 shows the corresponding offer curve of the foreign country that curves away from its M export axis. The autarky relative price of S in the foreign country is 3. If the terms of trade is 2, the foreign country will export 60 M in exchange for 30 S. At the improved $tt = 1$, the foreign country increases specialization in M exporting 80 in exchange for 80 S.

A higher relative price for M induces more specialization and export for the foreign country. Underlying the foreign offer curve are its PPF and indifference curves. The foreign offer curve bends away from its export axis.

EXAMPLE **4.1**   *Trends in the Terms of Trade*

The *tt* for oil-importing countries fell during the 1970s due to Organization of Petroleum Exporting Countries (OPEC) oil embargoes but improved after 1980

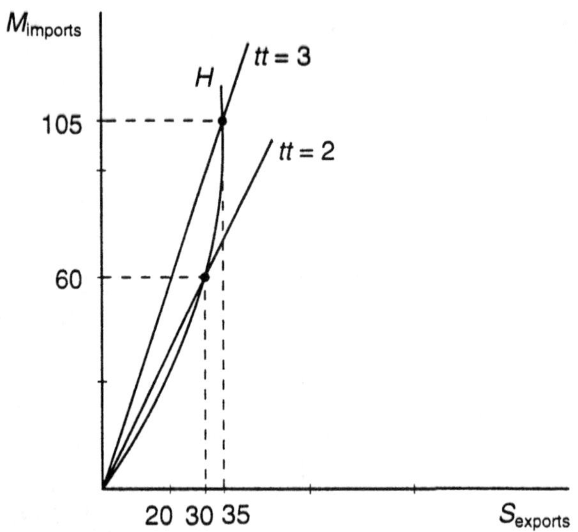

Figure 4.3
Home Offer Curve
The offer curve based on Figures 4.1 and 4.2 shows the increased level of trade due to better *tt*.

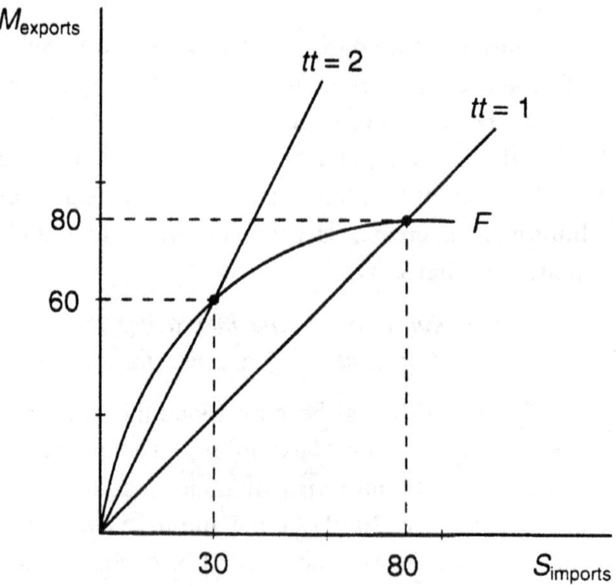

Figure 4.4
Foreign Offer Curve
As the *tt* improve for the foreign country, its exports of M increase.

and especially during the 1990s. Oil prices rose and *tt* fell during the 2000s with opposite moves during the 2010s before a crash in 2015. For developed countries (DCs) the *tt* for imported manufactures have improved due to increased production in less developed countries (LDCs) and newly industrialized countries (NICs).

Terms of Trade Equilibrium

With two countries, home imports equal foreign exports and vice versa at the equilibrium *tt*. In Figure 4.4 with *tt* = 3, no trade is offered by the foreign country because its exports are too cheap. In Figure 4.3 with *tt* = 1, no trade is offered by the home country for the same reason. These autarky prices in each country determine the limits to the *tt*.

At the equilibrium *tt*, the quantities of export offered by each country match the quantities of import the other wants. Home and foreign offer curves in Figure 4.5 illustrate this international equilibrium.

The tt and level of trade in the international equilibrium are determined where offer curves intersect.

If the international relative price of services were lower at *tt* = 1.5, there would be an international shortage of services *S* putting upward pressure on its price. There is also a surplus of *M* putting downward pressure on the price of *M*. The markets are stable as the *tt* and level of trade would tend toward the equilibrium.

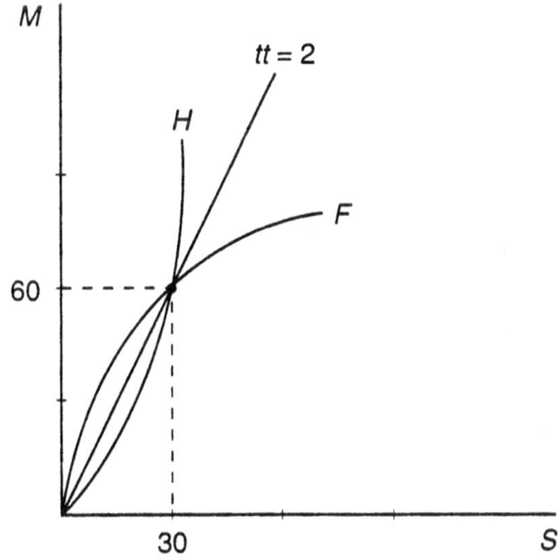

Figure 4.5
International Equilibrium
The *tt* and level of trade are determined where the home offer curve H meets the foreign offer curve F. At any other *tt*, the exports from one country do not match the imports of the other country.

EXAMPLE **4.2**   *The Terms of Trade of the Less Developed Countries*

International trade continues to grow over time. While trade in the LDCs is increasing, their *tt* have been falling during recent decades. As nonrenewable resources become scarcer, the *tt* for resource-rich LDCs will improve. LDCs want to become more involved in producing manufactures.

Shifting Offer Curves and the Terms of Trade

Offer curves change with the underlying condition of production or with evolving preferences. Suppose labor unions secure a new contract with higher wages and benefits in the manufacturing sector in the home country. As a result, manufactures would become more expensive to produce in the home country making it more open to trade.

Figure 4.6 pictures this expansion of the home offer curve. For each level of imported *M*, the home country offers more exported *S*. Expansion of the home offer curve results from this decreased supply of manufactures. The same shift could be due to increased demand for manufactures, decreased demand for services, or increased supply of services.

Figure 4.7 shows the expanded home offer curve will lower the international price of services. The *tt* fall for the home country to 1.75. Home exports rise to 40 *S* with imports rising to 70 *M*. The trade triangles of both countries expand.

An expanding offer curve lowers the tt and raises the level of trade.

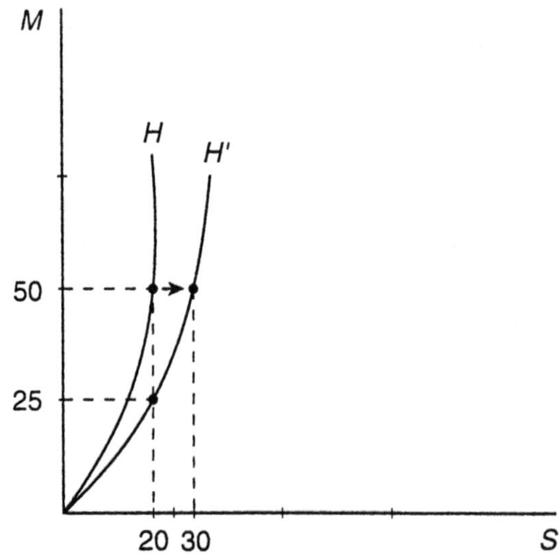

Figure 4.6
An Expanding Home Offer Curve
The home offer curve expands due to higher costs in manufacturing production or increased demand for *M*. The economy becomes more open to trade with the expansion.

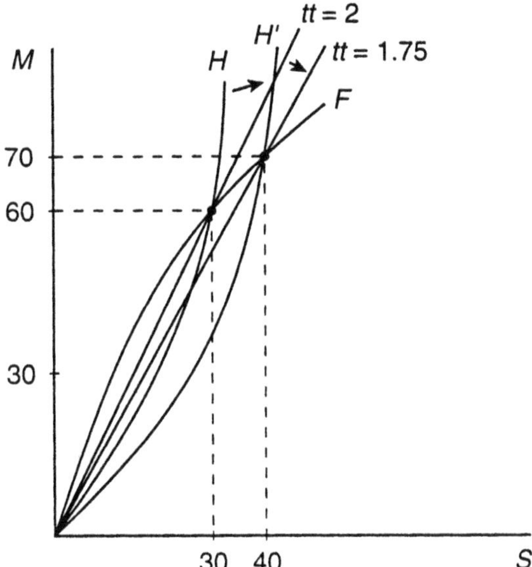

Figure 4.7
An Expanding Offer Curve and tt
A large country that wants to expand trade will suffer falling terms of trade. As the home offer curve expands from H to H', the *tt* fall from 2 to 1.75 while the level of trade increases.

Improved capability to produce exported services would have the same effect on the home offer curve. With investment or improved production technology in the export industry, the economy becomes more open to trade. The volume of trade increases as the *tt* decline. Increased efficiency in export industries lead to the falling price.

A shrinking of the offer curve occurs due to opposite changes. An offer curve can shrink due to falling import demand, reduction in export supply, increased demand for exported products, or increased supply of imported products. As the offer curve shifts closer to the export axis, the *tt* improve while the level of trade falls.

EXAMPLE **4.3**   *US Terms of Trade*

> The US *tt* have been constant over the recent decades with prices of imports and exports both trending upwards. The price of petroleum can raise import prices but also raise cost of production for exports. Smaller countries are more narrowly specialized and more exposed to changes in their *tt*.

EXAMPLE **4.4**   *Alfred Marshall and the Terms of Trade*

> Alfred Marshall was an English economist at the turn of the 20th century who developed many of the principles of microeconomics. Marshall wrote on economic issues. These edited remarks of Marshall (1926) are relevant today.

Before another century has passed there may remain only a few areas of rich minerals and raw products. Oil is a good example. With increasing scarcity, sellers will have the upper hand in international markets. Acting together, sellers will have a monopoly and restrict output to charge monopoly prices. This situation makes me regard the future of England with grave anxiety.

Discovery of oil in the North Sea turned England into an oil exporter after the 1980s.

Section A Problems

A1. Sketch the PPF and community indifference curves leading to the foreign offer curve in Figure 4.4.

A2. Show the offer curves of two countries that would not trade with each other.

A3. Explain why the equilibrium in Figure 4.5 is stable starting with a relative price of 2.5.

A4. Diagram the shift in Figure 4.5 if foreign demand for services decreases. What happens to the tt and level of trade?

A5. Show and explain what happens to the international equilibrium in Figure 4.5 with improved technology in home export supply and with increased foreign demand for home exports.

B. TARIFFS AND THE TERMS OF TRADE

When a large country imposes a tariff, the demand for its import falls on the international market improving its tt. A large country might gain as a result from a tariff. The foreign country, however, also has the option of imposing a tariff to improve its tt.

Large Country Gains from a Tariff

Figure 4.8 illustrates the potential of a large country to gain utility or income with a tariff. Autarky consumption and production are at point A. With trade, the country exporting services produces at P and trades along the terms of trade line tt to point T.

A tariff on manufactures pushes the economy to point P′ on the PPF. The reduced international demand for M lowers the relative price of M improving the terms of trade to tt'. The economy trades up along the new terms of trade line tt' from point P′. Consumers choose the tangent to the domestic price line at point T′ reflecting the high price of manufactures due to the tariff. Real income and the level of utility increase.

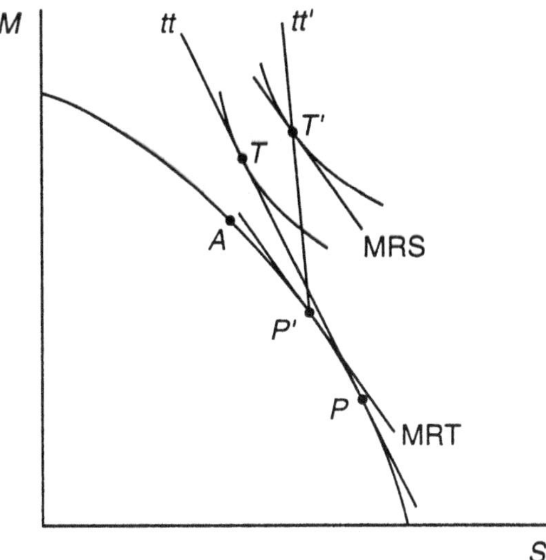

Figure 4.8
Improved tt with a Tariff
Autarky production and consumption occur at A. With free trade, the economy produces at P and consumes at T with *tt*. A tariff pushes the economy to P'. The relative price of exports rises to *tt'*. The economy trades along *tt'* to T'. At P' and T', MRT = MRS < *tt'*.

The terms of trade line *tt'* is not tangential to the PPF at P' since the tariff drives a wedge between relative prices inside and outside the country. The relative price of manufactures is higher inside the country.

A large country has the potential to improve its tt *with a tariff, raising utility compared to free trade.*

EXAMPLE **4.5**   *Britain as a Large Open Economy*

In the early 1800s, Britain protected its agriculture with the Corn Laws, tariffs on all grain imports. Economists argued that Britain should move to free trade but recognized the *tt* would fall since Britain was a large economy. Douglas Irwin (1988) estimates that lowering tariffs in 1841 from an average of 35% to 25% lowered the *tt* 3.5% and national income 0.4%. Efficiency gains were outweighed by the falling *tt*. British tariffs had fallen to 14% by the 1880s. When Europe and the US followed the example, world specialization and trade increased.

The Optimal Tariff

A large economy improves its *tt* with a tariff. In principle, there is an optimal tariff that maximizes utility. While a tariff reduces efficiency, the *tt* improve.

The marginal benefits from the improved *tt* may outweigh the marginal costs of lost efficiency.

Figure 4.9 illustrates trade indifference curves (TICs). Exports must be produced but are enjoyed by foreign consumers. More exports must be offset by more imports implying TICs slope upward. As exports rise, consumers want increasing imports implying TICs bend away from the export axis.

TIC I represents the autarky level of utility, and indifference curve IV the highest level. The large home economy can maximize utility subject to a fixed foreign offer curve. Suppose the home offer curve goes through point FT with free trade. The optimal tariff shrinks the home offer curve to go through the foreign offer curve at point OT. The highest level of utility on indifference curve IV is not attainable.

The optimal tariff maximizes utility subject to a given foreign offer curve assuming the foreign country does not retaliate.

Quotas and the Terms of Trade

A quota can have the same effect on the *tt* as a tariff by lowering the demand for import on the international market. If the home country imposes a quota, its offer curve is horizontal at the quota level. This restricted offer curve results in the same trade equilibrium as a tariff.

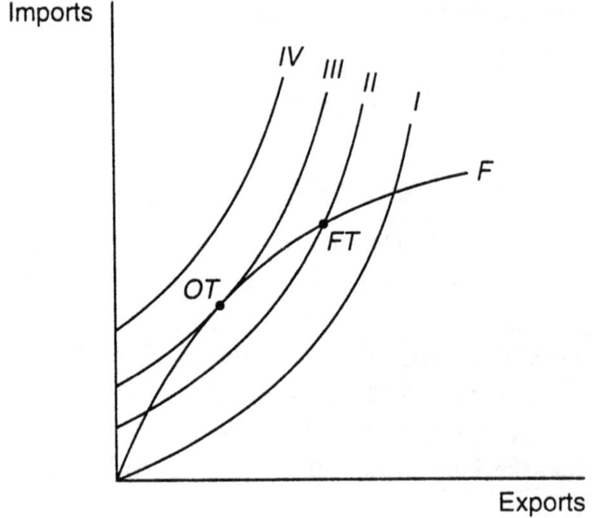

Figure 4.9
Trade Indifference Curves
TICs I through IV represent increasing preferences. An optimal tariff shifts the home offer curve through the optimal point OT on the foreign offer curve.

There is no tariff revenue with a quota. Deadweight losses (DWLs) are higher at the same *tt* and volume of trade. Another disadvantage of quotas is that all adjustments to changing market conditions are forced onto the price.

Tariff Wars

If the home country imposes a tariff, the foreign country can retaliate with its own tariff. This retaliation shrinks the foreign offer curve F. Foreign consumption of home exports falls, reducing the demand and price for home exports. The *tt* turn against the home country.

Figure 4.10 illustrates a tariff war as the volume of trade shrinks with each round of tariffs. The home country fires the opening shot, imposing a tariff based on offer curve F and shrinking its offer curve to H′. The international equilibrium moves from A to B as the *tt* improve for the home country.

The foreign country then imposes a tariff of its own based on home offer curve H′. The foreign offer curve contracts to F′, the international equilibrium moves to C, and the *tt* shift in favor of the foreign country.

The home country then imposes a higher tariff based on foreign offer curve F′ restricting its offer curve to H″, and so on. The result is a little change in the *tt* as the level of trade diminishes. Trade ceases when prohibitive tariffs are reached.

Optimal tariffs create gains at the expense of trading partners, reduce the level of trade, and invite retaliation.

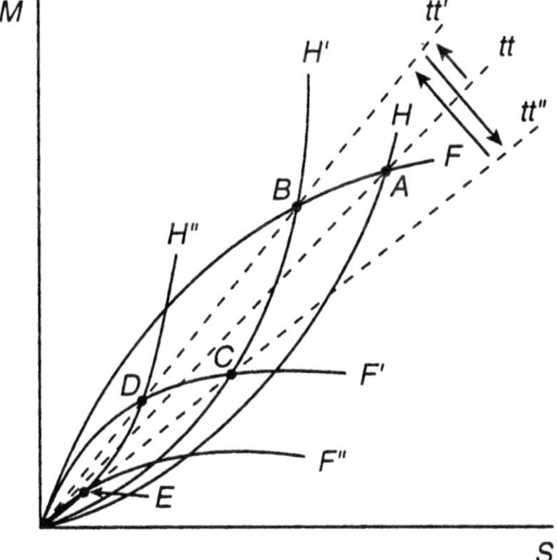

Figure 4.10
A Tariff War
The home country imposes a tariff shifting its offer curve from H to H′ reducing trade from A to B. The foreign nation retaliates with a tariff lowering trade to C. Subsequent retaliation lowers the level of trade to D and E.

EXAMPLE **4.6**   *Canada/US Tariff Wars*

> Canada and the US are prone to tariff wars. Alok Bohara, Kishore Gawande, and William Kaempfer (1998) examine the pattern of tariff retaliation from 1868 to 1970. When the US initiated tariffs, Canada reacted with tariffs. Canada would initiate tariffs but retreats without US reaction. Internal political issues initiated tariffs although the Canadian/US Free Trade Agreement and North American Free Trade Agreement (NAFTA) reduced tariff wars.

Optimal Tariffs in Practice

The World Trade Organization (WTO) has governed the international political economy since World War II. Nations are committed through the General Agreement on Tariffs and Trade (GATT) treaty to lower tariffs and protection. Any country stepping out of line is noticed by other countries. The WTO can impose penalties on countries breaking GATT rules. Average tariffs slowly decreased at least until the US presidential tariffs in 2018 led to similar increases worldwide.

Optimal tariffs are not part of the political process of setting tariffs, which is anything but scientific. Industries lobby for tariff protection paying politicians. Tariffs benefit the protected industry while hurting consumers as well as other industries.

Small countries have no incentive to impose tariffs. LDCs are exempt from WTO rules and are allowed to set their own tariffs. LDCs are typically small countries with an optimal tariff of zero.

Section B Problems

B1. Illustrate foreign gains from a tariff on services in a production frontier diagram based on Figure 4.8.

B2. Illustrate how a tariff war could eliminate trade.

B3. How is the optimal tariff similar to the optimal price for a monopoly?

EXAMPLE **4.7**   *US Energy Sources*

> US energy sources are mostly oil, natural gas, coal, and nuclear. Alternative energy sources such as solar, wind, and geothermal will eventually become economical as prices of nonrenewable fuels rise. Due to international environmental agreements, coal is declining and alternatives are rising.

C. TARIFFS IN GAME THEORY

Players in game theory have opposing goals and make strategic choices that determine the outcomes of games. Board games, cards, and sports are examples of strategic games. This section looks at tariff games between large trading countries that pursue tariffs to improve their *tt*.

The Prisoner's Dilemma of Tariffs

Consider two countries that trade in a game where one can gain with a tariff through improved *tt* at the expense of the other. If the gains of one country are exactly offset by the losses of the other, the game is called zero sum. Tariffs are a negative sum game due to the DWLs of tariffs.

Consider a simple tariff game with each country deciding whether to impose a tariff that lasts one year. The choices are free trade with a 0% tariff or protection with a 10% tariff. The countries announce their tariffs simultaneously.

Table 4.1 shows a payoff matrix with free trade by both countries resulting in incomes of 100. A tariff by one country increases its income by 20% but lowers income in the other by 40%. A home tariff with no foreign tariff results in home income of 120 and foreign income of 60. The game is symmetric as a foreign tariff with no home tariff raises foreign income to 120 as home income falls to 60.

If both nations impose tariffs, they both lose 20% with incomes of 80 in both countries. Global income is lower with multilateral tariffs than with a single tariff. If this game is repeated, each country develops a strategy to decide whether to impose a tariff for the coming year. While a country might promise free trade, the other might not trust it.

The situation in Table 4.1 is called a prisoner's dilemma. Police separate two suspected crime partners offering each a reduced sentence to squeal on the other. If they both keep quiet, they go free. The police tell each separately their partner has already confessed.

Tariffs are the dominant strategy since income with a tariff is larger regardless of what the opponent chooses. Multilateral tariffs are the Nash equilibrium defined by the mathematician John Nash when each player makes the best choice given a correct guess about the opponent.

The prisoner's dilemma illustrates why WTO negotiations are crucial to promote free trade. Each country is more willing to lower tariffs if it is assured that the other will do the same.

Table 4.1 Symmetric Negative Sum Tariff Game (foreign income, home income)

		Home Tariff	
		0%	**10%**
Foreign Tariff	**0%**	(100, 100)	(60, 120)
	10%	(120, 60)	(80, 80)

A country can signal a desire to move to free trade by unilaterally removing its tariff. This means a temporary loss of income if other keeps its tariff. The next round, it might follow suit with free trade. Free trade is an unstable equilibrium due to the temptation to gain at the expense of the other.

The persistence of tariffs is due to a prisoner's dilemma. Free trade is optimal for a country only if the other pursues free trade.

EXAMPLE **4.8**   *Multifiber Agreement and the Shirt Off Your Back*

The Multifiber Agreement (MFA) was an international market-sharing plan for textile and apparel trade. The MFA began in 1961 between Japan and the US and grew to encompass a wide range of products and many countries. Its quota schemes were inconsistent with WTO rules. Irene Trela and John Whalley (1995) point out that the quota allocation system awards existing firms. This "lock in" effect makes it difficult for new firms to enter the international market. The end of MFA resulted in increased competition and lower prices.

Tariff Reaction Functions

Each country has an optimal tariff given the tariff of the other country. The process of arriving at the tariff equilibrium is pictured by the reaction functions in Figure 4.11.

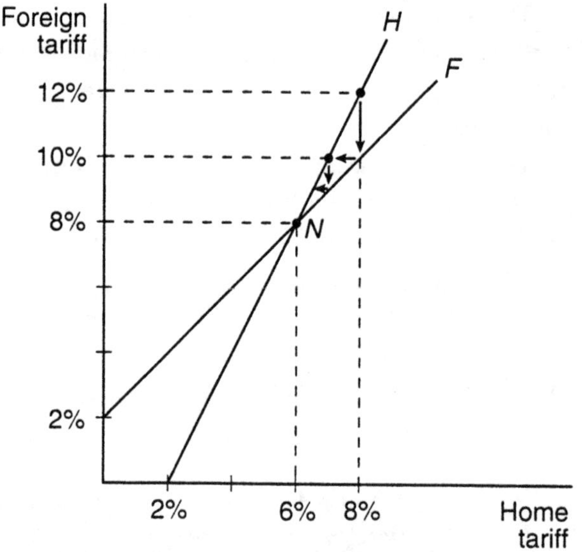

Figure 4.11
Tariff Reaction Functions
Each country reacts to a tariff from the other with its optimal tariff. Starting with a 12% foreign tariff, the home nation sets its tariff at 8%. The foreign nation responds to with 10% tariff. The adjustment process continues until the equilibrium is reached at point N with a 6% home tariff and 8% foreign tariff.

The home reaction function H shows the optimal home tariff on the horizontal axis for any given foreign tariff. With no foreign tariff, the optimal home tariff is 2%. If the foreign tariff is 12%, the optimal home tariff is 8%. The foreign reaction function F shows the optimal foreign tariff for any home tariff.

The home reaction function has a positive slope because a higher foreign tariff requires a higher optimal tariff in response. There is an international tariff equilibrium at point N where the two reaction functions intersect. Equilibrium tariffs are 6% and 8%.

EXAMPLE **4.9**   *The US and Canadian Equilibrium Tariffs*

Canada and the US trade but bicker over tariffs. James Markusen and Randall Wigle (1989) evaluate the impact of free trade between the two countries. Equilibrium tariffs are estimated to be 18% for the US and 6% for Canada. Tariffs are lower in the US than in Canada. The countries avoid the prisoner's dilemma by a progression of trade agreements.

Reaction functions shift with changing market conditions. If the home country becomes more efficient producing exports, the home reaction function shifts to the right. The home country chooses a higher tariff regardless of the foreign tariff. Increased demand for imports in the home country causes a similar shift. Decreased supply of exports or decreased demand for imports would shift the home reaction function left lowering both tariffs.

EXAMPLE **4.10**   *Shipping Cartel*

Shipping rates for LDCs add to the tariffs they face. Shipping rates add about 10% to the price of exports from LDCs and tariff rates about half that amount. International shipping prices are controlled by shipping cartels. Constant monitoring ensures the cartel members do not cheat. Such monopolistic practices would be illegal inside the US but are allowed for shipping.

Mixed Strategy Tariffs

A tariff game might not have an equilibrium. In Table 4.2, a tariff would help the home country given a foreign tariff with home income increasing from 97 to 98. When there is a foreign tariff, a home tariff improves the terms of trade.

Table 4.2 Mixed Strategy Tariff Game (foreign income, home income)

		Home Tariff	
		0%	**10%**
Foreign Tariff	**0%**	(100, 100)	(95, 99)
	10%	(101, 97)	(93, 98)

If the foreign country has no tariff, a home tariff could lower home income from 100 to 99. When there is no foreign tariff, a home tariff has little effect on the *tt*.

The situation of the foreign country is the reverse. A tariff hurts the foreign country if the home country has a tariff but raises income if the home country does not have a tariff.

This mixed strategy game has no equilibrium. If the foreign country chooses free trade, the home country would benefit following suit. If the home country picks free trade, the foreign country would benefit with a tariff.

The game in Table 4.2 is called chicken as the countries vacillate between free trade and tariffs. It would be optimal to pick a mixed strategy, randomly choosing free trade versus a tariff.

The outcome of a tariff game depends on country strategies. A tariff equilibrium can be stable or unstable.

EXAMPLE **4.11**   *Eliminating Tariffs*

Eliminating tariffs would benefit some countries but hurt others. Alan Deardorff and Robert Stern (1984) estimate exports for industrial countries would rise 4% with worldwide tariff elimination. Incomes would increase slightly, less than 1% in the US. Income in the EU would fall due to falling *tt*. LDCs would face modest losses. Japan, Australia, and Canada would enjoy small gains.

Section C Problems

C1. Develop a tariff game with a small foreign country and show the optimal tariff for the large home country.

C2. Explain the adjustment process to the equilibrium at point N in Figure 4.11 starting with a home tariff of 4%.

C3. Show and explain the effect on international equilibrium tariffs of an increase in foreign export supply.

EXAMPLE **4.12**   *Tariffs and the Great Depression*

The Great Depression was worsened by an international tariff war. International trade was decimated by the Smoot–Hawley Tariff Act that raised the average US tariff to 60% as described by Alfred Eckels (1998). Other countries followed suit with prohibitive tariffs. Republican President Hoover favored high tariffs while Democrat Roosevelt pushed for free trade. More recently, Republican Reagan advocated free trade but increased tariff protection. Republican Bush favored free trade and followed Mexico with lower tariffs. Democrat Clinton signed NAFTA despite labor union opposition. Republican W Bush talked free trade but imposed steel tariffs. Democrat Obama increased tariffs. The average tariff declined from the 1950s until Republican Trump radically raised it back to the 1950s level.

D. TRADE IN NONRENEWABLE RESOURCES

Nonrenewable resources such as oil and minerals with limited available stocks are highly traded on international markets. The *tt* involve the prices of nonrenewable resources based on optimal depletion. Their prices should increase over time at the rate of return (ROR) on other assets.

EXAMPLE 4.13   *The Future Fuel Bill*

> OPEC tries to maximize profit by managing its supply of nonrenewable petroleum. New discoveries and better technology increase supply and lower price. Demand shifts are due to economic activity and changing weather. Oil prices would continue to climb over the coming decades with variation due to shifts in supply and demand. James Griffin and David Teece (1982) estimate an oil import elasticity of -0.73 making oil imports inelastic. Rising oil prices would then increase import spending by importers and export revenue for OPEC.

Nonrenewable Resource Prices

Nonrenewable resources loom large in international economics and politics. OPEC oil embargoes caused economic upheavals during the 1970s and 1980s leading to fundamental changes in production and income redistribution.

The stock of a nonrenewable resource is like other assets such as stocks, bonds, and real estate. An asset produces a ROR as the ratio of return to value,

$$ROR = return/value$$

Money in the bank paying 3% interest with no inflation increases purchasing power 3% per year. A perpetuity bond paying $50 per year based on 3% interest has a present value of $1667 as its ROR = 0.03 = $50/$1667.

An oil well returning $30,000 per year with ROR of 3% would have a market value of $1 million. A crucial issue in deciding how much oil to sell this year is the expected price in the future. If the price is $80 per barrel and the ROR on assets is 3% then an expected price of $82 next year will leave you indifferent between selling oil this year and waiting to sell next year. Oil in the ground is "money in the bank" or should be treated that way.

The supply of oil is defined by its asset value. Owners deplete oil to increase price at the ROR of alternative assets. As the stock of oil is depleted, its price will rise as depletion falls.

> *The ROR determines the expected price paths for nonrenewable resources. The value of the stock of the resource should increase at the ROR of all assets.*

EXAMPLE **4.14**   *Oil Depletion*

During the 1970s, OPEC restricted production resulting in a price jump from $10 to $120 per barrel. Adjustments included more efficient cars and energy efficiency. Rising oil prices conserve oil in the ground. Proven oil reserves would last centuries at the current rates of consumption. Increasing prices and improving technology will lower consumption. As hydrocarbon fuels are exhausted, alternatives have to develop. Green energy policy aims to speed the transition to other energy sources. This may sound like an environmental activist but is an abridged quote from William Stanley Jevons in *The Coal Question* (1864):

> *Abundant fossil fuels are the source of mechanical motion and chemical change, a chief input in industry, the material source of energy, and part of everything we do. As we exhaust the fuels, it is worthwhile to consider the quantities remaining on earth.*

Energy Substitutes as Backstop Resources

The rising price of nonrenewable resources provides incentive to find substitutes. Green energy activists base pessimistic predictions of depleting resources on current prices and consumption, disregarding the role of markets in conservation. As resources become scarce, prices rise and consumption falls.

Backstop resources are close substitutes that can serve the purpose of a depleting resource. Solar, nuclear, wind, and geothermal are backstop resources for hydrocarbons. Coal and natural gas are nonrenewable but have very large reserves. Over time, technology for backstop resources improves.

US energy policy during the OPEC oil embargoes encouraged "energy independence" with subsidized investment in nuclear energy, increased coal consumption, and depletion of US oil reserves. Green energy policy aims to discourage all coal and gas as well as oil. A strategic US oil tariff would improve the *tt* and encourage backstop technologies. The unpopular drawback is fall in real income due to higher energy prices.

EXAMPLE **4.15**   *The Real Price of Oil*

The real price of oil in terms of other goods has been about constant since the 1880s. Increased demand has been met with increased supply leading to steady prices as consumption increases. Reserves of oil increase with price due to improving exploration, drilling, and extraction techniques. Prices of many products from plastics to chemicals depend on the price of oil.

Resource Cartels and the Terms of Trade

Oil producers formed OPEC to improve their *tt* by restricting oil exports. Figure 4.12 represents the trade between OPEC and DCs in the Organization for

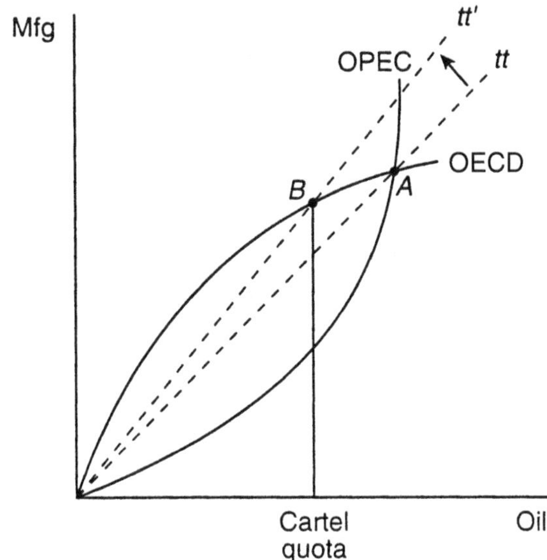

Figure 4.12
Cartel Quota and Price
A cartel quota improves the terms of trade from *tt* to *tt'* but the trade level falls from
A to B. The cartel must police the quota to avoid cheating at the high *tt'*.

Economic Cooperation and Development (OECD). The *tt* and volume of trade
at point A are based on optimal oil depletion. At point A, the expected return
on oil equals the expected return on other assets.

Suppose OPEC imposes an output restriction. The OPEC offer curve is cut
off at the cartel quota. The *tt* improve for OPEC to *tt'*. The relative price of oil
increases on the international market and the volume of trade falls.

Oil revenue might rise or fall with the quota since exports fall. There is
evidence from the embargoes that revenue rose for the first few years but returned
to previous levels over a decade. International cartels find it difficult to agree on
the quota for each member. A surplus would occur in Figure 4.12 as the high
price *tt'* makes it tempting for members to cheat on the cartel.

Cartels in rubber, coffee, tea, bananas, and various minerals have broken down
because of the inability to maintain quotas. The war between Iraq and Kuwait
stemmed from disagreement over OPEC strategy and their common pool of oil.

Oil exporters and importers use economic policy to influence the price of oil.
Embargoes, production subsidies, tariffs, subsidized research and development
(R&D) for energy research, auto efficiency, and emission standards are all aimed
to have effects on the international oil market. Similar trade policies aim to
influence other international resource markets.

EXAMPLE **4.16**   *Global Oil Production*

World output of petroleum has steadily increased since World War II. Saudi
Arabia is the single largest oil-producing country. Other OPEC members are Iran,

Venezuela, Algeria, Indonesia, Iraq, Kuwait, Libya, Nigeria, and UAE. China, Mexico, and Norway supply about 5% of the world output. The US' share of world output declined steadily starting in the 1970s, but recently increased due to fracking technology, increasing the yield.

Rates of Resource Utilization

Resource utilization varies across countries according to time preferences. LDCs are concerned with the immediate future and want income. This desire for quick income creates a high discount rate and faster resource depletion. Rich DCs discount the future at a lower rate and are more conservative with resources.

Figure 4.13 illustrates the depletion of a resource with high versus low discount rates. The country with a low discount rate realizes prices will rise in the future and is willing to wait. The country with a high discount rate is not willing to wait. Starting with equal stocks, the country with a high discount rate depletes its resource faster.

The discount rate of a resource owner determines how quickly the resource is depleted.

Oil exporters with different discount rates may form a cartel aiming to maximize income by restricting output. Cartels conserve resources by restricting output. Cartel members with high discount rates may agree to slow depletion if subsidized by others cartel members.

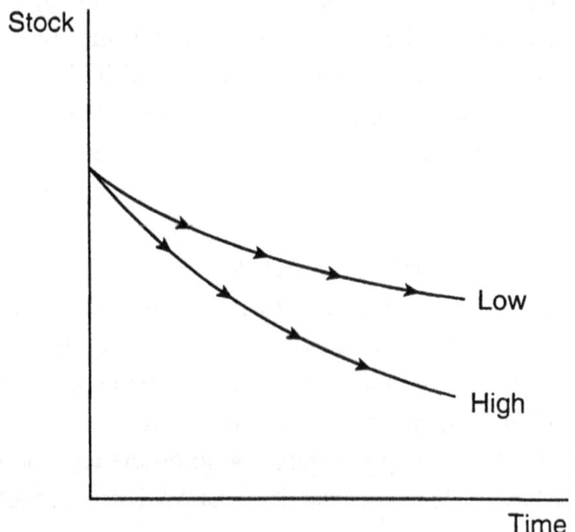

Figure 4.13
Nonrenewable Stocks and Discount Rates
A higher discount rate means quicker depletion of a natural resource.

EXAMPLE **4.17**   *Roller Coaster Oil*

The real price of oil would rise due to resource depletion, although improving technology increases reserves. Large areas of the world remain unexplored due to political and environmental issues. The real price of oil was stable through the 1950s and 1960s at about $10. OPEC embargoes led to $80 spikes during the 1970s and 1980s. Prices then stabilized at about $30 before beginning a climb during the 2000s with increased demand, the war in Iraq, and limited refining capacity. In 2015, the price crashed back below $30 but climbed back toward $80 as the US cut production. As a basis, the production cost is $30 in West Texas.

Section D Problems

D1. The interest rate is 4%, the present value of an oil well is $800,000, and the current price of oil is $100 per barrel. How many barrels would be sold this year with optimal depletion? How many barrels would be sold at $120?

D2. Find the path of prices over the next 10 years if the present price of oil is $100 and the real ROR is 6%. Compare this path with the example in the text of a 5% real ROR.

EXAMPLE **4.18**   *Major Oil Importers*

Japan and the EU are major oil importers, Japan importing all consumption and EU about 80% of its consumption. About 70% of imports in Japan come from the Persian Gulf, and 60% in the EU from OPEC. US imports come mainly from Mexico and Venezuela.

EXAMPLE **4.19**   *Resource Curse?*

Countries with an abundance of natural resources tend not to invest in capital, relying instead on resource income. This "resource curse" slows economic growth leaving income in the hands of the resource owners. Thorvaldur Gylfason (2004) examines data across countries and finds that resource-rich countries have lower investment, less trade, less foreign investment, more income inequality, less political liberty, and lower education. Oil-exporting Norway is an exception, but was a DC when oil was discovered. Zhenhui Xu (2000) shows processing resource products into finished goods has a positive effect on growth.

CONCLUSION

The *tt* contribute to determining national income and utility. Tariffs and other trade policies are not generally successful in improving the *tt*. Strategic tariff policies depend on the strategy of the other country. Trade policies aiming to affect international resource markets face the economics of optimal depletion. In practice, trade policies have proven ineffective to improve the *tt*.

Terms

Backstop resource	Optimal depletion rate
Cartel	Optimal tariff
Discount rate	Prisoner's dilemma
Dominant strategy	Real rate of return
International equilibrium	Repeated games
Nash equilibrium	Strategic tariff games
Offer curve	Tariff wars

MAIN POINTS

- The *tt* are determined between large countries through their production frontiers. Offer curves picture this interaction determining the *tt* and levels of trade.
- Tariffs can improve the *tt* for a large country by lowering the price of its import. While a large country might benefit from tariffs, its trading partners can retaliate leading to a tariff war.
- Game theory can predict the outcome of strategic tariff behavior. While free trade is optimal, tariffs present the challenge of a prisoner's dilemma.
- The *tt* for a nonrenewable resource can be predicted by optimal depletion treating the stock of the resource as an asset.

REVIEW PROBLEMS

1. Show and explain what happens to trade when the utility from imports increases in a large home country.
2. Show what happens when consumers in a large foreign country increase their demand for home exports.
3. Show and explain what happens to offer curves with increased investment in the foreign export industry.
4. Show and explain what happens when the foreign country supply of its export falls due to higher wages.
5. Evaluate what happens if both the home and foreign countries increase import demands.
6. Explain the remark "The tariff on oil imports in the 1950s was a policy of Drain America First."
7. Suppose the *tt* start at 1 and are improved 10% by respective tariffs. If each country responds to the other tariff with one of its own, find what happens to the *tt* after three rounds. Under threat of a trade war, should the home country wait for the foreign country to impose its tariff?
8. Suppose the foreign country has a policy of imposing a 4% tariff regardless of other countries. Diagram its reaction function. Given the home reaction function in Figure 4.11,

describe the adjustment process if the home country starts with a 3% tariff.

9. Illustrate the shift in the foreign reaction function when foreign demand for the home export falls in Figure 4.11. What happens to tariffs?

10. Illustrate a tariff equilibrium of free trade in a payoff table.

11. In Table 4.1, suppose payoffs to both countries with tariffs are ($80, $110). Predict and explain the outcome.

12. Show what happens in Figure 4.12 if OPEC imposes a tariff on manufactures. How is the outcome different from the cartel quota?

13. Why is it easier for cartels to form on primary products like oil, copper, and minerals, than on cars or engineering services?

14. The price of oil is $100 per barrel and 80,000 barrels are sold. If the interest rate is 2%, find the value of the oil deposit. Explain the difference if the interest rate is 3%.

15. Countries A and B each have oil reserves of 1 billion barrels. The discount rate of A is 10% while for B it is 2%. How much oil will each country sell this year?

READINGS

Ferdinand Banks (2004) *Energy Economics*, New York: Springer-Verlag. A sensible book on energy economics.

Robert Barro (1998) *Determinants of Economic Growth*, Cambridge: The MIT Press. A clear short book on economic growth.

Max Corden (1997) *Trade Policy and Economic Welfare*, Oxford: Clarendon Press. Neoclassical analysis of trade policy.

James Griffin and Henry Steele (1986) *Energy Economics and Policy*, New York: Academic Press. The economics of exhaustible resources.

Bernard Hoekman and Michel Kostecki (1995) *The Political Economy of the World Trading System: From GATT to WTO*, Oxford: Oxford University Press. Analysis of different interests at work in the evolution of trade agreements.

Farhad Rassekh (2004) The interplay of international trade, economic growth and income convergence: A brief intellectual history of recent developments, *Journal of International Trade and Economic Development*. A nice review of the theoretical and empirical literature.

Daniel Verdier (1994) *Democracy and International Trade: Britain, France, and the United States, 1860–1990*, Princeton University Press. A history of the ideals behind international trade.

MATHEMATICAL APPENDIX

The terms of trade (tt) are the price of exports relative to imports, $tt \equiv p_{exp}/p_{imp}$. Better tt mean a higher relative price of exports with an increase in tt. The tt between large countries are endogenously determined by their production possibilities and utility maximization with tt balancing trade in the international equilibrium. Better tt for the home country mean worse terms of trade $tt^* = 1/tt$ for the foreign country with a lower $tt^* = p^*_{exp}/p^*_{imp}$.

Suppose autarky prices are $p_S/p_M < p^*_S/p^*_M$ with relatively cheap S in the home country implying MRS = MRT < MRT* = MRS*. The home country would export S to the foreign country that exports M in return. Better tt induce a country to increase export production as consumption moves farther beyond its PPF.

Between two countries, each one imports what the other exports. Trade equalizes prices $p_S/p_M = ep_S^*/ep_M^*$ in the two countries. Trade moves the two countries to MRS = MRT = MRT* = MRS* on their production frontiers and indifference curves. Concave PPFs and strictly convex indifference curves imply a unique trade equilibrium.

The home offer curve $H = q_{exp}(q_{imp})$ is a function of the export a country offers as improved tt increase imports and the trade level. The offer curve H plots exports $q_{exp} = q_S - c_S$ on one axis versus imports $q_{imp} = c_M - q_M$ on the other summarizing the potential of the PPF and utility maximization. The offer curve is an increasing function as $dq_{exp}/dq_{imp} > 0$ with more exports offered and trade increasing as tt rises. The curvature is convex $d^2q_{exp}/dq_{imp}^2 < 0$ due to increasing marginal costs along the PPF and diminishing marginal utility of imports. Offer curves bend away from the "bad" export and toward the "good" import. Utility increases due to increased specialization and trade moving out along an offer curve.

The international equilibrium occurs where the home offer curve $H = q_{exp}(q_{imp})$ intersects the foreign offer curve $F = q_{exp}^*(q_{imp}^*)$. The tt are determined where the two offer curves intersect at $q_{exp} = q_{imp}^*$ and $q_{imp} = q_{exp}^*$ with both international markets clearing. Supplies and demands in both countries for both goods clear at the equilibrium tt.

A tariff shrinks the offer curve as the country trades less at any tt. A tariff lowers the level of trade but improves the tt. The contrived scarcity reduces demand for imports on the international market. The improved tt raises the possibility of increased utility due to a tariff. The optimal tariff t_{opt} maximizes utility taking advantage of the improved tt. While the level of trade decreases due to any tariff, there are optimal gains from trade at t_{opt}. A small country cannot influence its tt implying $t_{opt} = 0$.

A trade indifference curve (TIC) plots the level of utility in export–import space. Each TIC is an increasing convex in export–import space as imports are a good and exports a bad. More q_{exp} are given up at better tt with the higher q_{imp}. The optimal tariff maximizes utility on the highest TIC subject to the foreign offer curve F. The foreign country can retaliate leading to a tariff war that would make both countries worse off than with free trade.

The market for a nonrenewable resource N is characterized by a rising price p_N as the scarcity value of N increases due to the decreasing supply. The offer curve of a country exporting N, shrinks due to rising scarcity implying a decreasing level of trade and improved tt. Depending on the offer curve it faces, a resource depleting country can benefit due to increasing scarcity as the tt improve.

PRODUCTION AND TRADE

CHAPTER 5

Constant Cost Production and Trade

Preview

Comparative advantage was developed by English economist David Ricardo in the late 1700s in a political debate over tariffs. Ricardo showed the gains from trade in a simple example based on labor input to produce cloth and wine in England and Portugal. This chapter covers:

- Constant cost production with one input
- Gains from trade with constant cost production
- Relative wages and exchange rates in constant cost trade
- Complex trade with more than two countries and two goods

INTRODUCTION

Mercantilism was a popular economic doctrine in the 1700s at a time when international trade was increasing in England. Mercantilists advocated exports to accumulate gold and import tariffs to decrease wasting money on imports and increase wealth.

Adam Smith argued against mercantilism pointing out that wealth results from the capacity to produce valuable goods and services. Smith pointed out that international trade would lead to higher income and advocated free trade importing less expensive products from abroad and exporting the most efficient products with a high price abroad.

Ricardo came to realize that relative efficiency was the basis of gains from trade. A country that is the least efficient in producing every product nevertheless has comparative advantage in some products and can gain from trade. At the other extreme, a country that is the most efficient in producing every product can gain from trade.

Ricardo created a simple example with labor input in two goods comparing two trading countries. Constant costs are based on the fixed input per unit of output. The relative input levels in the two goods define comparative advantage as the opportunity cost of producing one more unit of a good in the lost output of the other. A country gains producing more of the good selected by relative efficiency. Importing the other good leads to the potential of increased consumption by not wasting input in either country.

This chapter develops constant cost production and trade revealing relationships for relative wages and exchange rates. With three or more countries and goods, relative price competition leads to diversified production and complex trade.

A. CONSTANT OPPORTUNITY COST IN PRODUCTION

Input in the Constant Cost Model

Assume a fixed amount of input is required to produce one unit of output. As an example, suppose the labor input per unit of output are $a_S = 2$ in services and $a_M = 3$ in manufactures. These constant inputs imply constant opportunity cost in production as one more unit of S lowers M by 2/3 of a unit.

The amount of the input $a_S S$ to produce 100 units of S is 200 workers. To produce 100 units of manufactures, M requires $a_M M = 300$ workers. If the total amount of labor available in the entire economy is 1200, the production possibility frontier (PPF) is $1200 = 2S + 3M$. The economy faces this linear PPF to produce the two goods. Producing 3 more units of S requires a reducing M output by 2 units.

The input represents a combination of capital, labor, and natural resources. Chapter 6 considers these inputs separately.

EXAMPLE **5.1**   *Inputs in Production*

Capital input is machinery, equipment, and infrastructure, such as streets and ports, involved in production. During the last half of the 20th century, the ratio of capital to labor K/L in the US economy grew 8%. Capital input per dollar of output rose 10% as the labor input decreased. While the mix of capital and labor slowly evolves, their bundle is the input with constant cost production.

Constant Cost Production Frontier

In Figure 5.1, if all the available input in a country goes into M production, the output would be $120/3 = 40$ M. If all the input goes into S production, the output would be $120/2 = 60$ S. In between is the linear PPF with same opportunity cost of lost M for an additional unit of S. The opportunity cost of one additional unit of S in terms of M is constant.

The domestic relative price of services is the slope of the PPF equal to $|-40/60| = 2/3$. This is the M given up to produce one more unit of S. This constant cost PPF is much simpler than the increasing cost PPF introduced in Chapter 3. In Chapter 6, separating labor and capital leads to the increasing cost PPF.

In autarky, consumers would maximize utility along the PPF at point A where $M = 20$ and $S = 30$. The utility function assumes consumers spend half their income on each good. At this point on the PPF, half of the input goes into producing each good.

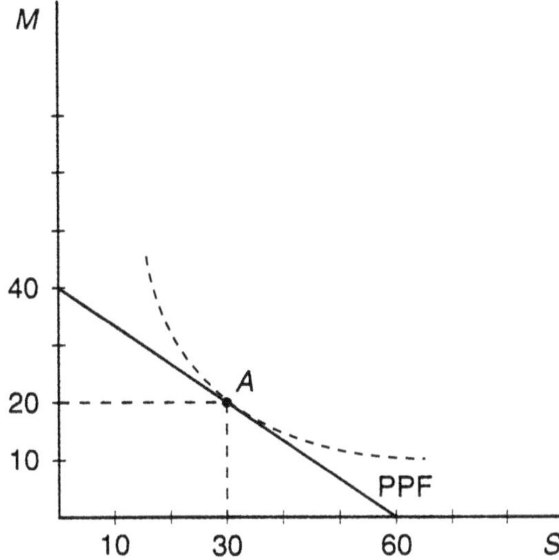

Figure 5.1
Constant Cost Production Frontier
Opportunity cost is constant along the linear PPF. The factor input is $F = 120$ with unit inputs $a_{LS} = 2$ and $a_{LM} = 3$. At point A, production and consumption are $(M, S) = (20, 30)$.

EXAMPLE **5.2**   *Evolving Inputs*

Improving technology requires investment in new capital equipment. An example is long-distance telephone calls per operator in the US rising from 64 per day in 1970 to 1300 in 1994. New digital switching systems accelerated the transition during the 1990s.

EXAMPLE **5.3**   *Input of Human Capital*

Human capital refers to education and training. In Japan, labor input per unit of output fell 90% from 1955 to 1995 partly due to the focus on education and training during the rebuilding after World War II.

Differences in Constant Cost Production

Suppose the foreign country has unit inputs $a_S{}^* = 6$ and $a_M{}^* = 4$ with available input of $F^* = 240$. This foreign production frontier PPF*, in Figure 5.2, has endpoints $M^* = 60$ and $S^* = 40$. The foreign relative price of services is $M^*/S^* = |{-}60/40| = 1.5$.

If foreign consumers also spend half their income on each good, the foreign input splits equally between the two sectors. Foreign consumption in autarky will be $120/6 = 20$ S and $120/4 = 30$ M.

Foreign inputs are higher for both goods, $a_S{}^* > a_S$ and $a_M{}^* > a_M$. The home country has the absolute advantage in both goods. Nevertheless, both countries gain from specialization according to comparative advantage. Comparative advantage is based on the autarky relative prices of services, 2/3 in the home country and 3/2 in the foreign country. The home country will want to import relatively cheap manufactures, and the foreign country relatively cheap services.

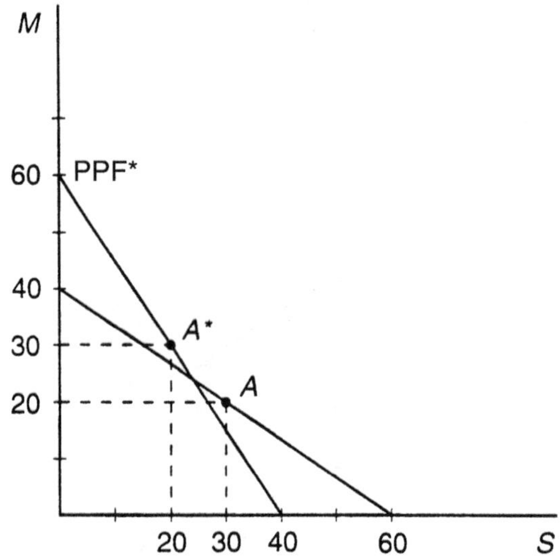

Figure 5.2
Autarky Production and Consumption
Foreign inputs are $a_S^* = 6$ and $a_M^* = 4$ with the available factor $F^* = 240$. Production and consumption in autarky are A* in the foreign country and A in the home country as in Figure 5.1. Services have a lower relative price M/S in the home country.

EXAMPLE **5.4**   *High-Tech Comparative Advantage*

Relative prices can be compared for different types of goods; for instance, the relative price of high-tech goods in terms of other manufactured goods M/H. Mordechai Kreinin (1985) compares these relative prices in the US, Japan, and Germany during the 1980s. The US had a comparative advantage relative to Japan, and Japan relative to Germany.

	US	Japan	Germany
M/H	0.90	0.95	1.08

EXAMPLE **5.5**   *Constant Cost*

The high wages below are due to high capital input and scarce labor. The present constant cost model is best applied to trade between the US and EU, or between Brazil and Mexico. The following two chapters will develop trade based on capital and labor inputs.

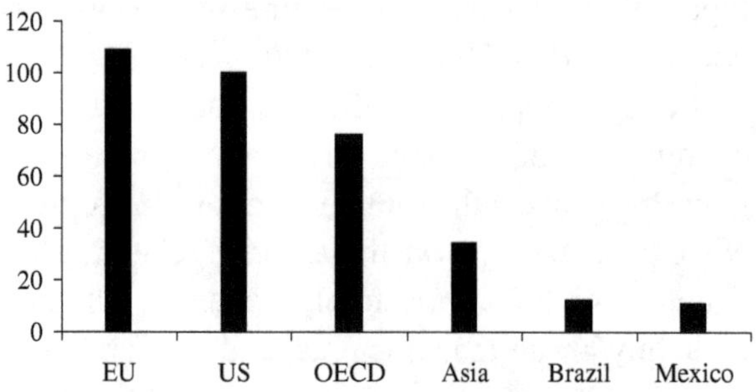

Section A Problems

A1. Draw the PPF for a country with unit labor inputs $a_S = 4$ and $a_M = 5$, and factor input $F = 220$. Find the relative price of S in terms of M.

A2. Draw the PPF with $a_S = 3$, $a_M = 1$, and $F = 60$. Find the relative price of S in terms of M in this country.

B. GAINS FROM TRADE WITH CONSTANT COSTS

Differences in relative prices between countries lead to competition with international traders exchanging products for gain. The result is international specialization leading to higher real income all around. Constant cost production provides a simple framework to illustrate relative price competition.

EXAMPLE **5.6**   *Output Shares*

Output in the US has trended toward services, now the dominant share of the economy. As late as 1980, the output share of manufacturing was 20%.

GDP shares

Agriculture, forestry, fishing, mining, utilities, construction	9%
Manufacturing	13%
Services	78%

Relative Prices and Specialization

Countries specialize in their comparative advantage products identified by comparative advantage. Figure 5.3 shows the home country in the previous section moving along its PPF to export services. The country enjoys gains with services traded at a price above its domestic relative price 2/3 on the PPF. The country specializes completely because there are only two goods. The foreign country must be large enough to supply the imported manufactures. Partial specialization can occur by trading with a small country. Trade among many countries and goods can lead to diversified production.

The international price of services is the terms of trade line $tt = 1$ in Figure 5.3. For the home country, this relative price of services is greater than its autarky relative price 2/3. For the foreign country, the terms of trade (tt) provide a higher relative price of its exported manufactures in the inverse S/M.

The limits to the tt are the autarky relative prices of the two traders, $3/2 > tt > 2/3$. In the late 1700s, John Stuart Mill showed how the tt are determined assuming consumers spend half their income on each product. Trade leads to the same prices in both countries short of transport costs and tariffs. The trade balance is zero (BOT = 0) with balanced trade between the two countries.

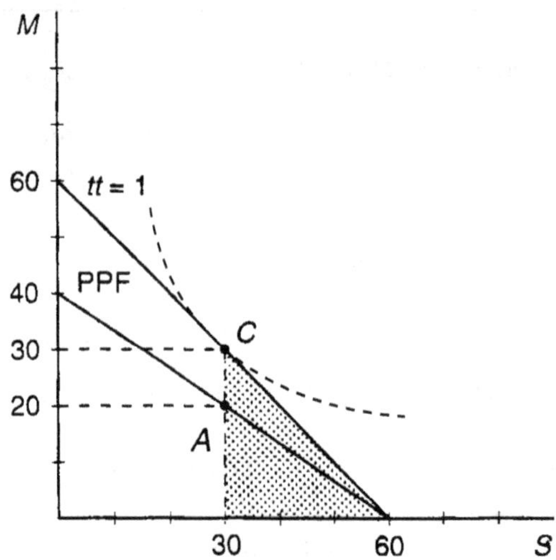

Figure 5.3
The Trade Triangle
Home consumers maximize utility on the terms of trade (*tt*) at $(M, S) = (30, 30)$. The shaded trade triangle starts at the point of specialization in *S*.

Based on Figure 5.3, exports of *M* from the foreign country trade for *S* from the home country at *tt* = 1. The home economy exports 30 *S* in exchange for 30 *M* imports. Home consumers maximize utility on the terms of trade line *tt*. The shaded trade triangle in Figure 5.3 shows 30 units of exported *S* and 30 units of imported *M*.

A country with more highly valued exports on the world market will enjoy greater gains from trade. If foreign consumers value services more than home consumers value manufactures, the *tt* favor the home country.

When a large country trades with a small one, the *tt* cannot vary much from the large country autarky relative price. The large country has to continue producing some of the importing good.

With many countries trading many goods, comparative advantage leads to incomplete specialization trading different goods with different countries. Relative prices lead to trade of one good for another diversifying production. Different exports go in different directions. The constant cost trade model leads to realistic predictions of trade.

Small countries gain more from trade with the tt farther from its autarky relative price. Large countries partially specialize to trade with small ones. Relative price competition leads to complex trade patterns.

The Real Gains from Trade

The real gains from trade are the value of consumption gauged at domestic relative prices. The real gains from trade at point C, in Figure 5.3, are measured by the domestic relative price $M/S = 2/3$. This domestic price is line *d*, in Figure 5.4, going through C. The line *d* is parallel to the PPF.

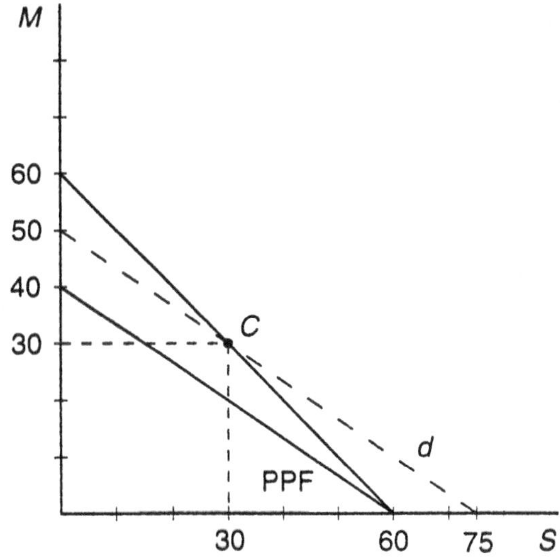

Figure 5.4
Real Gains from Trade
The consumption bundle at C with trade is valued at the domestic autarky prices on price line *d* parallel to the PPF. The value of consumption in terms of either good is found at the endpoints of price line *d*. Trade creates a 25% increase in real income.

The value of consumption at point C in terms of M is derived as $30M + (2/3 \times 30S) = 30M + 20M = 50M$. The 30 units of S consumed are converted to 20 units of M. Real income of 50 M is this 20 plus the 30 M consumed. The value of autarky consumption in terms of M is at the endpoint 40 on the M axis. The real gain from trade is the difference 10 M or an increase of 25% in real income.

In the foreign country, there are also real gains from trade. Specialization pushes it into producing manufactures. There are only two countries in the world with home imports equal to foreign exports. With many countries trading many goods, the same principle holds with all countries gaining real income.

EXAMPLE **5.7**   *The Capital, Labor, and Land of Ricardo*

Ricardo relied on models with capital, labor, and land to develop comparative advantage and the gains from trade as pointed out by Andrea Maneschi (1992). Tariff disputes between manufacturing capitalists, workers, and landowners were a major topic in the late 1700s when Ricardo developed comparative advantage. Not much has changed since then.

Section B Problems

B1. Diagram the foreign country in the example of this section. Show production point P*, the terms of trade line *tt*, consumption C*, and the trade triangle. Find the gains from *tt* of its export.

B2. Suppose the home country has $a_M = 4$ and $a_S = 5$ and the foreign country $a_M{}^* = 5$ and $a_S{}^* = 6$. Which country has the comparative advantage in S? Find the autarky relative prices of S in both countries and the limits to the *tt*. Predict the direction of trade.

EXAMPLE **5.8**   *Iron and Steel Labor Inputs*

During the 1970s, Japan switched from a large importer of iron and steel to a large exporter while the US and the UK became net importers. Investment in Japan led to lower labor inputs and production costs. Mordechai Kreinin (1984) reports these decreases in unit labor inputs between 1964 and 1984 as the US and UK became more efficient but lost their comparative advantages to the newcomer Japan.

US	UK	France	Germany	Japan
−16%	−16%	−55%	−56%	−72%

EXAMPLE **5.9**   *Labor Costs Around the Pacific Rim*

Wages and labor inputs determine labor cost. Susan Hickok and James Orr (1989) report a comparison of manufacturing labor costs around the Pacific Rim. While the US labor input a_{LM} is much lower than the other economies, the higher US wage result in a higher cost of labor per unit of output.

	Wages	a_{LM}	Unit Labor Cost
Thailand	$0.86	8.3	$7.14
Taiwan	$2.71	3.8	$10.30
South Korea	$2.65	4.3	$10.84
US	$13.90	1.0	$13.90

C. RELATIVE WAGES, EXCHANGE RATES, AND COMPLEX TRADE

Constant cost trade involves limits on relative wages and exchange rates across countries. The constant cost trade theory extended to many countries trading many products results in gains from trade with diversified production and complex trade patterns.

EXAMPLE **5.10**   *Revealed Comparative Advantage*

US exports are high-tech manufactures, business services, and some agricultural products. US imports are low-tech manufactures and various resource-based products. David Richardson and Chi Zhang (1999) document the US revealed comparative advantage in high-tech products.

Productivity and Factor Prices

The changing prices of goods due to trade influence input prices. Competition implies the price of a good equals average cost, $P = AC$. Consider the average cost of services in the home country. Cost is based on the input price w and unit input a_S. The price of exported services is,

$$P_S = wa_S = AC_S$$

The price of manufactures in the foreign country is stated in terms of w^* and the exchange rate $e = \$/peso$,

$$P_M = ew^*a_M^* = AC_M^*$$

The tt is the ratio of those two prices,

$$tt = P_S/P_M = wa_S/ew^*a_M^*.$$

The relative input price between the two countries then depends on the relative productivity and tt,

$$w/ew^* = (a_M^*/a_S)tt.$$

Improved productivity lowers the unit input and raises the relative factor price of a country. If the home factor becomes more productive a_S falls with less input required per unit of services output. The price w of the home input rises.

Consider how labor productivity depends on the quality and quantity of capital. With better machines and training, labor becomes more productive. As a_S declines w/ew^* increases.

Improved tt also increase w/ew^*. A higher relative price of services raises the home relative factor price. The tt depend partly on demand in the two countries. An increase in foreign country demand for services raises the relative price of the home input. As an example, when the demand for Japanese manufactures rose in the US during the 1970s, the tt and the relative wage fell in the US.

Higher productivity and better tt raise relative input price of a country.

EXAMPLE **5.11**   *Productivity and Costs*

Lower relative costs are associated with exports. Countries with lower wages also have lower labor productivity. Steve Golub (1995) examines the relationship between relative labor costs and bilateral trade flows for pairs of countries. In 1990, wages and labor productivity in Malaysia were both 15% of their levels in the US implying the unit labor costs were similar in the two countries.

Exchange Rates and Wages

For the home country to export services, its price must be lower than the foreign price. The price of home services is $P_S = wa_S$. In the foreign country, the dollar

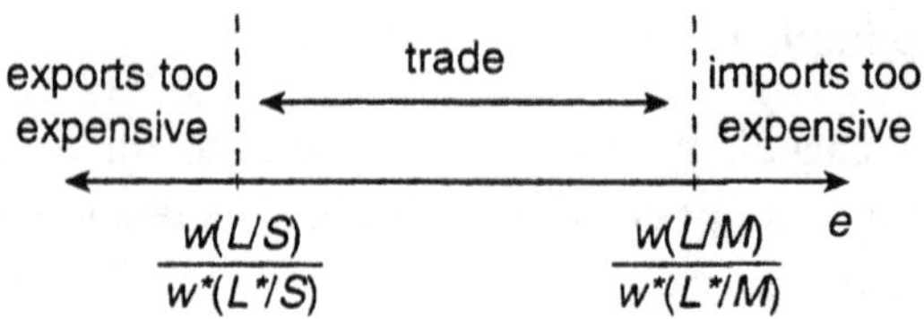

Figure 5.5
Limits to the Exchange Rate
If the exchange rate is too low, exports will cost too much abroad. If e is too high, imports will cost too much. This limited range of e is a necessary condition for trade.

price of the factor input is ew^* leading to the price of services produced in the foreign country $eP_S = ew^*a_S^*$.

For the home country to export services, $P_S < eP_S^*$ implies $wa_S < ew^*a_S^*$. The exchange rate e must satisfy the following condition for trade,

$$e > wa_S/w^*a_S^*$$

The dollar price of manufactures produced in the foreign country $ew^*a_M^*$ must also be less than the domestic price wa_{LM} leading to

$$wa_M/w^*a_M^* > e$$

For trade to take place, the exchange rate is bounded according to

$$wa_M/w^*a_M^* > e > wa_S/w^*a_S^*.$$

Figure 5.5 illustrates these limits to the exchange rate. For a given exchange rate, the home factor price can be only so high for export of S. Otherwise the home country loses its cost advantage. Given the gains from trade, the exchange rate will this range supporting trade.

Domestic factor prices are tied to foreign factor prices, the exchange rate, and productivities.

EXAMPLE **5.12**   *Wages and the Exchange Rate*

Dollar appreciation makes US exports more expensive abroad, lowers US exports, and might also lower wages. Baekin Cha and Daniel Himarios (1995) found dollar appreciation during the 1980s reduced wage growth but the subsequent depreciation had little effect. Between 1971 and 1988, the exchange rate affected wages even for nontraded construction and domestic services industries.

Trade with Three Goods

The three major categories of output are agriculture A, manufactures M, and services S. Consider the hypothetical inputs in Table 5.1. The opportunity cost of one unit of M in the home country is either 3/2 S or 3/4 A.

Table 5.1 Unit Labor Inputs with Three Products

	a_{LS}	a_{LM}	a_{LA}
Home	2	3	4
Foreign	3	4	2

S = services; M = manufactures; A = agriculture.

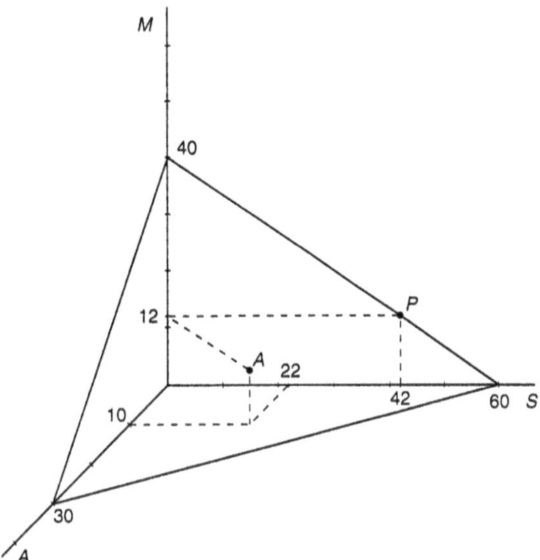

Figure 5.6
PPF with Three Goods
The inputs in Table 5.1 with F = 120 lead to this PPF. Autarky production and consumption occur at point A where $(M, S, A) = (12, 22, 10)$. The country could drop A production and move to point P = $(12, 42, 0)$. The country might continue production of A depending on country sizes and the different tt.

The inputs in services in the home relative to the foreign country is $a_S/a_S^* = 2/3$. It takes 2/3 as much input at home to produce the same output as one unit of foreign input. In manufacturing, it takes 3/4 of home input to match one foreign input. In agriculture, 2 units of home input are required.

The home economy has a comparative advantage in services. The foreign country has a comparative advantage in agriculture. Either country could export manufactures depending on country sizes and preferences. When there are many goods as in the world, most trade can go in either direction depending on relative price competition.

Figure 5.6 illustrates the home PPF given the factor endowment of 120. In autarky, domestic consumers determine production and consumption at point A. The 22 units of S and 10 units of A produced require 2 × 22 = 44 units of input in S and $4 \times 10 = 40$ in A. This leaves $120 - 84 = 36$ inputs to produce $36/3 = 12$ M.

The home country could drop A production and move to point P. Suppose M is nontraded with output remaining at 12. Service output rises to $84/2 = 42$ with the added 40 inputs from agriculture. At the tt, 1 unit of A for each exported S, the economy could trade 15 S and consume at point $(M, S, A) = (12, 27, 15)$.

With many products, each country exports toward the end of its productivity ranking. Middle products trade in the direction determined by the tt.

EXAMPLE **5.13**   *US Services Trade*

Major categories of US trade in services are listed below in descending order.

> Tourism, Affiliated services, Royalties, Passenger fares, Freight, Finance, Telecom, Insurance, Education, Construction and engineering

The US spends more than the rest of the world on freight. Royalties are important in World Trade Organization (WTO) negotiations. Affiliated services refer to transactions between multinational branch firms. Education of foreign students in US universities and financial services are growing as exports.

Trade with Many Countries

The constant cost trade model also applies to more than two countries. Consider the three countries with the unit inputs for M and S in Table 5.2. The relative price of services M/S is 2/3 in country 1, 3/4 in country 2, and 4/3 in country 3.

Country 1 has the lowest relative price of services at $M/S = 2/3$ and will export S. Country 3 has the highest relative price of services at $M/S = 4/3$ and will export M. Country 2 is in the middle and can trade in either direction depending on the tt. If $tt > 3/4$, country 2 will export S to country 3. If $tt < 3/4$, it will export M to 1. The limits to the tt from the extreme countries are,

$$4/3 > tt > 2/3.$$

When there are three countries trading three goods, the unit inputs predict at least some of the trade. Table 5.3 illustrates a situation for three countries producing three goods.

Table 5.2 Unit Labor Inputs with Three Countries

	a_{LS}	a_{LM}
Country 1	2	3
Country 2	3	4
Country 3	4	3

Table 5.3 Unit Inputs for Three Countries Trading Three Goods

	a_S	a_M	a_A
Country 1	2	3	4
Country 2	3	4	2
Country 3	4	2	3

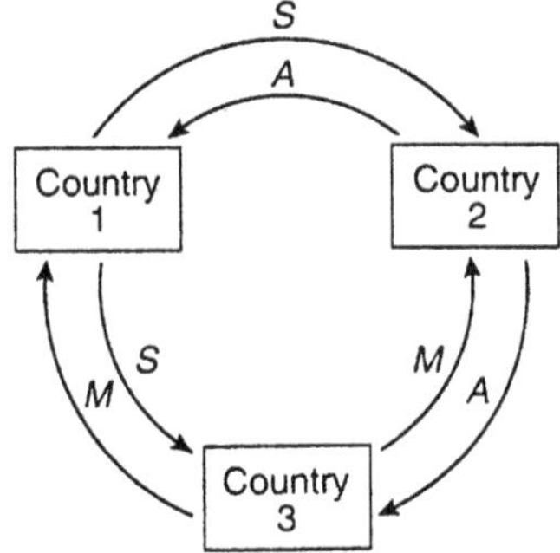

Figure 5.7
Trade Among Three Countries in Three Goods
Country 1 has the comparative advantage in S relative to the other countries, country 2 in A, and country 3 in M.

The relative prices M/S of services in terms of manufactures across the three countries are ranked $(2/3)_1 < (3/4)_2 < (2)_3$. Country 1 has the comparative advantage and will export S to country 3 in exchange for M. The relative price ranking for A/S is $(1/2)_1 < (4/3)_3 < (3/2)_2$ implying country 1 would export S to country 2 in exchange for A. For the relative price A/M the ranking $(2/3)_3 < (3/4)_1 < (2)_2$ implies country 3 exporting M to country 2 for imports of A.

Figure 5.7 shows this trade between the three countries in the three goods. Each country exports only one good based on extremes in the relative price rankings. Country 1 exports S to country 3 in exchange for M and to country 2 for A. Country 2 exports A to the other two countries, as does country 3 with M.

Trade will not be as simple as in Figure 5.7 given the middle country in each ranking can trade depending on the tt. In the first ranking, country 2 would export M to 1 in exchange for S given the tt $(2/3)_1 < tt_{12} < (3/4)_2$. Country 2 would then diversify producing M along with A to compete with country 3 exports of M to country 1.

Trade by the middle countries can lead to multiple exports, nontraded goods within a country, countries that do not trade with each other, and even two-way trade with a country importing and exporting the same good. These trade patterns are all familiar in world trade.

Inputs different from those in Table 5.3 can also break the link of a single efficient good for each country relative to every other good in every other country. Relative price competition leads to realistic trade patterns with gains from trade for each country.

Trade among many countries in many goods involves diversified production and complex patterns. Every country gains from trade based on comparative advantage and relative price competition.

EXAMPLE **5.14**   *R&D and Productivity*

Research and development (R&D) can lower unit inputs or raise productivity. Most R&D takes place in the developed countries (DCs). Japan's share of world R&D has increased while the EU's share has remained about constant, and the US' share has decreased over recent decades.

Section C Problems

C1. Assume the unit inputs $a_M^* = 5$, $a_A^* = 3$, $a_M = 2$, and $a_A = 3$ to find the international specialization. Find the relative wage w/ew^* if the *tt* are 1.
C2. Find the limits to the exchange rate with the inputs in Problem C1 when $w = \$10$ and $w^* = 1000$ pesos.
C3. If $w = \$16$, $e = \$/\pounds = 1.2$, and $w^* = \pounds10$, find dollar prices of the three goods using the inputs in Table 5.1. Predict the pattern of trade.
C4. Diagram PPF* with the inputs in Table 5.1 and $L^* = 228$.

EXAMPLE **5.15**   *International Wage Differences*

Assembly line wages vary across countries. Firms considering where to locate also consider transport costs, taxes, work habits, and infrastructure. Wage differences, however, can be overwhelming. The three highest and three lowest wage countries in 2000 are below.

Norway	$18.90
Switzerland	$18.10
Germany	$18.00
Hungary	$1.20
India	$0.40
Turkey	$0.40

D. APPLICATIONS OF CONSTANT COST THEORY

This section reviews applications and evidence on the constant cost trade model. One application is to distinguish between improving technology in a sector versus an increase in the total level of the input.

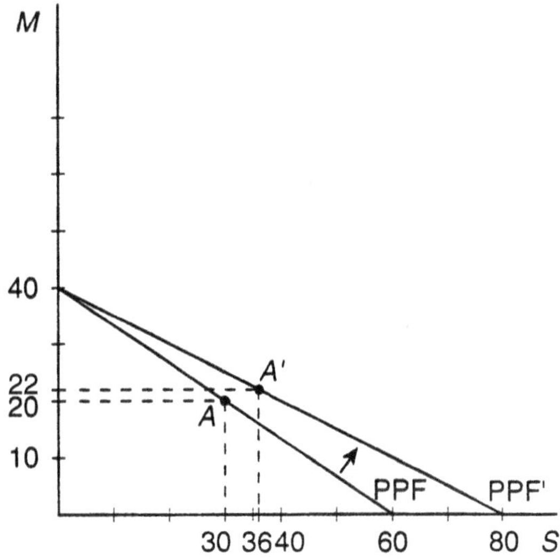

Figure 5.8
Improved Technology in Service Production
If a_S falls from 2 to 1.5, the maximum point along the S axis shifts to $120/1.5 = 80$. The economy can produce higher combinations of both goods. Production could jump from point A where $(M, S) = (20, 30)$ to A′ where $(M, S) = (22, 36)$.

Improved Technology Versus Input Growth

Improved technology occurs when the unit inputs in a sector or industry reduce. A decrease in a_S from 2 to 1.5 shifts the PPF in Figure 5.8 to PPF′,

$$120 = 1.5\, S + 3\, M$$

The total potential output in services increases from 60 to $120/1.5 = 80$. More of both goods will be produced due to the improved technology in one sector. The domestic relative price of services falls to $|{-40/80}| = 1/2$.

Growth in the amount of the input available in an economy creates a parallel outward shift of the PPF. Figure 5.9 illustrates an increase in the level of the input from 120 to 144. The unit inputs are the original $a_S = 2$ and $a_M = 3$. The equation for the new PPF′ in Figure 5.9 is,

$$144 = 2S + 3M$$

The maximum outputs of the two goods that could be produced are $144/2 = 72$ units of S or $144/3 = 48$ units of M. The relative price of S in terms of M remains at the original 2/3. The increased factor enables the economy to produce more of both goods.

Improved technology in a sector shift the PPF outward on that axis. Input growth causes an outward parallel shift of the PPF.

Improved technology in one sector expands the PPF in that direction, lowers the relative price of that good, and raises production potential.

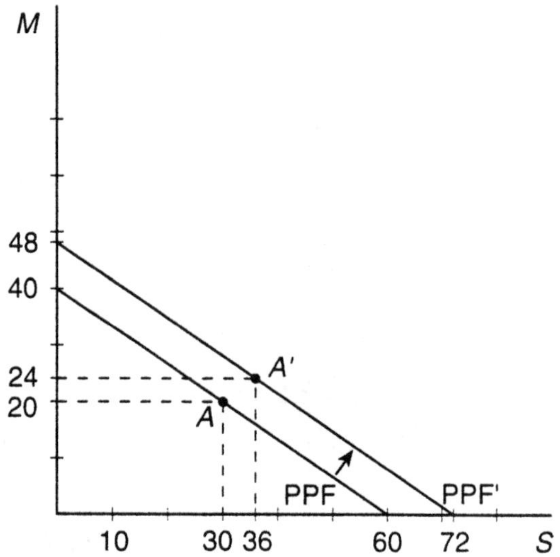

Figure 5.9
Input Growth
If the factor input grows from $F = 120$ to 144, the economy expands to a higher production frontier. The economy's output could rise from point A where $(M, S) = (20, 30)$ to point A' where $(M, S) = (24, 36)$.

EXAMPLE 5.16   *Improved Technology and Labor Inputs*

Matthew Shapiro (1987) reports the changes in unit labor inputs in US industries between 1974 and 1985. When unit labor inputs decline, the production frontier expands in the direction of those outputs. When unit inputs increase, as in mining and construction, the production frontier shrinks along those axes.

	$\%\Delta a_Q$
Communications	−2.3
Agriculture	−1.4
Manufacturing	−1.4
Construction	1.1
Mining	4.3

The Evidence on Constant Cost Trade Theory

Exports from the US and the UK in 1937 compared in G.D.A. MacDougall (1951) support constant cost trade as lower unit labor inputs were associated with higher export market shares. Numerous other studies confirm this association between unit inputs and net exports across many countries and goods.

Herbert Glejser, K. Goossens, and Eede Vanden (1982) compare countries in Europe before and after joining the EU. Countries with lower opportunity costs of goods tended to export those goods to other member countries.

Table 5.4 Unit Labor Inputs in High-Tech Products

	1963	1984
EU	1.25	1.46
US	1.00	1.06
Japan	1.76	0.92

High-tech products are distinguished by their high input of R&D. High-tech manufactures include electronics, chemicals, aircrafts, computers, and specialized machinery. Table 5.4 shows the change in unit labor inputs in high-tech products over two decades related to export growth in Japan. The EU declined in productivity as the US held its position. The improved technology in Japan was due to its investment in human and physical capital. The Japanese PPF expanded along the high-tech axis.

The US auto industry declined during the 1970s as imported cars from Japan rose from less than half a million in 1970 to almost 2.5 million by 1980. Japanese autos went from less than 5% to more than 20% of the US market. Starting in 1970, the US unit labor input was 1 with Japan at 1.5. By 1980, the US unit labor input rose to 1.15 primarily due to labor union work rules. US labor unions voted against robots on the assembly lines. Meanwhile, the unit input in Japan fell to 0.75 with heavy investment, more than tripling the stock of capital machinery and equipment over the decade.

EXAMPLE **5.17**   *US/China Trade*

Trade between China and the US has increased dramatically since 2000. Major US export categories are agricultural products as well as aircraft, fertilizer, and telecom equipment. Import categories are consumer goods, apparel, and electronics. The US-instituted discriminatory tariffs against China in 2018 due to unfair business practices including patent violations.

Section D Problems

D1. High-tech manufactures require skilled labor. Why might the US be able to produce relatively inexpensive high-tech goods?

D2. Investment spending in the US automobile industry lagged far behind its competitors in the 1970s. How does this account for the high cost of producing autos in the US during the 1980s?

D3. Start with the PPF in $a_S = 4$, $a_M = 5$, and $F = 220$. Technology changes in manufacturing to $a_M = 4.4$. Draw the new PPF' and explain whether technology improved.

D4. Suppose the economy in Problem D3 then grows to labor force $F = 260$. Diagram the new PPF.

CONCLUSION

The constant cost trade theory simplifies production assuming a constant level of a single input. Some questions arise. Why does a country have lower unit inputs? What could cause unit inputs to change? What happens if capital, labor, and resource inputs are separate in production? Chapter 6 turns to the factor proportions model of production to answer these questions.

EXAMPLE **5.18**   *Three-Way Trade*

Asia has trade surpluses with North America (NA) and the EU, while NA has deficits with the other two. The EU has a deficit with NA but a surplus with Asia. A good exercise is to complete a diagram similar to Figure 5.7. Asia exports manufactures while NA exports foodstuffs and raw materials. Asia and the EU ship more manufactures to NA than to each other.

Terms

Absolute advantage	Exchange rate limits
Comparative advantage	Limits to the terms of trade
Complete specialization	Mercantilism
Constant costs	Opportunity cost
Relative price competition	Relative prices
	Unit labor inputs

MAIN POINTS

- Constant cost production implies a linear PPF with slope equal to the ratio of unit inputs as the domestic relative price.
- The gains from trade the value of consumption at domestic relative prices.
- Wages and exchange rates have a limited range for trade to take place.
- The evidence provides some support for constant cost trade especially between countries with high and low incomes.
- Relative price competition in constant costs lead to realistic trade patterns among many countries trading many goods.

REVIEW PROBLEMS

1. In Figure 5.2, explain which country has a lower opportunity cost of manufactures.

2. Compare a country Gamma with $a_M = 4$ and $a_S = 5$ to the home country in Figure 5.1. Predict the trade pattern. Make a similar prediction for Gamma and the foreign country in Figure 5.2.

3. Labor forces are about 150 million in the US and 60 million in Japan. Find the amounts of high-tech goods these economies could produce over the years in Table 5.4, if a quarter of each labor force works in high-tech manufactures.

4. Suppose country H has $a_M = 4$, $a_S = 5$, and $L = 260$, and country F $a_M{}^* = 6$, $a_S{}^* = 5$, and $L^* = 300$. Find the comparative advantage. Suppose each country exports half its production to the other. Find the tt. Diagram the trade triangles.

5. Evaluate the gains from trade in Problem 4 in terms of good S. Evaluate the gains from trade for both countries in percentages. Which country enjoys the larger gains from trade?

6. Find the percentage gains from trade in the same example if the terms of trade are $M/S = 1$ with 30 units of S exported by F. Explain the difference in the gains from trade compared to Problem 5.

7. If the terms of trade are $tt = M/S = 1.4$ between the home and foreign countries in Figure 5.2, find the relative wage w/ew^* implied by trade. Find the relative wage if instead $tt = 0.7$. Explain the effect of trade on the relative wage.

8. Using the information in Problem 7, find w if $w^* = 1100$ ¥ and $e = \$/¥ = 0.008$. Compare and explain the limits to the exchange rate under the two tt.

9. In the home country, unit inputs are $a_M = 2$ for manufactures and $a_A = 3$ for agriculture. In the foreign country, unit inputs are $a_M{}^* = 4$ and $a_A{}^* = 5$. The terms of trade are $tt = A/M = 3/4$. Find relative wages implied by trade.

10. Find the limits to the exchange rate for the two countries in the previous problem.

11. Find the home wage w if the foreign wage $w^* = 10,000$ pesos and $e = 0.001$ in Problem 11. Show what happens to w if
    (a) tt falls for the home country to 7/10
    (b) Improved technology lowers a_M to 1.5.

12. Predict the pattern of trade for these unit inputs for three goods:

	Good 1	Good 2	Good 3
Home	3	5	3
Foreign	2	1	3

13. If the foreign wage is 2250 ¥ and the exchange rate $e = 0.008$ in Problem 12, find the home wage w that makes the price of the middle good the same in both economies. Using this wage, find the prices of the two traded goods in each country. Explain the direction of trade.

14. Find the limits to the exchange rate in Problem 13.

15. Consumer goods such as appliances and apparel require low levels of investment and high levels of unskilled labor. Why does the US have little cost advantage in consumer goods?

READINGS

William Allen (1965) *International Trade Theory: Hume to Ohlin*, New York: Random House. A short paperback with readings from the classics.

Ron Jones and Peter Kenen (1984) *Handbook of International Economics*, Vol. I, Amsterdam: North Holland. Surveys of international trade.

Andrea Maneschi (1998) *Comparative Advantage in International Trade: A Historical Perspective*, New York: Edward Elgar. An excellent historical review.

Michio Morishima (1989) *Ricardo's Economics: A General Equilibrium Theory of Distribution and Growth*, Cambridge: Cambridge University Press.
David Ricardo (1817) *The Principles of Political Economy and Taxation*, New York: Everyman's Library, 1969. Chapter 3 "On Foreign Trade" is Ricardo's own presentation.

MATHEMATICAL APPENDIX

This chapter presents the constant cost trade model with a single factor of production. The opportunity cost of an increase in the output of one good is the constant loss in other output. The amount of input per unit of good j output is a_j. Total input $F = \Sigma_j a_j x_j$ is fully employed across outputs x_j. The linear PPF for manufactures M and services S is $M = F/a_M - a_S(S/a_M)$ with slope $dM/dS = -a_S/a_M$ as the marginal rate of transformation (MRT).

The home country has an absolute advantage in S if $a_S < a_S{}^*$ and the foreign country in M if $a_M{}^* < a_M$. Absolute advantage is not necessary for export. Comparative advantage in the weaker relative efficiency $a_S/a_M < a_S{}^*/a_M{}^*$ is sufficient to predict home exports of S and foreign exports of M. The home MRT is less than the foreign MRT*.

The two countries must be similar in their sizes F and F* to completely specialize in their export. The home country exports S in exchange for M moving consumption beyond the PPF as does the foreign country exporting M. The world maximizes total output with efficient inputs. The tt depend partly on utility functions of the two countries. A necessary condition for trade is $a_S/a_M < tt < a_S{}^*/a_M{}^*$. The real gains from trade are the increase in income that would move consumers to the higher consumption bundle with trade. Home income in terms of good S is $c_S + (a_M/a_S)c_M$. Consumption of both c_S and c_M can increase with trade implying higher income evaluated at the autarky relative price a_M/a_S.

Competition implies prices $p_j = a_j w$ where w is the factor price. In the foreign country, $ep_j{}^* = a_j{}^*ew^*$. Export of S by the home country requires $a_S w < a_S{}^*ew^*$, and foreign M export $a_M w > a_M{}^*ew^*$. The relative wage is then restricted for trade to $a_S{}^*/a_S > w/ew^* > a_M{}^*/a_M$. Improving home export technology lowers a_S and raises the upper limit on the relative home wage. The same is true for foreign export technology. The exchange rate e is similarly restricted in $(a_M/a_M{}^*)(w/w^*) > e > (a_S/a_S{}^*)(w/w^*)$. The relative wage depends on the terms of trade as $tt = p_S/ep_M{}^* = a_S w/a_M{}^*ew^* = (a_S/a_M{}^*)(w/ew^*)$ implies $w/ew^* = (a_M{}^*/a_S)tt$. Improved tt for the home country raises w/ew^*. If foreign demand for services increase, the improved tt raises w/ew^*.

The gains from trade extend to any number of countries trading their efficient goods. For three countries and goods, relative price competition leads to complex trade patterns and diversified production. The relative price ranking for good j in terms of i across countries k, h, m in $a_i{}^k/a_j{}^k < a_i{}^h/a_j{}^h < a_i{}^m/a_j{}^m$ implies extreme country k would export i to extreme country m for j. Middle country h will export in the direction determined by the terms of trade tt_{ij}. Including the third good n, the three rankings i/j, i/n, and j/n lead to complex trade. There can be multiple exports, nontraded goods, nontrading countries, exports and imports of the same good, and separate trade groups.

The constant cost model illustrates expanded input as an increase in F shifts the PPF out from the origin like an increase in consumer income. The model also illustrates improved technology in good j with the lower unit input a_j expanding the PPF in along the j axis lowering the price of good j relative to any other good g in the input ratio a_j/a_g.

Introducing a second input previews the factor proportions model in Chapter 6. The two employment conditions with fixed unit inputs of capital K and labor L are $K = \Sigma_j a_{Kj} x_j$ and $L = \Sigma_j a_{Lj} x_j$. Capital is paid r and labor w leading to the competitive prices $p_j = a_{Kj} r + a_{Lj} w$ in the home country.

CHAPTER 6

Factor Proportions Production and Trade

Preview

The factor proportions model of production and trade starts with capital and labor as the factors of production for outputs of manufactures and services. Tariffs or changing international prices affect the capital return and the wage as the economy moves along the production frontier. The income redistribution due to trade and trade policy become the focus. Topics include:

* Specific factors of production
* Producing manufactures and services with capital and labor
* The general equilibrium of production
* Extensions and applications of factor proportions trade

INTRODUCTION

The economics of production is based on firms minimizing cost to hire inputs. Payments by firms to the factors of production provide the personal income in the economy for households to pay firms for goods and services. Factor markets along with product markets determine the output levels and factor prices in the general equilibrium.

A critical issue in international trade is the income redistribution due to tariffs and other trade policies that alter production. This chapter lays the foundation to determine whether capital or labor wins or loses due to trade policy. Results with skilled labor and natural resources are also discussed.

Each industry has its own specific capital input in Section A. In the rest of the chapter, capital moves with labor between industries along the production frontier. The abundance of capital and labor across countries largely determines exports. The intensity of capital and labor inputs are critical in the factor price adjustments to trade policy, to the winners and losers due to tariffs. Adjustments to labor migration and international capital movements are also examined.

A. SPECIFIC FACTORS OF PRODUCTION

Specific factors enter production in their industry only. As examples, trains are specific to the transport sector and surgeons to the medical industry. Changing

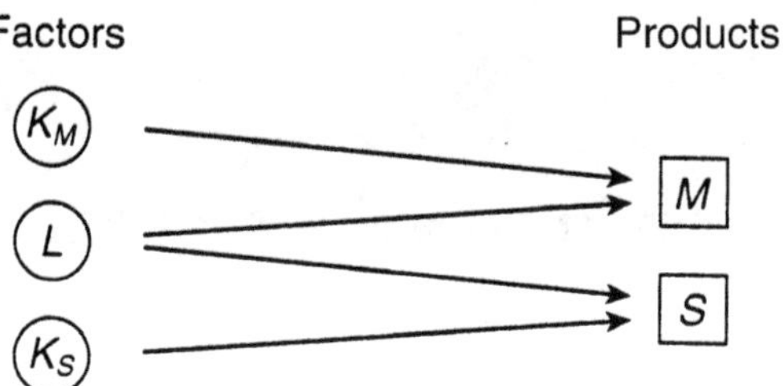

Figure 6.1
Sector-Specific Capital
Manufacturing M has specific capital K_M and services S has its separate K_S. The two outputs share labor L.

prices due to trade, tariffs, or subsidies have direct effects on specific factors in their industries. As an example, steel tariffs will affect the return to steel furnaces and other equipment designed specifically for steel production.

The Specific Factors Model of Production

Figure 6.1 shows a specific factor economy. Labor L is shared in manufactures M and services S production. Each sector has its own specific type of capital, K_M and K_S.

Factor Demand

Firms hire factors of production according to the revenue they produce. The demand for labor is the sum of demands for all firms hiring labor.

Diminishing marginal product (MP) is a fundamental property of all inputs in production. MP is the added output from an extra unit of an input. As the amount of any input increases, holding other inputs constant, its MP diminishes.

Firms hire an input according to marginal revenue product (MRP) as the marginal revenue (MR) of an added unit of the input,

$$MRP = MR \times MP.$$

MR is the marginal revenue of the addition to revenue and MP is the additional output making MRP the added revenue from an added unit of input. MRP slopes downward as in Figure 6.2 due to diminishing MP and nonincreasing MR. As one more unit of labor L is hired, MP diminishes. MR is constant for a price-taking firm but decreases with output for a firm that has market power.

The demand for labor is its MRP or demand as firms hire according to the revenue of the added worker.

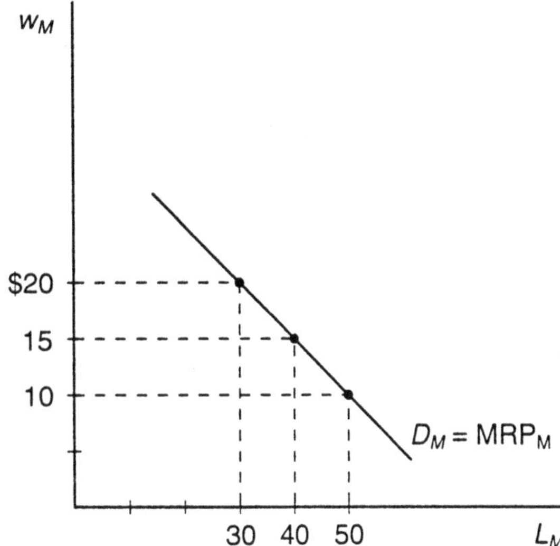

Figure 6.2
Demand for Labor in Manufactures
Labor demand slopes downward due to the diminishing *MP* in *MRP*. If w = $15, manufacturing firms hire 40 workers, but hire only 30 at $20.

The Market for Shared Labor

Figure 6.2 shows the demand for labor in manufacturing. Labor input L_M is measured on the horizontal axis. If the wage w_M is $20, then 30 units of L are hired. The output produced by the 30th worker is worth $20. If w_M = $15, hiring increases to 40 workers.

The demand for labor to produce services output is $D_S = MRP_S$ included in Figure 6.3 with the manufactures demand in Figure 6.2. The marginal revenue MR_S in services is based on the demand for services output. The economy has 100 workers along the bottom axis with labor in manufacturing measured from the left and labor in services L_S from the right.

Where the two demands meet in Figure 6.3, the equilibrium wage is $15 with 40 workers in manufacturing and 60 in services. If the wage were higher in manufacturing, labor would move there. If there were only 30 workers in M the wage would be $20 in M but only $10 in S. Labor would move from S to M until the wages equalize.

The mobility of labor ensures the same wage across industries.

Figure 6.4 shows increased the demand for labor D_S in services. The increase could be due to a higher price for services raising *MR* or to increased capital input raising the *MP* of labor.

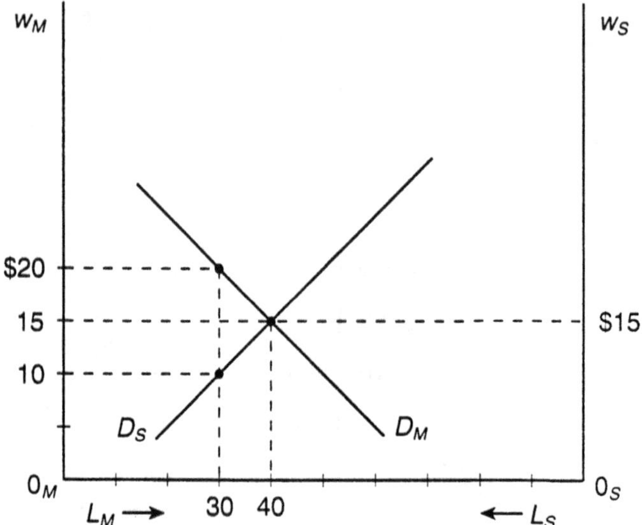

Figure 6.3
Equilibrium in the Labor Market
Labor in services L_S is measured from O_S with demand D_S sloping downward to the left. Services would hire 70 workers at $w = \$10$. The total L supply is 100. The wage $w = \$15$ in the labor market equilibrium with 40 workers are hired in M and 60 in S.

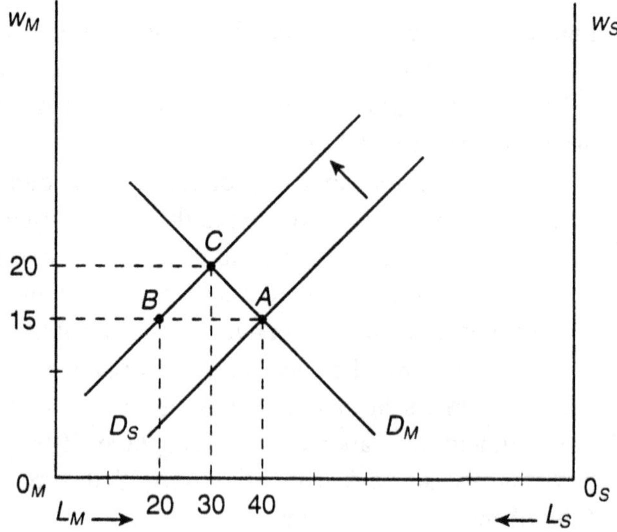

Figure 6.4
Increased Demand for Labor in Services
At $w = \$15$, the increase in labor demand in S creates the excess demand of 20 between A and B. The wage is bid up to $20 to move 10 workers from M to S. The labor market equilibrium moves from A to C.

At $w = \$15$, there is a labor shortage with the 40 workers demanded in manufacturing plus 80 in services. The wage bid up to \$20 moves 10 workers from manufacturing to services at the new equilibrium point C.

The economy adjusts to a higher price of services shifting labor with an increase in the wage.

EXAMPLE **6.1**   *Predicted Effects of North American Trade*

The specific factors model in John Francis and Henry Thompson (2009) predicts falling unskilled wages with moderate industrial output adjustments due to free trade in the US. Changes in investment, however, have much larger effects. Michael Kouparitsas (1997) predicts large increases in outputs and exports in Mexico as foreign capital comes into the economy.

Markets for Specific Capital Inputs

Demand for sector-specific capital is its *MRP*. When L moves into service production in Figure 6.4, the *MP* of capital K_S increases. The increased *MRP* raises the capital payment r_S in the service sector. In manufactures, the lost L lowers the *MP* of capital and r_M.

Figure 6.5 shows the market for sector-specific capital K_S in services with vertical supply S. Capital is fully utilized with its return r_S determined by demand

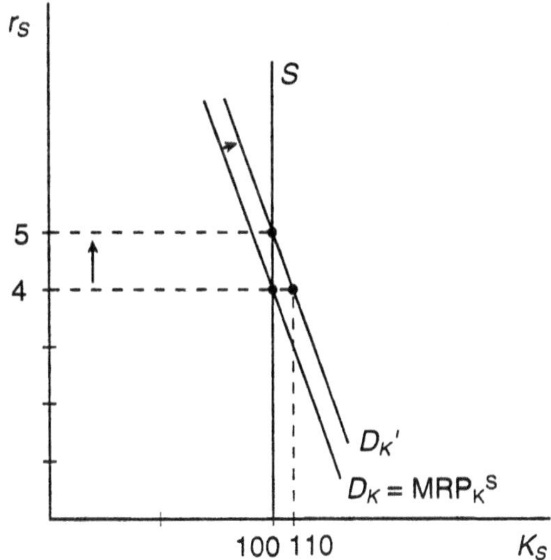

Figure 6.5
Market for Services Capital
The supply of capital in services is inelastic at the endowment 100. With capital demand D_K the capital payment is 4. When demand increases to $D_K{'}$ the return r_S increases to 5.

D_K. The increase in demand D_K could be due to a higher price of services raising MR or to incoming labor raising MP. Demand $D_K = MRP$ increases raising the capital return r_S.

In the market for manufacturing capital, the loss of labor lowers the MP of capital resulting in a lower MRP and capital return r_M. When labor leaves manufacturing, the marginal productivity of manufacturing capital falls.

When output prices change, the market for shared labor adjusts causing changes in demands for sector capital as the economy moves along its production possibility frontier (PPF).

EXAMPLE **6.2**   *Do Tariffs Protect Specific Factors?*

A tariff raises the return to specific capital if there is only one other input in the industry. A tariff on steel, for instance, could increase demand for labor and energy in domestic steel production but lowers capital demand as shown in Henry Thompson (1987). Gene Grossman and Jim Levinsohn (1989) find evidence that protected industries have higher-than-normal stock returns.

Trade and Specific Factor Income

Income is redistributed by changing prices due to trade. A decrease in the relative price of manufactures lowers M production but increases output of services. The return r_M to specific capital in manufacturing falls while r_S for specific capital in services rises. The wage w increases to attract labor into services production. Stockholders, management, and labor unions in manufacturing want their industry protected from foreign competition.

If both sectors share skilled labor as well as labor, the increased trade could increase the demand for shared skilled labor rather than capital in the expanding services sector. Demand for service capital and the return r_S would not increase.

EXAMPLE **6.3**   *Trade and Income Redistribution in Japan*

Three protected industries in Japan that expect falling prices due to import competition are business services, iron and steel, and natural resources. The projected impacts on wages in Henry Thompson (1994a) are for labor specific to industries assuming price decreases of 10% due to import competition. The falling prices lower the return to mobile capital by 5%. Wages in import-competing industries fall while other wages increase as capital moves into those industries:

Hydrocarbons	25%	Business services	−15%
Finance	15%	Iron and steel	−25%
Other wages	5%	Natural resources	−40%

Section A Problems

A1. The price of services is \$3 and the capital input 10 units. Draw the *MRP* of L if outputs of S from L are:

L	0	1	2	3	4	5
S	0	2.5	4.5	6	7	7.5

A2. The marginal product of L in M is 3.5 when $L = 1$, 2.5 when $L = 3$, and 1.5 when $L = 5$. The price of M is \$1.50. Draw this demand for L in manufacturing.

A3. Combine the labor demands in Problems A1 and A2 to determine the equilibrium wage and employment in each sector when the total labor endowment is 5.

B. CAPITAL AND LABOR MARKETS

This section introduces the factor proportions production and trade with capital K and labor L producing manufactures M and services S. These results were developed by Eli Heckscher and Bertil Ohlin in the 1930s and Abba Lerner and Paul Samuelson in the 1950s. The model leads to four fundamental propositions in trade theory.

Factor Abundance and Factor Intensity

Exports have low prices based on inputs that are less expensive in the exporters than in the importing countries. More abundant supply of a factor means its price will be lower. If the foreign country has abundant labor L the foreign wage will be lower than the home wage, $ew^* < w$. If the home country has abundant capital, its capital return will be lower, $r < er^*$. The abundance of factors of production provides a prediction of exports depending on the factor intensity in production.

Production of a good is labor intensive if it has a higher ratio of labor to capital input. Manufactures M is labor intensive, $K_M/L_M < K_s/L_s$. Services production S is capital intensive. Capital may include human capital as skilled labor.

The capital-abundant home country exports capital-intensive services S in exchange for labor-intensive manufactures M from the labor-abundant foreign country. Factor abundance generally explains relative factor prices leading to lower priced products intensive in lower priced factors. This simple link between factor abundance and factor intensity explains perhaps 3/4 of global trade.

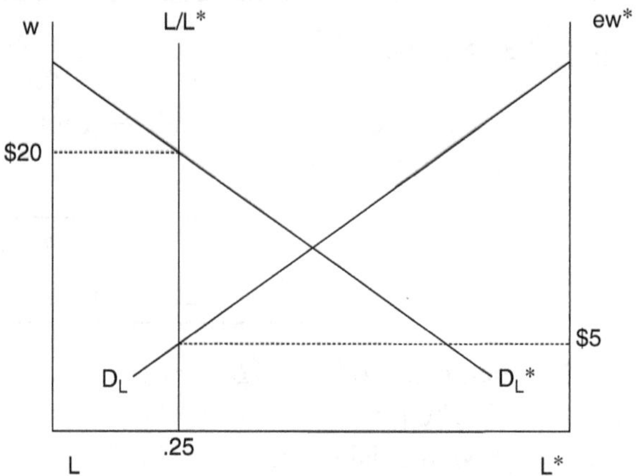

Figure 6.6
The International Labor Market
Demands for labor are similar in the home and foreign countries. Labor supply L in the home country is 25% of the total $L + L^*$. The labor-abundant foreign country has lower wages, $ew^* < w$. If e = \$/peso = ½ then w^* = 10 pesos.

Factor Markets and Product Markets

Figure 6.6 illustrates the labor market in the two countries with marginal revenue product MRP_L as demand D_L. Domestic labor L is measured from the left and foreign labor L^* from the right. The foreign demand for labor D_L^* slopes down as L^* increases. The base of the figure is the total $L + L^*$. The vertical line L/L^* indicates labor abundance as $L < L^*$ with 25% of total labor in the home country.

The two labor demands D_L and D_L^* imply $w > ew^*$ as w = \$20 and ew^* = \$5. The labor-abundant foreign country has a lower wage. Migration between the two countries is considered in Chapter 8.

EXAMPLE **6.4**   *US Output Growth*

Output increases with inputs of capital and labor. In the US, between 1940 and 1970, increases in the capital stock were not dramatic but output steadily responded. Since 1970, there has been higher growth in capital but slower growth in output per worker.

Figure 6.7 illustrates the related markets for labor-intensive manufactures. The demand for manufactures D_M is the same in both countries. The two supply curves are much different. The labor-abundant foreign country has a lower wage and higher supply of manufactures SM^*. The labor-scarce home country has higher wages w and lower supply S_M. In autarky, the price of manufactures is lower in the foreign country, $eP_M^* < P_M$. In the example, P_M = \$100 and eP_M = \$60.

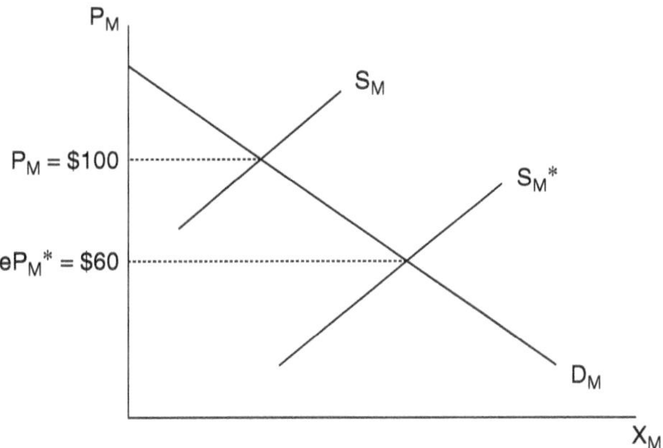

Figure 6.7
Labor Intensity and Abundance
With the same demand, the labor-abundant foreign country has a lower price of labor-intensive manufactures, $eP_M{}^* < P_M$. If $e = \frac{1}{2}$ then $P_M{}^* = 120$ pesos. The higher foreign supply comes from the lower foreign wage $ew^* < w$ in Figure 6.6.

The capital-abundant home country has a lower autarky price of services $Ps < eP_S{}^*$ due to its lower return to capital $r < r^*$. When trade opens between the two countries, the home country exports services and imports manufactures.

The fundamental prediction of factor proportions trade theory is that countries export products intensive in their abundant factor of production.

Free Trade and Factor Prices

Trade raises the prices of cheap exported goods and lowers prices of expensive import-competing goods. Consumers enjoy the low prices of imported goods while the import-competing industries reduce output. Export producers expand output with higher prices.

In the home country, the falling P_M lowers the demand for intensive labor in Figure 6.6. This decrease in demand lowers the wage w. Labor demand depends largely on manufactures output where it is the intensive input. Meanwhile, the rising price Ps of exported services raises the demand for intensive capital input. This increase in demand for capital raises the relatively low capital return r.

In the foreign country, the effects on factor demands are the opposite. Increased demand for cheap labor L^* to produce manufactures M^* raises the low ew^*. In Figure 6.6, the demand shifts lower the home wage below \$20 and raise the foreign wage above \$5. Production of import competing services S^* falls in the foreign country as does capital demand and r^*.

Trade raises the prices of the cheaper factors of production in each country leading to factor price convergence across countries.

Tariffs and Factor Prices

Tariffs move factor prices in the opposite directions from free trade. Tariffs raise the price for the import-competing industry, creating deadweight loss and shifting production away from exports. Tariffs redistribute income toward the scarce highly paid intensive factor in the import-competing industry. Tariffs raise the price of the factor that is higher than its price in the other country.

A tariff on imported manufactures in the home country raises the price of manufactures to $P_M = (1 + t)eP_M^*$. The higher price increases the demand for intensive labor raising labor demand D_L in Figure 6.6. The increased labor demand raises the home wage w that is already higher than the foreign wage ew^*.

Tariffs polarize factor prices between trading partners making the distribution of factor income more uneven across countries.

Section B Problems

B1. Diagram the international market for capital, like Figure 6.6, for labor. Explain which country is capital abundant. Explain the international difference between r and r^*.

B2. Diagram the international market for services, like Figure 6.7, for manufactures. Explain differences in supplies S_s and S_s^*. Predict the direction of trade based on P_s and eP_s^*.

B3. Create the example of trade between a resource-abundant foreign country and a labor-abundant home country. Assume similar capital endowments. Show the factor markets in each country and explain the differences in factor prices. Explain the differences in supplies of each product in each country.

C. FACTOR PROPORTIONS TRADE

Trade based on the production of two traded goods with the two factors capital and labor leads to some fundamental properties. Changes in the prices of the goods and in the available capital and labor inputs lead to adjustments in factor prices and outputs. The basic assumptions are cost minimization with full employment of factors and competitive pricing of the outputs.

Competitive Pricing

Figure 6.8 shows the cost structure of a competitive firm with the given market price $p = \$1$. The competitive firm can sell any amount of output at the market price. MR is the extra revenue increased output. For a competitive firm $MR = P$.

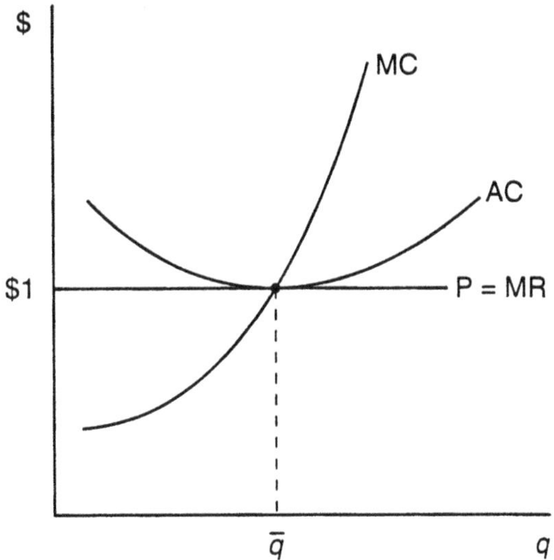

Figure 6.8
Price Taking Competition
A competitive firm takes the market price $P = \$1$. Competition implies MR equals price P. MC increases with output. Profit is maximized at the output where $MR = MC$ at the minimum average cost AC.

Marginal cost MC is the additional cost to produce one more unit of output. Profit is maximized where $MC = MR$.

Entry and exit of firms drive price to equal average cost (AC) of a typical firm. If the profit is positive, firms entering the industry increase supply, lowering price and raising input costs. If the profit is negative, the opposite occurs. AC is minimized for a competitive firm at the profit, maximizing the output.

Input Substitution

A ditch can be dug with shovels and a lot of labor or with substitution with a tractor and much less labor. The relative price of labor compared to the capital in the shovels and tractor determines the economical choice. Firms minimize cost combining K and L to produce output.

The isoquant in Figure 6.9 slopes downward with one input substituted for the other to keep the level of output constant. The firm can produce 1 unit of output with the different combinations of K and L.

The slope of the isoquant is the marginal rate of technical substitution ($MRTS$) of capital for labor. As capital input increases, the increasing $MRTS$ implies increasing capital is required to substitute for labor. The isoquant is based on the production function $q = q(K, L)$ relating inputs to output. Along an isoquant, the level of output q is constant.

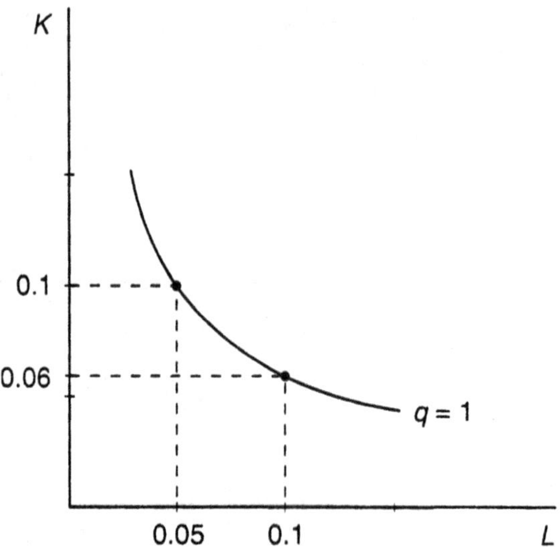

Figure 6.9
Unit Isoquant
Capital and labor are substituted along this unit isoquant where output $q = 1$. Two possible input combinations to produce $q = 1$ are $(K, L) = (0.1, 0.05)$ and $(0.06, 0.1)$.

EXAMPLE **6.5**   *Converging Labor Inputs*

Trade equalizing wages leads to input convergence. David Dollar and Edward Wolff (1988) examine convergence of manufacturing labor inputs across industrial countries between 1963 and 1982. The chart shows unit labor inputs relative to US manufacturing at 1. Italy used more than twice as much labor in 1963 but only 10% more by 1982. The UK converged quicker but from a lower level. Japan and Germany both converged to a much smaller extent.

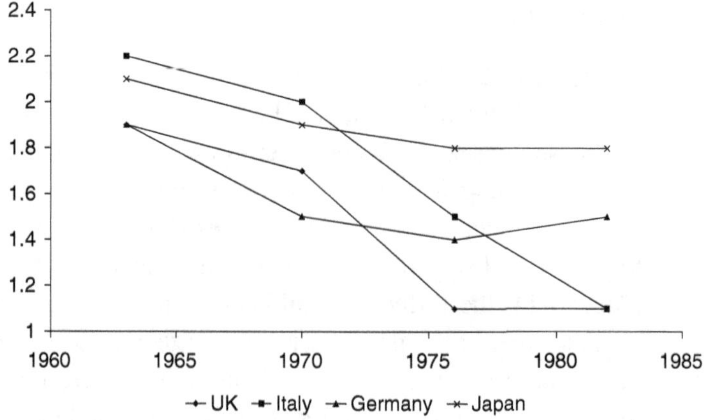

Cost Minimization

Suppose capital rent is $r = \$5$ and the wage $w = \$10$. Let a_{Kj} be the capital input and a_{Lj} the labor input per unit of good j. The cost c of producing one unit of output is

$$c = ra_{Kj} + wa_{Lj} = \$5a_{Kj} + \$10a_{Lj}$$

Competitive firms with zero profit have average cost equal to price,

$$P = \$1 = AC.$$

Figure 6.10 shows the isocost line with input combinations costing \$1. The labor that would cost \$1 if no capital is hired is $c/w = \$1/\$10 = 0.1$. The endpoint on the capital axis is $\$1/\$5 = 0.2$. The isocost line connects these endpoints. The slope of the isocost line is $-(c/r)/(c/w) = -w/r = -2$.

The firm finds the lowest isocost line to produce the optimal output. The unit isoquant and the \$1 isocost are tangent at this cost minimization where $MRTS = w/r$.

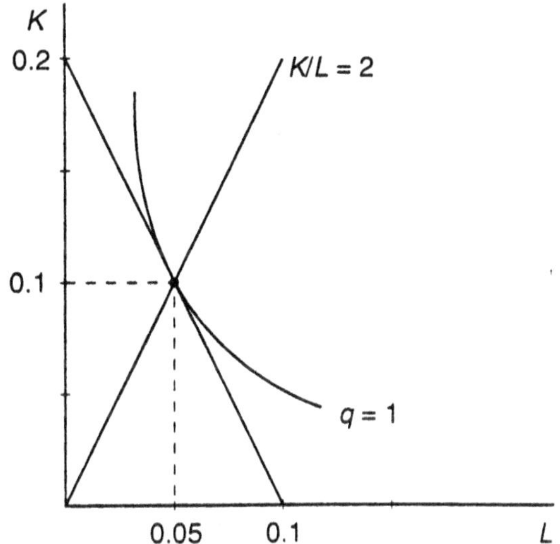

Figure 6.10
Cost Minimization
The firm wants to produce at minimum cost. Wages are \$10 and the return to capital is \$5. The firm looks for the isocost line tangent to the isoquant. Cost minimization implies $K/L = 2$.

Cost minimization leads to the input levels $L = 0.05$ and $K = 0.1$ to produce each unit of output. The expansion path shows this optimal capital/labor ratio. Along the expansion path, inputs proportionally increase with expanding output levels.

An increase in the wage w increases the slope of the isocost line causing substitution toward capital. The expansion path shifts to a higher K/L. If the capital rent r increases, the isocost line becomes flatter and K/L falls.

Firms minimize cost substituting away from a factor when its price increases.

Production of Two Goods

Figure 6.11 is the production diagram developed by Abba Lerner and Ivor Pearce. Unit value isoquants are $M = 1$ and $S = 1$ scaled to \$1. There is a single isocost line as capital and labor move freely between producing the two goods. Cost minimization leads to unit inputs $(a_{KS}, a_{LS}) = (0.1, 0.05)$ for S and $(a_{KM}, a_{LM}) = (0.04, 0.08)$ for M.

Expansion paths have the input ratios $k_S = 1/0.05 = 2$ and $k_M = 0.04/0.08 = 1/2$ where $k = K/L$. Manufactures production is labor intensive with its lower k and services capital intensive.

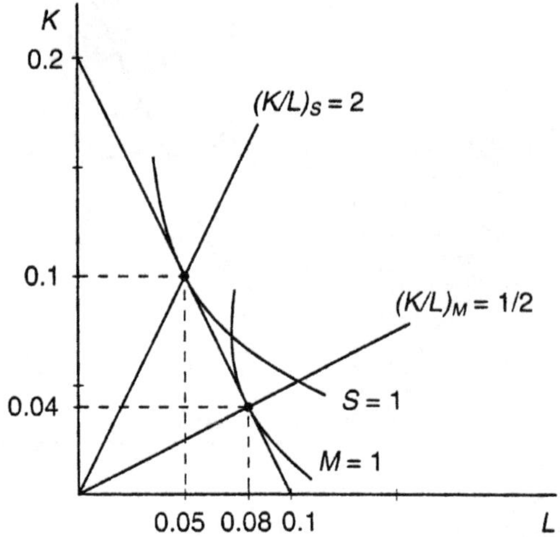

Figure 6.11
Two-by-Two Production
Both industries share the isocost line. Cost minimization leads to different K/L ratios. M is labor intensive and S capital intensive.

EXAMPLE **6.6**   *Competition and Income*

The 1999 *Global Competitiveness Report* surveyed 4000 business leaders to construct their competitiveness index. The top and bottom three economies are listed along with major US trading partners. More competitive economies have much higher income per capita in $000.

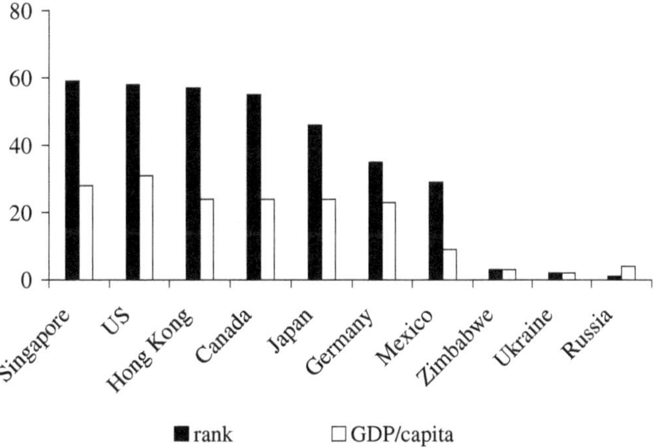

Outputs Levels

Figure 6.12 shows how outputs are determined by the endowments of capital and labor given cost minimization and full employment. The given amounts of inputs

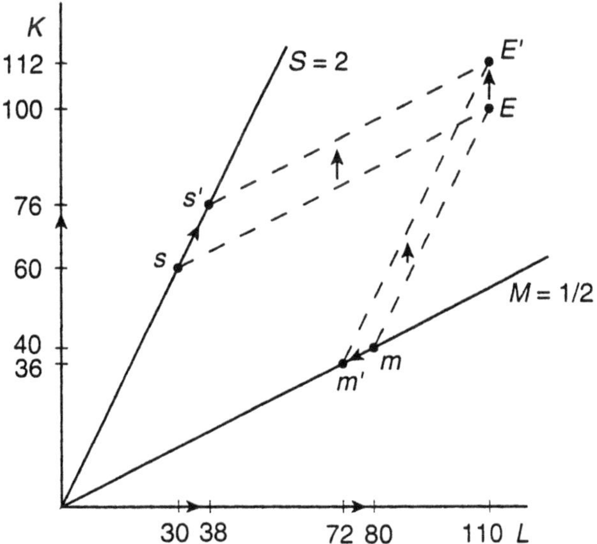

Figure 6.12
An Increase in Capital
When K increases, the economy moves toward the capital-intensive output. As K rises from 100 to 112, the production of S adds 16 K and 8 L. M output falls to m' as S rises to s'.

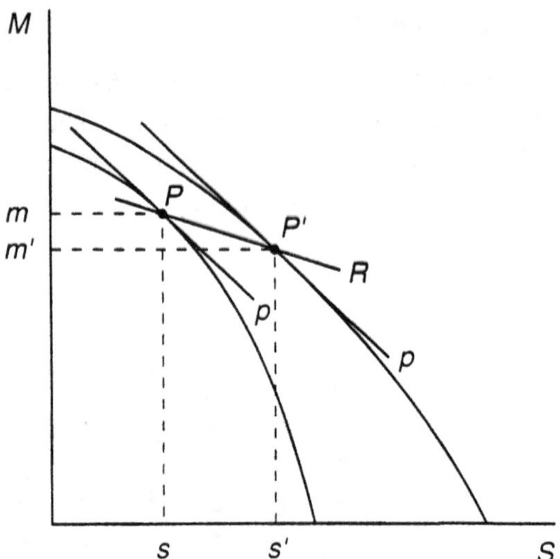

Figure 6.13
Rybczynski Line
An increase in K shifts the PPF out with a bias toward capital-intensive services. Connecting outputs is the Rybczynski line R for capital.

are $(K, L) = (100, 110)$ at point E. Completing the parallelogram determines the output levels along the expansion paths. The output levels m and s are unique and consistent with cost minimization and full employment.

An increase in capital shifts the endowment point E as in Figure 6.12. Services output rises to s' as manufactures falls to m'. Both capital and labor leave M production. If K increases to 112, the added K plus 4 more from manufactures move into the expanding production of S.

In Figure 6.13, the international relative price line p begins with production at point P. Outputs m and s correspond to Figure 6.12. When capital increases, the PPF shifts out biased toward capital-intensive services. The new production point P′ is where the new PPF is tangent to the price line p at output levels m' and s'. The Rybczynski line R connects these production points. In the early 1950s, T.M. Rybczynski proved that an increase in a factor raises the output using it intensively and lowers the other output.

EXAMPLE **6.7**   *Skilled Labor Content*

The US historically exports agricultural products. Robert Baldwin (1971) estimates that farm labor was 1.4 times more involved in export than in import-competing activity. Estimates of relative export involvement for skill types indicate the most skilled group, professionals, is most involved in exports, and the least skilled groups, operatives and laborers, are most involved in import competition. The middle skills, crafts and clerical, are in the middle between export and import competition.

Factor Abundance and Exports

A capital-abundant home country has a higher capital/labor ratio,

$$k > k^*,$$

making the foreign country labor abundant. If consumers in the two countries have similar preferences, they will want to consume the same ratio of outputs with free trade and equal prices. The capital-abundant home country exports capital-intensive services in exchange for labor-intensive manufacture.

This proposition developed by Eli Heckscher and Bertil Ohlin in the 1930s is part of fundamental intuition in trade:

Countries export products intensive in their abundant factors.

Factor Price Equalization

The isoquants in Figure 6.14 represent $1 of outputs S and M. When trade equalizes prices between countries, these unit value isoquants are the same in both countries. The isocost line and factor prices must then also be the same in the two countries.

Free trade between two factor proportions economies leads to equal prices for each factor in both countries.

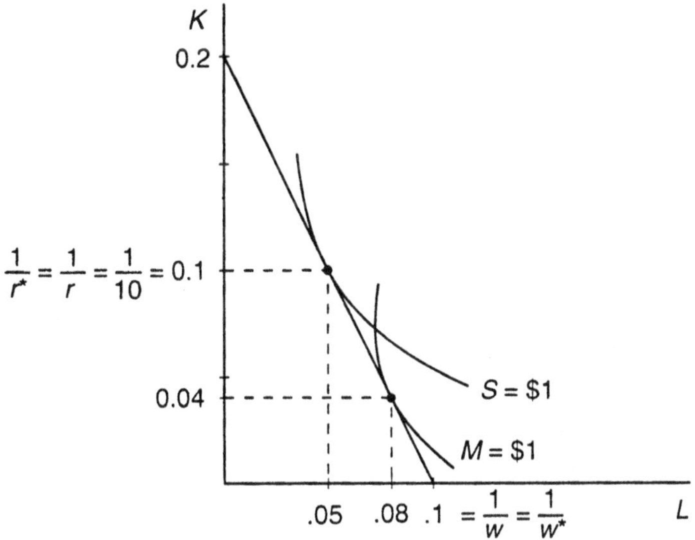

Figure 6.14
Factor Price Equalization
With free trade unit, isoquants are the same in each country. The unit isocost line is $c = 10\,L + 5\,K$. Wages are the same in both countries at $w = w^* = \$10$. Capital rents are also the same at $r = r^* = \$5$.

EXAMPLE **6.8**   *Skilled Labor Intensity*

Edward Leamer (1984) constructs industry rankings with inputs of capital K, labor L, and skilled labor S. Skilled labor includes professional, technical, and scientific workers. US industries are ranked according to S/L and S/K. The US abundance of skilled labor gives it cost advantage in products with high S/L and S/K ratios. US industries toward the top of the list prosper and export, while those toward the bottom face import competition.

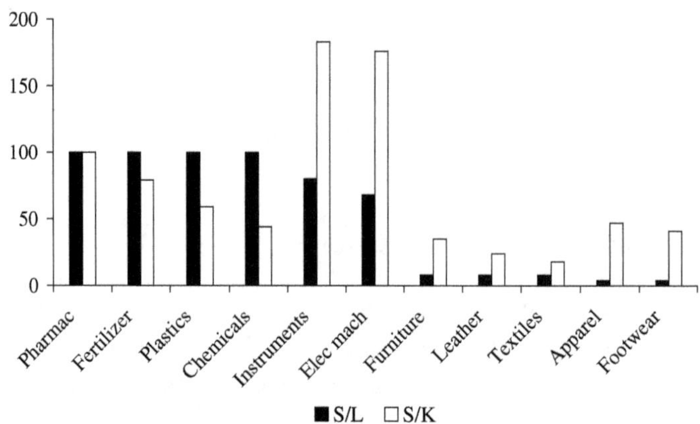

Factor price equalization is supported by the evidence that trade brings prices for similar productive factors closer together across countries. A labor-abundant country will have lower wages and less expensive labor-intensive products. If $ew^* < w$ due to abundant foreign labor, trade increases the demand D^* for labor in the foreign country raising w^*. Meanwhile labor demand D_L in the home country falls and w falls.

EXAMPLE **6.9**   *Trade and Convergence*

Increased trade causes both convergence of wages and per capita income as shown by Farhad Rassekh and Henry Thompson (1998). David Dollar and Edward Wolff (1993) find evidence of wage convergence. Jeffrey Williamson (1996) finds evidence of wage convergence in the 1800s. David Ben-David (1993) shows convergence of per capita income occurred with trade in Europe. Ben-David and Alok Bohara (1997) find per capita income convergence is stimulated by free trade agreements. Farhad Rassekh (1992) shows there has been convergence of per capita income among the Organisation for Economic Co-operation and Development (OECD) countries. For less developed countries (LDCs), the recommendation is free trade. Meanwhile unskilled labor in the developed countries (DCs) can expect falling wages and is encouraged to invest in becoming skilled.

Tariffs and Factor Prices

Protection drives the prices of similar factors across countries apart. If a tariff raises the home price of manufactures, the physical amount of the good worth $1 falls. The inputs required to make $1 of the manufactured good falls. The following property was proven by Wolfgang Stolper and Paul Samuelson in the early 1950s.

A tariff raises the price of the factor used intensively in the import-competing industry and lowers the other factor price.

In the cost minimization of Figure 6.14, a tariff on M pushes its unit isoquant toward the origin. The new equilibrium occurs at a higher wage w and lower capital return r. The price of already highly paid labor increases and the price of relatively cheap capital falls due to the tariff. The tariff results in more uneven income distribution across countries.

The increase in the relative price of labor causes both industries to become more capital intensive. The ratio of capital to labor rises in manufacturing and services. Output of protected labor-intensive manufacturing increases as output of capital-intensive services declines.

While the wage increases due to the tariff, workers pay higher prices for manufactures. The percentage wage increase is greater than the percentage increase in the price of manufactures. Labor enjoys higher real income in the magnification effect of Ron Jones.

EXAMPLE **6.10**   *Factor Price Convergence*

Farhad Rassekh and Henry Thompson (1993) review the status of factor price equalization FPE. While wages differ widely across countries, there is widespread evidence that trade leads to wage convergence.

EXAMPLE **6.11**   *Trade and Income Redistribution in Less Developed Countries*

Trade will raise the price of manufactures and lower the price of business services in LDCs. Henry Thompson (1995b) projects the effects of changing prices across LDCs in a factor proportions model combining a 10% increase in the price of manufactures with a 10% decrease in the price of business services. Wages of unskilled labor rise upwards by 50% while wages of skilled labor and the capital return fall.

Section C Problems

C1. Diagram a competitive manufacturing unit value isocost line if $w = \$2$, $r = \$3$, and $c = \$1$. Find capital input with 0.2 units of labor.

C2. Sketch the manufacturing unit value isoquant in Problem C1 and show the cost minimization. Draw the expansion path. What is k in manufacturing?

C3. Let point E in Figure 6.10 represent the home country. The foreign country has less capital and more labor. The two countries trade freely. Compare the different employments of K and L across sectors.

C4. Compare ratios of foreign outputs in Problem C3 with home outputs. Which country produces a higher ratio M/S? Which will export M if consumers in both countries have the same preferences?

C5. How would the switch from autarky to free trade affect payments to K and L for each country in Problem C4?

EXAMPLE 6.12   *Three-Way Trade*

When three countries produce three goods with three factors, Henry Thompson (2001) stresses the complexity of trade that does not have to balance between any two of them. Each country must export at least one product. All three might export two products. Tariffs raise the real income of at least one factor in each country. Factor intensity is important in adjustments to a tariff, but factor price substitution also plays a role.

D. APPLICATIONS OF FACTOR PROPORTIONS TRADE

This section covers some tests and extensions of the factor proportions theory.

Testing the Factor Proportions Trade Theory

Wassily Leontief (1953) examines the capital and labor content of US trade finding labor-intensive exports. The K/L ratio was 1.41 for export production and 1.82 for import-competing goods. The import of capital-intensive goods in the capital-abundant US is called the Leontief paradox.

Robert Baldwin (1971) finds the K/L ratio of US imports and exports were very similar excluding natural resource products. Baldwin also finds US exports were intensive in skilled labor.

Robert Stern and Keith Maskus (1981) find the Leontief paradox disappeared over time. Keith Maskus (1985) subsequently reports the paradox resurfaces with the US frequently being a net exporter of labor-intensive products.

Edward Leamer (1980) makes the point that products consumed in the US are much more labor intensive than exports. Francisco Casas and Kwan Choi (1985) estimate there would be no Leontief paradox balanced trade. William Branson and Nikolaos Monoyios (1977) show that the US exported goods intensive in skilled labor while importing unskilled labor-intensive goods.

Edward Leamer (1984) finds US exports are intensive in scientists, engineers, technicians, and draftsmen. Robert Stern and Keith Maskus (1981) also stress the role of skilled labor abundance.

EXAMPLE **6.13**   *North American Trade and Labor Supplies*

While trade between Mexico and the US might lower unskilled wages in the US, Kenneth Reinert and David Roland-Holst (1998) estimate wages can rise for all skills in all three countries with elastic labor supplies. North American trade is predicted to raise the average wage 1% in the US and 3% in Canada and Mexico given elastic labor skill supplies.

Applications of Factor Proportions Trade Theory

Hundreds of economies trade tens of thousands of goods and services making empirical analysis a challenge. Production involves various types of skilled labor, different vintages of capital input, and a wide variety of natural resource inputs. Factor intensity and factor abundance are a challenge in such applications.

Trade in business services is growing quickly. Skilled labor abundance in DCs is intensive in business services. The evolving pattern of specialization is a challenge to predict.

Computable general equilibrium (CGE) models of production and trade based on factor proportions theory predict the effects of protection, export subsidies, oil price shocks, exchange rate changes, and more across many products and inputs.

EXAMPLE **6.14**   *Industrial Factors Proportions Theory*

Links between prices of products and factors depend on factor intensity. Farhad Rassekh and Henry Thompson (1997) examine the factor intensities of nine industries across 12 DCs from 1970 to 1985. A high price for a labor-intensive good increases its share of output, raises the wage, and raises the capital-labor ratio. A high price for a capital-intensive good lowers the capital-labor ratio for five of the nine industries. Predictions of the specific factors model hold for seven of the industries. The ranking below compares capital intensity in thousands of dollars per worker. Canada has the most capital-intensive minerals industry. Canada and Japan have capital-intensive paper industries. US textile production is the most labor intensive. Germany has low capital intensities in chemicals and basic metals.

Production and Trade with Unemployment

Unemployment arises for various reasons. It takes time and resources to match firms and workers. Searching for a job is costly. Some labor markets require training and experience. Industries expand and contract with business cycles and international competition. Labor contracts create wage inflexibility. Unemployment benefits provide incentive to remain unemployed.

Firms hire labor according to marginal revenue product. If the minimum or contract wage is higher than the market wage, there is unemployment below the PPF.

In the probability wage model of James Harris and Michael Todaro (1970), rural wages w_R are low but everyone has a job in the rural area. Urban wages w_U are higher but there is only a probability P of finding a job. Workers in rural areas discount the high urban wage. If $P = 80\% = 0.8$ and $w_U = \$70$, the discounted urban wage is $0.80 \times \$70 = \$16$. If $w_R < \$16$, rural workers move to the urban area. Other considerations such as moving costs and tastes for urban versus rural life also influence decisions.

LDCs report high rates of unemployment but everyone is constantly working. In the DCs, workers draw unemployment benefits and work in the "underground" economy that actively produce valuable goods and services.

Minimum wage legislation and labor contracts create unemployment. A fall in the demand for labor results in either lower wages or unemployment. Neither is desirable but lower wages are less of a burden. Support for unskilled workers lessens incentive to become skilled. Flexibility in wages and hours worked would lead to more efficient labor markets.

Properties of trade theory are not much affected by unemployment.

EXAMPLE **6.15**   *Free Trade in Bolivia*

Free trade will impact production and factor prices in Bolivia, as examined by Hugo Toledo and Henry Thompson (2001) in an applied factor proportions model. Natural gas and manufacturing exports will expand while agriculture and services suffer import competition. Bolivian farmers will lose their protection in Mercosur. Bolivian business service industries are skilled labor intensive, government owned or subsidized, and inefficient. Skilled and unskilled labor will lose with free trade. Outputs in services and agriculture will fall. Capital in services and agriculture will suffer losses while capital owners in natural gas, manufacturing, and mining enjoy gains.

Factor Proportions with Constant Costs

The factor proportions model and the constant cost model are integrated by the constant cost endowment (CCE) model in Roy Ruffin (1988). Trade occurs between different skills of labor residing in different countries. Services S and manufactures M are produced by labor L or skilled labor H.

Figure 6.15 includes the constant cost unit labor inputs $a_{LM} = 1$, $a_{HM} = 2$, $a_{LS} = 2$, and $a_{HS} = 1$. The home country has an abundance of skilled labor, $(L, H) = (100, 400)$ and $(L^*, H^*) = (500, 50)$. Skilled labor at home can produce $400/2 = 200$ M. Home unskilled labor can produce an additional $100/1 = 100$ units of M. Alternatively the H at home could produce $400/1 = 400$ S and the L another $100/2 = 50$ S. Endpoints on the home PPF are 300 M and 450 S.

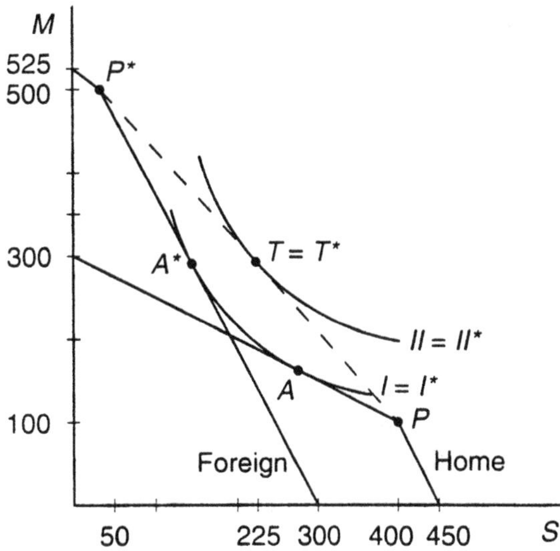

Figure 6.15
Constant Cost Factor Proportions
Each country specializes by producing the good with low input of its abundant factor, skilled labor in the home services, and unskilled labor in foreign manufacturing. The terms of trade are $tt = M/S = 200/175 = 8/7$. Each country consumes $(M, S) = (300, 225)$ beyond its PPF.

Starting at $M = 300$, skilled labor would begin producing S according to comparative advantage. If all available skilled labor produces S and only unskilled labor produces M output is at the pivot point $(M, S) = (100, 400)$. In autarky, consumers pick a point along the PPF. Home consumers maximize utility at point A with some skilled labor in manufacturing.

The foreign PPF* connects endpoints $M = 525$ and $S = 300$ with pivot point $(M, S) = (500, 50)$. Foreign consumers constrained to their PPF in autarky maximize utility at point A^*. Some foreign unskilled labor produces services.

Trade moves production to the pivot points with P and P^*. The terms of trade are the dotted line connecting pivot points. Abundant factors specialize according to comparative advantage. All skilled labor at home produces S and all of the unskilled labor in the foreign country produces M. The home country exports 175 units of S in exchange for 200 units of M from the foreign country. Both countries consume 300 M and 225 S at point $T = T^*$ with higher utility.

Income is more evenly distributed with trade. The home country has a relative abundance of skilled labor. Trade increases the price of cheap services with skilled labor pulled into services by a higher skilled wage. In the foreign country, trade increases the price of manufactures and the wage.

EXAMPLE **6.16**   *Evidence on Factor Abundance and Exports*

Edward Leamer (1984) examines links between factor endowments and exports in 47 countries producing the ten outputs of petroleum, raw materials, forest products, tropical agriculture, animal products, cereals, labor-intensive manufactures, capital-intensive manufactures, machinery, and chemicals. The 11 inputs are capital, professionals, unskilled labor, skilled labor, coal, minerals, oil, and four types of land. Countries abundant in capital and skilled labor are Belgium, France, Germany, Italy, Japan, the Netherlands, Sweden, Switzerland, UK, and the US exporting chemicals (capital and skilled labor intensive) and machinery (skilled labor intensive). Austria, India, Korea, and Spain export capital-intensive manufactures. Brazil, Colombia, Cyprus, Egypt, Finland, Greece, Malta, Sri Lanka, Thailand, and Turkey are labor abundant and export labor-intensive manufactures. LDCs are capital scarce and export tropical agricultural goods, raw materials, cereals, and animal products. Trade in agriculture, minerals, and oil is explained by the locations of land and natural resources.

EXAMPLE **6.17**   *Trade and Labor Skills*

Trade leads to gains but redistributes income. William Cline (1997) presents evidence that unskilled US manufacturing wages have fallen and suggests they will continue to fall. Skilled labor enjoys benefits due to increased trade as the US specializes in production intensive in skilled labor. The endowment ratio of skilled to unskilled labor has increased over decades as workers respond to market incentives by increasing education and training.

Section D Problems

D1. What is an explanation other than those in the text for the Leontief paradox?
D2. Use a 2 × 2 production diagram to illustrate the effects of increased unemployment benefits on outputs.

EXAMPLE **6.18**   *Labor along the PPF*

Trade moves the economy along its production frontier with labor and other factors of production moving toward export industries. Romain Wacziarg and Jessica Wallan (2004) examine trade liberalization from the 1970s to the 1990s across 25 LDCs and NICs. Labor market reactions vary. There was no movement between manufacturing, services, and agriculture but there was movement between industries and firms in manufacturing. Labor market adjustments were more dramatic following privatization of socialized industries.

EXAMPLE **6.19**   *Trade and the Wage Gap*

Skilled wages have increased relative to unskilled wages in the US with imports of unskilled-intensive products. Improved technology may also favor skilled labor. Robert Baldwin and Glen Cain (2000) find the US wage gap declined due to a net increase in the supply of skilled labor. Eli Berman, John Bound, and Stephen Machin (1998) find evidence of skill-biased technical change during the 1980s and suggest trade contributes. Robert Feenstra and Gordon Hanson (1999) find that 35% of the wage gap is explained by computers and 15% by outsourcing. Jonathan Haskel and Matthew Slaughter (2002) find evidence that sector-biased technical change in the skill-intensive industries best explains the wage gap. John Francis and Henry Thompson (2009) simulate a specific factors model with 458 industries, finding that trade lowers both skilled and unskilled wages widening the wage gap.

CONCLUSION

The factor proportions model of production and trade is the foundation of trade theory, production frontiers, and offer curves. Its basic assumption is competitive markets. Chapter 7 examines trade with noncompetitive pricing due to monopoly, monopolistic competition, and oligopoly. Each industrial structure has its own implications for trade and trade policy.

Terms

Computable general equilibrium	Isocost line
Constant cost	Isoquant
Cost minimization	Leontief paradox
Diminishing marginal productivity	Marginal cost (MC)
Entry and exit	Marginal product (MP)
Expansion paths	Marginal revenue (MR)
Factor abundance and scarcity	Marginal revenue product (MRP)
Factor demand	Price-taking firm
Factor intensity	Probability wage unemployment
Factor price equalization	Specific factors
Factor price substitution	

MAIN POINTS

- Tariffs raise the prices of factors specific to an industry but lower prices of factors specific to other industries. Shared factors may win or lose.

- The positive links between factor abundance, intensity, and exports are key to production and trade.
- Trade leads to factor price convergence between countries raising demand for abundant cheap factors in export production.
- Factor proportions theory predicts international trade and the effects of trade policy.

REVIEW PROBLEMS

1. In the specific factors economy from the problems in Section A, suppose the price of imported M rises to \$2.40 with a tariff. Show what happens in the labor market.

2. Diagram what happens in Problem 1 to markets for sector-specific capital inputs. Explain adjustments in outputs.

3. Suppose country A imposes a tariff on imported manufactures improving its terms of trade with B. Predict what happens to income distribution in B with the specific factors model.

4. Diagram the international capital market with a capital-abundant country with Figure 6.6 as a guide.

5. Diagram the international production of services with a capital-abundant home country similar to Figure 6.7.

6. Sketch the cost minimization with $w = \$2$, $r = \$3$, $c = \$1$, and 0.2 unit of L input. Find the capital input and sketch the unit value isoquant. Describe what happens if r falls to \$2.

7. Describe what happens to the cost minimization in Problem 7 if w rises to \$3.

8. Given factor prices $w = \$2$ and $r = \$3$ suppose 0.35 units of labor are employed in manufacturing to produce \$1 of output. Sketch the manufacturing cost minimization and the expansion path. Find K/L in manufacturing.

9. Draw the production diagram of the economy with the service sector in Problem 6 and the manufacturing sector in Problem 8.

10. Two economies have endowments $(K, L) = (100, 200)$ and $(K^*, L^*) = (110, 190)$. Given the technology in Problem 9, predict the pattern of trade. Explain which country is labor cheap.

11. If the foreign country described in Problem 8 imposes a tariff, explain what happens to w^* and r^*. Illustrate with a diagram. What happens to the K/L ratios in manufacturing and services?

12. Illustrate FPE using a production diagram when the home country has twice as much capital and half as much labor as the foreign country.

13. Draw the home PPF in the CCE model with endowment $(L, H) = (400, 500)$ and unit inputs in the text. Draw the foreign PPF* with endowment $(L^*, H^*) = (300, 600)$.

14. Find the terms of trade and consumption for the two economies in Problem 14. Explain the pattern of trade.

15. With three factors (capital, labor, natural resources) and two goods (manufactures, services), define factor intensity.

16. If agricultural output is added to Problem 15, define factor intensity and factor abundance.

READINGS

William Baumol, Richard Nelson, and Edward Wolff (1994) *Convergence of Productivity*, Oxford: Oxford University Press. History of convergence across countries.

Brian Berry, Edgar Conkling, and Michael Ray (1997) *The Global Economy in Transition*, New Jersey: Prentice-Hall. Graphical blend of geography, energy analysis, population dynamics, and economics.

Alan Deardorff and Robert Stern (1986) *The Michigan Model of World Production and Trade: Theory and Applications*, Cambridge: MIT Press. CGE model of production and trade.

Ronald Findlay (1988) *Factor Proportions, Trade, and Growth*, Cambridge: MIT Press. Clearly written short book.

Graff, Michael, A. G. Kenwood, and A. L. Lougheed (2013) *Growth of the International Economy, 1820–2015*, Routledge. A nice economic history.

Edward Leamer (1984) *Sources of International Comparative Advantage*, Cambridge: MIT Press, 1984. Quantitative basis of factor abundance and trade.

John Pool and Stephen Stamos (1994) *Exploring the Global Economy*, Shenandoah University: Durell Institute of Monetary Science. Short excursion into importance of international commerce.

David Richardson (1993) *Sizing Up US Export Disincentives*, Washington: Institute for International Economics. Policies diminishing exports.

MATHEMATICAL APPENDIX

Factor proportions trade is based on the abundance of factors of production and the factor intensity of goods. Suppose the home country H is capital abundant and the foreign country F is labor abundant in the relative endowment ranking $K/L > K^*/L^*$. For factor intensity, suppose manufacturing M is L intensive and services S capital intensive $a_{KS}/a_{LS} > a_{KM}/a_{LM}$, where a_{ij} is the amount of factor i input per unit of good j output.

Markets for inputs and outputs are competitive. The factors are fully employed, $K = \Sigma_j a_{Kj} x_j$ and $L = \Sigma_j a_{Lj} x_j$. Competitive pricing implies the price equals cost, $p_j = c_j = a_{Kj} r + a_{Lj} w$ for good j. These employment and pricing conditions lead to the static equilibrium factor prices $w = (a_{KS} p_M - a_{KM} p_S)/b$ and $r = (a_{LM} p_S - a_{LS} p_M)\,b$ along with outputs $x_M = (a_{LS} K - a_{KS} L)/b$ and $x_S = (a_{KM} L - a_{LM} K)/b$, where b is the factor intensity term $b \equiv a_{KS} a_{LM} - a_{KM} a_{LS} > 0$. Prices and endowments lead to positive factor prices and outputs in the static equilibrium. These conditions are the foundation for general equilibrium trade theory as well as computable general equilibrium (CGE) models.

Production and utility functions are assumed identical in both countries. As a result, differences in factor endowments account for the levels of production and trade in the static equilibrium. The assumptions can be relaxed without necessarily altering properties of the theory.

Turning to the comparative statics, a change dL in the labor endowment leads to adjustments in outputs and unit inputs according to $dL = \Sigma_j (a_{Lj} dx_j + x_j da_{Lj})$ with a similar expression for dK. Homothetic production implies the cost-minimizing inputs a_{ij} depend only on factor prices r and w. The change in the unit labor input is then $da_{Lj} = (\partial a_{Lj}/\partial r)dr + (\partial a_{Lj}/\partial w)dw$. The related cross price substitution of L with respect to a change r is $S_{Lr} = \Sigma_j x_j (\partial a_{Lj}/\partial r)dr > 0$ similar to a familiar factor price elasticity. The change in labor dL then expands to $dL = \Sigma_j a_{Lj} dx_j + S_{Lr} dr + S_{Lw} dw$ including the own wage effect S_{Lw} with a similar comparative static expression for dK.

Price changes are matched by changes in cost due to competition in production, $dp_j = dc_j = a_{Kj} dr + a_{Lj} dw$, given $r da_{Kj} + w da_{Lj} = 0$ due to cost minimization.

Shephard's lemma follows directly with inputs as first derivatives of the cost function, $\partial c_j/\partial r = a_{Kj}$ and $\partial c_j/\partial w = a_{Lj}$. Shephard's lemma implies cost functions are dual to production functions.

The conditions for changes in employment and pricing lead to the comparative static system,

$$
\begin{pmatrix}
S_{Kr} & S_{Kw} & a_{KS} & a_{KM} \\
S_{Lr} & S_{Lw} & a_{LS} & a_{LM} \\
a_{KS} & a_{LS} & 0 & 0 \\
a_{KM} & a_{LM} & 0 & 0
\end{pmatrix}
\begin{pmatrix}
\partial r \\
\partial w \\
\partial x_S \\
\partial x_M
\end{pmatrix}
=
\begin{pmatrix}
\partial K \\
\partial L \\
\partial p_S \\
\partial p_M
\end{pmatrix}
$$

Changes in endowments ∂K and ∂L and prices ∂p_S and ∂p_M lead to adjustments in factor prices ∂r and ∂w and outputs ∂x_S and ∂x_M. The determinant of the system is $\Delta = b^2 > 0$. Four theorems in the comparative statics relate to adjustments in factor prices and outputs to changes in prices and endowments.

A tariff on imported M raises the import-competing price p_M from $ep_M{}^*$ to $(1 + t)ep_M{}^*$. The comparative statics find the partial derivatives with $dp_M > 0$ and $dp_S = dK = dL = 0$. Factor prices adjust in the comparative statics according to $\partial r/\partial p_M = -a_{LS}b/\Delta < 0$ and $\partial w/\partial p_M = a_{KS}b/\Delta > 0$.

The Stolper–Samuelson theorem summarizes these factor price adjustments to price changes determined by factor intensity. An import tariff raises the price of the factor intensive in import-competing production. The Jones magnification effect follows as the percentage increase in w must be greater than the percentage increase in p_M as $(\partial w/\partial p_M)p_M/w = a_{KS}p_M/(a_{KS}p_M - a_{KM}p_S) > 1$. Labor benefits from the tariff with increased real income as the wage increases more than the average price of goods. Capital owners lose with r falling. Factor price adjustments to a change in the price of exported S is similar.

Outputs adjust along the concave production frontier with the tariff according to $\partial x_M/\partial p_M > 0$ and $\partial x_S/\partial p_M < 0$ in the comparative static solution due to substitution as S_{Kw}, $S_{Lr} > 0$ and S_{Kr}, $S_{Lw} < 0$. Movement along the concave PPF involves input substitution.

Factor endowments have no comparative static effects on factor prices as $\partial r/\partial K = \partial w/\partial K = \partial r/\partial L = \partial w/\partial L = 0$. This factor price equalization property implies the unintuitive result that foreign investment or labor migration do not affect factor prices. This result is due to the same number of factors and goods.

Changing endowments affect outputs in the comparative statics depending on factor intensity according to $\partial x_S/\partial K = a_{LM}/b > 0$, $\partial x_M/\partial K = -a_{LS}/b < 0$, $\partial x_S/\partial L = -a_{KM}/b < 0$, and $\partial x_M/\partial L = a_{KS}/b > 0$. The Rybczynski theorem states that each output increases with the endowment of its intensive factor and decreases with the other factor.

The Heckscher–Ohlin (HO) theorem relating endowments to trade follows from the Rybczynski theorem. The labor-abundant foreign country produces a higher ratio of L-intensive M. The same utility functions between the two countries imply equal consumption ratios with trade equalizing prices of goods. The K-abundant home country similarly exports K-intensive good S. Empirical studies show the HO theorem expanded to skilled labor and natural resources explains a good deal of observed trade.

The specific factors model introduces sector-specific capital input. Employment conditions are $K_M = a_{KM}x_M$ and $K_S = a_{KS}x_S$ for the two types of capital. Labor L is employed in both sectors. In the comparative static system, the capital of one sector is not employed by the other with no substitution between the two types of capital.

Changing endowments of K_M, K_S, or L affect factor prices r_M, r_S, and w. An increase in K_M lowers its own return $\partial r_M/\partial K_M < 0$ but raises the wage $\partial w/\partial K_M > 0$ as labor is attracted from the other sector. In sector S, the lost L lowers the marginal product of K as $\partial r_S/\partial K_M < 0$. Outputs adjust according to $\partial x_M/\partial K_M > 0$ and $\partial x_S/\partial K_M < 0$. Adjustments to changes in K_S are similar.

An increase in the labor endowment L lowers the wage $\partial w/\partial L < 0$ and raises both capital returns $\partial r_M/\partial L > 0$ and $\partial r_S/\partial L > 0$ as capital productivity increases. Both outputs increase due to an increase in L.

A tariff on imported M in the SF model raises r_M and w. Labor is attracted to import-competing production by the increased wage w. Capital in the import-competing sector benefits as the percentage increase in r_M is higher than any weighted average of price changes in the magnification effect. Labor may not come out ahead due to the neoclassical ambiguity as the higher price of imports erodes the purchasing power of labor income. The tariff lowers r_S as the other sector loses labor and output x_S falls.

These properties generalize to any number of factors and goods providing the theoretical foundation for trade theory. The comparative static properties are robust to parametric relaxation of the assumptions on employment and pricing. The success of factor proportions theory might be little surprise as production requires inputs. The underlying forces of competition tend to dominate noncompetitive legal or technical market conditions. Applied factor proportions and specific factors models based on observed factor shares and industry shares have sensible properties. The related detailed computable models provide detailed predictions on adjustments to tariffs, migration, and foreign investment.

CHAPTER 7

Industrial Organization and Trade

Preview

Industrial organization refers to different arrangements of firms in an industry. The four broad categories of industrial organization are competition, monopolistic competition, oligopoly, and monopoly.

A competitive industry has many price-taking firms producing a homogeneous product with free entry and exit and zero economic profit. At the other extreme is a monopoly, a single price-searching firm restricting the output to maximize profit. Monopolies are based on private ownership of a scarce resource or a government franchise. Oligopoly is when a small number of firms collude to form an effective monopoly. Monopolistic competition occurs when firms are price searchers although free entry and exit eliminate excess profit.

Topics in this chapter include:

- Tariffs on a foreign monopoly
- Trade with product differentiation and monopolistic competition
- Oligopoly collusion and strategy
- Other theories of trade

INTRODUCTION

A monopoly is a market with a single price-searching firm. A foreign monopolist, as the only source of a good, restricts output searching for the price that maximizes profit. Examples of monopoly power in international markets are scarce minerals and natural resources. The energy industry is characterized by monopolies franchised by governments wanting the transparent tax base.

An international monopoly can set different prices according to demand across importing countries. Buyers with higher or more inelastic demand pay a higher price.

An oligopoly is an industry with a few firms. An international oligopoly has firms in different countries with the output and price decisions of one firm affecting the others. Firms can collude to share monopoly profit. Collusion can break down into competitive pricing depending on firm strategies.

Monopolistic competition occurs in international markets when home or foreign firms have price-searching power in export markets. Free entry and exit of competing firms keep profit for the typical firm close to zero.

Differences in technology across countries can also be a source of trade. Some countries are better at developing new products leading to product cycles as copycat countries begin production. Increasing returns to scale with average cost decreasing as output increases can be a source of trade. Different income levels across countries account for trade in necessities versus luxury goods.

A. PRICE SEARCHING FIRMS AND TRADE

A firm that faces downward sloping demand searches for the price that maximizes profit. Optimal trade policy is different for markets with price-searching firms.

Price-Searching Firms

An industry with a single firm is a monopoly. A natural monopoly is based on average cost declining due to economies of scale until output meets demand. One firm is then the most efficient industrial organization as small starting firms are unable to compete. Natural monopolies are not very common.

A legal monopoly arises due to property rights or franchises that make competition illegal. Patents, franchises, licensing, and resource ownership establish property rights and legal monopolies. A production process may be patented ensuring other firms cannot copy a product or process. Copyright law ensures the property rights of authors, musicians, and movie producers. Patents and copyrights are a focus of the World Trade Organization (WTO).

The Organization of Petroleum Exporting Countries (OPEC) and other resource cartels try to establish international monopoly power based on property rights. Utility companies have the sole legal right to sell in their franchised area franchised by the government. In trade, foreign telecommunication firms are prohibited from entry. Licenses introduce some monopoly power by restricting free entry and competition. Foreign trained doctors and electricians as examples are prohibited from competing due to licensing.

A monopoly searches for the price and quantity combination that maximizes profit selecting a supply point on the demand curve. The profit maximizing price and quantity are found with marginal revenue (MR) and marginal cost (MC). If $MR > MC$, the monopoly will increase output and the opposite if $MC > MR$.

Figure 7.1 pictures the global gold market assuming a single mining firm. World demand for gold D constrains the monopoly. There are substitutes for gold such as silver jewelry, titanium input in industry, and real estate as an asset. At the price of $3,000 no gold is sold. MR lies below demand D as the monopolist lowers price to sell more.

Start with the inverse demand function $P = a - bQ$ where a and b are positive numbers. Total revenue is $TR = PQ = aQ - bQ^2$. MR is the change in TR for a change in Q, $dTR/dQ = MR = a - 2bQ$. The inverse demand function $P = 1,000 - 1/2Q$ leads to $MR = 1,000 - 10\,Q$ making MR twice as steep as the linear demand.

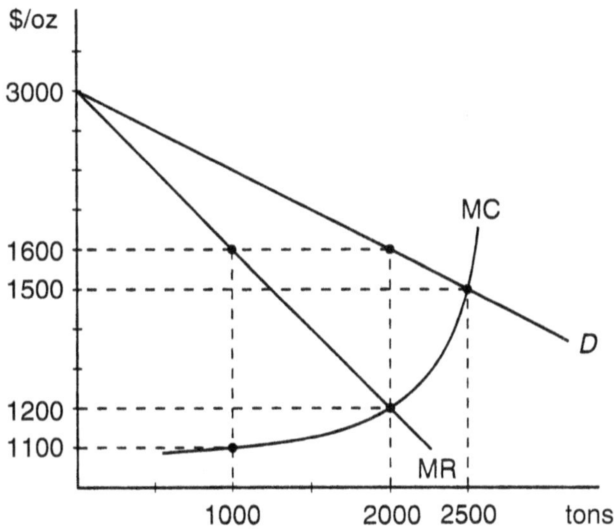

Figure 7.1
A Price-Searching Monopoly Exporter
The monopoly produces 2,000 where $MR = MC = \$1,200$. The price is set according
to demand at $P = \$1,600$.

Another constraint on monopoly pricing and output is the cost of production.
The monopoly has a certain amount of machinery and equipment to go along
with labor. Increasing gold output requires more labor, more wear and tear on
machinery and equipment, and more energy input.

MC increases with output sloping upward due to diminishing marginal products
in production. Additional workers add to total output but beyond the increments
decrease. Increasing output also raises demands for inputs increasing their prices.

At outputs below 2,000 tons, the MR from selling an extra unit of output is
larger than the MC of producing it. The monopolist raises profit by increasing
output and continues until $MR = MC = \$1,200$.

After finding the output that maximizes profit, the monopoly sets the price
of gold according to demand. The 2,000 tons can be sold at a price of $1,600
where output of 2,000 meets demand D.

*Price-searching firms maximize profit with the output where MR = MC setting
price according to demand to clear the market.*

EXAMPLE **7.1**   *A Snapshot of US Exporting Firms*

Manufacturing firms account for about 70% of US export revenue followed
by wholesalers, freight forwarders, transportation, services, business services,
engineering, management, gas and oil extraction, coal mining, and communications.
Large firms with 500 or more employees account for most of export revenue.
Intrafirm trade is almost half of merchandise export revenue. While most exporting
firms trade with only one foreign country, the few firms that export to 50 or
more countries account for about half of all merchandise export revenue.

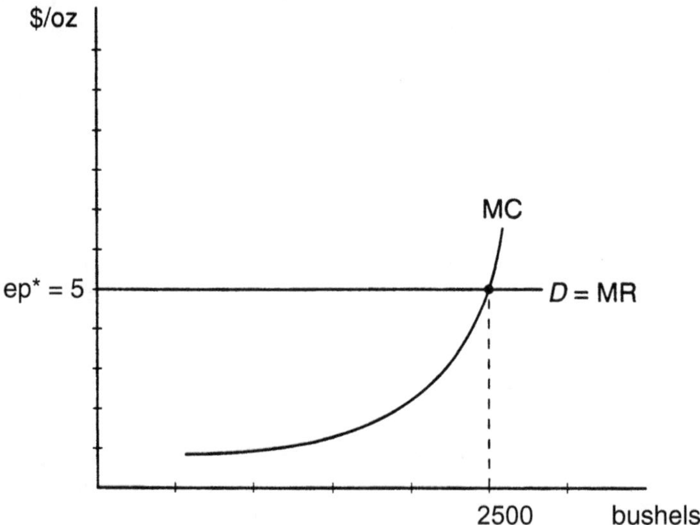

Figure 7.2
A Price-Taking Exporting Firm
The international price of corn is $5. The price-taking firm can sell any quantity at $5. The firm maximizes profit where $MR = MC$, producing 2,500 bushels.

Price-Taking Firms

A competitive industry is made up of many small firms that are price takers. Figure 7.2 pictures a price-taking firm in the international corn market. Competitive firms have no power to vary the international price of $5. MR is $5 as every bushel is sold at the same price. For competitive firms, $D = MR$ as the horizontal line at the market price. Profit is maximized where $MR = MC$ at a quantity of 2500.

Imagine marginal revenue $MR = D$ for the price searcher in Figure 7.1. The monopoly would maximize profit at $MR = MC$, setting $P = \$1500$ and selling $Q = 2,500$ as with competition in Figure 7.2. The monopoly restricts output and charges more compared to a competitive firm.

EXAMPLE **7.2**   *Trigger Prices for Steel*

During the 1960s, the US steel industry faced increased competition from Japan and Europe after their rebuilding from World War II. Their wages were about half those in the US. Ingo Walter (1983) estimates their production costs were 40% of the US. The import share in consumption rose from 5% in 1960 to 18% in 1980. US steel firms pressured the government, which pressured foreign governments to pressure their steel firms to agree to "voluntary" export restraints (VERs). The trigger price mechanism of 1978 stopped imports if the price of steel fell below the estimated cost and shipping. Trigger prices proved impossible to administer. After the 1980s, competition increased from newly industrialized economies including South Korea, Taiwan, Spain, and Latin America as well as some less developed countries (LDCs). Rather than depending on protection, the steel industry has become internationally competitive specializing in high-tech alloys.

Monopoly Profit

For a monopoly, entry of other firms is ruled out. In a competitive industry, profit attracts other firms, increasing supply and lowering price. Monopoly profit is the difference between price P and average cost AC at the optimal output. In Figure 7.3, profit is maximized where $MR = MC$ at $Q = 100$. Output is sold according to demand at $90.

For the lowest average cost, AC_1, with optimal output $Q = 100$, profit is found at $AC_1 = \$70$ with total cost $TC = AC \times Q = \$70 \times 100 = \$7,000$. With $P = \$90$ total revenue is $TR = \$9,000$. Profit π is the difference between total revenue and total cost in the lined area, $\pi = TR - TC = \$9,000 - \$7,000 = \$2,000$. Profit is positive as average revenue or price is greater than AC.

At the highest average cost AC_3, total cost $TC = \$110 \times 100 = \$11,000$ is greater than $TR = \$9,000$. With AC_3 there is a loss as $\pi = \$9,000 - \$11,000 = -\$2,000$ in the dotted area. A monopoly can operate for a time with loss if profit is expected in the future.

A monopolist would *shut down* if fixed costs were less than losses. When a firm shuts down it lays off labor and ceases operation but fixed costs including utilities and rent are paid. A monopolist may sell out liquidating its capital if it does not expect improved conditions.

With costs AC_2 profit is zero where $P = AC$. A price searcher is not guaranteed positive profit. Demand for the product and cost of production determine the level of profit.

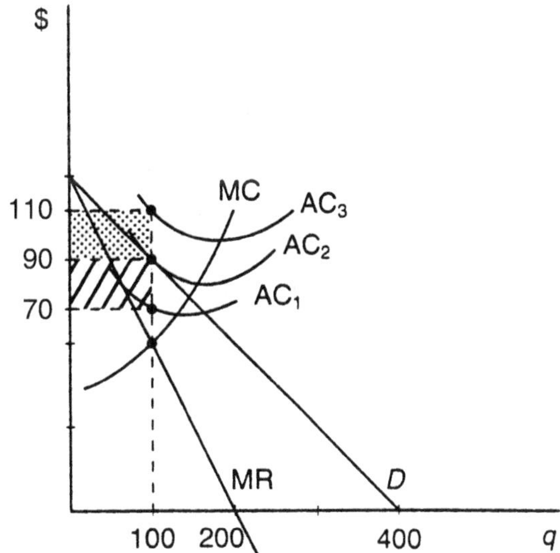

Figure 7.3
Monopoly Profit
Profit is maximized where $MR = MC$ at $q = 100$. Price is set at $15. Profit depends on average cost AC. At AC_1 $\pi = \$300$, at AC_3 $\pi = -\$300$, and at AC_2 $\pi = 0$.

EXAMPLE **7.3**   *US Trade Agreements*

The WTO continues to provide hearings for trade disputes. Organisation for Economic Co-operation and Development (OECD) discussions on investment and legal coordination continue. North American trade agreements are evolving. Negotiations for the Free Trade Area of the Americas (FTAA) continue. Asia-Pacific Economic Cooperation (APEC) is involved in talks over product standards. The Transatlantic Economic Partnership (TEP) coordinates legal issues between the US and the EU. The US Generalized System of Preferences (GSP) defines which tariff schedules apply to which countries. Textile market sharing quotas attempt to govern textile imports. The International Trade Commission (ITC) is the main administrator of all US trade agreements.

Tariffs on International Monopolies

A tariff may be optimal importing from an international monopolist. Domestic consumers pay a higher price but the domestic government taxes away some of the profit of the foreign monopoly converting it to tariff revenue.

In Figure 7.4, domestic demand is D. Costs for the foreign monopolist to sell in the home market are MC^* and AC^*. The monopolist would produce where $MR = MC^*$ at $Q = 100$ and $P = \$15$. Given $AC = \$12$, the profit for the foreign monopolist is $300.

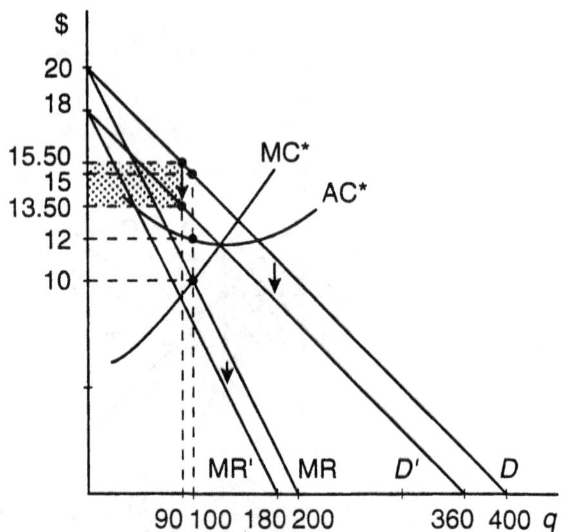

Figure 7.4
Tariff on a Foreign Monopoly
A tariff lowers demand with output falling from 100 to 90 and price from $15 to $13.50. Tariff revenue is $TR = \$2 \times 90 = \$180$. The lost consumer surplus of $47.50 is less than TR.

A \$2 tariff transfers some of that profit to the home government. The effective demand curve falls by \$2 to D' with MR falling to MR'. Output falls to 90 where MR' equals MC^*. Price in the domestic market rises to \$15.50 but the foreign monopolist receives only \$13.50.

The government collects tariff revenue in the shaded area \$2 × 90 = \$180. The size of the tariff revenue and the lost consumer surplus depend on demand and costs. In Figure 7.4, the transfer to the government is larger than the lost consumer surplus making the tariff optimal.

International Price Discrimination

An international price searcher that can distinguish among groups of buyers will increase profit by pricing according to demand of each group. This price discrimination implies consumers in countries with higher or more inelastic demand pay higher prices.

Figure 7.5 shows an international monopolist facing domestic and foreign demand D and D^* that have marginal revenues MR and MR^*. For simplicity, MC

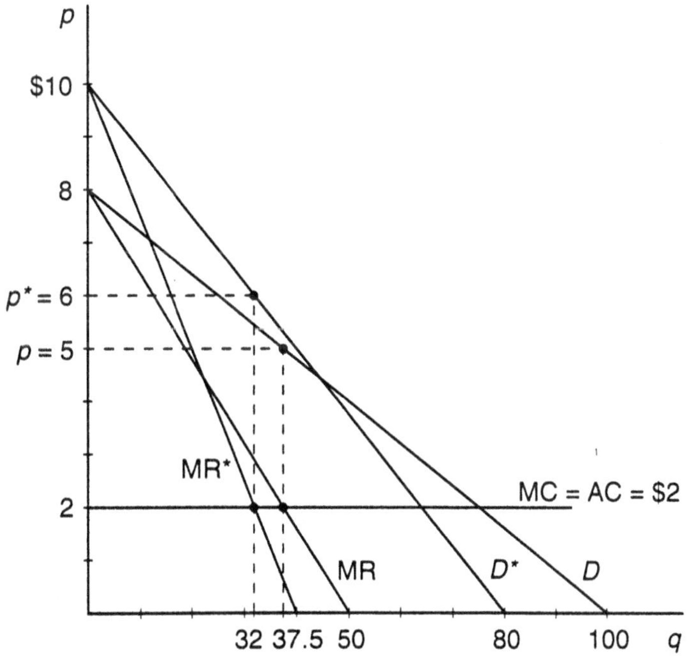

Figure 7.5
Price Discrimination by a Monopoly Exporter
This monopoly can discriminate between home demand D and foreign demand D^*. MC is constant at \$2. The monopolist equates MC with MR and MR^* selling 32 units abroad at \$6 and 37.5 units sold at home for \$5.

is held constant with each additional unit of output costing the same, making AC constant. Price discrimination means producing where $MC = MR$ for each group.

Profit maximization is 37.5 units of output in the home market and 32 in the foreign market. Foreign buyers with higher and more inelastic demand pay $6 while domestic buyers pay $5. Profit is higher than if the two demands are summed. Selling in the home market, the monopoly makes a profit of $3 per unit for a total of $3 × 37.5 = $112.50. Foreign profit is $4 × 32 = $128. Resale of products from the home country to the foreign country is ruled out.

International dumping refers to the predatory pricing of a foreign exporter temporarily selling below average cost to eliminate the competition of domestic firms. The foreign firm plans to enjoy monopoly profit later. The ITC hears dumping complaints and can award damages and import quotas. Other countries have similar antidumping policies.

Examples of dumping have been Japanese computer chips, European steel, Vietnamese catfish, and China in various goods. Detailed cost information is required to determine whether dumping takes place leading to arbitrary ITC decisions. International price competition is too sophisticated for ITC officials to police. Dumping allegations offers industry a nontariff trade barrier promoting lobbying.

EXAMPLE **7.4**   *ITC Protectionism*

The ITC hears cases and awards protection if foreign industries compete unfairly. Antidumping duties are regularly awarded. Countervailing duties are awarded for apparent foreign subsidies. Wendy Hansen and Thomas Prusa (1997) examine 744 dumping cases filed between 1980 and 1988. The steel industry has the highest probability of a favorable ruling. Industries with more Congressional representatives on the House Ways and Means Committee are more likely to receive protection. Political Action Committee donations increase the probability of a favorable ruling. Countries with growing market shares are more likely to be found guilty. Nonmarket economies are more likely to be found guilty. Western Europe was 17% less likely given to the threat of retaliation. Politics seem to dominate ITC decisions.

Dominant Firm Imports

Some industries have a dominant firm that sets the price with a competitive fringe of smaller firms that follow its lead. Suppose there is a dominant foreign exporter and a domestic fringe. The domestic firms follow the price set by the dominant foreign firm with a higher price leading to more domestic output.

Domestic demand D, in Figure 7.6, is the sum of foreign dominant firm DF^* and the residual domestic fringe supply FS. If the dominant firm sets

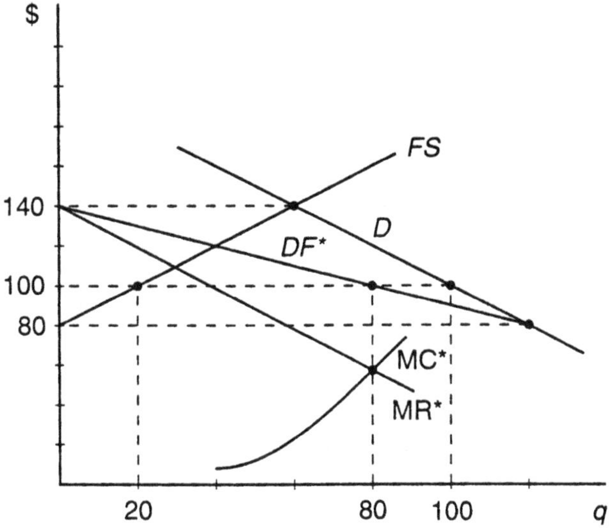

Figure 7.6
A Dominant Fringe Import Market
Domestic demand D is composed of the foreign dominant firm demand DF^* and domestic fringe supply FS. The dominant foreign firm produces where $MC^* = MR^*$ at P = \$100. Domestic fringe firms supply 20. A tariff taxes the foreign firm, stimulates the domestic fringe, and generates tariff revenue but costs domestic consumers.

the price below \$80 it captures the demand, leaving the domestic competitive fringe to supply nothing. Domestic fringe suppliers cannot produce for less than \$80.

The domestic fringe would completely take over the market at \$140. For any price between \$80 and \$140 the domestic fringe shares the market. Marginal revenue MR^* for the dominant firm is derived from DF^*. The dominant foreign firm maximizes profit where $MR^* = MC^*$ at $Q = 80$ and $P = \$100$ leaving a residual of 20 units for the domestic fringe on FS.

A tariff reduces output of the dominant firm and increases market share for the domestic fringe. Domestic consumers pay a higher price. The tariff produces revenue for the government. The tariff takes away some of the foreign profit. There can be net gains from the tariff depending on the conditions of demand and cost.

EXAMPLE **7.5**   *Import Quality Competition*

US imports have become more differentiated with lower quality products coming from low-wage countries as shown by Peter Schott (2004). About 3/4 of all products come from low-wage countries with more expensive varieties from high-wage countries. Shirts imported in 1994 from Japan were 30 times more expensive than those from the Philippines.

Section A Problems

A1. Explain whether a legal monopoly is more likely within a country or in international trade. What about natural monopolies?

A2. Why might a monopoly exporter operate at a loss pricing below their cost of production?

A3. Illustrate price discrimination with home consumers paying more. How might home consumers react? Would there be claims of dumping?

A4. Assume a foreign monopolist has constant marginal cost. Show the effects of a tariff including tariff revenue, lost profit, and consumer surplus.

B. INTRA-INDUSTRY TRADE

When the same good is exported and imported, it is called intra-industry trade. Exporting some products and importing others is inter-industry trade. This section examines the reasons for exporting and importing the same products.

Product Differentiation

Basic goods such as grains and metals are graded into standards. At the other extreme, cars and computers have a wide variety of characteristics. Categorizing goods is a challenge. Grains and fruits are not similar but are both food. Rice is different from barley although both are grains. Long-grain rice is different from short-grain rice. Inside any category there is a degree of product differentiation.

Sellers are familiar with their product as are buyers to some extent. Product categories are designed by governments interested in taxes and tariffs. Categories such as yarn, glass, medical products, alcoholic beverages, and telecommunications apparatus are broad. There is more product differentiation in broad categories.

Intra-Industry Trade

Intra-industry trade occurs when the same category of product is imported and exported. Cost differences in producing different qualities lead to intra-industry trade. A consumer buying a shirt evaluates the clothing service it provides. Higher quality implies more service but at a higher marginal cost.

Figure 7.7 illustrates marginal costs of two qualities along with demand D for services. Profit is maximized for each quality by producing where $MR = MC$. The firm decides whether to sell 10 units of the high-quality shirt for \$20 or 20 units of the low-quality shirt for \$15.

If production of the high-quality shirt is capital intensive, a capital-abundant country would specialize in that export. A labor-abundant country would specialize

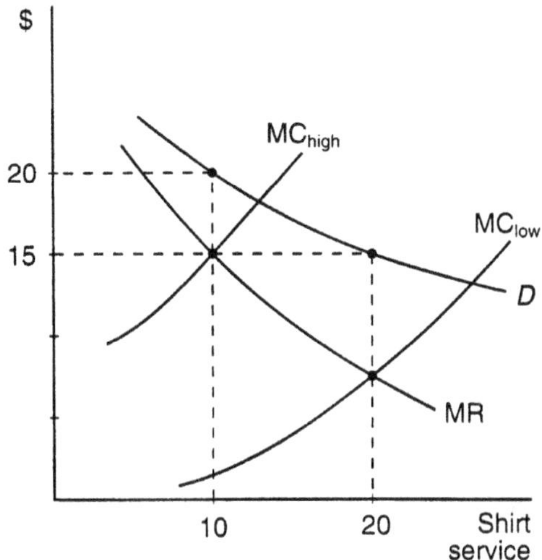

Figure 7.7
Quality Differentiation and Price
A high-quality shirt has higher cost of production than a low-quality version. This firm would produce one quality or the other at the corresponding P and Q.

in labor-intensive production of low-quality shirts. Consumers in each country want both types of shirts leading to intra-industry trade.

Intra-industry trade in the same product category can be the result of quality differences.

EXAMPLE **7.6**   *Intra-Industry Trade Index*

Trade within an industry depends on the level of aggregation. The index of intra-industry trade $I = (X - M)/(X + M)$ applies to import and export of the same category. A product that is only exported has $I = 1$ opposite to one that is only imported at $I = -1$. Equal export revenue and import spending for a good implies $I = 0$. For harvest machines at $I = 0.21$, these have a higher index than harvest machine parts at $I = 0.47$ due to the narrower category in parts. Herbert Grubel and Peter Lloyd (1975) show the level of intra-industry trade in Australia increases with the level of aggregation.

Another cause of intra-industry trade is international and domestic transport costs. International sea shipping from Europe to Florida is cheaper for some products than shipping by land from Pennsylvania to Florida. In the US, border regions are closer to other countries than to domestic regions on other borders. Texas is closer to Latin America than to New York. The US exports chemicals from California and imports them from the EU. Location and transport costs explain a good deal of observed import and export of the same good.

Products with high intra-industry trade include envelopes, transformers, plumbing fixtures, machine tool accessories, synthetic rubber, fans, and sheet metal. Goods that are more narrowly defined have less price dispersion and less intra-industry trade, for example, handbags, soap, radios, TV sets, leather gloves, costume jewelry, refrigerators, and vacuum cleaners. High-tech manufactures are more differentiated than primary products and agricultural goods. For this reason, developed countries (DCs) have more intra-industry trade than LDCs.

EXAMPLE **7.7**   *Price Dispersion*

Price dispersion within categories increases with the level of intra-industry trade. Elizabeth Wickham and Henry Thompson (1989) show larger, capital-abundant countries have more intra-industry trade. Smaller, labor-abundant countries produce more homogeneous raw products and basic manufactures.

Monopolistic Competition and Trade

Firms selling differentiated products have price-searching power although profit attracts competing firms. Firms face downward sloping demand because consumers recognize brand names. Entry reduces demand for firms in the industry and can lead to higher input prices. Free entry leads to zero profit. An industry with price-searching firms but zero profit is called monopolistic competition.

Figure 7.8 shows a firm with monopolistic competition and zero profit. The firm maximizes profit where $MC = MR$ producing 100 units of output with price $P = \$10 = AC$ equal to average cost.

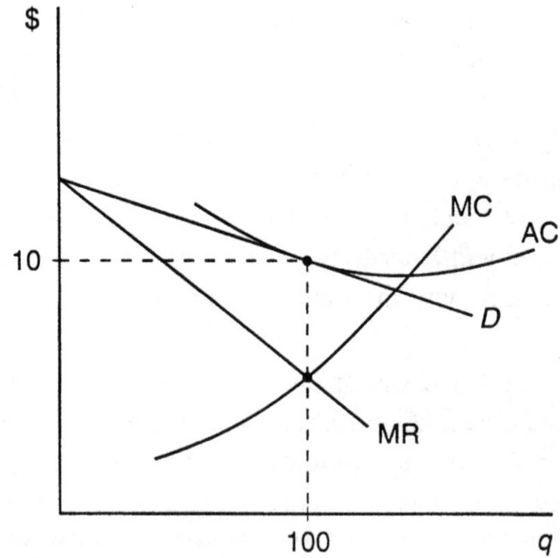

Figure 7.8
A Firm in Monopolistic Competition
The firm facing demand and *MR* maximizes profit where $MR = MC$ producing output $q = 100$ at $P = \$10$. Competition pushes cost to zero economic profit where $P = AC$.

If two firms with monopolistic competition are in different countries, there is intra-industry trade. Entry by foreign firms lowers the demand for domestic firms leading to zero profit. While a tariff would raise demand for the domestic firm, the foreign government could retaliate.

When a country opens to trade, domestic firms must compete with foreign firms. Suppose a protected domestic industry is making a positive profit but the country eliminates tariffs in a move toward free trade. Foreign firms enter the industry and drive domestic firms toward zero profit. The entering foreign firms make the domestic industry more competitive. In this way, free trade limits the market power of domestic firms encouraging more efficient production.

EXAMPLE **7.8**   *Intra-Industry Trade in Beer*

The high level of intra-industry beer trade in Jeffrey Karrenbrock (1990) finds France has the most intra-industry trade exporting a small share X/Q of its beer output. France and the US consume the highest ratio of imports M/C. Ireland and the Netherlands are highly involved in exports. Consumers in Denmark and Czechoslovakia enjoy no imports due to protection.

Section B Problems

B1. The US imports cars across a wide range of quality. How would a VER on Japanese imports affect the quality of Japanese imported cars? Predict what would happen to domestic quality.

B2. With three products (food, clothing, household goods) what would be the advantage of aggregating clothing and household goods into manufactured goods? Explain what could happen to the level of intra-industry trade.

B3. With monopolistic competition in an export industry that has negative profit, describe what will happen to the number of firms and profit of the typical firm.

EXAMPLE **7.9**   *Beer and Wine Trade*

Beer is locally produced and consumed all over the world. Wine is produced where grapes can be grown. Joshua Aizenman and Eileen Brooks (2005, *NBER Working Paper*) examine consumption across 38 countries and find wine consumption gaining on beer. Local tastes matter, however, with Latin Americans strongly preferring beer.

C. OLIGOPOLY TRADE

An industry with a few firms is an oligopoly. An international oligopoly has firms in different countries. An oligopoly can exhibit the full range of competition from near-perfect competition with zero economic profit to near monopoly pricing if the few firms can collude to make monopoly profit.

Oligopoly Collusion

The few firms in an oligopoly form a cartel to collude and share monopoly profit reducing output and raising price. Restricted entry keeps the number of firms low. One problem faced by the cartel is how to share the profit.

Collusion to set prices inside the US is illegal by the antitrust laws designed to limit monopoly power. Cartel collusion across international borders is legal. International cartels in primary products such as oil, rubber, coffee, tea, and bananas are successful at times limiting output among members to make monopoly profit.

EXAMPLE **7.10**   *Banana and Aircraft Export Taxes*

Export taxes are unconstitutional in the US after the colonists fought to quit sending export tax revenue to the King of England. Most other countries tax exports. Jessica Bailey and James Sood (1987) propose a banana export tax to maximize revenue in Latin America. The tax would effectively raise price to the monopoly level. Fewer bananas would be sold but export revenue would increase. The US has market power in aircraft and could tax exports if it were constitutional.

Oligopoly Demand

Figure 7.9 illustrates the dilemma facing a firm in an oligopoly. Demand facing the firm is elastic for prices above \$100. If the firm lowers the price, other

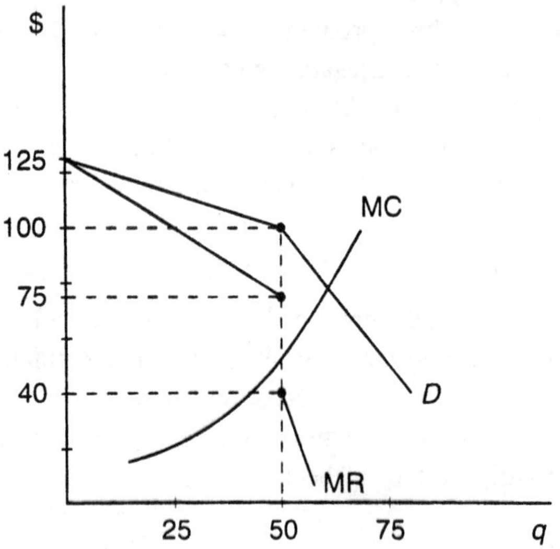

Figure 7.9
Kinked Oligopoly Demand
If the firm raises the price, competing firms do not follow suit making demand elastic. If the oligopolist lowers the price, the competition matches the reduction making demand inelastic. Revenue falls whether the firm lowers or raises the price.

firms do the same to keep from losing customers. Revenue falls with the price reduction. Demand is inelastic for prices below \$100.

The demand curve facing this firm is kinked. If the firm raises the price above \$100, consumers substitute for less-expensive output of the other firms in the cartel. Demand is elastic for price increases and revenue falls. If the firm lowers the price below \$100, the other firms lower their prices to keep from losing customers. Demand is inelastic for price decreases and revenue falls.

The kink in demand implies the break in marginal revenue. Each firm in an oligopoly faces the same dilemma as firms learn to keep price and output at the kink in demand. This oligopoly behavior can be the result of an explicit cartel agreement in an international market.

EXAMPLE 7.11   *Quotas and Domestic Downgrading*

Quotas can cause import-quality upgrading as foreign exporters increase revenue per unit sold. Examples include US imports of compact pickup trucks and cheese. Randy Beard and Henry Thompson (2003) show domestic-quality downgrading is necessary with a quota as the domestic firm relaxes reducing quality to the monopoly level. While foreign-quality upgrading is likely, domestic quality is bound to downgrade with a quota.

An International Duopoly

A duopoly is an oligopoly of two firms. A duopoly with a home firm and foreign firm is an international duopoly. Suppose each firm has the option of high or low output. The profit of each firm depends on its choice and the choice of the other firm. Game theory can predict how the two firms behave.

Table 7.1 presents an international duopoly game. Home profit is first in the parentheses. If the home firm produces high output and the foreign firm low output, home profit is \$2 million while the foreign firm loses \$1 million. If both firms produce high output, they break even with competitive zero profit. If the two firms collude and restrict output producing low levels, they split monopoly profit of \$2 million.

Collusion with low outputs is better than competing with high outputs although the temptation to cheat on the cartel presents a problem. If the foreign firm

Table 7.1   International Duopoly Profit
(\$mil Home, \$mil Foreign)

		Foreign Output	
		Low	High
	Low	(1, 1)	(−1, 2)
Home Output			
	High	(2, −1)	(0, 0)

cheats producing high output, it makes a profit of \$2 million while the home firm suffers a loss of −\$1 million.

Regardless of the choice of the foreign firm, the home firm benefits by producing high output. The game is symmetric as the same holds for the foreign firm. Given a correct guess about opponent behavior, each firm will produce high output and make zero profit. Competition is a stable equilibrium. The home firm could restrict its own output one year suffer and the loss. The foreign firm would notice the credibility of the cartel partner and restrict output as well. If they both continue to restrict output, the cartel is established.

EXAMPLE **7.12**   *International Aircraft Oligopoly*

The US remains the world leader in the aircraft industry with the EU and UK being major producers. Firms compete to design and sell new and more efficient aircrafts. The firms may price as a cartel in the military industrial complex described by President Eisenhower in the 1950s.

International Cartels

While the payoff for collusion can be large, cartels typically fall apart when demand and prices fall. The oil cartel OPEC has enjoyed more success and lasted longer than predicted when it formed during the 1970s. The problem facing OPEC is members want more than their allotted cartel quota.

The OPEC countries produce about a third of the world's output. Oil prices fell steadily during the 1990s. In 1999, the OPEC countries reached a quota agreement and prices rebounded. Prices since 2000 have been much more erratic due to refining problems, wars, and growing demand in China and India.

Oil prices will rise slowly due to increasing scarcity although extraction technology continues to improve. The price collapse in 2015 was due to fracking that greatly increases the amount of oil and gas that can be extracted. Green energy policy will raise the price of energy helping to maintain the OPEC cartel.

International cartels easily break down into competition. Members often have too much to gain by breaking the agreement and selling at the high price. Consumers benefit from the competitive prices of a cartel collapse.

The strategies of members determine the fate of international oligopolies.

The threat of entry makes oligopolies more competitive. Members may behave more competitively to discourage entry. Existing firms can discourage potential entrants by making a credible threat to lower price. Nonprice competition such as advertising can discourage entry. A contestable market with the threat of entry can be close to competitive.

EXAMPLE **7.13**   *Pricing to Market*

When a currency depreciates, prices of exports decrease in the foreign country. An exporter has the option of changing price to keep the foreign currency price of its export constant. Michael Knetter (1989) finds German exporters price to the US market. The dollar depreciation of the late 1980s did not affect the US trade deficit as prices of imports were kept constant. US exporters do not price to foreign markets.

Table 7.2   Boeing Subsidy ($bil Boeing, $bil Airbus)

		Airbus	
		Produce	**No**
Boeing	**Produce**	(−5, 5)	(100, 0)
	No	(0, 100)	(0, 0)

International Duopoly Subsidies

Suppose the US firm Boeing and the EU firm Airbus face the decision of whether to produce and export a new type of passenger jet. Paul Krugman (1987) examines such an international duopoly and suggests a US government subsidy would lead to a net gain.

Table 7.2 presents profits with and without production of the new passenger jet. The game is not symmetric. If Airbus produces, Boeing will not produce to avoid the loss of −$5 billion due to its disadvantage. Airbus does not suffer loss regardless and will produce regardless of Boeing. If they both produce, the industry is more competitive.

The US government subsidy to Boeing encourages production and keeps Airbus from gaining market share. One problem is that Boeing becomes reliant on subsidies. A more fundamental approach would be for Boeing to eliminate the asymmetric advantage of Airbus. Subsidizing the disadvantaged eliminates the incentive for Boeing to improve.

EXAMPLE **7.14**   *Export Market Competition*

Transport and electrical equipment exporters in Japan price to the US market as found by Richard Marston (1998). US exporters are less inclined to price to market. The evidence suggests exporters to the US sell in markets that are more competitive than the foreign market where US exporters sell their products.

Section C Problems

C1. Suppose cost rises for the firm in Figure 7.9. So *MC* intersects *MR* at \$100 where $q = 25$. Find the price. Explain how other firms in the industry would react. Find and explain the change in revenue.

C2. When OPEC income increased dramatically during the 1970s, the OPEC countries did not spend it all. Explain what had to happen.

C3. If the oil import elasticity is -0.6 and price increases from \$20 to \$22, find the percentage change in the level of imports. What are the two sources of this decrease? If OPEC raises price to \$40 find the reduction in imports. Explain what happens to OPEC revenue with these price increases.

D. OTHER THEORIES OF TRADE

Trade can arise due to differences in technology across countries, the new product cycle, increasing returns to scale, and income differences across countries. This section evaluates these different causes of international trade.

Trade Based on Differences in Technology

Technology refers to methods of combining inputs to produce outputs. Different countries might have access to different technologies that could be in patented machinery or especially skilled labor.

Figure 7.10 shows unit isoquants with two different technologies along isoquants t_1 or t_2. With technology t_1 point A at $(K, L) = (1.5, 4.5)$ and point B at $(4.5, 2)$ produce one unit of output. Technology t_2 mixes the inputs differently at $A' = (2, 5)$ or at $B' = (5, 1)$. Points B and B' illustrate the different cost-minimizing inputs for the same relative input price.

If two countries have identical factor endowments and production functions with the same number of consumers, there would be no reason to trade. If the home country has better technology for producing services, both would benefit from trade.

The constant cost model based on fixed inputs in production essentially assumes differences in technology. The factor proportions model looks at the abundance of capital and labor as the key to explaining trade. Differences in technology as a cause of trade is a challenge to isolate.

Capital is mobile across countries with multinational firms providing the same technology around the world. College students worldwide become familiar with the latest technology. The general availability of the latest technology suggests differences in technology do not account for much trade. The available capital, labor, skilled labor, and natural resources account for trade.

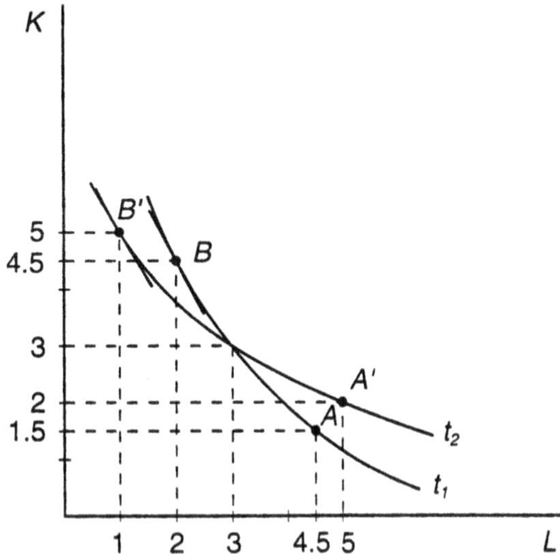

Figure 7.10
Production with Different Technologies
Isoquants t_1 and t_2 represent different technologies. Less of both inputs is possible comparing A and A'. Cost-minimizing inputs can vary as illustrated by B and B'. Different technologies across countries can lead to trade.

EXAMPLE **7.15**   *Tariffs Worldwide*

Average tariffs on all imports are low in the DCs but are much higher in the LDCs. Theory suggests the large countries could gain from tariffs while the small countries have nothing to gain except tariff revenue by the government. Some examples of average tariffs are:

EU	UK	Japan	US	Mexico	Brazil	Gabon	Bermuda
1.7%	1.9%	2.3%	1.9%	3.3%	13.6%	18.6%	22.3%

Product Cycle Trade

The product cycle predicts exports of new products from DCs to the rest of the world. Over time, production of the products moves to DCs with lower wages. Products cycle in this manner from DCs to the rest of the world.

The DCs account for over 90% of worldwide spending on research and development R&D.

US	EU	Russia	Japan	Other DCs
33%	20%	18%	15%	5%

Exports from DCs are intensive in R&D. Exports of products with high levels of R&D relate to the product cycle.

Figure 7.11 pictures the product cycle with new products unveiled at times 1 and 2. The R&D country exports the new products enjoying a monopoly power

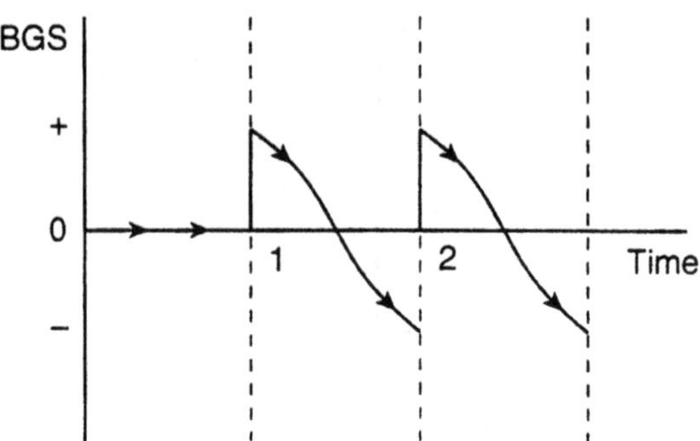

Figure 7.11
Trade in the Product Cycle
The R&D country introduces new products at times 1 and 2 with a trade surplus exporting a new good. Over time, other countries produce it at lower cost.

for a time. Production slowly moves to NICs and LDCs, where production costs are lower. There is no international legal system to enforce patents and copyrights. Soon the DC becomes a net importer of the good and moves into a trade deficit until the next innovation.

Products cycle from new to old as production moves away from the innovative countries. R&D countries are net exporters of new products.

Product cycles describe trade in some products. Although the weight of the product cycle in total trade is not high, transitory profit from new goods can be substantial. International patent enforcement would lengthen the lengths of the cycles.

EXAMPLE **7.16**   *Research and Development High-Tech Exports*

The US has almost half of the R&D scientists in the world. The US has a comparative advantage in developing new products and consistent export surpluses in high-tech products. The EU and Japan have increased their levels of R&D. The rest of the world has less than 10% of all R&D scientists.

EXAMPLE **7.17**   *International Intellectual Property Rights*

International intellectual property rights (IPRs) of patent protection would raise the level of trade. Keith Maskus and Mohan Penubarti (1995) find evidence across LDCs that increased patent protection increases the level of trade. Foreign firms with patents avoid trading with countries where their product could be copied and produced locally.

Trade due to Increasing Returns to Scale

Returns to scale refer to how the size of a firm matters in *AC*. Constant returns to scale (CRS) refer to proportional changes in inputs and output, with doubling the levels of all inputs doubling the output. Increasing returns to scale (IRS)

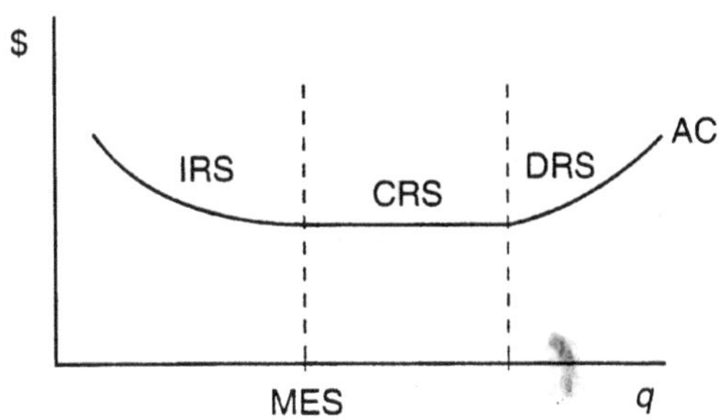

Figure 7.12
Returns to Scale
Decreasing AC reflects IRS up to the MES. AC is constant in the region of CRS. Increasing AC is consistent with DRS.

result in more than a proportional increase in output. Decreasing returns to scale (DRS) occurs if the increase in output is less than proportional.

Returns to scale can be external or internal to the firm. External influences include the available transportation, communication, and utility infrastructure. The availability of local suppliers and educated skilled workers are also external to the firm. Internal returns to scale occur inside the firm as machinery and other resources are utilized more efficiently.

Figure 7.12 shows the long-run AC curve decreasing up to the minimum efficient scale (MES) of the firm. AC is declining in the region of IRS with the firm not as efficient utilizing inputs but approaching MES. Over a range of output after reaching MES, the firm has CRS with AC constant. The AC curve rises at higher outputs reflecting DRS. As the firm expands, DRS might occur due to problems of organization or communication inside the firm.

With IRS, a firm would be below its *MES* and should grow. A firm producing output less than MES could not compete with other firms at MES. Firms operating above MES would not survive at that high level of output. Firms typically observed must be operating in the region with efficient scale and minimized average cost consistent with CRS.

Two countries with IRS in different products have the incentive to specialize in one product or the other and trade to increase export levels. With specialization, world output would be higher and both countries would enjoy higher income. While this situation is feasible, IRS does not seem to be a major reason for international trade.

While increasing returns to scale may play a role in some specialization and trade, firms and industries generally operate at MES with constant returns.

EXAMPLE **7.18**   *Factor Endowments or Increasing Returns?*

Available factors of production explain trade but IRS might as well. Donald Davis and David Weinstein (1995, 1998) find that factor endowments explain more trade than IRS. Geography is important as transport costs and borders account for a good deal of trade.

Income Effects and Trade

Countries with higher income consume more services and luxury goods, while those with low income spend on necessities. Income levels contribute to determining the trade pattern based on demand.

Income elasticity is the percentage change in quantity demanded for a 1% change in income,

$$E_I = \%\Delta Q / \%\Delta Y$$

Normal goods have a positive income elasticity with quantity demand increasing in income. If $0 < E_I < 1$, the good is a necessity like food, transportation, housing, and clothing. If $E_I > 1$, the good is a luxury such as steak, foreign travel, imported cheese, and restaurant meals. If $E_I < 0$ the good is inferior with consumers avoiding it as their income increases as with public transport, used cars, and red beans as a protein source.

Figure 7.13 illustrates a pattern of trade between DCs and LDCs based on income elasticities. If production is uniform across countries, the LDCs would be importers of necessities and inferior goods with the DCs importing luxury goods.

High-income countries tend to import luxury goods while low-income countries tend to import necessities and inferior goods.

Linda Hunter and James Markusen (1988) study income in 34 countries and trade in 10 commodities reporting the income elasticities. Food, furniture, fuel, and education are necessities. A 10% increase in income would raise the quantity of food consumed by 5%, furniture by 8%, fuel and power by 8%, and education by 9%. All other goods are luxuries. A 10% increase in income brings about a 19% increase in medical services, for instance. Recreation is a luxury

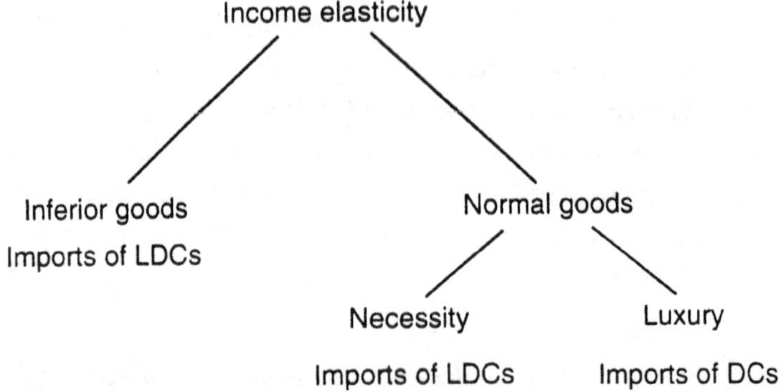

Figure 7.13
Income Elasticity and Trade
LDCs tend to import inferior goods and necessities. DCs tend to import luxury goods.

good. The influence of income on consumption patterns is significant but there is little influence of income on trade.

The Bottom Line on Other Trade Theories

The supplemental theories in this section contribute to an overall understanding of trade and apply to some observed trade. Factor proportions (FP) theory remains the fundamental explanation for international trade. The relative abundance of productive capital, labor as well as skilled labor, and natural resources provides the fundamental explanation for specialization and trade. The right inputs are required for production.

EXAMPLE **7.19**   *Trade in Coca*

The tropical Chapare region in Bolivia specializes in coca leaf for cocaine and traditional medicine. Hugo Toledo (2005) compares the cost of illegal versus legal production. Small farmers earn $3,000 per acre selling coca leaves versus $1,000 with government programs to grow pineapples, bananas, and peppers. Countries wanting to control cocaine imports could subsidize the difference.

Section D Problems

D1. Draw the production possibility frontiers (PPFs) of a home country with better technology for producing food and a foreign country with better technology for producing clothing. Show the pattern of specialization and trade.

D2. Explain whether it would be wise for a DC to spend resources protecting its steel industry or developing new steel products.

D3. What do income elasticities predict regarding international trade in inferior goods?

EXAMPLE **7.20**   *Regional Competition in Mexico*

Large countries are made up of economic regions that adjust differently to trade. Mexico opened to trade in 1985 after decades of misguided import substitution policy and nationalized industries as reviewed in Gordon Hanson (1998). With trade, industry became competitive and moved north toward the US border due to transport costs. Northern Mexico is an economic region integrated with the southwestern US that has little in common with the rest of Mexico or the US.

CONCLUSION

Competition is the dominant industrial organization in trade especially including monopolistic competition. Oligopoly characterizes international markets for oil, minerals, computer software, advanced weapons, and similar trade based on limited ownership of inputs. FP theory based on competitive pricing explains most international trade although various other theories provide insight into some types of trade. Chapter 8 turns to the causes and effects of international movements of labor and capital, followed by Chapter 9 on how countries are integrating their economies.

Terms

Cartel quota	Luxury good
Collusion	Minimum efficient scale (*MES*)
Contestable market	Monopolistic competition
Credible threat	Necessity
Dominant and fringe firms	Oligopoly
Income elasticity	Price discrimination and dumping
Inferior good	Price taker versus price searcher
International duopoly	Product cycle
International monopoly	Product differentiation
Intra-industry trade	Returns to scale
Kinked oligopoly demand curve	Technology and trade
Legal versus natural monopoly	Trigger prices

MAIN POINTS

- A price-searching monopoly restricts output and raises the price relative to a competitive firm. A tariff on imports from a foreign monopolist turns some of its profit into tariff revenue and may generate net gains for the importing country.
- Product differentiation can lead to intra-industry trade in a monopolistically competitive industry. The level of product differentiation and intra-industry trade decrease as products are disaggregated.
- Firms in an international oligopoly have the incentive to collude in a cartel to gain monopoly profit. Depending on payoffs and strategies, oligopolies can share monopoly profit or be competitive with zero economic profit.
- Other theories apply to some observed international trade, including differences in technology, product cycles, increasing returns to scale, and income elasticities of demand.

REVIEW PROBLEMS

1. Complete Figure 7.1 including an AC curve for a domestic firm with profit of $300,000. Illustrate zero profit for a foreign firm. Which firm has higher costs?

2. Suppose higher energy costs raise the home firm cost in Figure 7.1 dropping the output to 1,000. Find the price. Is the demand elastic? If all output is exported, what happens to export revenue?

3. Suppose a monopolist has two plants, one in the US and one in Mexico. The Mexico plant has lower unit costs. Which plant will produce more? How does the monopolist determine the price of its export to the EU?

4. Find monopoly profit in the example of price discrimination in Figure 7.5 separating domestic and foreign profit.

5. The following costs were estimated for steel production in the US and Japan by a famous analyst of the steel industry, Peter Marcus. Numbers are costs per ton for labor, capital machinery, and material inputs:

	Labor	Capital	Inputs
US	$209	$134	$330
Japan	$97	$171	$291

Which country spent more on labor input? What are two possible reasons? If it costs $100 per ton to ship steel to the US, find the cost of Japanese steel in the US, assuming Japanese profit is zero. If Japanese producers make 2% profit, find the price. Where will US producers want to set the trigger price?

6. With the cost data in Problem 5, suppose the ratio of wages to capital rent (w/r) is 1 in Japan and 1.4 in the US. Explain labor-intensive production.

7. Explain which categories of goods are likely to have more intra-industry trade:
    yarn or medical products
    computers or laptop computers.

8. An international industry has a dominant domestic firm and a competitive foreign fringe. At a price below $3, the foreign fringe cannot compete. At prices above $10, the fringe takes over the market. Diagram this market with an international price of $7. Show the effects of an increase in domestic costs.

9. Find the index I of intra-industry trade in Example 7.3 for the following product categories. Figures are millions of dollars for the US in 1985. Explain the likely cause of the different levels of intra-industry trade.

	Exports	Imports
Footwear	$128	$354
Cotton	$1671	$258
Leather	$287	$425
Leather goods	$121	$374
Toys and games	$271	$2,968
Automotive electric equipment	$443	$568

10. This hypothetical duopoly between Saudi Arabia and Russia in the international oil market is based on economic profit in millions of dollars. The first figure in parentheses is Saudi Arabia. Find the equilibrium. Is it stable? Who has the greater incentive to cheat on a cartel agreement? How can the other discourage cartel cheating?

(Saudi Arabia, Russia)

		Russia	
		Low	High
Saudi Arabian	Low	(30, 10)	(−20, 40)
	High	(40, −30)	(0, 0)

11. Classify the following as internal or external returns to scale:
    a. Workers in the firm become more experienced
    b. A better port is built closer to the factory
    c. New imported machines lower unit costs
    d. Local schools improve
    e. Internet service improves

12. Show what happens over time to the PPF as a country specializes in manufactures when there are external IRS. Explain the change in level of trade.

READINGS

Roger Blair and David Kaserman (1985) *Antitrust Economics*, Chicago: Irwin. Tools of industrial organization and regulation.

Yves Bourdet (1988) *International Integration, Market Structure and Prices*, London: Routledge. Range of issues on international industrial integration and market structures.

Paul Krugman, ed. (1986) *Strategic Trade Policy and the New International Economics*, Cambridge: MIT Press. Some "new" trade theory.

Stefan Linder (1961) *An Essay on Trade and Transformation*, New York: Wiley. Linder's original.

Gerald Meier (1988) *The International Environment of Business*, Oxford: Oxford University Press. International political and business institutions.

Ryuzo Sato and Paul Wachtel, eds. (1987) *Trade Friction and Prospects for Japan and the United States*, Cambridge: Cambridge University Press. Collection of articles.

P. K. Michael Tharakan and Jacob Kol, eds. (1987) *Intra-industry Trade: Theory, Evidence, and Extensions*, New York: Macmillan. Articles on intra-industry trade.

MATHEMATICAL APPENDIX

Price-searching firms with monopoly power based on ownership of natural resources or patents carry weight in trade. A foreign firm with market power faces demand $D_j(p_j)$ in the home country selling output q_j at price p_j to maximize profit $\pi_j{}^* = R_j{}^* - c_j{}^*$ where revenue is $R_j{}^* = p_j q_j = e p_j{}^* q_j$ and total cost is $c_j{}^* = c_j{}^*(q_j{}^*)$. To maximize $\pi_j{}^*$ the foreign exporter sets marginal revenue $MR_j{}^* = dR_j{}^*/dq_j = p_j + (dq_j/dp_j)p_j$ equal to marginal cost $MC_j{}^* = dc_j{}^*/dq_j$. The level of $\pi_j{}^*$ depends on average cost $AC_j{}^* = c_j{}^*/q_j$ as $\pi_j{}^* = (p_j - AC_j{}^*)q_j$.

A country importing 'from a foreign monopoly can convert some of the $\pi_j{}^*$ to tariff revenue TR_j. The tariff effectively lowers demand leading a lower price $e p_j{}^*$ although $p_j = (1 + t)e p_j{}^*$. The reduced import lowers consumer surplus CS_j but the government gains tariff revenue TR_j. The tariff creates a net gain if $TR_j > -dCS_j$ that depends on domestic demand $D_j(p_j)$ and monopoly marginal cost $MC_j{}^*$.

Monopolistic competition is based on downward sloping demand but free entry and exit drives p_j to $AC_j{}^*$ leaving no potential for net gain from a tariff.

International price discrimination refers to an exporting monopoly that can separate demand $D_j{}^k(p_j{}^k)$ in two countries to maximize profit $\pi_j{}^*$. The price-discriminating exporter sets optimal prices $p_j{}^1 \neq e p_j{}^2$. The country with higher or more inelastic demand pays a higher price.

Another form of imperfect competition is a dominant firm in an industry that can set price p_D sharing the market with a competitive fringe of competitive firms producing at cost. A country importing from a foreign dominant firm can use a tariff to convert some of the foreign profit π^* into TR. Any domestic fringe firms would benefit from the higher price $(1 + t)e p_j{}^*$ due to a tariff.

Product differentiation refers to differences in quality or other characteristics for the same category of good. In most categories, most countries both export and import. The index of intra-industry trade $I_j = (X_j - M_j)/(X_j + M_j)$ ranges from 1 with all exports to -1 with all imports. The highest level of intra-industry trade at zero $I_j = 0$ where $X_j = M_j$, assuming both are not approaching zero. Increasing the number of categories of goods greatly reduces I_j. If a differentiated good requires differentiated factors of production, the principles of FP theory apply.

Monopolistic competition implies firms facing downward sloping demand are forced into competition by the potential entry and exit of competing firms. The result is price p_j equals to AC_j implying $\pi_j = 0$ eliminating the motivation for tariffs with a positive π_j^*.

International oligopolies are industries with a few exporting firms in different countries. If a firm lowers its price, demands for the other firms fall. If a firm raises its price, the others will not follow. A tariff on imports from an oligopoly may lead to the same gains as a tariff on a foreign monopoly.

Other theories of industrial organization in the last section start with different production functions laying the basis for trade based on technology differences. Product cycle theory considers goods cycling from new to old with exports of new goods by innovative countries and exports of old goods by copycat countries with lower costs. Returns to scale can play a role as increasing returns or falling AC favor exports. Income effects in demand suggest high-income countries import luxury goods, while low-income countries import inferior goods.

INTERNATIONAL ECONOMIC INTEGRATION

CHAPTER 8

International Migration and Capital Movement

Preview

Labor and capital moving across borders in pursuit of higher income alter the patterns of production and income distribution in the host country as well as the source country. Immigration is the main source of population growth for developed countries (DCs). Migrant worker remittances are critical shares of income in some countries. Foreign capital is the source of economic growth in less-developed countries (LDCs). The main topics of this chapter are:

- The causes and effects of labor migration
- Foreign capital, production, and income
- Income redistribution due to migration and foreign capital
- The effects of international migration and capital on trade

INTRODUCTION

People emigrating from their home country are typically leaving for higher income in other countries. The difference in income must be larger than the costs of relocation. Capital also moves between countries due to differences in returns. Governments aim to control migration and capital movement based on the income redistribution and adjustments in production.

Labor immigration lowers the wage for competing labor due to the increased supply but raises the return to capital and other labor groups. Doctors, for instance, benefit from the immigration of nurses. When foreign capital enters a country, the capital return falls but the wage rises. International factor movements have the opposite effects in the source countries. Migration and foreign investment policy influence the international movement of labor and capital.

The adjustments to migration and foreign capital involve product markets as well as factor markets. This chapter focuses on the causes as well as the effects of international factor movement.

A. INTERNATIONAL MIGRATION

A comparison of labor markets across countries reveals the fundamental cause and effect of migration. The capital market as well as the labor market are affected by migration.

Marginal Revenue Product and Marginal Factor Cost

A firm makes revenue selling the output produced by the factors it hires. Factor demand is the value of what the factor contributes to production. The marginal revenue product (*MRP*) of a factor equals the marginal revenue (*MR*) of output times the marginal product (*MP*) of the added input,

$$MRP = MR \times MP$$

MRP is the revenue due to an added unit of the input. Suppose price P and *MR* are constant at the competitive market price \$2. If the *MP* of an extra worker is 5 units of the output of the firm, $MRP = \$2 \times 5 = \$10$.

A firm will hire an input if the value of what it produces is greater than its cost. Marginal factor cost (*MFC*) is the cost to hire an extra unit of input. The necessary condition to hire a worker is $MRP > MFC$.

In a competitive labor market, firms can hire any number of workers at the market wage. The wage then equals *MFC*. If the *MFC* of an extra worker is \$40 per hour and the *MRP* is \$30, the firm increases profit by \$10 per hour hiring the worker.

EXAMPLE **8.1**   *A Land of Immigrants*

The US is populated by immigrants mainly during periods of large immigration. The annual immigration averaged 1% of the population from 1850 to World War I. That scale of immigration would populate a city as large as Minneapolis, as happened during 2022. During the early 1900s, about one million people immigrated every year, a number reached recently. San Antonio is projected to become the second largest US city due to immigration.

Labor Demand and Supply

Figure 8.1 shows labor demand as *MRP* with 30 million hired at $MFC = \$5$ and 10 million at $MFC = \$15$. Labor demand slopes downward based on diminishing marginal productivity. With labor supply perfectly inelastic as shown, workers would accept any wage. Labor supply slopes upward at low wages and may bend backward at high wages as workers choose to enjoy more leisure.

The labor market clears where demand equals supply where $w = \$15$. If the wage is over \$15, the labor surplus induces workers to accept a lower wage. At a wage below \$15, there is a labor shortage and firms compete for workers offering a higher wage.

Labor markets clear at the market wage where demand equals supply.

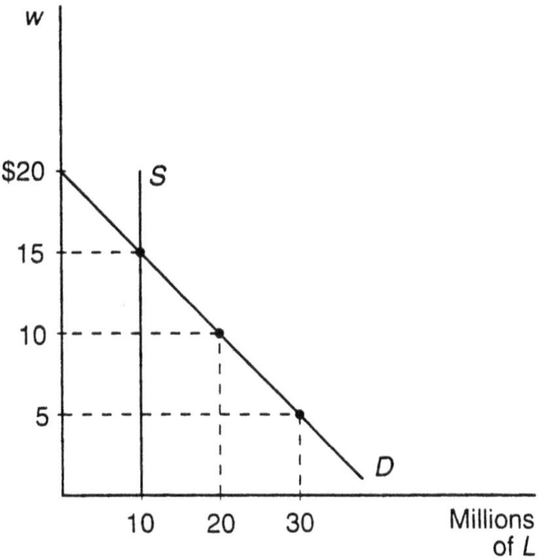

Figure 8.1
Labor Market
With inelastic labor supply S this labor market clears at the market wage $w = \$15$.

EXAMPLE **8.2**   *International Labor Growth*

Birth rates are the highest among the already labor-abundant LDCs. While free trade would raise LDC wages, migration pressure promises to continue. Labor growth rates in DCs are declining due to emigration.

International Labor Market

Figure 8.2 pictures the international labor market developed by economist Stanley Jevons in the late 1800s. The vertical axis w measures domestic wages related to domestic demand D. Foreign labor demand D^* is measured from the right on the vertical axis ew^* as the foreign wage in terms of the domestic currency.

The length of the bottom axis represents total labor in both countries, here 40 million workers. Home labor L is measured from the left and foreign labor L^* from the right.

The vertical supply line S/S^* indicates a labor force of 10 million in the home country. The demands for labor are the same in this example. The home wage is found where home demand intersects the low supply at $15. The abundant foreign labor supply of 30 leads to the low $5 foreign wage.

With open migration and zero relocation costs, foreign workers would migrate to the home country for the higher wage. This emigration decreases the foreign

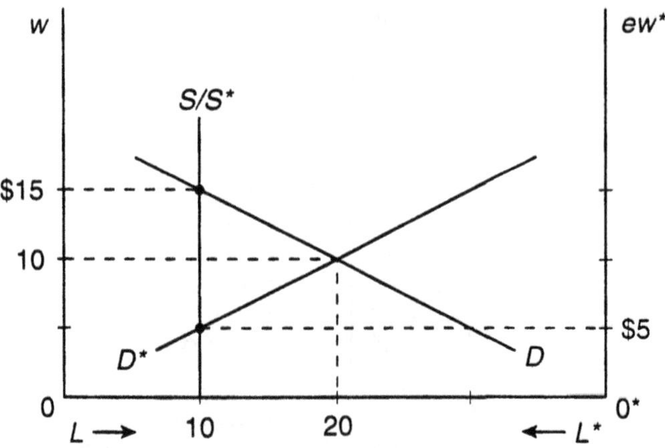

Figure 8.2
International Labor Market
The home labor market has demand D and wage w. The foreign labor market with demand D^* and wage ew^* is measured from 0^*. The labor supplies are 10 million in the home country and 30 million in the foreign country on supply line S/S^*. The home wage is \$15 and the foreign wage \$5.

labor supply increasing the scarce home supply. The supply line in Figure 8.2 moves to the right due to migration.

Other things equal, migration would continue until wages are equal at \$10 with 20 million workers in each country. The world output increases as labor moves to the capital-abundant country where it has higher MP.

Immigration expands host country resources expanding the production frontier. The host gains as the source country loses. The migrating labor gains and typically repatriates some of its earnings.

EXAMPLE **8.3**   *Recent US Immigration*

Immigration increased since 1970 to over 1 million per year — the level of the early 1900s before the disruptions of two World Wars and the Great Depression. Since 1950, immigration has grown steadily and now accounts for population growth. The result will be a much different population after a few generations.

Trade as a Substitute for Migration

Trade encourages wage equalization or at least convergence across countries. Trade increases local demand for relatively cheap factors of production. Trade substitutes for migration while tariffs increase the incentive for migration.

In the international labor market of Figure 8.3, the foreign country is labor cheap. Autarky labor demands are D_A and D_A^* with labor supplies $L = 10$ and $L^* = 30$. Trade leads the foreign country to export labor-intensive products. The higher price of labor-intensive products increases demand for labor from D_A^*

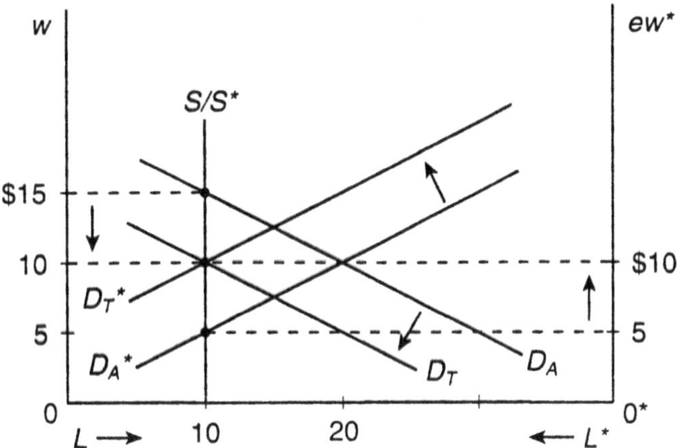

Figure 8.3
Trade and Wages
Trade increases labor demand in the labor-cheap foreign country from D_A* rises to D_T*.
Labor demand in the home country falls from D_A to D_T. Trade equalizes wages at $10.

to $D*$. As the price of labor-intensive products in the home country decreases, labor demand falls from D_A to D_T. The equilibrium with free trade occurs where D_T intersects D_T* at $w = ew* = \$10$.

Trade raises the wage in the labor-cheap country and lowers the wage in the capital-rich country, shifting labor demands. Labor migration shifts supplies.

International trade substitutes for migration, both leading toward equal wages across countries. The rising wages in poor countries due to exports of labor-intensive products reduces the incentive to emigrate.

Trade may be preferred to migration in the DCs. The choice faced by DCs is whether to import manufactured products or labor from LDCs. Illegal immigration remains a problem. Trade decreases the incentive for legal and illegal migration.

Migration raises international efficiency as labor moves to where it is more productive. Free trade creates similar efficiency gains through specialized production. Labor-scarce countries can discourage immigration with trade. Migration is more costly — moving products is simpler than moving people.

EXAMPLE **8.4**   *Early US Immigrants*

Immigration to the American colonies was open to Europeans. The population in 1790 was close to 4 million, including about 700,000 African slaves. The English, Irish, and Germans immigrated as indentured servants serving up to 14 years. When the slave trade ended in 1808, Africans and Asians were excluded from immigration. Until 1850, immigrants were English, Scotch-Irish, Dutch, German, and north Europeans. Between 1850 and the early 1900s, immigrants were central or southern Europeans, including nearly one million French Canadians fleeing religious persecution in Canada.

Legal Immigration

The high variation in labor skills suggests that there are markets for different types of labor. A high level of demand and low level of supply favor a higher wage. People making the highest wage are the most productive in expanding industries. People making the lowest wage are the least productive in declining industries.

Table 8.1 shows the skill groups of labor in US Census data. Groups are listed from the highest to the lowest paid. Lower wages might be due to immigration or falling demand due to import competition.

The lowest paid labor groups have the most immigrants. Immigration contributes to depressing the wages of less skilled workers. Unions favor strict enforcement of tight immigration laws. Firms hiring immigrants benefit from the low wages. The more skilled groups enjoy higher productivity and wages with unskilled immigration.

The wages for immigrating unskilled workers are much higher than in their source nations. DCs have a scarcity of labor and large amounts of cooperating capital, skilled labor, and natural resources. High levels of cooperating inputs imply higher productivity and wages compared to the labor-abundant source countries.

The wage in a skill group is lowered by its own immigration. As an example, immigration of foreign doctors was eliminated in the 1970s. The American Medical Association lobbied for the cutoff arguing that foreign-trained doctors are unreliable. The reduced supply helped maintain the high wages of doctors.

DCs attract skilled workers from around the world. Brain drain refers to emigration of skilled workers from LDCs. Resources spent by LDCs to train engineers, scientists, doctors, and other skills are wasted if the workers emigrate to a DC. Students from LDCs sent to study in the DCs often stay to work. Brain drain hinders growth in source nations. Skilled labor is scarce in the LDCs but there is not enough capital for skilled workers to be highly paid. Skilled workers in LDCs are underemployed by unproductive governments.

Table 8.1 US Census Skilled Labor Groups

L1 = professionals

L2 = craft, repair

L3 = transportation

L4 = machine operators

L5 = administrative, sales

L6 = handlers, laborers

L7 = agricultural, forestry, fishing

L8 = janitors, restaurant workers

An example of wage effects is an influx of Vietnamese political refugees to the US in the 1970s. Many went into shrimping along the Texas Gulf Coast, lowering wages and the price of shrimp.

When workers immigrate, payments to capital and natural resources are also affected. Groups hurt by immigration want stricter quotas while groups helped favor immigration.

Income redistribution caused by migration is key to understanding why some groups favor and others oppose immigration.

EXAMPLE **8.5**   *US Immigrant Population*

The chart shows the population in millions of descendants of the immigrants in each time period with a conservative 1% growth rate. The sum nearly equals the US population. About 40% of the total has immigrated since 1900 with the largest group between 1900 and 1920.

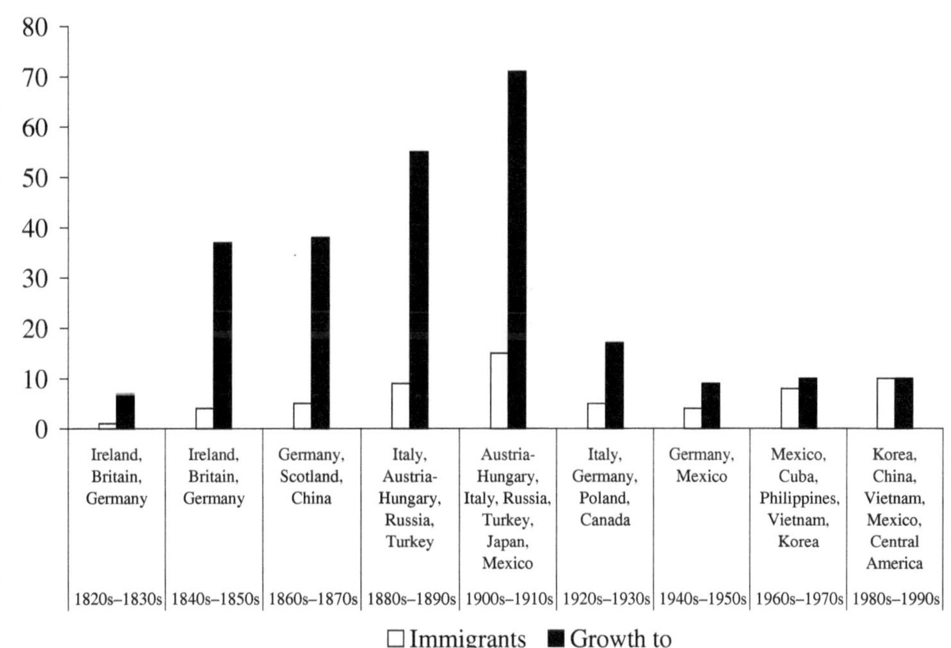

Illegal Immigration

Many workers enter DCs as illegal immigrants. The risk of being detained must be part of the decision to migrate illegally as the benefits must outweigh the costs. Part of the cost depends on the probability of being caught. While laws penalize firms hiring illegal immigrants, enforcement is uneven. There is a lot to gain through immigration for the employers as well as the migrants.

Illegal immigration can be reduced by lowering marginal benefits or raising marginal costs. The marginal benefit (*MB*) curve in Figure 8.4 illustrates the

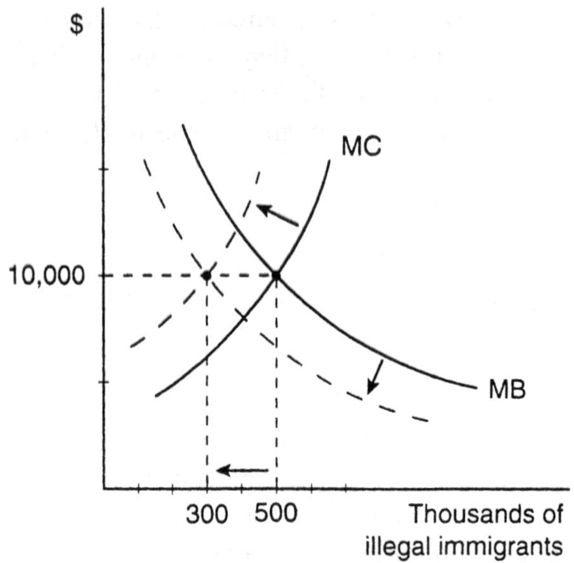

Figure 8.4
Decreasing Illegal Immigration
MB represents the marginal benefit for the migrant, and *MC* the marginal cost. Illegal immigration can be controlled by lowering *MB* or raising *MC*.

difference between wages in the host and source countries. As illegal workers enter, wages fall in the host country. *MB* slopes downward. The marginal cost *MC* schedule reflects the cost of relocation and the probability cost of a penalty if caught. The *MC* rises with the number of illegal immigrants.

Making it more difficult to hire illegal workers would reduce *MB*. Trade reduces *MB* by lowering the international wage difference. International investment attracts capital to low-wage countries and lowers *MB*. Increased patrolling of the border and stiffer penalties for illegal labor raise *MC*.

The main cause of illegal immigration is the higher wage. Trade and international investment reduce the incentives for illegal migration.

EXAMPLE **8.6**   *Migrants Worldwide*

Migrants are 3% of the world population. Remittance payments are 0.2% of world income. Immigration to DCs occurs at a rate of 0.2% of the population. In the US, migrants are 12% of the population with an immigration rate of 0.5% and 5% of GDP going to remittance payments. Australia has the largest stock of immigrants at 23% of the population.

EXAMPLE **8.7**   *Sources of Illegal Immigration*

Almost all immigration to the US from Europe is legal while more than half from Mexico is illegal. Europe is the largest foreign-born (FB) group. Asia counts for just over half as many FB residents as Europe and now has more immigration. Illegal FB immigrants from Mexico, Central America, and the Caribbean are about half the size of the legals.

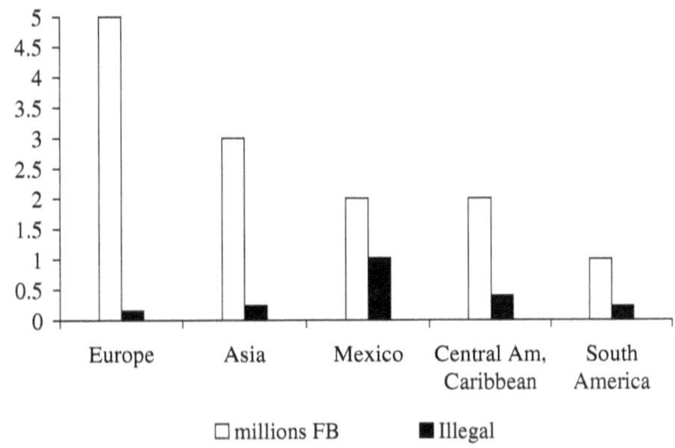

Section A Problems

A1. Find the wage in each country that would result from migration of 5 million to the home country in Figure 8.2.

A2. Suppose the relocation and readjustment cost is $2/hour in Figure 8.2. Find the equilibrium distribution of labor between the two countries. How many workers emigrate from the foreign country?

A3. Name one other way to reduce illegal immigration in Figure 8.4.

B. INTERNATIONAL CAPITAL

Capital moves between countries in search of higher returns. Capital is more mobile internationally than labor because the owners do not have to move with their capital. International capital is critical for production and trade.

International Capital Markets

Capital machinery and equipment combine with labor and energy to produce output. LDCs rely on DCs for capital to build manufacturing industries and develop natural resources. Capital also flows between DCs as with the foreign capital accounting for growth of the US automobile industry since the 1980s. International capital earnings can be repatriated to the source country. Paul Romer (1994) shows import restrictions on capital goods diminish production.

In the host country, incoming capital raises labor productivity and expands the production frontier. When foreign capital enters, the wage rises but the capital return falls. Incoming capital stimulates economic growth. Jong-Wha Lee (1994) finds that foreign capital provides more growth stimulus than domestic capital.

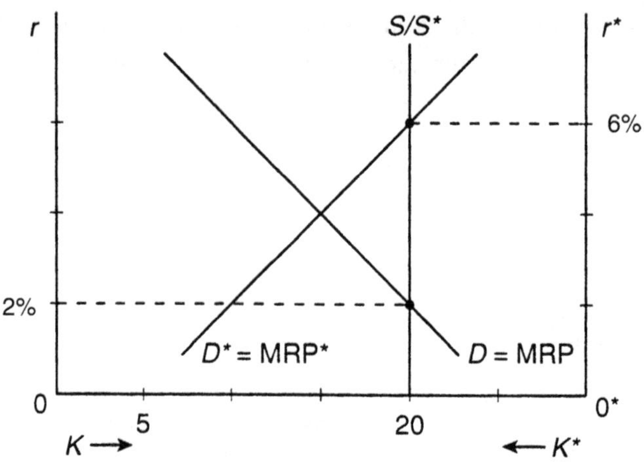

Figure 8.5
International Capital Market
Domestic capital demand D has return r. Foreign capital demand D^* measured from origin 0^* has return r^*. The relative supply line S/S^* has 20 units of capital at home and 10 in the foreign country. Capital returns are $r = 2\%$ and $r^* = 6\%$.

Figure 8.5 presents the international capital market. The structure of the international capital market is like the international labor market.

The domestic capital market is plotted from the left. The MP of capital diminishes for given levels of labor. Foreign capital demand is plotted from the right.

The rate of return r is the return divided by the capital stock. A 3% rate of return on the \$100,000 worth of physical capital means the capital produced \$3000 of output during the year. This 3% rate is the competitive rental for the capital.

In Figure 8.5, there are 20 units of capital at home and 10 units abroad. The return to capital is 2% at home where capital is abundant and 6% in the foreign country where it is scarce.

The difference in the two returns diminishes if capital moves between the two countries. Policy may limit foreign investment. In the DCs, there are appeals to keep foreigners from buying farmland and skyscrapers. LDCs limit foreign investment by requiring majority domestic ownership.

Capital moving to the foreign economy in Figure 8.5 shifts the supply line left. The rate r^* in the foreign country declines as r in the home country rises. Capital returns converge due to the international capital movement.

Restrictions on foreign capital in the host are due to the desire of capital owners to keep their input scarce and return high. In the source country, labor groups want to keep capital from leaving to maintain the marginal product of labor.

Owners of home capital in Figure 8.6 want to move their capital to the foreign country. International capital market equilibrium is reached with five units of capital moving from the home to the foreign country. Each country then has a stock of 15 at the international 4% rate.

International differences in capital returns are due primarily to differences in supplies. If free to move, capital moves toward an international equilibrium with equal returns across countries.

EXAMPLE **8.8**   *Foreign Capital in the US*

The US owns more than twice as much capital abroad as foreigners own in the US. The US holds net credit positions with Canada and Latin America, but net debit positions with Europe and Japan. Foreign firms invest in the US jumping tariffs to locate close to US consumers or producers. Foreign capital increases labor productivity and wages.

Trade as a Substitute for International Capital

Trade substitutes for international capital. DCs export capital-intensive business services and high-tech manufactures. Trade increases the price of these exports raising demand for capital and the return. Trade lowers the capital return in the capital-scarce countries that import the capital-intensive goods. Trade leads to more equal capital returns across countries.

International capital movements equalize returns across countries. Trade substitutes for capital movement by bringing returns to capital closer across countries.

EXAMPLE **8.9**   *Foreign Capital and Trade*

International capital movement has been growing faster than trade. Linda Goldberg and Michael Klein (1999) investigate effects of foreign capital serves on trade in Latin America. Capital from the US shifts manufacturing toward more capital-intensive production and exports.

US Foreign Direct Investment

Foreign direct investment (FDI) in the Balance of Payments (BOP) tracks international capital movements. FDI from the US goes to subsidiaries that are mostly totally owned. Table 8.2 shows the largest shares of FDI across industries and host countries. Manufacturing, finance, and hydrocarbon industries account for about 80% of FDI. Europe, Canada, and Latin America account for about the same percentage.

Each country presents its own legal and policy issues. Some countries are much more open to foreign capital than others. Mexico has been relaxing its restrictions on foreign capital after the introduction of free trade in North America.

Table 8.2 Distribution of US FDI

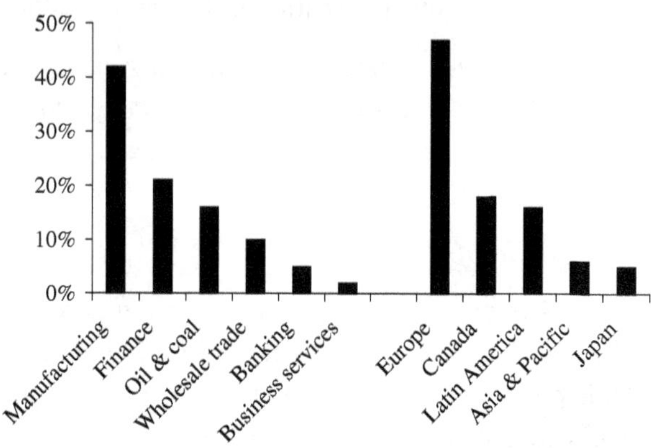

The largest owners of foreign capital inside the US are Canada, the Netherlands, the UK, Japan, Germany, France, and Switzerland. Many familiar companies are foreign owned: Budweiser, Shell, A&P, Mack Trucks, Carnation, and Nestle. About 20% of all foreign assets in the US are the result of FDI.

EXAMPLE **8.10**   *Foreign Capital between the US and Japan*

Foreign capital between the US and Japan is the result of protectionism, investment incentives, trade, and local practice. The US has invested capital in oil and manufacture in Japan. In contrast, Japan focuses on wholesale trade and banking investment in the US. The largest US manufacturing FDI is in chemicals. The US has a net negative capital position with Japan.

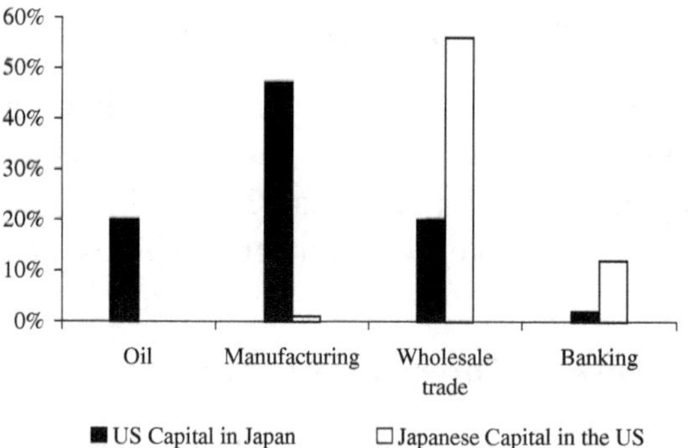

International Loans and Capital

Productive capital includes equipment, machinery, and structures that differs across industries. Firms borrow or spend retained earnings to buy productive capital inputs. In business and journalism, the term "capital markets" refers to credit markets. Borrowing by firms relates the international credit market developed in Chapter 11 to the international market for productive capital input.

There are links between international capital movements and the international credit market. If a US engineering company wants to establish a branch operation in England it can apply its own funds from the US or it can borrow in the credit market. The international credit market is based on borrowers in one country and lenders in another.

EXAMPLE 8.11 *FDI from DCs to LDCs*

Capital moving from DCs to LDCs has steadily increased since the 1980s. Firms in the DCs prefer to operate branch plants in the LDCs. Foreign capital in the LDCs is largely in the form of foreign direct investment FDI.

Section B Problems

B1. Illustrate and explain the effects of trade in Figure 8.5 leading to an international capital return of 4%.

B2. Show and explain what would happen to the international pattern of capital returns in Figure 8.5 with labor emigration from the foreign country.

EXAMPLE 8.12 *Foreign versus Home Capital Stocks*

The stock of US-owned capital in foreign countries remains ahead of the stock of foreign-owned capital in the US. Prices of tangible assets such as machinery, equipment, structures, land, and inventories as well as intangible assets such as patents and trademarks represent the discounted present value of the streams of expected profit in the future.

C. FACTOR MOVEMENTS AND INCOME REDISTRIBUTION

International movements of labor or capital lead to adjustments in factor prices as well as outputs, exports, and imports. Income redistribution typically determines who favors or is opposed to migration and capital movements. This section focuses on the income redistribution due to migration and foreign capital.

Factor Market Effects of Migration and Foreign Capital

An incoming factor increase raises national income but reduces its own return. Outputs adjust affecting factor productivities leading to adjustments in other factor prices. If the other factor price rises, the two are called *factor friends*. Two factors are *factor enemies* with a negative effect.

Figure 8.6 shows the market for factor F with price f. Migration of F shifts its supply. International movements of other factors affect the marginal productivity of F and demand. If immigrating unskilled labor raises the marginal product

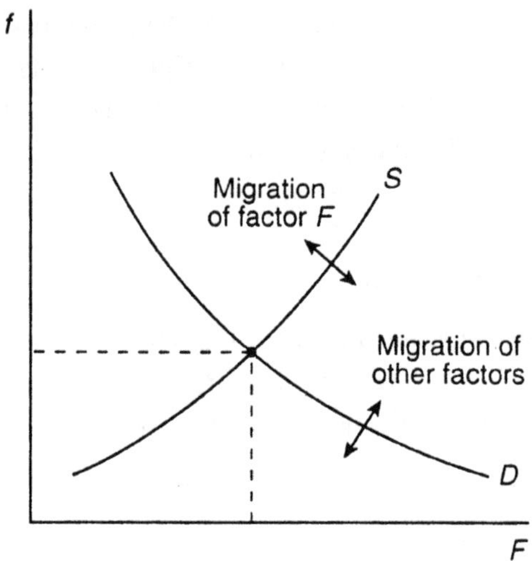

Figure 8.6
Factor Market Shifts
The domestic market for factor F is influenced by international factor movements. When the factor migrates, supply shifts. When other factors migrate, productivity and demand shift.

of F rises due to output changes, the two are factor friends. If another factor suffers falling MP, the two are factor enemies.

> *The international increase of a factor raises prices of its factor friends and lowers prices of its factor enemies.*

Labor Skills and Migration

The lowest paid groups of labor are unskilled handlers, laborers, agricultural workers, janitors, and restaurant workers. Higher skilled or semi-skilled groups include professionals, craft workers, transport workers, operators, and managers. The markets for these various skill groups are separate but related. Immigration of any one skill group affects the wages of the others.

The MPs of capital and natural resources are also affected by immigration. The effects of immigration on income distribution between these skill groups and capital depend on factor intensity and substitution as outputs adjust across the economy.

As a rule, unskilled labor is a factor friend of skilled labor and capital. Immigration of unskilled labor raises those marginal products. The skilled wage and capital return rise as the unskilled wage falls. Labor unions representing unskilled labor have long opposed immigration. Hispanic groups are strongly opposed to increased immigration.

The local effects of immigration can be large. Construction wages in Houston and farm wages in California are kept low by the supply of immigrants. Wages of restaurant workers around the country are another example. Across regions, the Sun Belt benefits from immigration.

Demographics of the US will be much different after 50 years due to immigration. The various minority groups will soon make up most of the population. The population is shifting to the south and west due to open shop labor market policy. Immigration is playing a role as labor moves around the country changing the pattern of production and trade.

International movement of labor and capital raise world output and distribute income more equitably. Of course, not every group benefits from international factor movement. Factor mobility as well as trade lead toward similar incomes for similar productive factors regardless of location.

A trading country effectively exports its cheap factors. International factor movements effectively export the cheap factors of production.

EXAMPLE **8.13**   *Immigrants Income*

Asian immigrant households in the US have higher income than other immigrant groups and the native-born population as well. Immigrants from Mexico have the lowest income with about a third on government assistance, double the rate of the native population. Immigrants from Europe have about the same income as native born. Labor skills explain most of these income differences.

Foreign Capital as a Specific Factor

Incoming international capital goes into a particular industry such as Korean car plants in the US and Dutch oil refineries in Africa.

Figure 8.7 shows the market for sector-specific capital in manufactures M. With supply S at 10 the capital return is 4%. Figure 8.8 shows the market for labor manufactures M and services S. The equilibrium wage is $10 with 20 million workers in manufacturing and 30 million in services indicated by the supply line S.

Incoming foreign capital increases the supply of capital in manufactures to S' in Figure 8.7. The result is a decrease in the capital return to $r = 3\%$. In Figure 8.8, labor demand increases in manufacturing as the incoming capital boosts the MP of labor. The wage in manufactures w_M jumps to $14. Workers move to manufacturing causing w_S to rise as well with w_M settling to $12. Labor supply shifts to S' with 5 million workers moving from services to manufactures.

The incoming capital in manufactures lowers the MP of capital in services due to the departing labor. The return to capital specific to services falls. Owners of capital in manufactures oppose the foreign capital while owners of capital in services are in favor. Labor favors foreign capital in either sector due to the wage increase.

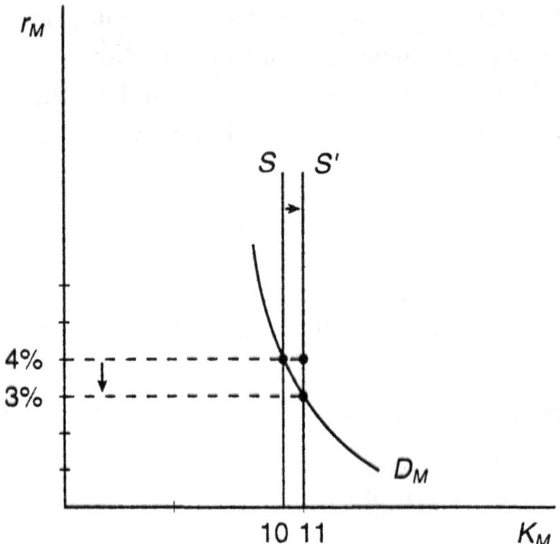

Figure 8.7
Incoming Foreign Capital in Manufactures
When the supply of capital K_M in manufactures increases from S to S' due to foreign capital, r_M falls from 4% to 3% along demand D_M.

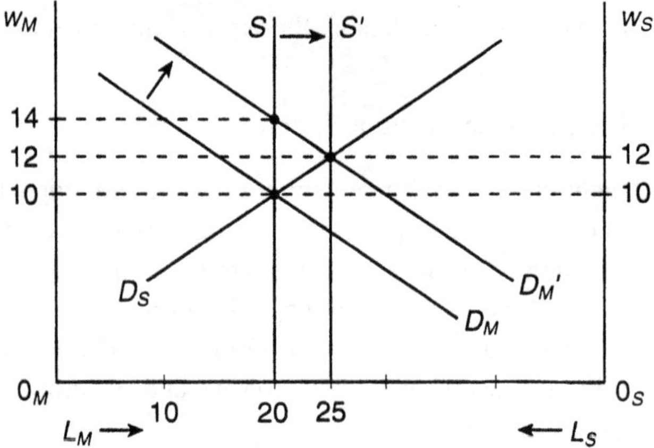

Figure 8.8
Foreign Capital and Labor
Labor productivity rises in manufacturing with foreign capital. Demand for labor in manufacturing rises from D_M to D_M'. Wages increase from \$10 to \$12 across the economy as 5 million workers move to manufacturing.

EXAMPLE **8.14**   *Mariel Immigration*

The labor force in Miami increased by 7% in 1980 when 62,000 workers fled Cuba from the port of Mariel. David Card (1989) shows this immigration had little effect on wages in Miami. Even among unskilled workers competing directly with the immigrants, there was no decline and no increase in unemployment. Production of goods intensive in unskilled labor, especially textiles and apparel, increased. The Mariel immigration suggests the main effect is on the pattern of production. Ethan Lewis (2004) finds evidence that the immigration of unskilled Cubans slowed adoption of computer technology.

Income Redistribution in Computable General Equilibrium Models

Computable general equilibrium (CGE) models predict adjustments in product markets and factor markets due to changes in the labor force or capital inputs. CGE models simulate the income redistribution due to international migration and capital movement.

CGE simulations indicate migration and foreign capital have small effects on income distribution at least beyond local effects. Skilled labor and capital benefit when unskilled labor immigrates, explaining the lack of persistent opposition to immigration.

In CGE models, skilled labor and capital prove to be weak enemies. Incoming foreign capital lowers the skilled wage along with the capital return. Unskilled labor benefits from foreign capital as it works more with machinery and equipment in manufacturing and construction.

The effects of migration and international capital movement have small effects on wages and capital returns but large effects across industrial outputs. Effects vary across labor skills.

EXAMPLE **8.15**   *Winners and Losers Due to Immigration*

Wages for unskilled workers are lower in Mexico than in the US. Clark Reynolds and Robert McClery (1988) calculate the gains and losses due to immigration from Mexico. Skilled wages and especially the capital return rise while unskilled wages fall. Capital includes land with US landowners especially benefiting from immigrant labor. In Mexico, the remaining unskilled workers enjoy higher wages as both skilled labor and capital lose.

Section C Problems

C1. Illustrate the effects of unskilled immigration on the markets for unskilled labor, skilled labor, and capital in factor markets based on Figure 8.6.
C2. Suppose immigration increases the supply of unskilled workers by 5% with the elasticities 0.5 for the skilled wage and −0.8 for the unskilled wage. Find the new wages assuming the skilled wage starts at $80,000 and the unskilled wage at $30,000.

EXAMPLE **8.16**   *Foreign Capital and Wages*

Foreign capital raises labor productivity but with uneven effects across labor skills and regions. Robert Feenstra and Gordon Hanson (1997) find evidence that foreign capital coming into Mexico from 1975 to 1988 raised skilled wages in the maquiladora factories of northern Mexico. Foreign capital outsourcing by multinationals shifted production toward products intensive in skilled labor. Foreign capital accounts for over half of the increase in skilled wages. Anna Falzoni, Giovanni Brunno, and Rosario Crino (2004) find all wages increase due to foreign capital in Poland, Hungary, and the Czech Republic during the 1990s.

D. FACTOR MOVEMENTS AND TRADE

International movements of labor and capital affect the pattern of production and trade as well as factor prices. The evidence suggests these output adjustments are stronger than the factor price adjustments.

Output Adjustments in the Factor Proportions Model

An increased supply of one factor of production raises output intensive in that factor and lowers other output as other factors are attracted to the expanding sector. The levels of imports and exports also adjust.

Figure 8.9 shows the expansion paths for services and manufactures with inputs of skilled labor S and unskilled labor U. Services use skilled labor intensively. Point E is the starting endowment of 100 for each labor group. Outputs of S and M are on the two expansion paths projected from point E.

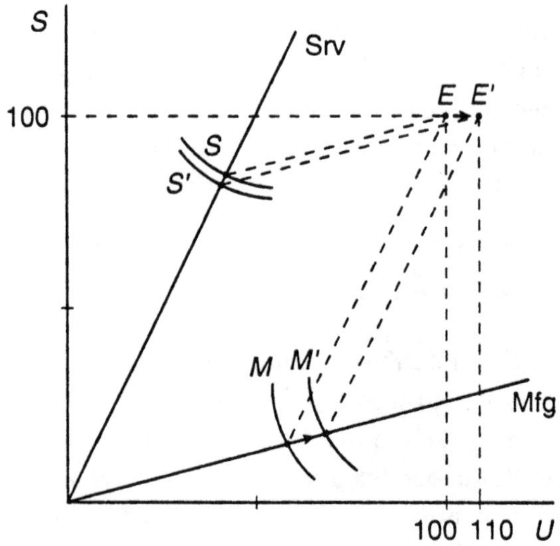

Figure 8.9
Production and Immigration of Unskilled Labor
Immigration of unskilled labor shifts the endowment from E to E'. Unskilled intensive production of M increases as S decreases. If S is exported, both exports and imports fall. If M is exported, both exports and imports rise.

Immigration of unskilled labor moves the endowment point from E to E' with an increase of 10%. Projecting from E' the new outputs are M' and S'. Production shifts toward labor-intensive manufactures as both types of labor leave services. All immigrating unskilled workers plus some from services move into manufactures. Skilled labor leaves services as well.

Immigration of unskilled labor lowers its wage but raises the skilled wage. The evidence suggests these changes in factor prices are small. In a small open economy, the prices of traded services and manufactures do not change.

If manufactures are imported, immigration of unskilled labor increases import-competing production and lowers imports. Immigration of unskilled labor substitutes for trade.

If manufactures are exported, the immigration of unskilled labor raises the level of trade. The country becomes more abundant in unskilled labor, intensive in export production. Imports of manufactures, however, are more likely as the immigrating unskilled labor would be attracted by the relatively high unskilled wage.

Immigration is expected to lower the level of trade based on factor abundance and intensity.

EXAMPLE **8.17**   *Immigration, Foreign Capital, and Trade*

Kar-Yui Wong (1995) estimates the effects of immigration and foreign capital on US production of traded goods. Immigration increases exports of nondurable goods and services. A 1% increase in the labor force has strong effects with an increase of 2.2% in exports and 1.5% in durable good exports. Imports also increase due to the increase in consumption. Changes in capital input have smaller elasticities on exports and imports.

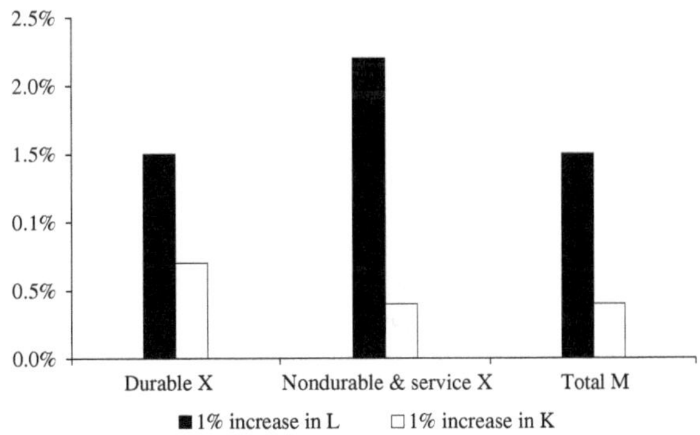

Output Adjustments With Specific Factors

Sector-specific capital combining with shared labor leads to different adjustments to foreign capital. Figure 8.10 shows the expansion paths for manufactures M and services S. Supplies of the two capitals are the vertical lines $K_M = 10$ and $K_S = 10$. Production of M employs 20 million workers at the capital/labor ratio

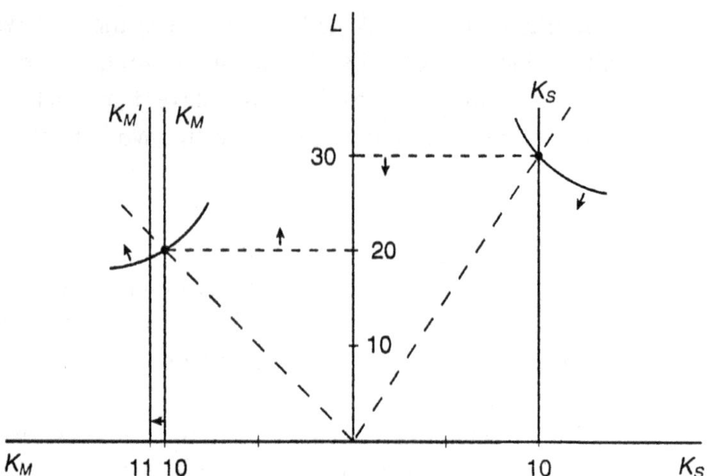

Figure 8.10
Foreign Manufacturing Capital and Outputs
Foreign capital coming into M attracts labor from the production of S. While the output of M rises, output of S falls.

$K/L = 1/2$. Services employs the other 30 million workers at $K/L = 1/3$. The 50 million workers in the economy are split between the two sectors.

Incoming foreign capital increases supply in manufacturing from 10 to 11 raising the output of M. Labor is attracted to M with the higher marginal product and wage. As labor leaves S production falls. In services, the decreased labor input lowers the MP and return to capital.

Immigration would increase both outputs with shared incoming labor. The wage falls but both capital returns increase.

Foreign sector–specific capital raises sector output drawing labor away from the rest of the economy.

Simulated Output Adjustments

The three major classifications of output are agriculture A, manufactures M, and services S. Labor is split into the eight skill groups in Table 8.1. Table 8.3 presents the simulated elasticities of outputs with respect to immigration of these eight labor skills and an increase in capital.

Adjustments are larger in the sector where a factor is intensive. Agriculture is capital intensive with capital including land as well as extensive machinery and equipment. Capital owners receive 58% of the income in agriculture. A 5% increase in the capital stock resulting from incoming foreign capital results in an elastic 13.5% increase in agricultural output.

Another strong adjustment is immigration amounting to 1% of agricultural workers L7 raises agricultural output by 0.9%. As the US is a net exporter of agricultural products, immigration of agricultural labor increases exports.

Table 8.3 Output Elasticities of Migration and Investment

| | **1% Increase in Supply of** | | | | | | | | |
	L1	**L2**	**L3**	**L4**	**L5**	**L6**	**L7**	**L8**	**K**
A	1.4	0	0	−0.2	−1.0	0	0.9	−0.2	2.7
M	−0.5	0.7	0.1	1.8	−0.5	0	0	−0.1	−0.4
S	0.5	0	0	−0.3	0.5	0	0	0.1	0.3

Source: Henry Thompson (1991).

Operators L4 are intensive in manufactures receiving 29% of the income. Immigration of L4 workers would cause manufactures output to rise while services and agriculture fall. Manufactures is highly elastic with respect to the supply of operators. Immigration amounting to an increase of 10% operators would spur manufacturing output by 18%.

Majorities of the labor groups of professionals L1, craft L3, and sales L5 are employed in services. Professionals and sales receive 27% and 21% of the income in the services sector. The largest output effects on the service sector come from immigration of these two skilled groups. The US is a net exporter of services with skilled labor immigration increasing specialization and exports.

The strong adjustments across outputs to international movements of labor and capital are tied closely to factor intensity.

EXAMPLE **8.18** *Foreign Capital by State*

The foreign capital stock in the US increased over five times from 1980 to 2020 when foreign firms employed 6% of the US labor force. States with more than 8% of the labor force employed by foreign multinational firms are Kentucky, New Hampshire, New Jersey, South Carolina, Massachusetts, and Wisconsin. Other states in the Midwest, Northeast, and South are not far behind.

Section D Problems

D1. Show what happens in Figure 8.10 with emigration of skilled labor. If services are exported, predict what will happen to exports and imports.

D2. Predict what happens to production and trade with outflows of skilled labor from a DC. Compare these adjustments with what would happen in an LDC.

EXAMPLE **8.19** *Immigrant Remittances to Mexico*

Mexico accounts for a third of the foreign workers in the US. Their remittance payments are a source of income for Mexico. Catalina Amuedo-Dorantes, Cynthia Bansak, and Susan Pozo (2005) review the evidence from a survey of Mexican workers reporting remittances support families, meet goals for saving, and pay debts. Undocumented workers with low education and family members in Mexico remit a larger share of their income. Remittances are declining as income in Mexico increases with the immigrants staying longer and becoming residents.

EXAMPLE **8.20**   *Foreign Capital Up and Down*

Foreign capital increased around the world through the 1990s but slowed during the 2000s due to concerns over recession, protectionism, and terrorism. Only about a third of global capital goes to LDCs. The largest recipients are the US, China, the EU, and Asia-Pacific. Weak government policy including uneven property rights restrict international capital movement.

CONCLUSION

International migration and capital movement are important to the global economy. Outputs and factor prices inside host and source countries adjust to these factor movements. Output adjustments are larger that adjustments in wages and capital returns. Countries integrate their economies through trade, migration, and foreign direct investment. Chapter 9 discusses this process of international economic integration.

Terms

Brain drain	International capital mobility
Capital depreciation	International factor markets
Emigration, immigration	Legal and illegal migration
Factor friends, enemies	Labor skills migration
Foreign capital	Marginal factor cost (*MFC*)
Host and source countries	Marginal revenue product (*MRP*) Remittances

MAIN POINTS

- Workers respond to international wage differences by migrating to countries with higher wages. Migration leads to converging wages across countries. International trade substitutes for migration due to converging wages.
- Capital moves between countries for a higher return. International capital movement leads to the convergence of capital returns.
- When labor or capital enter a country, national income rises but the price of that factor falls. Factor friends gain while factor enemies lose income. International factor movements redistribute income.
- International migration and capital movement strongly affect the pattern of production and trade.

REVIEW PROBLEMS

1. Illustrate the adjustment to trade with wages equalizing at $10 in Figure 8.2.
2. What else could the different wages of the labor groups in Table 8.1 reflect other than the skills and training to enter each group?
3. Predict how foreign capital coming into the auto industry would affect wages of the labor groups in Table 8.1.
4. Given the trend of unskilled labor immigration, predict adjustments in the pattern of production and trade.
5. If capital owners in the US traded their capital evenly with capital owners in the EU, what would be the effect?
6. Explain how the industries in Table 8.2 with substantial foreign investment compare with comparative advantage of the US.
7. Explain which groups in an economy most favor restricting foreign investment. Which groups should oppose restrictions?
8. Services includes categories such as wholesale trade and banking as in Example 8.10. What have been the effects on income redistribution and outputs of this foreign capital?
9. Predict what will happen to wages of the various types of labor in Table 8.1 with the emigration of professionals.
10. Explain what happens to the income of the various types of labor and sector-specific capital when a foreign firm opens a new factory.
11. What happens to the long-run distribution of income when US firms open factories in Mexico? What would be the difference if the plant opened on the US side of the border with Mexicans allowed to cross for work?
12. Explain whether it is more likely that the US would join a common market with free trade and free movements of labor and capital with Canada or Mexico.
13. With higher birth rates among unskilled immigrants in the West and South, predict what will happen to the pattern of trade inside the US.
14. Free trade zones (FTZs) attract foreign firms by eliminating tariffs. Explain whether FTZs promote or inhibit trade.
15. Describe the output effects on the three sectors A, M, and S with 10% immigration of machine operators L4 in Table 8.3. Predict the effects on imports and exports.

READINGS

Barry Chaswick, ed. (1982) *The Gateway: US Immigration Issues and Policies*, Washington: American Policy Institute. Studies on immigration.

Edward Graham and Paul Krugman (1991) *Foreign Direct Investment in the United States*, Washington: Institute for International Economics. Loads of information and detail on FDI.

International Migration Review, New York: Center for Migration Studies. Journal on Migration. "The New Refugee," *US News and World Report*, October 23, 1989. A startling look at migration.

Kaz Miyagiwa (1990) *International Capital Mobility and National Welfare*, New York: Garland. Review of theory.

John Shoven and John Whalley (1984) Applied general equilibrium models of taxation and international trade, *Journal of Economic Literature*. A nice survey of CGE models as they began to evolve.

Julian Simon (1999) *The Economic Consequences of Immigration*, London: Blackwell. Economic analysis of immigration.

Aad van Mourik (1994) *Wages and European Integration*, Maastricht: BIV Publications. Detailed analysis of integration.

MATHEMATICAL APPENDIX

Differences between the home wage w and the foreign wage ew^* are the main reason for migration. The wage w in the labor market depends on demand $D_L = MRP_L$. The marginal revenue $MR = dR/dQ$ of output Q and marginal product $MP_L = dQ/dL$ of labor lead to MRP_L as the change in revenue from the marginal worker in $MRP_L = MR \times MP_L = dR/dL$.

In a competitive labor market, labor is paid marginal revenue product $w = MRP_L$. In the foreign country, $ew^* = MRP_L^*$. If D_L and D_L^* are similar, higher foreign labor supply $S_L^* > S_L$ would imply $w > ew^*$. A higher home wage would also arise with similar supplies $S_L = S_L^*$ and higher labor productivity $D_L > D_L^*$.

A large enough difference $w - ew^*$ provides incentive for foreign labor to emigrate. Where C_M is the total cost of migration, $w - ew^* > C_M$ leads to migration to the home country.

Assuming skilled labor or natural resource input as a third factor, migration raises L and ew^* lowering L^* and w. The model includes a third factor in the general equilibrium system of the Chapter 6 Appendix. With only two factors, migration has no effect, given the same number of factors and goods. In applied general equilibrium simulations, the effects of migration on wages are found to be small. The empirical evidence also points to small effects of migration on wages as outputs do most of the adjusting to migration.

Every country has immigration laws limiting or controlling migration. Illegal immigration nevertheless occurs if $w - ew^*$ is large enough. Part of the cost C_M of illegal migration is the probability of the penalty if caught.

In the low-wage foreign country, free trade raises the price of labor-intensive exports raising MRP_L^* and ew^*. In the high-wage home country, the falling prices of labor-intensive goods lower MRP_L and w. Trade diminishes the incentive to migrate by decreasing the difference $w - ew^*$.

International capital movements are similar based on the difference in capital returns, $r^* - r > 0$. Aside from risk and legal restrictions, capital would move to the capital-scarce foreign country increasing K^* and decreasing K. Trade increases capital demand in the capital abundant home country reducing the incentive for capital movement as $r - r^*$ decreases. Trade diminishes the incentives for international movement of capital and labor.

In the specific factors model, capital movement affects primarily its sector. Suppose home capital in manufacturing K_M moves to the foreign country increasing K_M^*. The foreign capital return falls as $\partial r_M^*/\partial K_M^* < 0$ due to the increased capital supply while the foreign wage increases $\partial ew^*/\partial K_M^* > 0$ due to the increased MP_L^*. Labor is attracted to M^* lowering the marginal product of K in the other sector, $\partial r_S^*/\partial K_M^* < 0$. Outputs adjust accordingly $\partial x_M^*/\partial K_M^* > 0$ and $\partial x_S^*/\partial K_M^* < 0$. The decrease of K_M in the home country has the opposite effects, $r_M\uparrow$, $w\downarrow$, $r_S\uparrow$, $x_M\downarrow$, and $x_S\uparrow$. These effects can be analyzed in a general equilibrium model based on the Chapter 6 Appendix.

Production and trade also adjust due to migration and capital movement. Immigration increases labor-intensive output. Incoming capital increases capital-intensive output. These effects can be derived in the general equilibrium model of the Chapter 6 Appendix. Migration and capital movement decrease trade based on factor abundance and intensity.

CHAPTER 9

International Economic Integration

Preview

The degree of integration of countries has accelerated over recent decades due to the increased levels of trade and international capital. Economic integration increases with lower barriers to trade and foreign capital across borders. The result is higher income all around although there are losers as well as winners in every country. Political opposition to trade and international capital will persist. Topics in this chapter include:

- Multinational firms (MNFs) involved in trade and international capital
- Policy regarding international externalities in production
- International political economy and policy
- Policy steps of economic integration countries can take

INTRODUCTION

Countries are becoming increasingly connected due to improved transportation and communication as economies increase their dependence on each other. International trade and capital generate gains all around but redistribute income leading to political disagreements over trade and investment policy.

Multinational firms (MNFs) have branch operations in different countries bringing in production techniques and skilled labor. Governments restrict MNFs motivated by protectionist lobby spending. The capital of MNF lowers the return in the host country explaining some of the political opposition. Labor in the host benefits from MNFs due to increased labor demand. There are examples of foreign MNFs inside the US in the automobile, airplane, metal, and pharmaceutical industries.

International pollution can motivate economic coordination across countries. There are no pollution taxes or courts to settle liability involving the negative externalities of pollution. As an example, water pollution from factories in Germany harms Poland that has no appeal to an international agency or court to file suit for damages.

Governments can take policy steps to increase economic integration subject to different pressure groups helped or harmed by each step. Governments want to protect supportive industries but are looking for broad support from the public. Economic integration progresses through steps as governments give up local political power in favor of raising income.

A. MULTINATIONAL FIRMS

An MNF is based on headquarters in one country with branch operations in other countries. MNFs rely on international capital and are typically involved in trade.

International Marketing

A firm wanting to sell its product in other countries has four options that require increasing degrees of familiarity with the foreign markets:

- Produce at home and export
- License agreements with foreign firms
- Joint ventures with foreign firms
- Become an MNF with a branch plants.

The choice is based on transport costs, contacts among foreign firms, levels of protection, local economies of scale, fixed costs of a branch plant, relative cost of foreign labor, home and foreign skilled labor, the level and elasticity of foreign demand, and familiarity with the foreign legal system.

Licensing with a foreign firm is one way for a domestic firm to begin production in a foreign country. If the source firm has a special production process, licensing allows the transfer of technology. The branch firm attaches its label to the product and receives a royalty. Licensing requires trusting the foreign firm.

Joint ventures are the next step with an agreement between firms to share management, production processes, and market information. One firm might be better at research and development, and the other in management and marketing. Both firms can end up better off by operating as a single firm. The firm's specific input or production process might be based on a patent. International patent protection remains a challenging issue in the World Trade Organization (WTO).

A firm wanting to protect its production process can set up its own MNF branch plant operation in the foreign country. This step requires the most familiarity with the foreign country.

The four options for a firm wanting to sell its product in foreign markets are to export, license, enter a joint venture, and become an MNF.

EXAMPLE **9.1**   *MNFs in Business Services*

Over recent decades, a large part of MNF growth has occurred in business services. About half of the outward investment in the US goes into business services. For other developed countries (DCs) the percentage is about one third. Most investment coming into the US is also in business services.

International Entrepreneurs

DCs have an abundance of entrepreneurs who organize firms and manage economic decisions. This comparative advantage is revealed in the net export of business services from DCs.

An increase in MNF activity lowers the return to entrepreneurs inside the host country although labor benefits with higher wages. Firms in an industry must compete with new MNF branch plants. There is political pressure in both directions wanting to encourage and limit MNFs.

The US automobile industry provides an example of how MNFs force the domestic industry to become more competitive. Foreign MNFs since the 1980s have made domestic car makers more efficient. The quality of cars has increased dramatically over the past 30 years due to competition from MNFs. There is little difference in domestic value added between domestic and foreign cars produced inside the US.

EXAMPLE **9.2**   *MNFs in the US*

There are more Japanese MNF branch operations inside the US than from any other country. The UK has about half as many branch operations as Japan, and Canada and the EU about a third each.

Multinational Firm Horizontal Integration

Horizontal integration occurs when a firm produces the same product at different locations. A horizontally integrated MNF decides how much to produce in each branch plant. The MNF in Figure 9.1 maximizes profit where marginal revenue (MR) equals marginal cost (MC) in both its domestic and branch plants. The foreign branch has lower marginal cost MC^*.

Optimal outputs involve equating each MC with MR to maximize profit where $MR = MC = MC^* = \$5$. The domestic output of 10 plus foreign output of 20 adds to total output of 30. At any price above \$5, the two quantities from the MC and MC^* would add to more than the quantity on the MR curve. The output of 30 is sold according to demand at \$10. Output is higher at the lower cost plant.

A horizontally integrated MNF produces more output at lower cost plants.

The firm might continue to operate the higher-cost plant even though all production could be shifted to the foreign plant where $MC^* = MR$ at $Q = 25$. The profit of each location would depend on its average cost (AC). Profit could be higher operating in both plants. Transport costs might also be an incentive to keep plants operating since customers could be closer to one plant or the other.

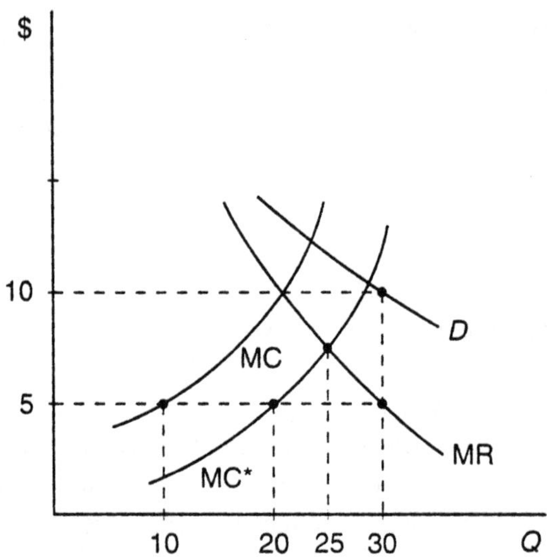

Figure 9.1
Horizontal MNF Integration
The MNF produces the same product in two countries equating *MR* with *MC* and *MC**, setting the price according to demand. The foreign plant has lower costs and produces 20 units while the higher cost home plant produces 10 units. Total output is 30 where $MR = \$5 = MC$ and P = \$10.

One plant could be located closer to a natural resource. There might be costs of shutting down the domestic plant. The domestic plant might be headquarters to train foreign managers. If the firm expects costs to change at home or abroad, it may want to operate the branch plants as a hedge.

EXAMPLE **9.3**   *Foreign MNFs in the US*

Foreign investment in the US is spread across industries. Ed Ray (1991) finds foreign MNFs go into large firms with market power in large growing industries intensive in skilled labor and capital. Capital inflow increases when the dollar depreciates. Foreign MNFs tend to avoid labor unions, not lobby for protection, and focus on business services.

Multinational Firm Vertical Integration

Multinational vertical integration occurs when an MNF produces an intermediate product in the host plant and uses it in the home plant to produce the final product. Natural resource products from the host country could be shipped to the home source country for processing or assembly.

Figure 9.2 shows a vertically integrated MNF with demand and *MR* for furniture *F* on the left. Part of the *MC* of producing furniture is the lumber *L*, produced in the foreign branch on the right side of the diagram. The demand

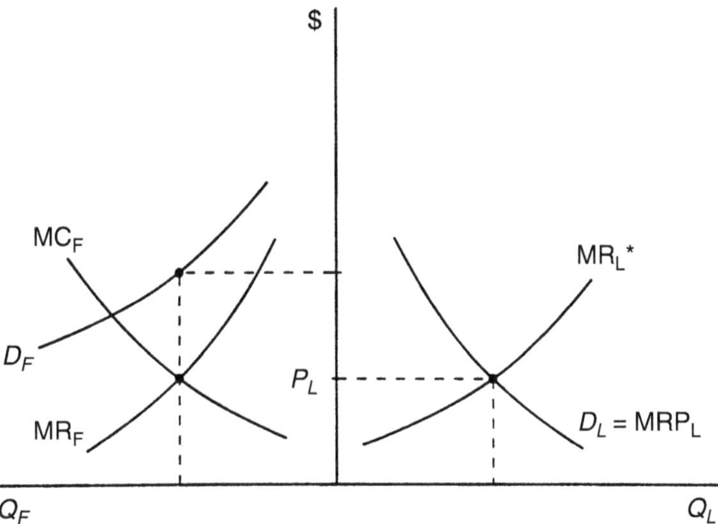

Figure 9.2
Vertical MNF Integration
This MNF producing furniture F is vertically integrated producing lumber L in the
foreign country. Lumber demand is derived from upstream furniture demand. Increased
furniture demand would raise its price and the MRP and price of lumber.

for lumber L is marginal revenue product (MRP), the MR of the furniture times
the marginal product of lumber.

The demand for lumber is derived from the demand for furniture since the
MR of the lumber depends on the price of furniture. The firm ships the lumber
from its foreign branch operation to the home assembly plant.

*An MNF avoids the market through vertical integration by producing its own
raw materials or components in foreign branch plants.*

The MNF can transfer the price-buying components from its own foreign
branch operations. The foreign branch firm will appear to be less profitable with
less tariff paid on the imported intermediate product understating the price of
the import. The firm avoids the market where price is transparent. The transfer
price of the lumber in Figure 9.2 would be less than its price. If the transfer
price of the components is overstated, the foreign branch firm will appear more
profitable. MNFs transfer prices to shift profit to the country with lower taxes.

*Transfer pricing provides an incentive to establish a foreign branch in a
low-tax country.*

EXAMPLE **9.4**   *Obstacles to MNFs*

A survey by the World Bank indicates a ranking of obstacles to international
commerce. Taxes top the list. Corruption involving paying government officials
or locals for "protection" is next on the list. Financing ranks third as it can be

more difficult in some countries. Poor infrastructure resulting from inefficient government is next on the list. Last on the list is crime and theft.

Section A Problems

A1. Explain why the domestic automobile industry disagrees with the domestic electronic industry on foreign MNF car factories. Predict whether domestic consumers should favor MNF plants.

A2. Speculate on whether a textile factory or an insurance company would be more likely to license a foreign operation. Explain which would be more likely to set up an MNF branch.

EXAMPLE **9.5**   *Do MNFs Promote Growth?*

MNFs spur economic growth. Theodore Moran, Edward Graham, and Magnus Blomström (2005) find evidence of more benefits in countries with high human capital, sophisticated private sectors, competition, and free trade and investment. Mandatory joint ventures with domestic firms are a hindrance to MNFs. Tax incentives also discourage MNFs.

B. INTERNATIONAL EXTERNALITIES

Negative production externalities occur when some of the costs of producing a good are paid by others. Pollution is the primary example of a negative production externality harming those nearby. Air and water pollution can cross borders leading to international externalities. International positive externalities occur when the benefits from one country spill over to other countries, for example, airports, parks, and public health policies.

Negative Production Externalities

A negative production externality occurs when a firm does not pay all its production cost. Pollution is a negative externality. People near a polluting firm pay part of the cost of production, suffering dirty air and water, frequently painting their houses, and replacing rusted cars.

The economic solution to pollution is in Figure 9.3. Demand facing the firm is D and MR. Marginal private cost (MPC) is the explicit costs of labor, capital, energy, intermediate inputs, and raw materials considered by the firm. The implicit costs of pollution is the \$6 distance between MPC and marginal social cost (MSC). A firm insensitive to the external pollution costs produces where $MR = MPC$ at 12 units of output and a price of \$20.

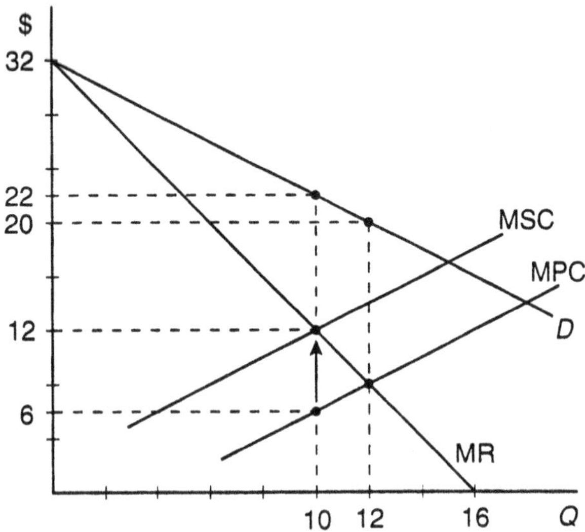

Figure 9.3
Negative Production Externality
The difference between *MSC*s and *MPC*s is external pollution cost of $6 per unit. A myopic profit maximizer disregards external cost producing where $MPC = MR$ at $Q = 10$ and $P = \$20$. A pollution tax of $6 per unit of output raises *MPC* to *MSC* restricting output to 10 and raising price to $P = \$22$.

Firms that want goodwill operate on the *MSC* schedule restricting output to 10 and raising price to $22. The $6 difference could be spent on research and development (R&D) to lower pollution. A firm that ignores *MSC* might suffer bad publicity and lower profit.

Negative externalities are the costs of production not explicitly paid by the firm. Firms interested only in short-run profit ignore external costs.

If the firm is responsible or liable for the costs it imposes on others, it will cut The output to the social optimum. With robust civil liability, property rights govern pollution as the polluter can be sued for damages.

Residents could pay the firm to produce the optional amount of pollution through negotiations. According to the Coase theorem, the socially optimal output is reached given costless negotiation. Those paying the external costs may not be aware of the costs. Negotiation is more costly for international externalities.

The government can tax a firm into internalizing its external costs. The tax equals the difference between *MPC* and *MSC*. In Figure 9.3, a tax of $6 per unit of output forces the *MPC* up to *MSC*. The pollution tax forces the firm to explicitly consider the cost of pollution, restricting the output to 10 at a price of $22. The resulting tax revenue is $6 \times 10 = \$60$. Revenue of the firm with the tax is $\$160 = \$220 - \$60$. The tax is an economical solution to pollution.

The US Environmental Protection Agency (EPA) uses command and control to limit pollution with little regard to costs. Firms in the US face fines when sampling turns up pollution outside limits. Firms avoid fines by installing what EPA determines the Best Available Technology (BAT). The production of BAT introduces potential conflicts of interest for EPA administrators.

Civil liability would lead to efficient pollution levels. Pollution taxes are an economic solution to pollution. Command and control policy is an inefficient method of pollution control.

International Externalities

International externalities across borders are more difficult as the external costs are paid across borders. Countries have different legal systems and pollution policies. There are few international legal precedents that offer remedies for international externalities. There is no international civil liability. Cooperation among governments, industries, and citizens groups across countries is more difficult than within a country. Awareness of the negative externalities with the desire for goodwill and ultimate profit can be effective.

International externalities pose a problem in that civil liability and pollution taxes cannot be applied.

Different pollution control standards have been cited as an influence on the decision of where to locate branch plants. DCs typically have stricter environmental enforcement than less-developed countries (LDCs). Relaxed standards may attract industry. One goal of the WTO is consistent international pollution standards.

All pollution can be eliminated but the costs increase. Benefits must be weighed against costs. Pollution control adds to the cost of production. For LDCs, the cost of pollution control may outweigh the benefits of income. As incomes rise, the demand for clean air and water increases. There is evidence polluting production has been moved from DCs to LDCs.

EXAMPLE **9.6**   *International Environmental Agreements*

Various international treaties address pollution. The Basel Convention controls the movement of industrial waste across borders. The Biodiversity Convention is an agreement to preserve wildlife diversity. The Convention on International Trade in Endangered Species of World Fauna and Flora requires permits on trade in some species. The Climate Change Convention encourages countries to stabilize carbon dioxide emissions. The London Convention regulates dumping of hazardous waste at sea. The Montreal Protocol on Substances That Deplete the Ozone Layer phases out trade in some chemicals. The Nuclear Test Ban Treaty aims to control the production of nuclear waste. The International Whaling

Agreement has the goal of preserving whale species. The US has signed all but the Basel Convention and the Biodiversity Convention, making the rest the law of the land. Countries that have signed all agreements are Austria, Brazil, Canada, Denmark, Finland, Italy, the Netherlands, Norway, Poland, South Africa, Spain, Switzerland, and the UK. Japan has signed all except the whaling agreement.

Positive International Externalities

Positive externalities are benefits enjoyed by someone other than the decision maker. Positive international externalities cross borders. Education provides an example of a positive externality. LDCs send their brightest students abroad to study. International trade in education services has positive externalities.

Another example of an international positive externality occurs around oil rigs providing breeding grounds for fish in the sea. Other examples of products with positive international externalities are electricity, telecommunication, the internet, roads, water, sewer, radio, and television.

With a positive externality, *MSC* is less than *MPC*. Spillover benefits make social costs less than private costs. A firm that does not consider its positive spillover produces too little output. Those enjoying the external benefits would compensate the firm to increase output. The government can subsidize the firm to increase production. The aim of policy is to match *MPC* with *MSC*.

Positive international externalities require policy coordination between partner governments.

International Public Goods

Public goods such as police, national defense, public health, parks, roads, highways, docks, and safe air travel create positive externalities. Public goods suffer the free rider problem of people enjoying the product without paying. Markets fail to provide sufficient public goods because those enjoying the product do not directly pay. Nonexclusion is a characteristic of public goods.

Governments provide public goods that may be undersupplied especially close to borders. Parks close to a border might be used heavily by foreign citizens. Governments reduce the supply of public goods close to the border.

Some public goods cross national borders. Police, military, public health, ports, and airports benefit citizens of neighboring countries. International externalities and public goods raise political issues. There are efforts to integrate international electricity systems. International telecommunication and the internet face local protectionism. Highways that cross borders require international coordination. Defense spending in one country affects its neighbors.

The solution to an international externality or public good requires international political cooperation.

EXAMPLE **9.7**   *TRIPs and IPRs*

> The WTO oversees Trade-Related Intellectual Property Rights (TRIPs) to oversee international disputes on Intellectual Property Rights (IPRs). International trade and investment depend on a successful IPR system. The TRIPs agreement sets minimum standards and settles disputes imposing penalties on violators.

Section B Problems

B1. Find the revenue of the firm in Figure 9.3 without the pollution tax. Introducing the tax, find the tax revenue and firm revenue.

B2. Suppose pollution standards limit the output of the firm in Figure 9.3 to 10 units. Contrast this outcome with the pollution tax.

B3. Comment on the claim that "International pollution is harmful to the environment and should be totally eliminated."

C. INTERNATIONAL POLITICAL ECONOMY

Political decisions that affect economies are made by international organizations including the International Monetary Fund (IMF), General Agreement on Tariffs and Trade (GATT), WTO, and the World Bank. Political agreements and treaties are made between countries, especially trading partners. Income redistribution is the connecting thread in international policy.

EXAMPLE **9.8**   *Unfair Competition, But How Much?*

> US trade law allows countervailing tariffs imposed on subsidized exports from another country. The concept is fair value based on the cost of production. For imports causing material damage, duties can be imposed regardless of trade agreements. Kenneth Kelly and Morris Morkre (1998) find impacts of imports determined as unfair caused revenue of competing domestic industries to fall by under 5%.

International Political Economy and Income

International political economy attempts to influence income distribution across countries. DCs supporting the status quo are politically conservative. LDCs want to redistribute income with some calling for a new economic order.

Laws and customs inside any successful country are accepted and defined. Ownership of goods and resources is settled by property rights of the legal system. Damages are awarded if a firm or individual is negligent. Such everyday legal affairs are more difficult to settle internationally due to the lack of a legal system across borders. International legal practice is a developing field due to the increasing levels of international trade and capital.

International political economy is concerned with the laws and practices between countries that affect income distribution.

One example of an international political agreement is the Bretton Woods fixed exchange rate system of the 1950s and 1960s. Stable exchange rates allowed international trade and finance to grow steadily without the added risk of unexpected exchange rates changes. The US dollar was undervalued making US products cheap abroad and foreign products expensive in the US. One result was the US chronic trade surpluses during the 1950s.

Another international political institution is the IMF that manages exchange rates and overseeing finances. The IMF is a bank for government central banks, imposing constraints on government deficit spending.

Another active international political agreement is the GATT and its enforcement arm the WTO. The countries signed to GATT agree to lower their tariffs on a regular schedule. Governments are subject to protectionist lobby spending without GATT. Negotiations organized by the WTO to hear complaints on tariff disputes can impose penalties on countries violating the treaty. Decisions of the WTO have the status of international law.

Protectionism, foreign exchange controls, limits on international investment, and migration laws are tools of international political economy. Every government would like to use policy to distribute more income its own way leading to constant tension.

EXAMPLE **9.9**   *Regional Versus Global Free Trade*

Regional free trade agreements eliminating tariffs inside the groups might divert trade from the rest of the world (ROW). Kym Anderson and Hege Norheim (1993) show that trade is increasing both within and between regional blocs. Trade is returning to its high levels of the late 1920s before the protectionism of the Great Depression and World War II. Regional trade agreements seem to encourage the overall growth of trade.

International Public Choice

Governments might act on the principle of majority rule basing policy on a majority of voters. Given a choice of policies affecting trade, foreign investment, and migration, voters would want to choose policies distributing more income their way.

Voters may be inconsistent in their choices due to the paradox of voting. Suppose there is a choice between three restrictive policies,

* protect industries competing with imports
* restrict foreign investment
* restrict immigration.

Table 9.1   Policy Preferences

	Voting Groups		
	A	**B**	**C**
Protection	1	3	2
Restrict foreign investment	2	1	3
Restrict immigration	3	2	1

Suppose three groups of voters rank their preferences in Table 9.1. Each group knows how the policies will redistribute income, ranking the policies according to their own advantage.

If there is a vote between protection and restricting foreign investment, B restricts foreign investment while A and C choose protection. If there is a vote between restricting foreign investment or immigration, C restricts immigration but both A and B restrict foreign investment. Protection is preferred to restricting foreign investment, which is preferred to restricting immigration. With a vote between protection and restricting immigration, A chooses protection while B and C choose to restrict immigration.

The paradox of voting in public choice explains why politics seems irrational.

Voters seem apathetic but could be politically inactive because of rational ignorance. Becoming familiar with issues such as protection takes effort. Any benefit that would come from an informed vote may be outweighed by the costs of becoming informed. Trade policies have concentrated benefits and dispersed costs. The average voter may remain rationally ignorant on trade issues. Rational ignorance is tied to the free rider problem as the average voter may assume well-informed voters are likely to determine the outcome.

Principles of public choice are crucial for understanding political economy. International economic policy is open to inequities created by special interest groups and logrolling. Lawmakers logroll trading votes on issues. A representative from Iowa, for instance, may agree to vote for a new highway in Los Angeles provided the California representative votes for a new post office in Des Moines. Neither keeps the interests of the entire country nor economic efficiency in mind. International negotiators enter into similar agreements.

EXAMPLE **9.10**   *The Escape Clause*

While the US is committed to reduce protectionism by the GATT treaty, industries can apply for temporary protection. The US International Trade Commission (ITC) has the authority to award protection by the escape clause. Appeals examine available evidence on costs. If the ITC decides a foreign firm is dumping, tariffs or quotas are imposed on their products imported into the US. Gary Hufbauer, Diane Berliner, and Kimberly Elliott (1986) document the substantial gains from the escape clause in shoes, steel, televisions, bolts, and motorcycles.

International Political Economy and Growth

The developed North is abundant in capital and skilled labor, and the less developed South in labor and natural resources. For global efficiency, the North would specialize in services and high-tech manufactures and the South in labor-intensive manufacturing and resource products. There are gains in both regions with increased specialization and trade.

This international specialization is painful for the North's manufacturing. Imagine how protection looks to the LDCs as they try to specialize and export labor-intensive manufactures in the face of protection.

The opening of trade in manufactures remains a central issue in international political economy. Adjustment in the North may be less painful with gradual reduction of protection. Workers can receive trade adjustment assistance to retrain and relocate.

The WTO has fundamental effects on international political economy. Countries are committed to systematic reduction in trade barriers. The WTO has been successful in lowering tariffs.

The IMF is as a bank for national central banks. The IMF makes loans to governments that have foreign exchange shortages. The IMF has its own currency, the Special Drawing Right (SDR), accepted by central banks. The SDR is part of the monetary base of every country.

The IMF was formed at the end of World War II for stability in international monetary policy. Prior to World War I, countries were on the gold standard. Exchange rates were stable. The 1920s and 1930s were different with each country pursuing its own monetary policy. Exchange rates fluctuated hurting international commerce.

After World War II, countries met in Bretton Woods, New Hampshire, to promote cooperative monetary policy. Until 1958, the dollar was the stable international currency. The US government traded gold for dollars. The system began to unravel in the 1960s as countries pursued independent monetary policies. Germany revalued the mark while the UK and France devalued the pound and franc. Money supply growth in the US rose to finance the Vietnam War. In 1973, Nixon ended the fixed exchange rate system by pulling the dollar off of the gold exchange standard.

The IMF has since been a lender of last resort for central banks. The insurance provided by the IMF creates a moral hazard problem. If bailouts are readily available, central banks can afford to be more careless. The IMF has become heavily involved in loans to LDCs imposing policy on borrowers. The IMF provides a forum for international bankruptcy. The IMF can provide a stable anchor for floating exchange rates with the SDR. The IMF verifies accounting and financial reporting, provides financial data, and publishes research on international banking and finance.

EXAMPLE **9.11**   *International IPRs*

> IPRs involve protection of private property, one of the principles of English common law. Keith Maskus (2000) discusses international IPRs in the WTO negotiations. IPRs promote innovation because the owner enjoys monopoly power. IPRs may restrict the spread of technology. DCs have trade surpluses on IPR products. Patents and copyrights are involved with 20% of total US trade. The WTO hears complaints on IPR violations with international actions taken on CD piracy, pharmaceutical patent infringement, and pirated books.

EXAMPLE **9.12**   *Beef Sandwich Cut the Cheese and Mustard*

> Some cattle in the US are fed growth hormones. Scientific evidence finds no associated health problems for the cattle or for people eating the beef. Nevertheless, the EU bans imports of US beef on the grounds that it is unhealthy. The competition is certainly unhealthy for EU ranchers. The WTO has ruled that there is no reason to ban the beef. The US retaliated with tariffs on cheese, pork, and mustard from the EU.

Section C Problems

C1. Explain the roles of the major organizations of international political economy.

C2. Illustrate the pattern of trade and the gains from trade between the North and South with a production possibilities frontier for each region. Show the effects of Northern protection of its traditional industries. Discuss the income redistribution in both regions that would occur with free trade.

EXAMPLE **9.13**   *Mexico Libre*

> During the 1990s, Mexico made a dramatic switch in trade policy after decades of misguided import substitution and socialized industries. Mexico has become more open and competitive in free trade agreements with Chile, the North American Free Trade Agreement (NAFTA), Columbia, Venezuela, Bolivia, Costa Rica, Nicaragua, and the EU. Productivity and income are rising substantially in Mexico.

D. ECONOMIC INTEGRATION

A nation involves government, borders, territory, language, culture, history, flags, currencies, border patrol, and armies. International economics suggests there are gains to eliminating barriers to international trade raising the question how integrated a country should become with the ROW. International economic integration involves policy steps of free trade, investment, and labor migration. Through the political steps of economic integration global economic efficiency improves and the political characteristics of a country change.

The four steps of international economic integration are:

- Free Trade Area (FTA)
- Customs Union (CU)
- Common Market (CM)
- Monetary Union (MU)

EXAMPLE **9.14**   *The US–Mexico Connection*

The economies of the US and Mexico are intertwined with trade between the two involving intermediate products. The largest trade categories are transport equipment, computers, and electrical equipment highly traded in both directions suggesting an economic integration. The US also exports chemicals and machinery. The main other exports of Mexico are oil and apparel.

Free Trade Area

Protectionism is costly but difficult for governments to avoid because protected industries lobby politicians with cash and business deals. Some countries form FTAs eliminating tariffs on each other. The US, Canada, and Mexico agreed to lower protection in North America. The industries enjoying gains are export industries and those importing intermediate products, while import-competing industries must become more competitive to survive. Consumers enjoy higher income and utility.

This FTA is the first step toward economic integration, removing tariffs and the temptation of industry to lobby for protectionism with political payoffs.

Countries forming an FTA to eliminate the political economy of tariffs and protectionism.

A few tariffs remain between the US, Canada, and Mexico. The governments gave up some tax revenue as national incomes increase. FTAs take trade policy out of the hands of shortsighted politicians and industrial lobbyists.

There is concern that the world is breaking up into regional FTA blocs that might decrease global trade. If country A lowers its tariff for country B but not for C, some exports from C could be diverted.

NAFTA was a watershed as tariffs have been the hallmark of US trade policy. The GATT treaty and the WTO have slowly led the US toward free trade since World War II. Canada and the US were fumbling toward an FTA when Mexico approached them in the early 1990s. When NAFTA became a treaty, the Congress lost the leverage to exchange tariffs for lobby spending and associated private business deals.

NAFTA was renegotiated and labelled the US-Mexico-Canada Agreement (USMCA) in 2020. By either name, it remains a successful FTA. Environmental clauses monitor industrial pollution in all three countries. An FTA takes a big step away from the political economy of special interest lobbying.

EXAMPLE **9.15**   *Steps to the EU*

The EU has taken a half century to evolve toward free trade, free investment, and open migration. The EU including common taxes and commercial law slowly took shape in political steps:

1951	France, Germany, Italy, Belgium, the Netherlands, Luxembourg form the European Coal and Steel Community by treaty
1957	These six countries sign the Treaty of Rome to establish the European Community (EC)
1968	The EC removes internal tariffs and establishes a CU
1972	Denmark, Ireland, and the UK join the "snake" exchange rate
1985	Spain and Portugal join the EC
1986	Single European Act set up a CM
1992	Start of the CM with free mobility of labor and capital
1999	Start of the euro MU

Customs Union

The next step toward international economic integration is a CU with common external tariffs. The step to a CU is much harder because each country has different industries facing international competition from the ROW. An industry not facing competition from a neighboring country inside an FTA might from the ROW.

A CU is an FTA with common tariffs for the ROW.

Imports can jump tariffs in an FTA going first to the country with the lowest tariff and then shipped to the higher tariff country inside the FTA. If Germany has a 25% tariff on shoes from the ROW and France a 10% tariff, French importers will buy Brazilian shoes in France and ship them to Germany. An FTA must become a CU to avoid tariff jumping.

An FTA is easier to form between countries with fewer common industries because there is less pressure for protection. A CU is easier to form for member countries with more common industries because they can agree on protection from the ROW. The step to a CU makes forming an FTA a challenge.

EXAMPLE **9.16**   *Projected Gains From Integration*

Trade within the EU increases specialization across countries. Alasdair Smith and Anthony Venables (1988) project gains for German and Italian appliance industries, but losses in those industries across the rest of the EU. Winning industries are office machines, fibers, autos, and footwear. Predicted gains in income are less than 5%. These sorts of gains and losses at the industry level occur with overall increased income due to trade.

EXAMPLE **9.17**   *The CU of the EFTA*

The European Free Trade Association (EFTA) is a CU that includes Austria, Finland, Iceland, Norway, Sweden, and Switzerland. The EFTA is the largest trading partner of the EU followed by the US. The EU is by far the largest trading partner of EFTA. The relatively small EFTA gains due to improved terms of trade with the EU.

Common Market

The next step in international integration is a CM eliminating restrictions on the international movement of capital and labor. The EU is a CM with workers and firms free to move among countries. The EU also has uniform policy for migration and international capital with the ROW. The UK was a member of the CM but left over disagreement about the ROW migration policy.

There has been some discussion of a CM between the US and Canada. Both countries have relatively open immigration policies with little pressure on their border suggesting a CM would be feasible. Still, the political step of open the border to migration and multinational firm operation faces a political challenge as there would have to be common policies for the ROW.

Given the free trade and free factor mobility in a CM, the countries are almost economically integrated. The competitive markets across countries create similar living standards inside a CM.

EXAMPLE **9.18**   *The FTAA*

NAFTA established free trade between Canada, Mexico, and the US. The Andean Pact and Mercosur did the same for South America. There are also free trade agreements in Central America and the Caribbean. Efforts have started to tie them together in a Free Trade Area of the Americas (FTAA). While all countries would benefit through the free trade and investment, there would be losers in each country. Open migration policy will certainly meet political resistance in North America as will open investment policy especially in Latin America. This political resistance can be understood by factor scarcity and factor prices.

EXAMPLE **9.19**   *The CM of ASEAN*

> Workers and firms freely move inside a CM. The Association of South East Asian Nations (ASEAN) is made up of Japan, China, South Korea, and the "tiger economies" of Southeast Asia including Brunei, Cambodia, Laos, Indonesia, Malaysia, Myanmar, the Philippines, Singapore, Thailand, and Vietnam. The ASEAN is slowly progressing to become a CM with open migration of skilled labor.

Monetary Union

The final step of economic integration is an MU with the same currency across countries. The step to an MU is the most difficult because each of the governments will lose the power to print money. Government spending is popular while taxes are not, leading to constraints for a government balancing its budget. Printing or creating new money allows the government to spend more than its tax revenue.

Adoption of the euro in 1999 made the EU into an MU. Germany had low inflation since World War II while France, Italy, Spain, and Greece had high inflation. This wide difference in government styles made it seem unlikely that the euro would succeed. The euro ended the ability of governments to spend freshly created money bringing fiscal discipline to the high-inflation countries. These topics will be a main focus in Chapters 10–13 on open economy macroeconomics and finance.

EXAMPLE **9.20**   *Hey Buddy, Can You Spare an SDR?*

> The IMF is the bank for government central banks, essentially a bank for the banks of the banks. The SDR is the currency of the IMF for accounting defined in terms of a basket of world currencies. Central banks can borrow SDR from the IMF. If the SDR were introduced for international transactions, central banks would begin to lose their ability to print money to cover government deficits. Foreign exchange markets would become unnecessary. Ultimately, the SDR would be eliminating inflation as the IMF has no spending goals. It seems very unlikely that governments would relinquish the ability to spend more than collected in taxes.

Comparative Economic Systems

The difference between the economic systems of capitalism and socialism is ownership of productive capital and natural resources. Private ownership of factors of production and decentralized decisions characterize capitalism. Government ownership and centralized command and control characterize socialism.

During the last half of the 20th century, the Soviet Union, China, Cuba, Eastern Europe, and others had socialist economies based on material balance planning. Priorities for final goods and services were planned and allocated although a wide range of consumer products were produced and allocated by markets. International trade was controlled by the government and carried out largely by barter.

In contrast, the US is a capitalist economy based on market allocation. Production proving efficiency continues while inefficient activity ceases. The US is partly socialized with public housing, medical care, and support for some industries. Utility firms are government franchised monopolies. Nevertheless, markets determine most production and international trade.

Countries in Eastern Europe closed to international trade and investment since World War II have become open to international markets. Foreign investment and trade between the Western capitalist economies and socialist Eastern Europe is increasing. Russia has shaken off some of its socialist traditions but remains largely a command-and-control economy. China has a socialist political economy based on government control.

The LDCs in South America, Africa, and Asia are making their choices on economic systems. Market economies rely on free trade and investment. Socialist economies rely on government planning restricting commerce. The LDCs would benefit more from becoming market oriented if the DCs would eliminate tariffs on their exports.

Nations choose economic systems along the spectrum from market capitalism to command-and-control socialism.

Economic integration has been proceeding slowly worldwide with numerous FTA, CU, CM, and even MU agreements in effect. The move toward capitalism and economic integration in Central and Eastern Europe since the 2000s has had dramatic effects on development. The most powerful influences are increased investment and improved communication with trade continuing to grow. Most people in the world live in poverty and many others live by standards well below the DCs. Getting more of the world into the mainstream of competitive economic activity is the challenge for political economy.

EXAMPLE **9.21**   *The CCP in the WTO*

The integration of the very large LDC of China into the world economy is having large impacts. The Chinese Communist Party (CCP) runs the socialist economy that was totally closed to the world following World War II. China negotiated for 13 years before becoming a member of the WTO in 2001. The import competition from China has eliminated labor-intensive industries in the US and other DCs. The choice faced by LDCs and newly industrial countries (NICs) around the world is whether to become more socialist or market oriented.

Section D Problems

D1. Eastern European countries were integrated closely with Russia in the Soviet Union. Explain how they benefit economically when the Soviet Union disintegrated.

D2. Explain whether two countries could have free international movements of labor and capital without an FTA.

D3. Make use of factor abundance, factor intensity, and manufacturing wages to contrast US trade with Canada versus Latin America in Example 9.18.

EXAMPLE **9.22**   *Dump Dumping*

Antidumping laws are a relic of protectionism. No firm will sell its output at a loss for very long with competitive dumping to drive others out of business. The real issue is whether US industry and labor groups will face international competition. Antidumping laws offer protection that lowers productivity and income. Chile correctly claims US dumping laws are protectionist.

CONCLUSION

Free trade and investment remain the fundamental goal of international political economy. The trend toward international economic integration is improving living standards around the world. Strategic international economic policy aiming for short-term gains is best avoided.

Terms

Branch plant	Licensing agreement
Common market (CM)	Marginal social cost
Customs union (CU)	Monetary union (MU)
Externalities	Multinational firm (MNF)
Free rider problem	Paradox of voting
Free trade area (FTA)	Public goods
Horizontal and vertical integration	Rational ignorance
International externality	Transfer pricing
Joint venture	

MAIN POINTS

- MNFs increase international economic integration through trade and investment.
- International externalities call for economic policy coordination between countries.
- International political economy examines the causes and effects of political choice. Income redistribution is the main result of policy choices.
- Countries integrate through steps to promote trade and investment with each operating along the spectrum from capitalism to socialism.

REVIEW PROBLEMS

1. Explain why the US has many MNF branches in construction, business services, and oil production.
2. Analyze what happens with a multiplant firm similar to Figure 9.1 if costs are the same in each plant.
3. Explain how price discrimination between foreign and domestic markets could lead a firm to establish an MNF branch.
4. Analyze what happens to the vertically integrated MNF in Figure 9.2 if costs rise in the foreign country with a new labor contract in the electronic component industry.
5. Smoke from a factory in country A falls across the border onto country B. Explain three ways to control this problem.
6. How can a government host encourage the positive externalities that come with MNF activity? How will domestic firms react?
7. The EU acts like a single nation and the separate countries in Europe like the states in the US. Predict whether this sort of international cooperation can spread to Asia and Africa.
8. Illustrate North and South trade with offer curves including protectionism in the North. What happens to the volume and terms of trade if this protectionism is lifted?
9. Speculate on why economic integration has not been successful in Africa or Japan.
10. What would be the economic effects of an FTA between the US and Japan? A CU? A CM? An MU? What are the politics of such agreements?
11. Answer the same questions as #10 for the US and the EU.
12. Predict what would happen if the MU between states in the US were eliminated and each state government could print its own currency.
13. What would be the consequences for the US if an FTA was formed for North, Central, and South America? A CU? A CM? An MU?

READINGS

Jeffrey Arpan and David Ricks, eds. (1990) *Directory of Foreign Manufacturers in the US*, Atlanta: Georgia State University Business Press. Detailed data on foreign MNFs in the US.

James Buchanan and Gordon Tullock (1962) *The Calculus of Consent*, Ann Arbor: University of Michigan Press. The classic in public choice economics.

John Carrol, ed. (1988) *International Environmental Diplomacy*, Cambridge: Cambridge University Press. Articles on the international politics.

James Cassing and Steve Husted, eds. (1988) *Capital, Technology, and Labor in the Global Economy*, Washington: The AEI Press. Globalization of production and technology.

Harold Crookell (1990) *Canadian-American Trade and Investment under the Free Trade Agreement*, New York: Quorum Books. Changes for the two countries.

Stephen Easton (1989) Free trade, nationalism, and the common man: The Free Trade Agreement between Canada and the US, *Contemporary Policy Issues*. Free trade from a Canadian viewpoint.

Jeffry Frieden and David Lake, eds. (1987) *International Political Economy: Perspective on Global Wealth and Power*, New York: St. Martin's Press. Articles on international political economy.

Paul Gregory and Robert Stuart (2003) *Comparing Economic Systems in the 21st Century*, Cengage Learning. Perspective on different economic systems.

Gary Hufbauer and Jeffrey Schott (1994) *Western Hemisphere Economic Integration*, Washington: Institute for International Economics. Economic integration in North and South America.

Melvyn Kraus, ed. (1973) *The Economics of Integration*, London: George Allen and Unwin Ltd. Articles on economic integration.

Nora Lustig, Barry Bosworth, and Robert Lawrence, eds. (1992) *Assessing the Impact of North American Free Trade*, Washington: Institute for International Economics. Articles on assessing NAFTA.

Philip Martin (1993) *Trade and Migration: NAFTA and Agriculture*, Washington: Institute for International Economics. Migrant workers and NAFTA.

Tom Tietenberg (1994) *Environmental and Natural Resource Economics*, New York: Harper-Collins. Very good on production externalities.

MATHEMATICAL APPENDIX

A multinational firm (MNF) with horizontal integration has branches in the home and foreign countries with marginal costs MC and MC* that determine the optimal outputs Q and Q*. The MNF faces demand D(P) and marginal revenue MR(P) producing where MR = MC = MC* based on equating quantity demanded with the sum of outputs, D(P) = Q + Q*.

An MNF with vertical integration produces an intermediate good I* in one country for the production of the finished good F in the home country. The marginal cost MC_F of the finished good depends in part on the cost eP_I* of the intermediate good. Demand D_F and marginal revenue MR_F of the finished good determine output Q_F as well as Q_I*. The intrafirm transfer price P_I* of the intermediate good inside the firm is not observed and can be stated to minimize tax in the two countries.

The costs of production for MNF branch plants are based on taxes and policies in the two countries. The ability of footloose MNFs to choose locations introduces tax competition that lowers tax rates. MNF investment from other countries makes other home firms more competitive. Free Trade Areas (FTAs) include MNF policy.

A negative production externality E introduces a difference between Marginal Social Cost MSC and Marginal Private Cost MPC, E = MSC − MPC. The firm pays MPC but others must pay E with overproduction the result. The economic solution is the tax t = E, forcing the firm to pay the externality. Liability for damage can reach the same solution. When E crosses a border, the tax or liability solutions are unavailable but can be part of FTA agreements.

Public goods supported by taxpayers are available for anyone inside the country. When the benefits B of a public good cross the border, there is no basis for collecting tax T = B. The financing of such shared public goods can be part of FTA agreements.

International political economy includes issues of public choice as some groups win due to trade while others lose. Game theory quantifies the interdependent gains and losses leading to strategies for groups in policy negotiations. The examples of public choice negotiations in the text are transparent.

Four steps of international integration are FTA eliminating tariffs, Customs Unions (CU) avoiding tariff jumping, Common Market (CM) with free migration and investment, and Monetary Union (MU) with a common currency.

CHAPTER 10

The Balance of Payments

Preview

This chapter introduces the balance of payments (*BOP*) and its accounts that record international transactions for trade and investment. Trade deficits and surpluses occur when export revenue does not equal import spending. International lending and borrowing are important for economic growth and stability. *BOP* and the government budget may be interrelated. This chapter introduces some of the fundamentals of open economy macroeconomics including:

- Import elasticities and trade balance
- Different accounts in *BOP*
- Government budget and *BOP*
- Monetary policy and *BOP*

INTRODUCTION

An increase in the price of an import lowers the quantity of import, perhaps enough to lower import spending. As prices change, the trade balance depends on import price elasticities since the imports of one country are the exports of others. Changes in the prices of traded goods such as oil, food, and machinery can be critical for importers as well as exporters.

Trade balances can be positive or negative as countries may not spend on imports what they earn from exports during a given year. The current account (*CA*) in the balance of payments (*BOP*s) includes trade in goods and services plus net interest payments. A deficit in *CA* implies borrowing in the capital account (*KA*) of *BOP*. This chapter describes adjustments in *CA* and *KA*.

Fiscal policy refers to government spending and taxes in the government budget. Monetary policy refers to the government control of money supply. Fiscal and monetary policies affect not only the macroeconomy, but also the *BOP* accounts. This chapter lays the foundation for open economy macroeconomics.

A. ELASTICITIES AND THE TRADE BALANCE

Changing prices of traded goods affect export revenue X and import spending M. Imports and exports of merchandise enter the balance of trade (BOT). The balance on goods and services (*BGS*) adds trade in services (TS) to BOT, BGS = BOT + TS. The trade balance may refer to BOT or to *BGS*.

Changing Export Prices and *BGS*

An increase in the price of exports raises the output and export revenue but domestic consumers pay the higher price. In Figure 10.1, at the world price of $10, exports are 100 units of services S. The output is 200 with 100 consumed. Exporters in the small open economy can export any amount at the international price. If price rises to $12, domestic consumers lower consumption to 75 and firms increase output to 225 with exports expanding to 150.

Selling more services at higher price increases the export revenue. The level of exports rises by 50, raising the export revenue X from $1,000 to $1,800 as total revenue of domestic firms rises from $2,000 to $2,700. Domestic consumers must pay the higher price and reduce their level of consumption as a result. Consumers spend $900 on 75 units, less than the previous $1,000 spending on 100 units.

A higher export price is illustrated by the increased excess demand XD^* of the foreign country in Figure 10.2. The higher price in Figure 10.1 could be due to the increased XD^* in Figure 10.2.

An increase in the price of exports raises export revenue X and BGS.

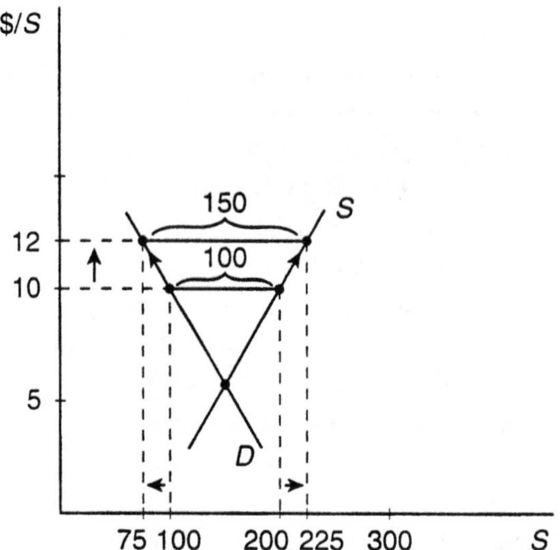

Figure 10.1
Increased Price of Exports
When the price of services rises from $10 to $12 exports increase from 100 to 150. Producer surplus rises as consumer surplus falls.

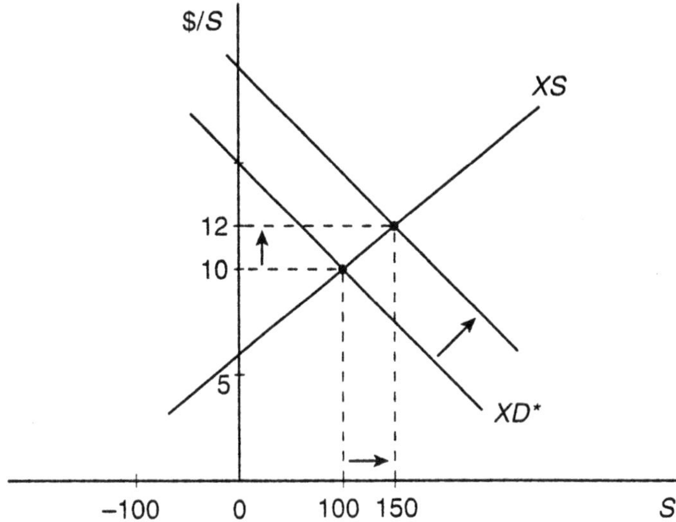

Figure 10.2
Increased Foreign Excess Demand
An increase in foreign excess demand XD^* raises the international price from \$10 to \$12 and the quantity exported from 100 to 150.

EXAMPLE 10.1   *A Price Taking Exporter*

Bangladesh has a very high export elasticity in textiles and apparel products according to Arvind Panagariya, Shekhar Shah, and Deepak Mishra (2001). A small increase in the price of these products leads to a large increase in exports. Domestic production increases substantially as domestic consumption falls leading to a very elastic effect on exports.

Import Prices and *BGS*

Imports are opposite to exports with an inverse relation to price. An increase in the price of an import lowers the quantity demanded and raises the quantity supplied by import-competing industry. Examples of increased import prices include the tripled price of oil during the 1970s due to Organization of Petroleum Exporting Countries (OPEC), droughts in Brazil driving up the price of coffee, and dollar depreciation during the 1980s, raising the price of cars from Europe and Japan.

In Figure 10.3, the price of imported manufactures increases from \$5 to \$7.50. The quantity demanded falls from 300 to 250 although spending by domestic consumers increases from \$1500 to \$1875. The quantity supplied domestically rises from 100 to 150. Revenue of domestic firms rises from \$500 to \$1,125. Import spending falls from \$1,000 to \$750, raising the *BGS*. Import spending would rise with inelastic imports.

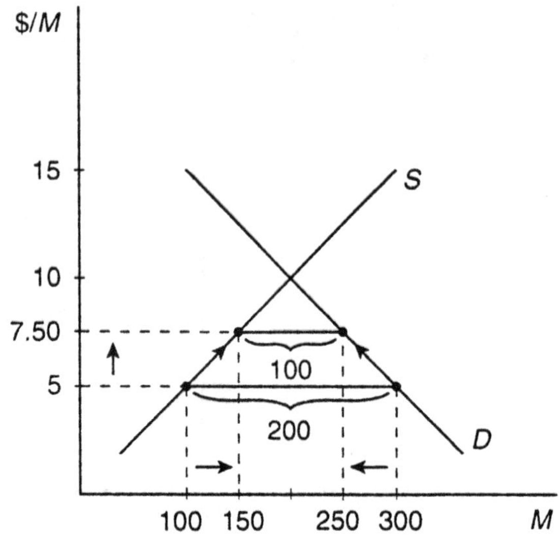

Figure 10.3
Higher Import Prices
An increase in the price of imports from $5 to $7.50 increases quantity supplied from 100 to 150. Quantity demanded falls from 300 to 250. Imports fall from 200 to 100. Import spending falls with elastic import.

Import Elasticity

If there is little opportunity to adjust to a change in the price of an import, import demand is inelastic. An increased price then raises import spending. During the 1970s, at the time of the oil price increases, consumers were driving large inefficient cars. Imports were inelastic leading to increased OPEC export revenue. With the consistently high price of oil, cars became much more fuel efficient. Houses were better insulated as heating and cooling technology improved. Oil consumption fell considerably as the quantity of oil supplied domestically increased. OPEC learned about import elasticity as their export revenue began to fall, as imports proved elastic.

The import elasticity summarizes the relationship between import prices and spending,

$$\varepsilon_{imp} = |(\%\Delta Q_{imp})/(\%\Delta P_{imp})|.$$

The symbol $\%\Delta X$ refers to the percentage change in X. Quantity Q_{imp} and price P_{imp} are inversely related. To find percentage changes, subtract the original level from the new one and divide by the average. In Figure 10.3, $\%\Delta Q_{imp} = (100 - 200)/150 = -0.667 = -66.7\%$ and $\%\Delta P_{imp} = (\$7.50 - \$5)/\$6.25 = 0.4 = 40\%$. The import elasticity in Figure 10.3 is then $|-66.7\%/40\%| = 1.67$.

If the import elasticity is greater than 1, the elastic import demand implies an increase in price lowers import spending. If the import elasticity is less than 1, the change in the level of imports is not large enough to offset a price change.

Countries have different import elasticities — higher for goods with more elastic supply, more available substitutes, and larger budget shares.

EXAMPLE 10.2   *BGS Deficit*

Since the 1970s, BGS of the US has steadily become more negative. Export revenue has fallen due to competition in machinery, transport equipment, and metals. Meanwhile import spending increased with the rising price of oil. The trade surplus in services is not large enough to offset the merchandise deficit.

The Terms of Trade and BGS

The terms of trade (tt) are the price of exports relative to imports. Consider a country exporting services in exchange for manufactures at the international price of \$5 for M and \$10 for S. The terms of trade are $tt = \$10/\$5 = 2$. The increase in the international price of S to \$12 in Figure 10.1 improves tt to $\$12/\$5 = 2.4$.

Suppose the home country increases its supply of services, shifting XS as shown in Figure 10.4. The country sells more services as exports rise from 100 to 140. The change in export revenue X depends on the foreign import elasticity. The price of services falls from \$10 to \$8 raising the export revenue from \$1000 to \$1120. Foreign import demand is elastic in this example.

Export revenue would fall if the foreign import demand were inelastic. Improved technology in service production or an increase in the number of firms will then lower export revenue X. If the level of exports rose to only 115 given

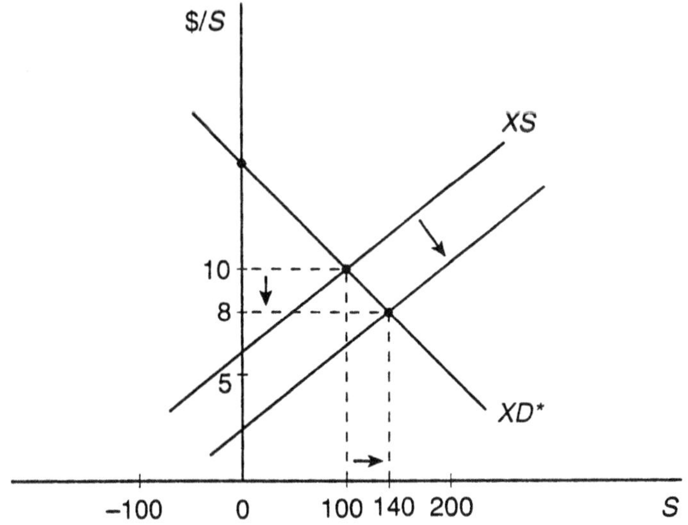

Figure 10.4
Improved Technology and Export Revenue
Increased excess supply of services drives down the price of exports and increases exports. The change in export revenue depends on foreign import elasticity.

the same price decrease, the export revenue would fall to \$920. This decrease seems paradoxical because improved technology and more firms sounds like good news for services production. This declining revenue summarizes the history of improved efficiency in the production of agriculture.

EXAMPLE **10.3**   *Markets Effects of the FX Rate*

Exchange rates have effects on many markets. Nathan Childs and Michael Hammig (1987) trace regional exports of corn, wheat, soybeans, and rice from the US between 1968 and 1984. While soybean exports are sensitive to the exchange rate, corn exports are not. Similarly, rice and wheat exports to Europe and Asia are sensitive while exports to Latin America are not. The effects of the exchange rate are felt after a few years in these markets because of planning, planting, and harvesting.

Section A Problems

A1. Based on Figure 10.1, suppose P_{exp} falls to \$8 raising the quantity demanded to 125 and decreasing the quantity supplied to 175. Diagram this change in the export market and find export revenue X.

A2. In Figure 10.3, suppose the quantity demanded falls to 270 and quantity the supplied rises to 130 when the P_{imp} rises to \$7.50. Find the import elasticity ε_{imp}. Explain what happens to BOT with this increase in P_{imp}.

A3. Diagram an example of improved technology in export production and the international price decline based on Figure 10.4 that does not change export revenue.

B. CURRENT ACCOUNT AND CAPITAL ACCOUNT

The two components of the *BOP* are *CA* and *KA*. *CA* records trade and interest payments, and *KA* international investment. Incoming cash is recorded as a positive credit and outgoing cash as a negative debit. Export revenue X is a credit and import spending M a debit.

Borrowing is a credit in *KA* although future interest payments must be made in *CA*. Wealth holders can accumulate assets. If an investor in the home country buys a foreign asset, a debit is entered in *KA*. *KA* reports international borrowing and lending.

EXAMPLE **10.4**   *Japan Inc.*

International trade and investment in Japan described by Naohiro Amaya (1988) has a unique structure. Savings rates are very high relative to other countries although young wealthy *shinjinrui* are beginning to spend more. Trade is a challenge as the *keiretsu* business system entails dealing in closed groups. The education system encourages discipline rather than innovation leading to difficulty for firms dealing with international competition.

BOP Accounts

BOP is the balance sheet for a country as the sum of *CA* and *KA*,

$$BOP = CA + KA$$

Transactions involving current goods, services, and interest payments enter the *CA*. Investment transactions involving borrowing and lending enter the *KA*.

The two components of *CA* are the *BGS* and Net Investment Income (NII) recording payments on previous investments,

$$CA = BGS + NII$$

BGS is broken down into BOT in goods plus TS,

$$BGS = BOT + TS$$

International transactions for business services in TS include transportation, insurance, engineering, construction, and banking. Figure 10.5 pictures the *BOP* accounts.

Since 1990, TS of the US has been positive and growing but the larger BOT has been negative and falling. The recent negative *BGS* of the US has been trending downward. NII is positive and increasing, reflecting the net incoming payments on foreign assets. The positive NII indicates more international assets are held inside the country than domestic assets held outside.

KA is the sum of direct investment (DI) and portfolio investment (PI),

$$KA = DI + PI$$

International investment spending by multinational firms (MNFs) in plant and equipment is DI due to control over operations. International investment by wealth holders who have no control over the foreign operation is considered to be PI.

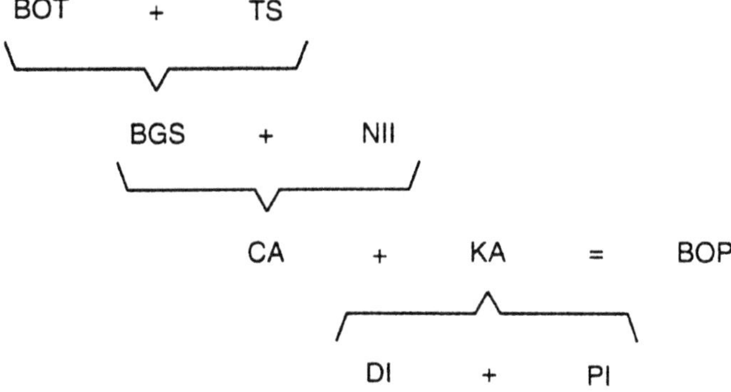

Figure 10.5
Components of the Balance of Payments

In practice, DI is reported for 10%, 25%, and 50% ownership of firms. Roy Ruffin and Farhad Rassekh (1987) find that DI and PI are perfect substitutes as an increase of $1 in PI results in a loss of $1 of DI. The implication is that the contribution to the management of branch operations goes beyond the percentage of stock ownership.

EXAMPLE 10.5   *Recent History of BGS in the US*

BGS of the US was nearly zero from 1950 until the 1980s when oil import spending led to a growing deficit that reversed to balanced trade by 1990. Increased imports of labor-intenstive manufactures then led to an increasing trade deficit that stabilized by 2010.

Trends in the US *BOP*

The most apparent trend in the *BOP* is the growing BOT deficit with the most recent surplus in 1975. Domestic import-competing industries use the BOT deficit to argue for protection. The economy has specialized less in labor-intensive manufactures and more in services. The offsetting surplus in TS does not make the news as much as the BOT deficit.

CA in the US is small relative to gross domestic product (GDP). Current account balances vary widely across countries, up to ±20% of GDP. From the 1950s through the 1970s, the *CA* of the US was less than 0.5% of GDP. The typical macroeconomics textbook included little international economics. During the 1980s, *CA* turned toward deficit peaking at 4% of GDP in 1987 with imports 11% of GDP and exports 7%.

KA of the US typically has a deficit in DI as US firms establish foreign branch operations. DI involves management with the investment. Recent surpluses in DI have been due to foreign MNF investment.

There is no clear trend since the 1970s in PI even though the US remains a safe haven for investors. The volatility of PI reflects increased competition in global financial markets. The New York Stock Exchange competes with financial centers worldwide as investors diversify portfolios across countries.

A *CA* surplus in one country must be balanced by *CA* deficits of others. Taiwan, Japan, Germany, and China have *CA* surpluses. One component of the recent *KA* surpluses in the US has been net official inflow with foreign central banks buying US government bonds.

BOP data are estimated by surveys that have large margins of error. The statistical discrepancy some years is as large as the *BGS*. Countries underestimate export revenue. Estimates of US exports to Canada are less than Canadian estimates of imports from the US. If that margin of error is applied to all trade, the *BGS* deficit disappears.

EXAMPLE 10.6   *FDI and International Capital*

> Foreign direct investment (FDI) has been slow and steady relative to PI as reported by Robert Lipsey (2000). During the 1980s, the US switched from the dominant source of FDI to the dominant host. For less-developed countries (LDCs), the main source of investment has been FDI. Worldwide FDI was about one third of total international investment in 1994. There is a good deal of FDI from Japan to low-wage Asian countries.

Section B Problems

B1. US firms own and operate branch plants in Central America where apparel is exported to the US by the MNF branch plants that manage, invest, and retain profit. Should this apparel be counted as imports?

B2. A Korean carmaker that exports to the US decides to invest $100 million to build a plant in the US. Predict the subsequent effects on the *BOP* and NII.

B3. Trade figures for Mexico in 1990 were $X = 26.7$, $M = 29.8$, TS $= -5.7$, NII $= 3.5$, and $KA = 8.8$ in $billion. Find the BOT, *CA*, and *BOP*.

EXAMPLE 10.7   *Components of the US BGS*

> The four components of *BGS* have been growing but import spending the fastest. The *BGS* was nearly in balance through the 1970s but import spending on goods began to accelerate with the rising oil prices in the 1980s. The North American Free Trade Agreement (NAFTA) and the World Trade Organization (WTO) trade agreements during the 1990s increased spending on manufactured imports. Exports of services are expanding but more slowly. The *BGS* was near zero through the 1970s before the dip in the 1980s followed by recovery to near zero by 1992 before a steady decline.

C. DEFICITS AND SURPLUSES IN THE *BOP*

> Countries borrow and lend in the international credit market. A CA deficit requires borrowing or selling assets in the credit market. A CA surplus is the opposite as the cash is loaned and assets purchased. Governments as well as private firms and individuals.

EXAMPLE 10.8   *Too Easy Debt for LDCs*

> It has been too easy for LDC governments to borrow. LDC debt totaled 35 times the GDP in 2000. A reasonable level of debt is about one year of income. Debt service payments of the LDCs account for one-fifth of their exports. Lenders

presume LDC governments will not default but the excessive debt will lead to bankruptcy.

International Debt and Equity

Households can spend more or less than their income for a given year. Firms borrow to invest in capital goods and train labor. Firms assume debt by selling bonds or create equity by selling stock. Bonds are a promise to pay a certain amount of cash at a future date. Stocks entitle a share of future profit representing ownership of the firm. Governments also have budget deficits funded by the borrowing of selling bonds.

A country is made up of its households, firms, and government. Deficits and surpluses in the yearly *CA* are expected. If a country spends more on imports than it receives from exports, it borrows or spends wealth. Borrowing is typical for young and growing consumers and firms given the potential for future income. International lending and borrowing facilitate growth.

EXAMPLE 10.9   *The Growing KA*

The US invests in the rest of the world as it invests in the US with *KA* reporting net investment. Both outflow and inflow have grown especially during the 1990s. US investors prefer FDI in foreign countries. Foreign investors prefer portfolio investment in the US. The *KA* has been positive since the 1980s implying a future decline in NII will. The incoming net investment raises US productivity.

The International Credit Market

A household, firm, or country making more income than it spends must save and become a lender. A period of individual saving typically happens at the peak of careers after education and before retirement. Firms with positive profit retain earnings to invest in new capital or become lenders. Countries with surpluses in their *CA* lend the surplus on the international credit market. The credit market for loanable funds involves lending and borrowing.

Households, firms, and countries will be borrowers or lenders. Managed debt with a purpose has potential to increase income for all.

People have different habits and desires regarding wealth accumulation. Some firms want to expand while others want stable production and size. Countries vary in their desire for growth and wealth. Financial planning involves defining goals for the future.

EXAMPLE 10.10   *Baby Boom CA and KA*

Baby boomers were born in the evidently busy years following World War II leading to the largest population group born between 1945 and 1955. Michael Bryan and Susan Bryne (1988) examine the baby boom influence on US trade and foreign investment. Boomers entered the labor force in the 1970s with high earning potential leading to *CA* deficits and *KA* surpluses. Expect the opposite as boomers retire.

A Borrowing Country

Trade deficits in the US ranging since the 1980s are evidence of a growing economy and international borrowing. Imported capital goods raise productivity and the standard of living. Growing countries borrow to accumulate capital goods with foreign investors seeing a good place for their funds.

A *CA* deficit reflects a *KA* surplus with a country borrowing to create debt or selling stock as equity. This debt and equity will be paid by future production. The ability to borrow indicates international investors see a country with high potential for the future.

EXAMPLE 10.11   *Government Spending and Deficit*

Each government decides on services to provide and levies taxes to pay for them. The ratio G/GDP is rising worldwide. Portugal, Italy, Greece, and Spain, as the PIGS, are famous for their very high G/GDP leading to government deficits and debt. The US has about the average G/GDP but large government deficits. Sweden and a few other countries have balanced their government budgets. A government deficit is financed by selling bonds as promises to pay or by creating more money supply.

Increased Foreign Assets

Foreign-owned assets in the US are increasing with recent *KA* surpluses as foreign investors buy US stocks, bonds, and real estate. Investors expect the US to grow reflected by the *KA* surpluses.

Foreigners own about 10% of the gross capital stock in the US. The US has historically bought more into the rest of the world than vice versa. MNFs continue to expand and invest around the world. International asset diversification has increased dramatically. The growing international lending and borrowing is a sign of a healthy global economy.

Section C Problems

C1. As the average age of the population rises from 30 to 50 predict what will happen to *CA* and *KA*.

C2. Explain whether Brazil or Austria would be more likely to have a *BGS* deficit.

C3. Diagram the international excess supply and excess demand for credit. What is the price of a loan? Show what happens if the borrowing country limits the quantity of foreign loans.

EXAMPLE 10.12   *The Ups and Downs of NII*

While receipts on US assets abroad have steadily increased since the 1960s, outpayments on foreign assets inside the US have grown faster. The net effect on the NII is a slow increase, stabilizing after the 1990s. The increasing levels of interest income in both directions reflect healthy economic activity.

D. EFFECTS OF FISCAL AND MONETARY POLICY

International trade and finance are affected by macroeconomic policy:

- fiscal policy as government spending and taxes
- monetary policy as control of the money supply

Fiscal and monetary policy affect the *BOP*. Economists differ in opinions about fiscal and monetary policy with some favoring active policy intervention to deal with unemployment and inflation while others favor market adjustments and a balanced government budget. This section introduces macroeconomic policy as it relates to international trade and finance.

Government Budget Constraint

The government produces public goods such as police, water and sewage, fire departments, highways, national defense, roads, health inspectors, and parks. Clean air, rivers, and oceans are also considered public goods. Governments play a positive role by providing public goods that might not be provided by the market economy. Markets fail to produce public goods due to free riders who do not pay and cannot be excluded. Decisions on government spending should be based on the costs and benefits of a program or project.

Taxes provide revenue for the government to produce public goods. When the government spends more than its tax revenue, the deficit creates debt if the government borrows by selling bonds. A bond is a promise to pay face value to the bondholder at a future date. Government bonds are bought by lenders willing to forego consumption in favor of the interest and higher consumption in the future.

Bonds are bought by consumers, firms, the central bank, foreign investors, foreign governments, or foreign central banks exchanging cash now for the promise of more cash later. If a bond is bought by a central bank, it pays with newly created money. A government deficit then increases the money supply, a form of monetary policy.

When a household or firm buys government bonds, private funds are transferred to the public sector. Government spending grows as consumption and investment spending fall. The demand for credit increases as the government borrows increasing the interest rate as the price of a loan.

The government budget constraint reflects its cash flows. Let B represent total outstanding bonds in the government debt. The government must pay interest expense rB where r is the interest rate. Total government spending is $G + rB$. Subtracting taxes leads to the budget deficit as $G + rB - T$ that must be financed by selling bonds ΔB or raising the money supply ΔM_S.

The government budget constraint is then,

$$G + rB - T = \Delta B + \Delta M_S$$

Tax revenue T comes mainly from income taxes and profit taxes in developed countries (DCs). Compared to an income tax, a sales tax would result in more saving investment and lead to higher economic growth. Tariff revenue is an important source of revenue for LDCs.

EXAMPLE 10.13   *International Stocks and Bonds*

The US holds a lower level of private assets in foreign countries than the foreign-owned assets in the US. Assets of the US abroad are in DI, PI, government bonds, and real estate. The Western Hemisphere has the largest share of bond holdings inside the US. The EU accounts for most of the stock holdings inside the US.

Fiscal Policy in the Open Macroeconomy

An increasing interest rate other things equal attracts foreign investment. The demand for home currency in the foreign exchange (FX) market increases, appreciating the currency favoring a trade deficit. This link between government and trade called the twin deficits has mixed evidence as other influences can dominate the FX market.

Government deficit spending can lead to a trade deficit if the higher interest rate attracts foreign investment appreciating the currency.

Figure 10.6 summarizes these channels of fiscal and monetary policy. Foreign purchase of government bonds can cause appreciation. Inflation resulting from expansionary monetary policy depreciates the currency. The effect of increased government spending on BOT depends on the composition of imports consumed by the government relative to the private sector.

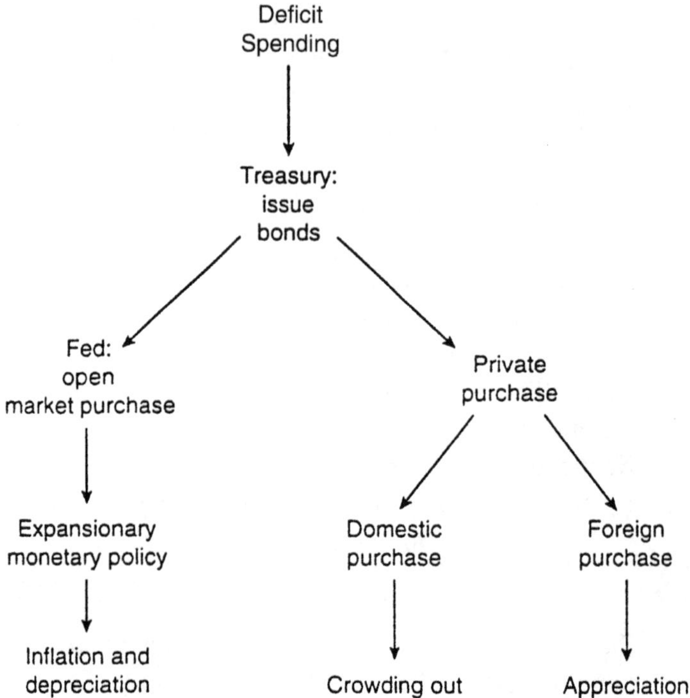

Figure 10.6
International Effects of Deficit Spending

EXAMPLE 10.14   *Interest Expense on US National Debt*

Interest payment on the national debt has risen to almost 20% of US government spending as taxpayers pay US bondholders who previously lent money to the government. About 10% of the national debt is held by foreigners.

Monetary Policy and the *BOP*

Monetary policy can affect international trade and finance. Inflation occurs when the money supply grows faster than output. Inflation can have real effects through the credit market and FX markets, but has little effect if correctly anticipated. Steady growth in the money supply leads to low or zero inflation.

Business cycles are alternating periods of recessions and booms. Foreign business cycles can affect the domestic economy through trade. There is disagreement about whether business cycles should be the target of policy.

Figure 10.7 shows an idealized cycle of recession and expansion. The frequency of a business cycle is measured from peak to peak. There are various theories of business cycles.

Central banks manage the money supply in attempt to influence the business cycle. Expanding the money supply encourages investment spending to ease a

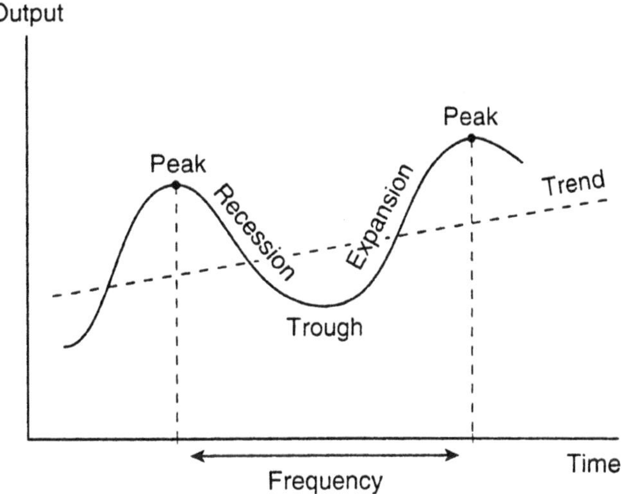

Figure 10.7
The Business Cycle
Output may cycle around the underlying trend. Expansions lead from troughs to peaks
with recessions leading back to troughs.

recession. The Fed can also lower the discount rate it charges commercial banks
for loans.

The goal of monetary policy should be a reliable money supply with zero
or low inflation leading to a stable currency on the foreign exchange market.
Steady growth of the money supply leads to a stable exchange rate. Traders and
investors are more successful when the price levels and exchange rate are stable.

Section D Problems

D1. Describe how funds are borrowed from a domestic and a foreign lender
when the government has a deficit. Explain how the foreign exchange rate is
affected in each case.

D2. When the government sells bonds to a foreign resident, what are the present
and future effects on the *BOP*?

D3. Explain how a government surplus might affect the BOT.

CONCLUSION

International markets for goods, services, and assets are steadily growing as
countries become integrated in trade and finance and more dependent on each
another. In most countries, the exchange rate makes the daily news, affecting
routine economic decisions, profit across industries, prices of goods and services,
and tourism. Chapter 11 studies the foreign exchange market.

Terms

Active versus passive policy	Export elasticity
Balance of payments (*BOP*)	Fiscal versus monetary policies
Balance of trade (BOT)	Government deficits and debt
Balance on goods and services (*BGS*)	Government bonds
Business cycles	Import price elasticity
Capital account (*KA*)	Inflation
Current account (*CA*)	Money supply
International debt and equity	Portfolio investment (PI)
Net investment income (NII)	Trade in services (TS)
Direct investment (DI)	

MAIN POINTS

- Import elasticities determine how changing prices affect the trade balance.
- *BOP* reports transactions for goods, services, and interest payments in the *CA* and for international investment in the *KA*.
- *CA* deficits are typical for growing countries that borrow to build their capital input.
- Government deficit spending reduces private spending affecting the interest rate and the FX rate.

REVIEW PROBLEMS

1. Predict what will happen to foreign excess demand when lower prices are expected for home exports due to improved foreign technology. Explain happens to international prices, the level of exports, and export revenue.

2. Explain what will happen in the international market for manufactured goods when domestic income rises. Explain what happens to the international price, the level of imports, and import spending.

3. Explain what happens to import spending if the increase in import price to $7.50 in Figure 10.3 causes the quantity demanded to fall to 250 while domestic quantity supplied rises to 116.67.

4. If the price of *M* is $5 and the price of *S* is $12.50, find the relative price of *M* as the *tt* for the exporter of *M*. Find *tt* if the price of *S* falls to $7.50.

5. Find the import elasticity and explain what happens to import spending when the quantity of imports rises from 100 to 125 with a fall in price from $10 to $8. Find the elasticity if imports rise to 110 and to 130.

6. Find the *BOP* account figures for the most recent year.

7. Explain current and expected future changes in the *BOP* when an investor in the US buys stock on the Tokyo exchange.

8. Suppose a US firm wants to open a branch plant in Costa Rica. It could transfer $1 million of retained earnings to a bank in Costa Rica to build the plant. Another option is to offer

stock worth \$500,000 in Costa Rica to raise funds. Describe the *BOP* entries for the US and Costa Rica under each option.

9. A saying is that the way to get ahead is to spend "other people's money". Explain the analogy with the *BOP* accounts.

10. Why do wealth holders diversify internationally?

11. Assume you were forced to live without borrowing or lending. How would your life be affected? How does this apply to countries?

12. During the expansion and recession phases of the business cycle, explain whether there would be BOT surpluses or deficits.

13. Justify whether you think Congress should consider the marginal costs and benefits of each newly proposed spending program.

14. Explain the effect reducing import tariffs and imposing export taxes on the BOT.

15. Predict how a war in the Mideast would affect the *BOP* accounts of the US.

READINGS

Robert Barro (1996) *Macroeconomics*, New York: McGraw-Hill. Analysis of monetary and fiscal policies.

John Pool and Stephen Stamos (1989) *International Economic Policy: Beyond the Trade and Debt Crisis*, Lexington: Lexington Books. Facts on government and international debt.

Francisco Rivera-Batiz and Luis Rivera-Batiz (1985) *International Finance and Open Economy Macroeconomics*, New York: Macmillan. Macroeconomics for an open economy.

James Rock, ed. (1991) *Debt and Twin Deficits Debate*, Mountain View: Mayfield Publishing. Links between the government deficit and the trade deficit.

World Economic Outlook, Washington: IMF. A bi-annual publication on monetary developments, current and capital account balances, interest rates, exchange rates, and the international oil market.

MATHEMATICAL APPENDIX

The balance of trade (BOT) in manufactures plus trade in services (TS) is referred to as the trade balance. In bookkeeping, export revenue X is a positive entry bringing in cash. Import spending M is a negative entry with cash leaving the country. The balance on goods and services is BGS = BOT + TS = X − M.

A trade surplus BGS = X − M > 0 means a net cash inflow from the trade of goods and services during the year. A trade deficit BOT < 0 implies X < M and a net outflow of cash.

An increase in the price P_X of exports raises the quantity Q_X of exports as the domestic quantity supplied Q_S increases and domestic quantity demanded Q_D falls. The BOT increases with an increase in P_X as $X = P_X Q_X$ increases.

An increase in the price P_M of imports lowers Q_M leaving the change in import spending $M = P_M Q_M$ ambiguous with P_M and Q_M moving in opposite directions. The import elasticity ε_M summarizes this property. Elastic imports $\varepsilon_M < -1$ imply an increase in p_M lowers M. Inelastic imports $-1 > \varepsilon_M > 0$ imply M increases due to an increase in p_M. The import elasticity includes the demand and supply elasticities.

The current account (CA) adds net investment income (NII) from payments on foreign assets to the BGS. NII is income from home-owned foreign capital K_F minus payments to foreign-owned capital K_H^* in the home country. Where r and r^* are the rates of return, $NII = r^*K_F - rK_H^*$.

The balance of payments (BOP) adds the capital account (KA) of the net flow of investment $KA = \Delta K_H^* - \Delta K_F$ to the CA. KA can be separated into direct investment (DI) and portfolio investment (PI). In principle, DI involves management or control by the foreign investor while PI does not. In practice, control of firms is difficult to assess.

If $CA < 0$, the country loses cash from trade and interest payments borrowing or selling assets with a capital account surplus $KA > 0$. The opposite occurs in a lending country when $CA > 0$ leads to a buildup of cash as $KA < 0$.

Summing the accounts, $BOP = CA + KA = (BOT + NII) + (DI + PI)$. If $BOP > 0$, there is net inflow of money into the country, while $BOP < 0$ implies a cash outflow.

Another important macroeconomic variable involved in the international flow of money is the government budget, $B_G = T - G - rB + \Delta B + \Delta M_S$, where $T =$ tax revenue, $G =$ government spending, $rB =$ interest payment on government debt B, and $M_S =$ money supply.

Changes ΔB in debt or ΔM_S in money supply must offset any difference between spending $G + rB$ and revenue T. If $T - (G + rB) < 0$, the government has a primary deficit that must be offset by borrowing as selling bonds $\Delta B > 0$ or by covering the spending with newly created money supply $\Delta M_S > 0$.

Selling bonds means $\Delta B > 0$ to generate revenue to cover deficit spending but adding future payments rB to the future budget constraint. Bond prices fall implying higher interest rates leading to foreign investment inflow that appreciates the domestic currency favoring a trade deficit. There is weak evidence of these twin deficits.

Increasing the money supply $\Delta M_S > 0$ has the disadvantage of inflation unless output growth keeps pace with money growth. Raising taxes T to cover the deficit is never a popular option.

Fiscal policy refers to the control of G and T as well as the financing ΔB involving debt and higher interest payments rB in the future. Monetary policy refers to ΔM_S to cover deficits and control inflation. The government budget B_G is included with the BOP along with output Y, the interest rate r, the wage w, and the foreign exchange (FX) rate as the major variables in macroeconomics.

CHAPTER 11

Foreign Exchange Rates

Preview

International trade and investment involve a buyer of a product or asset trading currencies in the foreign exchange (FX) market to pay the seller. Brokers and traders in banks and investment firms make the FX market. Traders want to hedge exchange rate risk in the forward and future currency markets. Currencies are traded in commodity markets. Transactions in the FX market add up to US gross domestic product every three days. This chapter covers the basics of the FX market including:

- Supply and demand of FX
- Floating versus fixed FX rates
- Arbitrage and risk in the FX markets
- Relative money supplies and FX rates

INTRODUCTION

Trading goods, services, and assets between countries involves buying and selling currencies in the foreign exchange (FX) market. Transactions exchange mediums of exchange in the largest market of the world.

Domestic buyers of foreign products and assets demand the currency supplied by foreign buyers in the FX market. Supplies and demands determine floating market FX rates. Some governments fix their fixed exchange rates with price controls leading to surpluses and shortages. Trading takes place in the forward and futures FX markets to avoid the risk of changing exchange rates.

The electronic global interbank network links private banks, brokers, traders, and speculators. Figure 11.1 summarizes these FX market links.

FX platforms on the internet allow small private traders into the market. Large-scale traders and investors buy and sell FX through banks. Brokers stay busy trying to match buyers and sellers. The FX market offers a higher return but also more risk than bond and stock markets. The future and forward exchange rates moderate the risk faced by traders and investors and provide a platform for speculators.

The three major traded currencies are the US dollar, EU euro, and Japanese yen. These rates float freely with no control by the three governments. Many

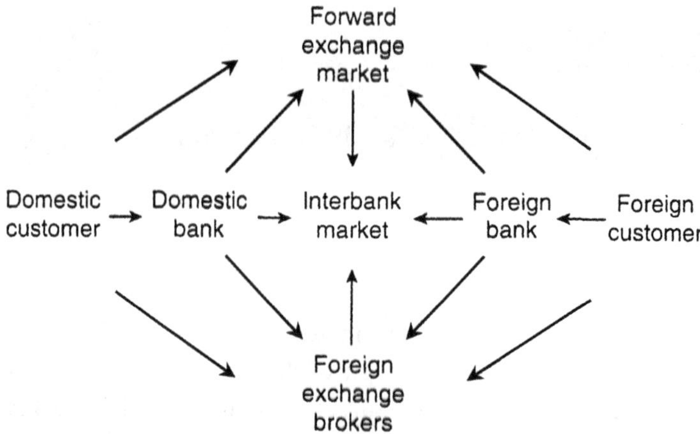

Figure 11.1
The FX Market

currencies define their exchange rate with a peg to one of these three. Other countries have fixed exchange rates set by government price floors and ceilings leading to surpluses and shortages of FX reserves. Binding constraints and licenses for FX trading provide profit to central banks. Parallel black markets operate for some currencies far out of line with their market value.

A government can undervalue its fixed exchange rate to raise the trade balance due to higher prices for imports and lower prices for exports to other countries. An undervalued currency is equivalent to a tax on imports. Other governments overvalue their currencies to encourage foreign investment but harming import-competing industry. Fixed exchange rates are not sustainable due to shortage or surplus of foreign currency.

A relatively high growth rate in money supply leads to depreciation. Differences in money supply growth rates explain long-term trends in exchange rates. Short-term changes in exchange rates are difficult to predict introducing a degree of risk or uncertainty to international trade and investment.

A. THE FOREIGN EXCHANGE MARKET

Supply and demand in the FX market are linked to export and import price elasticities. Depreciation refers to a falling price for a currency in terms of other currencies, and appreciation to a rising price. Exchange rates affect the trade balance over time depending on contracts of exporters and importers.

The FX Market

An importer sells domestic currency and buys foreign currency on the FX market. Consider a US importer buying a car from Japan. The importer can go through a bank to buy the yen to transfer to the bank of the Japanese exporter. Banks and import agencies specialize in currency transactions along with the paperwork of customs to pay tariffs.

Suppose the exchange rate between the dollar and yen is $/¥ = 0.008. Price is expressed in the home currency as with any commodity such as $/car or $/apple. At the exchange rate $/¥ = 0.008, one dollar will trade for 1/0.008 = 125 yen. If the price of an imported M is ¥625 the dollar price is $0.008/¥ × ¥625 = $5. The decision to import is based partly on the FX rate.

If $/¥ falls to 0.005 the dollar price of ¥625 falls to $3.13. The appreciating dollar lowers the price of the import increasing quantity demanded. If imports are elastic, import spending rises along with the quantity of yen demanded.

An inverse relationship between $/¥ and the quantity of yen demanded is shown in the FX demand in Figure 11.2. The decrease in $/¥ from 0.008 to 0.005 increases the quantity of yen demanded from 20 to 30 trillion. The downward sloping demand for yen is based on elastic imports.

On the supply side of Figure 11.2, Japanese importers buy US exports and sell yen. If the price of an export is $/S = 10 the price in Japan is 10/0.008 = 1250 yen at $/¥ = 0.008. If the yen depreciates to $/¥ = 0.005 the yen price rises to 10/0.005 = 2000 yen lowering the quantity of services demanded. If import demand is elastic, import spending and the quantity of yen supplied in the FX market fall. In Figure 11.2, the quantity of yen supplied falls from 20 to 10 trillion on the upward sloping supply curve.

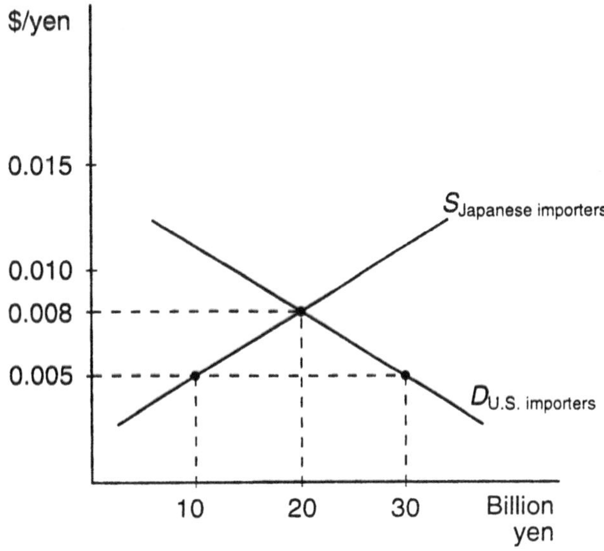

Figure 11.2
The Foreign Exchange Market
Demand D for FX comes from buyers of foreign products in the home country. Supply S is based on foreign buyers of home products.

The market exchange rate clears with the quantity of yen supplied equal to the quantity demanded. At the equilibrium $/¥ = 0.008 the quantity traded is 20 billion yen.

Supply and demand for foreign currency in the FX market determine the price of foreign currency in terms of home currency.

EXAMPLE 11.1   *FX Rates*

Exchange rates are traded on websites as well as in banks and at currency exchanges in airports and close to borders. In some countries, exchange rates are front-page news with busy exchange windows on the street. Examples of exchange rates are $/yen = $/¥ = 0.008 with one yen worth almost a penny, $/euro = $/€ = 1.09, $/pound = $/£ = 1.23, and $/COP = 0.00026 or $1 worth 3,846 Colombian pesos.

Depreciation

Depreciation occurs when the foreign currency price of the home currency falls. Depreciation of the yen refers to $/¥ falling. Depreciation lowers the purchasing power of the yen to buy products from the US and raises the purchasing power of the dollar over exports from Japan.

Shifts in the FX market are due to shifts in traded products and assets. Consider an increase in the demand for copper from Chile due to increased construction in the US. Figure 11.3 shows the resulting increase in the demand

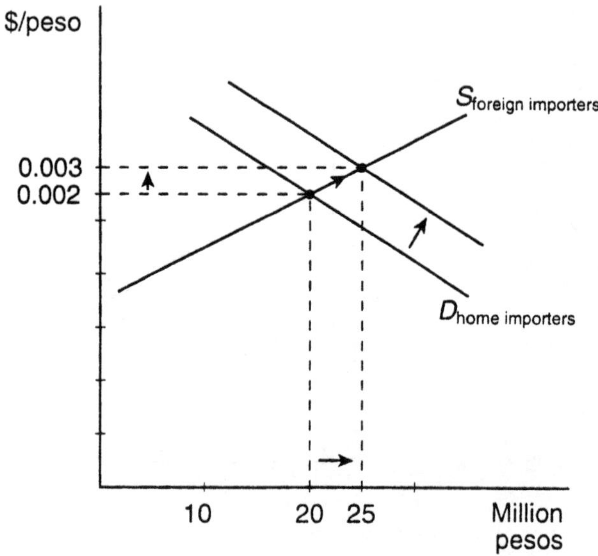

Figure 11.3
Increased Demand for Imports and Foreign Currency
The increased demand for imports raises demand for pesos and the exchange rate from $/peso = 0.002 to 0.003. The quantity of pesos traded rises from 20 to 25 million.

for pesos. The quantity of pesos traded in the FX market increases. The peso appreciates from $/peso = 0.002 to 0.003.

Increased demand for copper raising its price in the copper market is amplified by the dollar depreciation in Figure 11.3. Suppose the price of copper starts at 2000 pesos per pound or peso/lb = 2000. At the original exchange rate $/peso = 0.002 the dollar price is $4 per pound at $/lb = 4. The peso appreciation to 0.003 raises that dollar price to 0.003 × 2000 = $6.

The increased demand for copper also raises the price of copper in Chile, say from peso/lb = 2000 to 2500. The result would the price of imported copper rising to 0.003 × 2500 = $7.50 including the dollar depreciation.

Depreciation from any other source would also makes imports more expensive. Suppose the central banks and the IMF announce a plan to depreciate the dollar. If traders and investors expect dollar depreciation, demand for the dollar decreases and supply increases, depreciating the dollar right away. When the dollar depreciates, imports become more expensive for the US.

Dollar depreciation lowers import spending M given elastic imports. Dollar depreciation also lowers the price of imports from the US in other countries raising US export revenue. Depreciation then leads to an increase in the trade balance.

Depreciation raises the balance on goods and services (*BGS*) if imports of the home and foreign countries added together are elastic. This condition derived by economists Alfred Marshal and Abba Lerner holds, given enough time for markets to adjust to price changes.

The Marshall–Lerner condition is that depreciation raises the trade balance.

EXAMPLE 11.2   *A Yen for the ¥*

The Japanese yen has appreciated over 200% since the 1970s with $/¥ rising from 0.003 to 0.01. The reasons are the slower growth of the money supply in Japan given its balanced government budget. Meanwhile, the US has government deficit spending supported by fast money supply growth. Holding yen is more attractive than holding dollars.

Depreciation and the balance on goods and services

The exchange rate affects the trade *BGS*,

$$BGS = p_X\, q_X - e p_M^*q_M.$$

The average price of exports is p_X = $/export. Imports priced in the average foreign currency F at p_M^* = F/import are converted to their price in the domestic currency by the exchange rate e = $/F$.

Depreciation as an increase in the price of foreign currency e would increase import spending depending on how much imports q_M fall due to their higher price. The foreign currency price $p_M{}^*$ would also fall due to decreased demand for foreign country exports. Depreciation raises q_X due to the lower price of home exports in the foreign currency country. The dollar price of exports p_X would also increase due to increased demand. The overall effect of e on BGS considering all elasticities is generally positive given enough time for market adjustments.

Depreciation raises the trade balance if the export elasticity plus the negative of the import elasticity is greater than one.

The large exchange rate swings since the 1980s provide ample experiments of depreciation and trade balance adjustments. These effects vary across countries and over time. Overall, the evidence suggests depreciation raises the trade balance.

The J Curve

Depreciation requires time to have a positive effect on the trade balance. A temporary deficit is likely due to the higher domestic currency price of imports at least for a surprise depreciation. The J curve tracks how the trade balance reacts to depreciation over time.

Figure 11.4 illustrates a J curve for depreciation at time d. Contracts for delivery at time d are based on the expected exchange rate. During this contract period, the BGS deficit increases. With quantities fixed by contract, depreciation lowers the trade balance due to the higher price of imports. Over time, the level of imports falls as the level of exports rises. During the pass-through period, the trade balance increases.

Depreciation may cause a temporary trade deficit due to set contracts before it raises the trade balance.

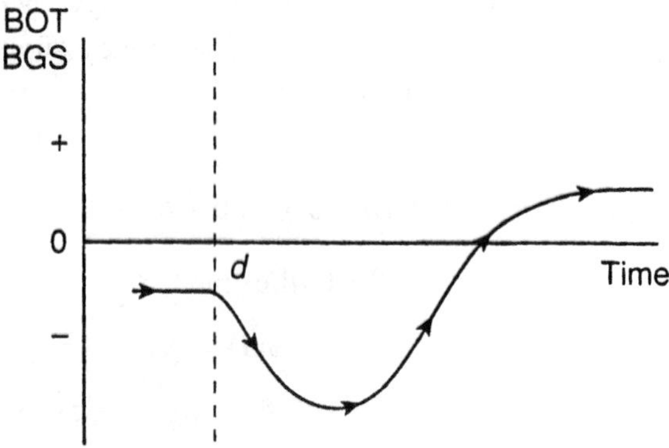

Figure 11.4
The J Curve of a Depreciation
A surprise depreciation at time d temporarily worsens the trade balance given contracts for export and import. Over time, export revenue rises and import spending falls.

EXAMPLE 11.3   *Appreciation and Manufacturing Industries*

The exchange rate affects the price of exported manufactures but also the price of imported intermediate products. Between 1995 and 1998, the dollar appreciated by almost one third against trading partners. Linda Goldberg and Keith Crockett (1998) examine the effects on exports as well as input purchases across US manufacturing industries. Those most hurt were instruments, machinery and equipment, electronic and electrical equipment, tobacco products, and chemicals. Appreciation benefited industries that import intermediate products such as leather, refined petroleum, printing and publishing, fabricated metals, and furniture and fixtures.

Market Shifts and the Exchange Rate

Underlying shifts in supply and demand across trading countries affect their exchange rate. For instance, rising income in the foreign country raises import demand leading to an increase in supply of foreign currency in the FX market. Figure 11.5 shows this increased supply of foreign currency depreciates the Brazilian real (pronounced *re-al*) and increase in the level trading in the FX market. The depreciation raises prices of imports in Brazil, reinforcing underlying increase in the product markets.

The balancing effect of the FX market provides more reason to allow it to operate freely. Changes in the exchange rate work in the same direction as changes in underlying market prices.

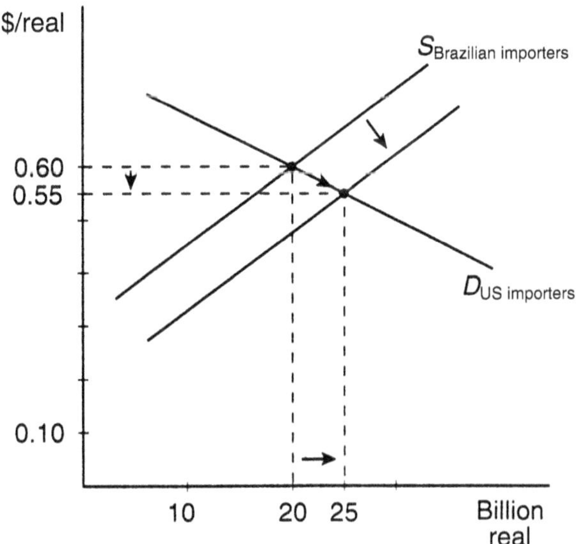

Figure 11.5
Increased Supply of Foreign Currency
This increase in the supply of Brazilian real comes from increased demand for US exports in Brazil. The real falls from $0.60 to $0.55 as the quantity traded rises. Appreciation rises the price of US exports in Brazil reinforcing price effects in the product markets.

EXAMPLE 11.4   *FX Rate Effects on Local Industries*

Between 1975 and 1990, the dollar exchange rate had periods of large swings due to the energy crisis and erratic monetary policies. Henry Thompson and Kamal Upadhyaya (1998) examine the effects of exchange rate changes on chemicals and primary metals in Alabama. The chemicals industry producing petrochemicals exports a quarter of its output. Primary metals exports about a fifth of its output. Chemical output declined with dollar appreciation between 1981 and 1985, followed by an increase with depreciation from 1985 to 1990. Primary metals production rebounded with the dollar depreciation following 1985. Over the sample, every 10% appreciation lowered chemicals output by 2.8% and price by 1.4%, and metals output by 2.1% and price by 2.9%. In the other direction, dollar depreciation of 10% raised revenue of chemicals by 4.2% and metals by 5.0%.

Section A Problems

A1. Find the dollar prices of imported cars costing ¥880,000 when the $/¥ falls from 0.009 to 0.008. Explain whether this is dollar appreciation or depreciation.

A2. Illustrate the FX market for the euro with the equilibrium exchange rate $/€ = 0.85. Suppose the US announces it will eliminate all restrictions on European imports after six months. Diagram the immediate effects on the exchange rate. Explain what happens to the price of EU products in the US.

A3. Suppose a US petrochemical company discovers an efficient way to export liquid petroleum gas to Europe. Illustrate the effect on the $/€ market.

A4. Explain the effect of a surprise appreciation of the yuan on the trade surplus in China with J curve adjustment.

B. FIXED EXCHANGE RATES

Governments try to influence international trade and investment for a variety of political and economic reasons. The government sets an exchange rate floor or ceiling with a fixed exchange rate to control prices of exports, imports, and international assets. This section examines:

- Fixed exchange rates and FX reserves
- FX licenses
- Black market exchange rates
- The pros and cons of fixed exchange rates

Fixed Exchange Rates

Governments overprice or underprice their currencies for various reasons. An overpriced currency makes imports cheaper for consumers and firms importing

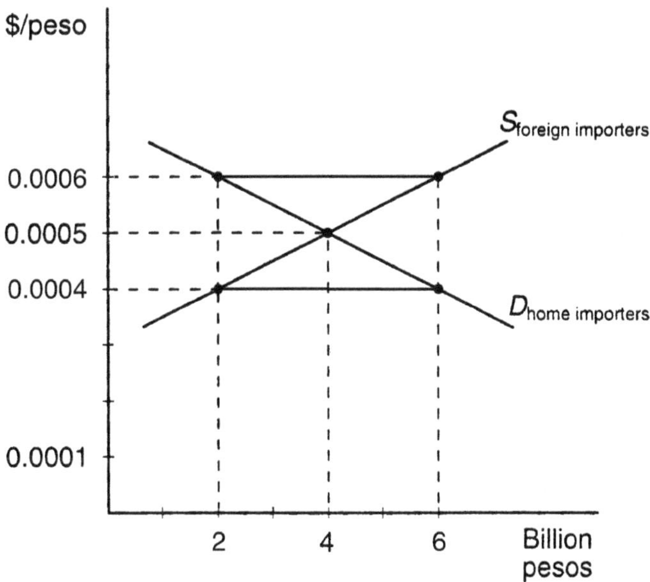

Figure 11.6
A Fixed Exchange Rate
At the fixed exchange rate $/peso = 0.0006, the peso central bank reduces its dollar reserves by $2.4 million. At the fixed exchange rate $/peso = 0.0004, the central bank dollar reserves increase by $1.6 million.

intermediate products and capital goods. An underpriced currency leads to a trade surplus with increased FX reserves for the government central bank. In Figure 11.6, the market equilibrium exchange rate is $/peso = 0.0005.

Suppose the peso government fixes the exchange rate at 0.0006. The result is a surplus of 4 billion pesos equivalent to a shortage of $2.4 million. The peso central bank could sell its dollar FX reserves. Supporting the peso by depleting FX reserves implies a loss for the peso government as the price of dollars is too low. The artificially high exchange rate will collapse as the central bank depletes its dollar reserves.

EXAMPLE 11.5   *Rigged FX Rates*

Most governments exercise the monopoly power of a fixed exchange rate. About 150 currencies are fixed, with 50 tied to the dollar, euro, or yen, and another 50 to a basket of currencies. The monopoly government bank controls FX trade to maximize profit as a source of tax revenue.

Suppose the peso government chooses to undervalue the peso in Figure 11.6 to stimulate exports. The undervalued $/peso = 0.0004 lowers the dollar price of exports from the peso country. At that fixed rate, the peso central bank would increase its FX reserves absorbing the surplus dollars due to the trade surplus. The expensive imports in the peso country make the undervalued exchange rate unpopular suggesting it will not last long.

> *Fixed exchange rates help some groups in the economy and hurt others. Fixed exchange rates cannot last indefinitely.*

EXAMPLE 11.6   *Views on the FX System*

Differing views on exchange rates are expressed by economists in the *Journal of Economic Perspectives* (Winter, 1988). Ronald McKinnon favors fixed exchange rates managed by central bank focus on stability. John Williamson agrees that exchange rate swings are disruptive and favors exchange rate target zones managed by central bank trading. Rudiger Dornbusch thinks the market rates work well making the point that there are no inherently correct levels to fix or target exchange rates.

FX Licenses

One way to sustain the FX price of a currency without having to deplete or build FX reserves is to limit imports with foreign exchange licenses. Figure 11.7 shows a license for 2 billion pesos making peso supply perfectly inelastic at that level. Importers in the peso country are unable to buy more dollars. If demand for pesos falls, the government would lower the number of licenses to keep the value of the peso at $0.0006.

The license gives the central bank a margin buying dollars at a low price from US importers and selling dollars at a higher price to exporters in the peso country. In Figure 11.7, the peso bank buys dollars at pesos/$ = $1/e$ = 1667 and sells dollars at pesos/$ = 2500. The central bank creates pesos as well.

Over time, this rigged foreign exchange market becomes unpopular. Importers pay higher prices with a deadweight loss in the import market spending 0.8 million pesos. Exporters too are frustrated with export revenue of 1.2 million pesos. With a market exchange rate, import spending and export revenue would jump to 2 million pesos.

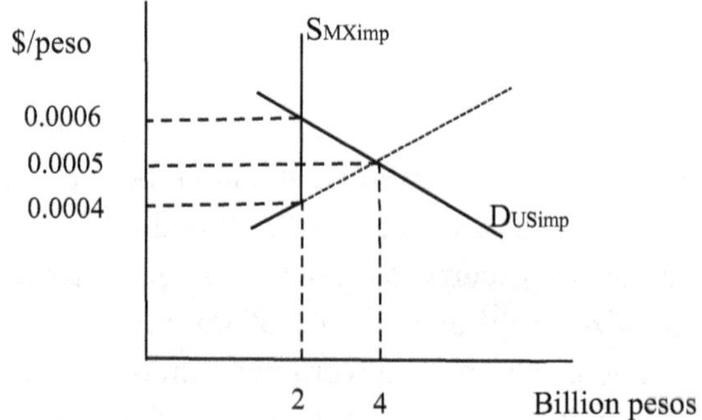

Figure 11.7
FX License
The peso government licenses the right to sell pesos at 2 billion creating a margin between the exchange rate for importers and exporters.

To support their currency, the peso government can also curtail foreign tourism by restricting the amount of cash citizens can take when leaving the country or limiting withdrawal from foreign ATMs. Another option is to limit the purchase of foreign assets.

EXAMPLE 11.7   *Devaluation and the Balance of Trade*

A decrease in a fixed exchange rate is called a devaluation. Governments must reset fixed exchange rates when inflation rates vary. Daniel Himarios (1989) reports on the effects of 60 devaluations of fixed exchange rates prior to 1973. Devaluations raised the trade balance in 80% of the devaluations with immediate increases followed by lagged effects over a few years. Similar results occurred for 15 countries with fixed exchange rates between 1975 and 1984. In Salvador, France, Greece, and Zambia, there were J curves with immediate trade deficits followed by surpluses. Murli Buluswar, Henry Thompson, and Kamal Upadhyaya (1996) find there were no effects of devaluations in India.

Black Market Exchange Rates

Black market rates arise if a fixed exchange rate is far enough from the underlying market rate to make the penalty if caught worth the risk. Black market rates tempt tourists, importers, and investors when fixed rates are too far out of line.

An artificially high fixed rate would fall ensuring nobody will want to hold the currency for a long time. Merchants dealing with tourists might be happy to accept foreign currency in the black market depending on the penalties and chances of being caught.

Black market transactions can be unofficially allowed in a parallel exchange market. The official market then operates alongside the black market with some transactions settled at the official rate. Others enjoy the higher purchasing power of a hard currency.

EXAMPLE 11.8   *Appreciation and Labor Demand*

The strong dollar appreciation from 1980 to 1985 reduced import prices and labor demand across 38 import-competing industries in the US as shown by Ana Revenga (1992). The falling labor demand lowered the wage by 1.5% even with the labor force falling 6%.

Fixed Versus Floating

While floating exchange rates introduce risk and uncertainty, fixed exchange rates have issues as well. An artificially high rate requires the central bank to deplete its foreign exchange reserves at a loss. An artificially low rate frustrates consumers of imports and expands foreign exchange reserves. The debate over fixed versus floating exchange rates has a long history.

With the gold standard of the late 1800s, currencies were defined in terms of gold implying stable exchange rates if the governments traded gold for their currency at the set price. The 20th century brought two World Wars and a long depression disrupting international trade and investment. The Bretton Woods fixed exchange rate system introduced at the end of World War II, endured with the US the dominant economy and the dollar defined in terms of gold. The International Monetary Fund (IMF) monitored the central bank behavior. Low US money supply growth in the US led to a steady price level and stable exchange rates.

The jump in oil prices during the 1970s and 1980s led to large current account deficits for oil importers. Increased government spending eased the resulting recessions but led to inflation. The Bretton Woods fixed exchange rate system collapsed. The German mark and Japanese yen provided some stability with their low money supply growth and low inflation.

The floating dollar dropped 13% from 1974 to 1979 before rising 63% by 1985 and then falling 62% by 1990 relative to trading partners. Starting at $/yen = 0.05 in 1974, a Japanese car priced at ¥2,000,000 was priced at $20,000 before jumping to $22,600 and then falling to $14,200 only to shoot back to $23,000.

The last three decades of the 20th century were characterized by LDCs defaulting on their government debt, the emergence of Japan, the collapse of the Soviet Union, the euro monetary union, expanding foreign investment, large differences in inflation, and wild FX movements. The growing level and intensity of international transactions eliminated any chance to return to a system of fixed or target zone exchange rates.

The active FX markets of the early 21st century also eliminated management by central banks. Failed attempts by central banks to control exchange rates only increased the level of uncertainty in the markets. Each country chooses its money supply growth determining its inflation rate through a political and economic process. Depreciation and appreciation of floating exchange rates reflect the underlying money supply growth and inflation.

EXAMPLE 11.9   *Economist Views on FX Rate Policy*

Peter Kenen argues governments should intervene to stop runs on FX markets. Ronald McKinnon argues for active management of FX rates. John Williamson favors active intervention and coordinated central bank action. Jacob Frankel believes reliable fiscal and monetary policies should be the focus. Martin Feldstein trusts the competitive FX market to reveal currency values.

Section B Problems

B1. China undervalues its yuan currency. Diagram the FX market for yuan with a fixed exchange rate. Explain whether the undervalued yuan is a price floor or price ceiling. Explain the resulting change in foreign exchange reserves in China.

B2. How could the Chinese government use FX licensing to keep the yuan undervalued? How could it make profit from the license?

B3. Justify your opinion on fixed versus floating exchange rates.

C. FOREIGN EXCHANGE TRADING

Traders in the FX market aim to buy at a low price and sell at a higher price. Topics in this section include how traders form the FX rate expectations, exchange rate stability, and the stabilizing influence of triangular arbitrage.

FX Rate Expectations

Expected price changes are self-fulfilling in FX markets as in all markets. If a currency is expected to appreciate, potential buyers buy it now increasing demand while potential sellers wait to sell later, decreasing the supply. The increased demand and decreased supply appreciate the currency right away.

A lot of the daily FX rate changes is due to changing expectations. Some traders are looking for short-term gains. Others focus on long-term gains favoring bonds or stocks in currencies expected to appreciate. Investors with cash in high-inflation countries switch to low-inflation countries to avoid their holding the depreciating currency.

Market expectations explain the dollar depreciation that started in 1985 when the central banks of Germany, France, Britain, Japan, and the US announced they would act together to sell dollars. Investors and traders expected the dollar to depreciate, leading to the depreciation. While the volume of central bank dollar sales ended up being trivial compared to the size of the market, the change in expectations led to decreased demand and increased supply on the FX market.

In 1989, the dollar appreciated even though the dollar sales by central banks from their FX reverses continued. The central bank action was shown to be pointless. Ultimately the differences in money supply growth across countries determined inflation rates and FX rates. Currencies with higher inflation rates ultimately depreciate in the FX market.

EXAMPLE 11.10   *Chartists Versus Fundamentalists*

Chartists look for predictable FX rate behavior in time series including trends, break points, shoulders, cliffs, spikes, and bubbles. Fundamentalists focus on the news relying on the underlying theory and empirical analysis. An increase in the relative growth rate of a money supply leads to depreciation of that currency. Jeffrey Frenkel and Kenneth Froot (1990) report there are more chartists than fundamentalists among FX traders. Most FX trading takes place between large banks and investment houses although the market share of small traders is increasing.

FX Rate Speculation

Debate continues over speculation and erratic behavior in FX markets. Milton Friedman made the point during the debate over terminating the Bretton Woods fixed exchange system that speculative trading would stabilize the FX market. Profitable speculators diminish exchange rate volatility. Unprofitable speculators disappear.

Figure 11.8 shows the effect of profitable speculation in the market for yen at two different times. The \$/¥ exchange rate is e_0 at time 0 and e_1 at a later time 1. The shift in the market is the decreased supply from S_0 to S_1.

Speculators who correctly anticipate the market shift will buy yen now at e_0 and sell them later at e_1 making a profit. These speculators dampen exchange rate variation as the increase in D_0 raises e_0 and the increase in S_1 lowers e_1. Any unprofitable speculators would increase e variation but soon be out of business. Profitable speculation transfers the yen from a time when they are plentiful to a time when they are scarce.

Detractors argue speculators jump on bandwagons creating speculative bubbles. If the yen is appreciating, speculators buy yen expecting the trend to continue pushing the yen faster and further. When the climb stops, speculators all rush to sell yen causing a crash. Strategic traders want to appear to be anticipating a boom only to create a bubble and sell at the peak.

While the debate will continue, exchange rate speculation will remain an important part of the international economy. Fixed exchange rates and central bank management also cause speculation with all of it in one direction resulting in sharp collapses or explosions. The floating exchange rate system, based on a competitive market with many buyers and sellers, remains the only viable option.

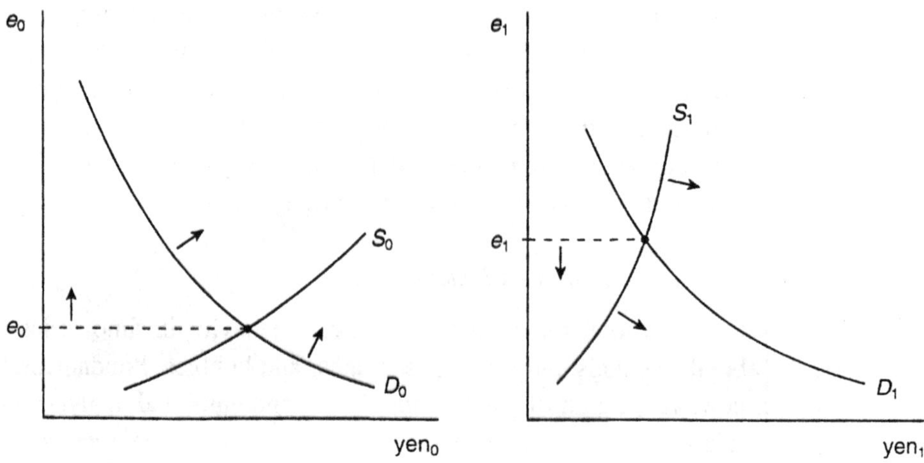

Figure 11.8
Profitable Speculation
Speculators at time 0 who anticipate the increase to e_1 buy yen increasing D_0 and e_0. At time 1 they sell yen increasing S_1 and lowering e_1. Exchange rate variation diminishes.

EXAMPLE 11.11   *The Currency Game*

> The top ranked investment fund managers actively trade currencies reporting sizeable gains and losses. Trading currencies is riskier with a higher average return than trading bonds and stocks. Exchange rates depend on the politics of money supply control across central banks with differing in goals and modes of operation. International politics can also affect FX rates.

EXAMPLE 11.12   *FX Intervention by the Fed*

> Trading of FX reserves by the Federal Reserve Bank is a small fraction of the FX market. The New York Fed summarizes its FX intervention in an abridged report from 1998:
>
>> The Fed successfully intervened in the FX market on June 17 buying yen worth $833 million. The yen fell 4.1% against the dollar during the previous quarter. The intervention was carried out in coordination with the central bank of Japan. As a result, the yen strengthened.
>
> The report could mention the daily volume of trading more than 100 times its yen purchase. The Fed had $14 billion of FX reserves at the time, a drop in the daily bucket of FX transactions. The only hope is a psychological effect on traders.

Stability of Exchange Markets

The slopes of supply and demand in the FX market depend on import elasticities. The evidence suggests import demand is elastic given enough time to adjust to price changes. The FX market may be unstable due to inelastic imports over short time periods.

The FX market in Figure 11.2 has a stable equilibrium. An exchange rate above \$/¥ = 0.008 implies a surplus of yen that leads to a falling rate. At \$/¥ = 0.009, expanding yen inventories lead to selling bidding price down. At \$/¥ = 0.007, buyers would line up for yen and sellers would raise the rate.

An unstable FX market occurs with inelastic imports. Figure 11.9 shows a downward sloping supply that would result from inelastic imports in Japan. A lower \$/¥ rate implies a higher price of imports in Japan. Inelastic imports imply an increase in the quantity of yen along the supply curve. The supply of yen slopes downward during the contract period of the J curve. At \$/¥ = 0.009, the shortage bids \$/¥ up. At \$/¥ = 0.007, the excess supply of yen leads to \$/¥ falling further. The market exchange rate would be unstable in this situation.

From one day to the next, there can be substantial exchange rate movements. Traders are essentially searching for the market equilibrium. The short-term movement in the exchange rate leads some traders to profit while others suffer loss. The high risk and returns keep the traders busy.

Large swings in the dollar occurred during the 1980s. The dollar appreciated by 87% from 1980 to 1985 followed by 42% depreciation up to 1988. The large

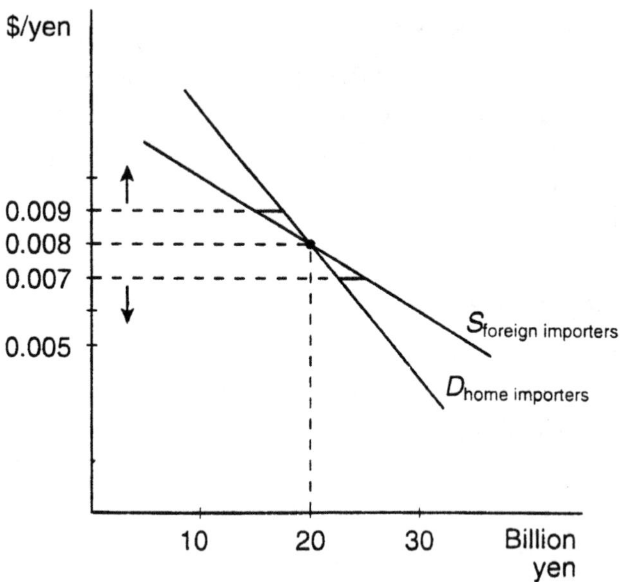

Figure 11.9
An Unstable FX Market
At any rate above 0.008, the shortage raises the exchange rate. At any lower price, the surplus lowers the exchange rate. The exchange rate would continue its rise or fall without bound.

dollar appreciation during the early 1980s raised import spending and lowered export revenue indicating import elasticity. The recession at the time can be attributed to low export production and falling prices of imports. As the dollar depreciated after 1985 import prices rose and export revenue climbed. The US experienced trade surpluses by early 1991.

Exchange rates can be volatile over short time periods due to inelastic imports and exports indicated by the contract period in the J curve.

EXAMPLE 11.13   *Predicting FX Rates*

Economists are often asked to do the impossible and will gladly do so for a fee. The popular press is full of descriptions of FX markets. *The Economist* reported in May 1989 that the dollar appreciated due to rising US exports even as slowing output growth led to an expected decrease in inflation and dollar appreciation. While no single theory will explain all exchange rate movements, differences in money supply growth rates explain long-term trends.

EXAMPLE 11.14   *FX Trading Banks*

An October 1999 issue of *FX Week* reports the FX revenue of US banks for the third quarter. Citigroup reports the largest FX revenue of $358 million followed by Chase Manhattan at $199 million, and Bank of America with $138 million. FX traders enjoy an active market earning commissions on volume. One trader commented that good movement during the latter part of the quarter kept the FX desks busy with volatility below the Asian and Russian episodes of the previous year.

Triangular Arbitrage

The banks, brokers, and traders in the FX market operate through online interbank links. Brokers make the market matching buyers and sellers. The FX market is highly competitive with traders operating on small price margins on large contracts. Any differences in cross rates disappear quickly due to triangular arbitrage.

Suppose market rates are $/€ = 1.09, ¥/€ = 136, and $/¥ = 0.009. A trader with $1000 dollars would buy €917, trade them for ¥124,771, and simultaneously trade the yen for $1,123 making a profit of $123. Note that the cross rate $/¥ = 1.09/136 = 0.008 is less than the market rate 0.009 indicating the underpriced yen. Triangular arbitrage increases demand for yen pushing the cross rate in line with the market.

Continuous triangular arbitrage keeps exchange rates in line with each other. Among the three currencies, there are two independent rates. Among the 150 or so currencies in the world, there are 149 or so independent exchange rates to keep traders busy.

These days many banks have an active FX trading desk. In larger US cities, especially near the Canadian and Mexican borders, foreign currency circulates along with the dollar with traders in downtown FX windows. Airports have FX windows where travelers buy and sell currency. There is active FX trading online with traders pursuing various strategies to predict exchange rate movements.

EXAMPLE 11.15   *Growth in the FX Market*

The volume of trade in the FX market has grown more than 10% annually since the early 1990s with the volume of exports a small fraction of the volume of FX trading. Spot FX transactions are about one third of total FX transaction with more trading on forward and futures markets. Trading occurs geographically in three major centers, with London handling the greatest volume, New York, the center of trading in the Americas, and Tokyo, the center in Asia. The FX market operates around the clock.

Section C Problems

C1. Start with $1,000 and make a profit from triangular arbitrage given the South Korean won/$ = 1050, the peso/$ = 175, and the won/peso = 5.95.

C2. Suppose the demand for yen slopes upward due to the inelastic demand for Japanese bonds. Diagram and explain the behavior in this unstable $/yen market with upward sloping demand.

D. FOREIGN EXCHANGE RISK

Yearly exchange rates reflect higher inflation rates across countries with depreciating currencies. The time horizon to predict FX rates is months or years. International commerce operates on a shorter time frame introducing FX risk and uncertainty.

EXAMPLE 11.16   *Euro Exchange Risk*

The dollar price $/€ of the euro fell 15% right away when the euro was introduced in 1999. US exports became that much more expensive in Europe and European imports in the US that much cheaper. Over the following 10 years, foreign exchange risk persisted with $/€ ranging from 0.85 to 1.50. The supply of euros is controlled by the EU government in Belgium. Without the ability to create money, each national government in Europe balances its budget or nearly so. The goal of low inflation in the EU has led to a narrowing range for variation in $/€ and much less exchange risk.

Inflation and Exchange Rates

Inflation is an increase in the average price level of all goods and services. The price level P = $/good is the average price of all goods and services. Its inverse $1/P$ = goods/$ represents the purchasing power of the dollar.

Currencies have mostly inflated since the 1950s with consumers and firms adjusting to the inflation. Periods of deflation with falling price levels have occurred throughout history with little economic impact.

If one currency is expected to inflate more than another, interest rates reflect the difference. The real interest rate is the return on an investment after the lost purchasing power due to inflation. The real interest rate is consistent over time and across countries. The nominal interest rate, the real interest rate plus an inflation premium, varies much more over time and across countries.

The Fisher equation is,

$$I = r + \pi$$

Irving Fisher developed this relationship during the early 1900s with i as the nominal interest rate, r the real interest rate, and π the expected inflation rate. With i = 6% as the nominal interest rate $100 becomes $106 after a year. If inflation is 5% the purchasing power of $106 reduces to $101 revealing the real interest rate of 1%.

Suppose expected inflation is 25% for the peso and 5% for the dollar. Rational expectations are based on theory and history as well as any information about monetary policies for the coming year. A 28% nominal interest rate in pesos is consistent with a real interest rate of 3% and a nominal interest rate of 8% in dollars. Investing at those nominal interest rates yields the same purchasing power at the end of the year. The expected increase in purchasing power from investing in either country is 3%.

Nominal interest rates are observed but not expected inflation. The difference between nominal interest rates in two countries is the market expectation of the difference between the two inflation rates assuming competitive exchange rates and financial markets. If nominal interest rates are 28% for the peso and 8% for the dollar, the peso has a 28% − 8% = 20% discount against the dollar.

Holding foreign currency involves foreign exchange risk. International investors diversify currency holdings to dissipate exchange risk. Currencies can be ranked according to their potentials for unexpected depreciation.

Nominal interest rates are higher in countries with currencies that have higher expected inflation revealing market discounts.

EXAMPLE 11.17   *An Era of Dollar Appreciation*

The weight of each country in US trade leads to an exchange rate index of the dollar. Country i trade $T_i = X_i + M_i$ leads to the sum T for all countries. The weight of country i is its share $W_i = T_i/T$. The trade weighted exchange rate is $e = W_1e_1 + \cdots + W_ne_n$. From 1973 when floating exchange rates started until 1981, the dollar remained at about $e = 30$ before it began appreciating to 100 by 1998. This appreciation reflects the slower money supply growth in the US compared to its trading partners over 25 years.

EXAMPLE 11.18   *One Peso Crash*

The Mexican government tries to support the peso above its market rate creating a surplus of pesos as in Figure 11.6. To meet this dollar shortage in 1994 FX reserves in Mexico fell 70%. The supply of pesos continued to grow with the peso overvalued. The government devalued the peso by 15% leading to speculation of a peso crash. Over three months the peso fell 50%.

Forward and Future Exchange

Risk arises in international transactions due to unexpected changes in exchange rates. Contracts for goods and services are written for future delivery. There is also risk for investors holding assets denominated in foreign currency. To avoid this FX risk, traders and investors can hedge in the forward exchange market making a contract to buy or sell foreign currency at a date in the future for an exchange rate stated today. The supply and demand in the forward exchange market are from traders and investors wanting to settle prices of transactions or earnings in their own currency.

Future contracts for standard quantities of foreign currencies at set time intervals are regularly traded. Transaction costs for future contracts are very low. Future exchange rates provide unbiased predictors of exchange rates reflecting what market participants expect the exchange rate to become. Rapidly inflating currencies are discounted with forward exchange rates below spot rates. Currencies expected to have lower inflation have premiums.

Speculators trade foreign exchange when they believe the exchange rate will turn out to be different from the forward rate. Suppose the current spot rate for South Korean won is won/\$ = 760 and the three-month future rate is 780. A speculator expecting the won to drop to 800 will sign a contract to sell won at the forward rate of 780. Based on expectation, the plan is to buy won in the spot market at 800. This speculation is leveraged as the only payment is a small fee for the contract.

Forward and future FX markets offer hedgers a way to avoid risk, and speculators a way to assume risk.

EXAMPLE 11.19   *FX Futures*

Futures contracts are for standard quantities of foreign currency at specified dates. One example is contracts for 12.5 million yen every Wednesday. Speculators match wits with futures contracts with FX alongside gold, oil, cotton, and beef. The quotes below are for 30-day futures contracts. A trader could buy or sell yen at yen/\$ = 94.94. The spot rate yen/\$ = 106 indicated investors expected the yen to depreciate. Speculators buy future contracts hoping to outguess the market. The change column shows the percentage change from the previous day.

	Price	Change
¥ FUTURE	94.94	0.14%
£ FUTURE	162.06	0.05%
C\$ FUTURE	68.19	−0.06%
GOLD 100 OZ FUTURE	289.30	−0.58%
CRUDE OIL FUTURE	23.00	0.61%
COTTON FUTURE	51.11	0.02%

Section D Problems

D1. Suppose current price levels are $P = \$/\text{good} = 100$ and $P^* = \text{€}/\text{good} = 150$. If the same goods are consumed in each country with free trade, what is the current exchange rate \$/€? Five years later it turns out that $P = 120$

and $P^* = 160$. What should the exchange rate be? Explain which currency depreciated.

D2. Suppose the nominal interest rate is 12% and inflation is 9%. Find the real interest rate. Starting with $100 find the nominal and real return to saving. If expected inflation rises to 15% but the real interest rate does not change, find the nominal interest rate. Find the nominal and real returns to $100.

EXAMPLE 11.20   *Volatile Central Banks*

Central banks intervene in FX markets in attempts to stabilize the exchange rates of their currency. Richard Baillie and William Osterberg (1997) find evidence that intervention is destabilizing. Daily FX interventions by the US, German, and Japanese central banks only increase the variation of exchange rates. The reason is that traders view the central banks as unpredictable.

CONCLUSION

The FX market is a vast deep market with growing numbers of participating firms and consumers. The evidence suggests fixed exchange rates and government controls on the FX market are counterproductive. As countries integrate into the world economy, the FX market becomes more critical. The influence of the exchange rate on daily economic life cannot be overlooked. Chapter 12 turns attention to the important role of money.

Terms

Black market FX rate	Future and forward contracts
Cross FX rate	Import license FX
Discounts and premiums on FX	J curve
Expected inflation	Managed FX rate
Fischer equation	Market exchange rate
Fixed exchange rate	Marshall–Lerner condition
Forward exchange rate	Parallel exchange markets
FX reserves	Real and nominal interest rates
FX risk	Spot exchange rate
FX speculation	Triangular arbitrage

MAIN POINTS

- FX markets are large, busy, efficient, and vital for every country.
- The demand for FX comes from domestic imports of foreign products and assets, and supply from foreign importers of domestic products and assets.

- A depreciating currency raises the domestic price of foreign goods and lowers the foreign price of domestic goods. Depreciation raises the trade balance assuming enough time for markets to adjust to the price changes.
- Governments artificially set fixed exchange rates for political reasons. Theory and evidence strongly recommend relying on market exchange rates.
- High inflation rates are associated with depreciating currencies and high nominal interest rates. Currencies expected to depreciate are discounted in the forward and future exchange rate markets.

REVIEW PROBLEMS

1. Suppose domestic demand for Japanese cars is $Q = 10{,}000 - P$ where P is the dollar price. Find the quantity of Japanese cars at a price of 1 million yen demanded when the exchange rate is $1/e =$ yen/\$ $= 110$ and then 125. Plot the quantity of yen demanded to buy cars at these two exchange rates.

2. Find yen prices of US rice costing \$4.50 per bushel when the yen/\$ exchange rate is 110 and then 125. Given demand for rice $Q = 9{,}000{,}000 - 10{,}000\,P*$ where $P*$ is the yen price, find the quantity of yen supplied in the FX market at the two exchange rates. Plot the corresponding supply of yen.

3. Start with \$1000 and make a profit facing exchange rates won/peso = 6.05, won/\$ = 1050, and \$/peso = 0.00571.

4. Suppose the EU launches a large number of communications satellites. Given that the US exports telecommunications services, diagram the effect on the FX market.

5. Find the short-run percentage change in import spending and export revenue that would be due to 5% depreciation with import elasticity 0.3 and export elasticity 0.4. Describe what happens to the trade balance.

6. If the import elasticity is 1.5 and the export elasticity is 1.2 find the long-run percentage change in export revenue and import spending due to the 5% depreciation. Compare the trade balance to the previous problem.

7. Illustrate the effect on the FX market of a binding limit on cash that can be taken on foreign travel.

8. Explain how a central bank supporting its currency by buying the surplus of its own currency amounts to a tax on its citizens.

9. Which groups of economic agents demand pesos in the forward market? What happens to the quantity of pesos demanded when the forward price of pesos rises? Who supplies pesos forward in the market?

10. "Despite repeated central bank intervention, the US dollar rallied to highs of 1.71 marks, 151 yen, and \$1.62/pound." Illustrate what was happening in an FX market diagram.

11. Suppose the spot exchange rate for Kuwait dinar is \$/dinar $= 3.60$ and the six-month forward rate is 3.65. Explain whether the dinar has a forward premium or discount.

12. In the example of Korean won in the text, calculate profit if the speculator signs a contract to sell 10 million won and the spot rate turns out to be exactly what was expected. Find profit in dollars if the spot rate instead falls to 750 won/\$.

READINGS

Paul Krugman (1989) *Exchange Rate Instability*, Cambridge: The MIT Press. Examines the surprising volatility of exchange rates during the 1980s.

Mike Melvin (1989) *International Money and Finance*, New York: Harper & Row. Lively text with excellent coverage of the FX market.

Leland Yeager (1976) *International Monetary Relations*, New York: Harper & Row. A classic. Federal Reserve Bank Bulletins. Monthly bulletins with analysis of the FX market, available online. Trading FX is possible on a number of internet platforms.

MATHEMATICAL APPENDIX

Foreign exchange (FX) rates are the prices of foreign currencies in the home currency, for instance, the price of euros $e = \$/€$ or yen $\$/¥$ in dollars. Demand for FX D_{FX} is derived from home import demand $D_M(ep_X{}^*, Z)$ where $p_X{}^* = €/$ exp* is the price of exports in the foreign currency and $ep_X{}^* = \$/exp^* = \$/imp$. Import demand D_M includes domestic quantity demanded Q_D on the demand curve minus quantity supplied Q_S on the supply curve of the product, $D_M = Q_D - Q_S$. Any variable Z affecting demand or supply of the product shifts D_{FX}.

Supply of FX S_{FX} is similarly derived from foreign import demand $S_M{}^*(p_X/e, Z)$ where $p_X = \$/exp$ is the price of home exports and any variable Z^* shifting $S_{M*} = Q_S{}^* - Q_D{}^*$ affects S_{FX}.

FX rates influence transactions across the border involving goods in the Balance of Trade (BOT), Trade in Services (TS) that includes tourism, Net Investment Income (NII) in the Current Account (CA), and traded international assets in the Capital Account (KA). The effect of an exogenous change in e on the balance of payments (BOP) includes these components. Floating exchange rate theory treats e as an endogenous variable.

Denote home currency depreciation or foreign currency appreciation as $e\uparrow$. Depreciation raises the price of imports $p_M = ep_X{}^* = \$/M$ lowering D_M as Q_D falls and Q_S increases. Elastic import demand D_M with demand D_{FX} decreasing in e is likely given the negative price elasticity ε_D of demand and positive price elasticity ε_S of supply. Similarly, supply $S_{FX}{}^*$ has a positive slope if foreign import demand $D_M{}^*$ is price elastic with the FX supplied by foreign importers.

The FX market clears at the market rate e_{mkt} where $D_{FX}(ep_X{}^*,\ldots) = S_{FX}{}^*(p_X/e,\ldots)$. Any change in demands for traded products and assets shifting D_M or $S_M{}^*$ imply shifts in D_{FX} or $S_{FX}{}^*$ and adjustments of e_{mkt}.

In the home country, depreciation $e\uparrow$ implies $\$/imp\uparrow$ leading to a decrease in import spending M given elastic imports. In the foreign country, $e\uparrow$ implying $p_M{}^* = €/exp\downarrow$ leads to $X\uparrow$ assuming elastic foreign imports. Depreciation $e\uparrow$ then raises balance on goods and services (BGS) $= p_Xq_X - ep_M{}^*q_M$ assuming $q_X\uparrow$ and $q_M\downarrow$ are large enough to offset $e\uparrow$. The J curve effect of a surprise depreciation $e\uparrow$ is possible over a short amount of time as contracts may be set implying an immediate BGS$\downarrow$ followed by BGS$\uparrow$ to a higher level.

A government can "fix" its exchange rate e_F with a franchised monopoly central bank (CB). An underpriced currency $e_F > e_{mkt}$ raises export revenue and increases FX holdings of the CB but hurts consumers and industries importing intermediate products. An overvalued currency $e_F < e_{mkt}$ helps import-competing industries and may attract foreign investors with underpriced home assets but depletes FX holdings of the CB. A fixed e_F tends to be unstable. Governments also attempt to manage their FX rate through licensed traders, quotas on the volume of FX trades, and CB buying or selling FX.

International trade and investment require long-term contracts that lead to hedging in FX at the forward exchange rate f. In the forward exchange market, traders and investors make contracts to buy or sell FX at a future date. The forward f eliminates the risk of e changing before a planned transaction takes place.

Foreign currency can be considered an asset leading to speculative buying and selling based on the expected spot rate Ee. The forward FX market clears where $D_f = S_f$ where Ee = f. Changes in Ee shift both the forward FX rate f as well as the spot FX demand and supply. The futures exchange market is a commodity market offering standard quantities and timings of FX transactions.

Inelastic imports in the short term imply FX rate instability with D_{FX} or S_{FX} having the same slope and e diverging away from the equilibrium e_{mkt}. Exchange rate volatility increases in higher frequency data. Changes in Ee also generate the observed high variation in e. Opposition to floating exchange rates is based on this short term volatility.

Inflation and depreciation go together as an inflating peso with a rising price level P_{peso} = peso/good would lower desire to hold pesos leading to $D_{pesos}\downarrow$ and \$/peso$\downarrow$.

Triangular arbitrage \$/€ = (\$/¥)(¥/€) ties FX rates together as \$/€ remains stable with \$/¥$\downarrow$ and ¥/€$\uparrow$.

CHAPTER 12

International Money and Finance

Preview

Money supplies across countries affect interest rates and exchange rates that are tied to international borrowing and lending in financial markets. This chapter covers topics in international money and finance including:

- Loanable funds market and capital account
- Exchange rates and international financial markets
- The functions and history of money
- Money supplies, inflation rates, and exchange rates

INTRODUCTION

Money is the medium of exchange for transactions with cash, bank cards, credit cards, and checks. The foreign exchange (FX) market involves the exchange of mediums of exchange.

Lending and borrowing are carried out in money terms with the interest rate as the cost of borrowing and the return to lending. International finance involves exchange rates at the times of the loan and repayment.

The consumers, firms, and government of a country can be net lenders or borrowers in the international credit market. Each country would have its own loanable funds market but enjoys net benefits through the international market. International interest rates are the result of lending and borrowing across countries.

Money as the unit of account for international trade and investment involves the exchange rate. Money is a store of value for future transactions depending on its inflation rate. An inflating currency is a poor store of value depreciating in the FX market.

International financial flows are reported in the capital account of the balance of payments. Net investment income in the current account is the payment on international loans. Borrowing countries have capital account surpluses with cash inflow but current account deficits later. Lending countries have capital account deficits and net investment income surpluses in the future.

Trade deficits and international borrowing are signals that a country is expected to grow. Less-develop countries (LDCs) must borrow to acquire capital goods. The debt is expected to be repaid as output expands.

Stocks, bonds, certificates of deposit, futures contracts, options, swaps, and overnight paper are financial instruments in international finance. Active international arbitrage occurs among financial intermediaries including banks, investment houses, and brokers. This international arbitrage involves the FX market.

The role of government in international financial markets is to manage deficit spending and control money supply growth. If the money supply grows fast relative to the rest of the world, the currency depreciates. Government deficit spending leads to money creation and inflation. Governments balancing their fiscal budget have low inflation rates and stable exchange rates encouraging international lending and borrowing.

A. INTERNATIONAL CREDIT MARKETS

This section introduces the international credit market based on borrowing and lending between countries.

EXAMPLE 12.1   *International Financial Markets in the 1890s*

International credit became highly developed during the 1890s leading to economic growth around the world. The two World Wars and the Great Depression disrupted international financial markets during the first half of the 20th century. International investment relative to world output reached lows during the 1950s and 1960s but has increased since the late 1970s but still not reaching the high level of the 1890s.

Two Senses of "Capital"

"Capital" has two meanings in economics. Capital in microeconomics is an input in production, the machinery and structures combined with labor and natural resources to produce output. In finance, capital refers to the credit involved with lending and borrowing. The two meanings are connected. When a firm borrows from a bank or sells bonds and stocks, it invests in machinery and equipment to increase future production. Debt and equity purchase new productive capital.

Consumers can expand consumption beyond income by borrowing. Governments can increase spending beyond tax revenue by selling bonds. If a firm lacks cash for a worthwhile investment project, it can borrow in the credit market.

A firm deciding whether to invest in a project looks at its rate of return. Suppose a new machine is expected to create net profit of $40K for one year. If the machine costs $1 million, its rate of return is 4%.

To determine whether investing in the machine is worthwhile, consider the opportunity cost of the $1 million. If the interest rate is 3% with no inflation, the firm with $1 million cash on hand could become a lender and earn $30K.

The machine offers a higher return. At a market interest rate of 5%, the firm could earn $50K and should not invest in the machine.

A firm with no cash on hand could borrow to invest in the machine. A net borrowing cost of $35K would make the borrowing worthwhile. Borrowing cost of $45K would rule out the borrowing. Higher interest rates increase the cost of borrowing and discourage investment. Financial capital is turned into productive capital when firms borrow to invest in new plant and equipment.

Investment spending varies inversely with the interest rate. A higher interest rate leads to less investment spending.

EXAMPLE 12.2   *Emerging Stock Markets*

Financial capital is transformed into productive capital when firms sell stocks and bonds to spend on investment projects. The major international stock markets are in New York, Tokyo, and London. Stocks are increasingly traded by small brokers not connected to the major exchanges. There is a high degree of variation in returns across emerging stock markets. Emerging stock markets have high average rates of return but also high risk.

Credit Market

An increase in the interest rate lowers the quantity of loans demanded and increases the quantity of saving. The market for loanable funds (LF) includes demand and supply for credit in Figure 12.1.

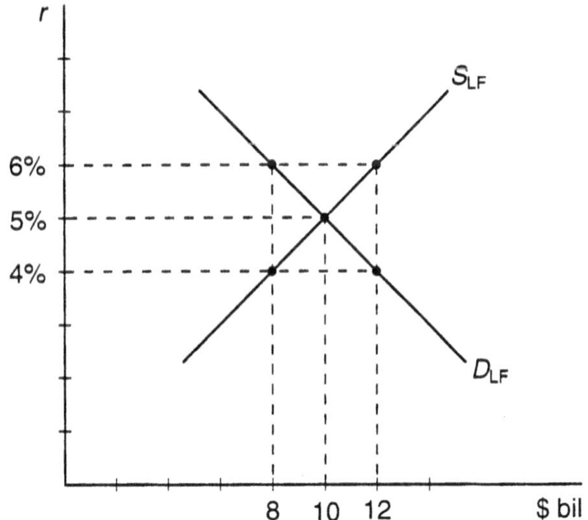

Figure 12.1
The Domestic Credit Market
The demand for loanable funds D_{LF} shows the ranking of investment projects. Supply S_{LF} comes from households and firms with cash on hand. Competitive market equilibrium is $r = 5\%$ with $Q_{LF} = \$10\text{bil} = D_{LF} = S_{LF}$.

The real interest rate r is the price of borrowing and the return to lending. The real interest rate is the nominal interest rate minus expected inflation in the Fisher equation,

$$r = i - \pi$$

If $r = 5\%$, saving \$100 today results in \$105 of purchasing power next year. Borrowing \$100 will cost \$105 next year. Lending \$100 will result in \$105 available to spend next year.

At $r = 4\%$, the quantity of loans demanded at \$12 billion is greater than the quantity supplied at \$8 billion. Financial intermediaries perceive this shortage and ration by increasing the interest rate. At $r = 6\%$, there would be surplus of \$4 billion spurring banks to lower the interest rate. At the market equilibrium of 5% the quantity of credit supplied equals the quantity demanded.

EXAMPLE **12.3**   *International Defaults*

Bad loans, debt problems, default, and bankruptcy are familiar issues especially involving loans to governments. Barry Eichengreen (1991) surveys the history of bad debt. Latin American governments defaulted in the 1820s, followed by US states during the 1830s and 1840s. Latin American governments defaulted again in the 1880s along with Egypt, Greece, and Turkey. During the Great Depression of the 1930s, every debtor country defaulted. Default is a better option than struggling to pay back bad loans. Lenders tend to make new loans due to the high potential returns. While bankruptcy laws accommodate default inside countries, there are no international bankruptcy laws.

The International Credit Market

International financial intermediation occurs as banks try to match borrowers with lenders in different countries. A small open economy can borrow or lend at the international interest rate. In Figure 12.1, the small open economy would borrow \$4 billion at the international interest rate of 4%. This inflow would be a capital account surplus, $KA > 0$. If instead the world interest rate were 6%, there would be lending with a deficit of \$4 billion, $KA < 0$.

The international loanable funds market between two large economies is pictured in Figure 12.2. As with the excess supply and demand of a product, the international price is determined between the two countries. The home excess demand XD is derived from the credit market in Figure 12.1.

The foreign country has its own supply and demand with different lenders and borrowers. Note that the foreign autarky interest rate $r^* = 3\%$ is less than the home autarky interest rate $r = 5\%$. At $r = 4\%$ the home excess demand equals foreign excess supply, $XD = XS^*$. The home country borrows \$4 billion from the foreign country.

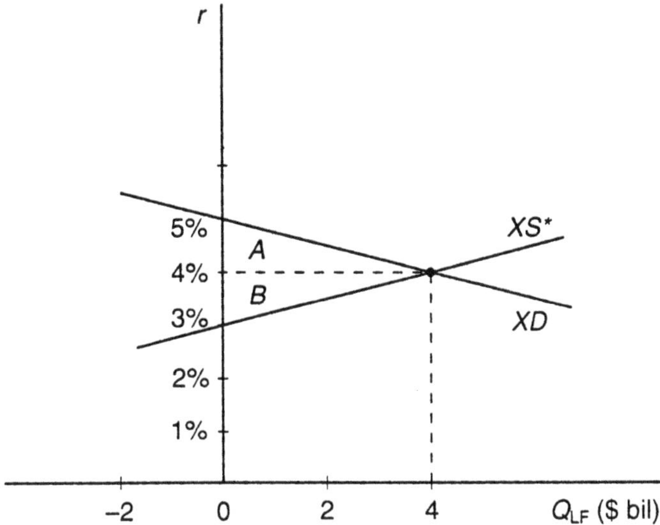

Figure 12.2
The International Credit Market
The home excess demand XD for credit derived from Figure 12.1 has the autarky $r = 5\%$. Excess supply XS^* of the foreign country has autarky $r^* = 3\%$. The international equilibrium $r = 4\%$ leads to \$4 billion of loans from the foreign to the borrowing home country.

A small open economy takes the international interest rate. Large economies lend and borrow at the interest rate clearing the international credit market.

Home borrowers and foreign lenders are better off with international credit in Figure 12.2 compared to autarky. Home lenders and foreign borrowers would be better off in autarky. There are total surplus gains—area A for the home country and B for the foreign country.

The net gain for the home country is the area between XD and the international interest rate of \$20 million. The foreign net gain is the area between foreign XS^* and the international interest rate 4%, area B equal to \$20 million. International gains from the credit market are \$40 million.

International Investment Accounting

Financial flows enter the capital account (KA) of the balance of payments (BOP) as foreign investment. Borrowing countries report positive numbers for KA surpluses, and lending countries negative numbers for KA deficits.

Net investment income (NII) resulting from KA investments also enters the BOP. Suppose home investors have a stock of \$2,200 billion invested abroad while foreigners have \$1,675 billion invested at home. If the international interest rate is 4% then $0.04 \times \$2,200$ billion $= \$88$ billion is received as investment income while $0.04 \times \$1675$ billion $= \$67$ billion is paid. The NII is then $21 billion. This was the NII surplus reported by the US in 1998.

Estimates of the *KA* and NII are done by survey. Some years it is not clear whether the US is a net debtor or creditor due to the statistical discrepancy. The rapid expansion of international financial activity has made government surveys less reliable. Multinational firms (MNFs) account for an increasing share of international financial transactions. Transactions within firms are difficult to track. International banks have complicated the accounting process.

A typical arrangement would be a branch of a US bank in Mexico buying $1 million of newly issued stock for an industrial plant in a free trade zone on the Texas border employing Mexicans who walk daily across a bridge. A bank in Spain owns 49% of the stock of the Mexican bank. Investors in Texas hold 60% of the deposits in the Mexican bank. Machinery bought for the assembly line is assembled by a firm based in Michigan that imports components from Taiwan and employs skilled labor from Panama. Imagine the national income accounting steps to capture this activity.

International Financial Policy

Governments trying to control or influence international financial flows can place direct controls on international investment. LDCs and newly industrial countries (NICs) often forbid the outflow of investment, a policy debated in the developed countries (DCs). Many governments are reluctant to allow investment inflows fearing the influence of foreign interests.

One concern is the share of gross domestic product (GDP) that is paid abroad as interest earnings. Markets naturally determine whether there has been too much borrowing. A country borrowing only for consumption will lose the ability to repay the debt. A country borrowing for capital investment will be able to produce output to repay the debt. Competitive financial markets, not governments or politicians, should govern financial flows.

Governments often attempt to protect their own financial industries leading to losses for the country due to the inefficiency. Foreign investment in banking is not allowed in some countries. While there will always be political pressure for controls on international investment, competition leads banks to become more efficient.

EXAMPLE 12.4   *Global Financial Instability*

International trade and finance slow during a financial crisis. Frederic Mishkin (1999) notes that lending slows, interest rates rise, and uncertainties increase during financial crises. Gerard Caprio and Patrick Honohan (1999) find political interference in bank regulation is apparent in every financial crisis. Jeffrey Sachs (1995) advocates an international bankruptcy court. Paul Krugman (1998) advocates capital outflow controls. Barry Eichengreen (1999) advocates capital inflow controls. Sebastian Edwards (1999) shows such capital controls are ineffective. Henry Kaufman (1998) advocates the International Monetary Fund (IMF) as an international financial regulator. Jeffrey Garten (1998) proposes a single world currency and a central bank. Kenneth Rogoff (1999) advocates equity financing. Stanley Fischer (1999) points to the need for transparent international credit standards. International competition improves the efficiency of banking systems. Balanced government budgets would diminish instability.

Section A Problems

A1. Draw a foreign credit market that leads to the foreign excess supply in Figure 12.2.

A2. Find the investment income due on the international loans in Figure 12.2. Explain which country makes the payment.

A3. Find NII given a 5% interest rate at home and a 6% interest rate abroad with home-owned investment stock abroad of $1470 billion and foreign-owned stock at home of $1346 billion. Explain whether there is a surplus or deficit in NII.

A4. Find the KA and NII in Problem A3 if there is a 5% increase in the home-owned stock abroad combined with an increase of 39% in the foreign-owned capital stock at home.

EXAMPLE 12.5   *LDC Defaults*

The Organization of Petroleum Exporting Countries (OPEC) oil embargoes of the 1970s and 1980s created high OPEC profit and a large surplus of credit. These funds filtered into loans to LDC governments from international banks with the perception that default would be impossible. Nominal interest rates were very high due to high inflation rates. The LDCs suffered in the worldwide recession due to high oil prices. Interest rates began to fall. Paying back the loans became impossible for LDC governments leading to default. In a number of publications, Rudiger Dornbusch and Franco Modigliani proposed paying the debt in LDC currencies. Some of the debt was forgiven with taxpayers in DCs bailing out the LDC governments and the international banks. A better option is to let inefficient banks go bankrupt with their stockholders suffering a loss. The same can be said about the financial crises and bailouts of the 2010s.

B. FOREIGN EXCHANGE RATES AND INTERNATIONAL FINANCE

International financial transactions involve the FX market. Changes or expected changes in exchange rates affect prices of financial assets across countries. In the opposite direction, the changing flows of foreign investment affect exchange rates.

International Portfolios

International financial transactions are carried out electronically between large international banks and financial intermediaries. Traders adjust portfolios internationally to spread risk and to avoid overexposure in a particular currency.

International financial transactions occur due to foreign direct investment (FDI) and international portfolio diversification. Banks and financial intermediaries arbitrage across credit and exchange markets making profitable transactions across currencies and interest rates.

Exchange rates affect stock prices, bond markets, and other financial assets. International financial transactions in turn affect exchange rates.

Suppose the nominal interest rate is 20% in the peso country. The price of a perpetuity bond paying 100,000 pesos per year indefinitely would be 100,000/0.2 = 500,000 pesos as 500,000 pesos would earn 100,000 pesos interest every year. Suppose the current spot exchange rate is e = $/pesos = 0.002. To keep it simple, suppose the dollar and peso countries have the same inflation rate. The dollar price of this perpetuity bond would be $0.002 \times 500,000 = \$1000$. An unexpected peso devaluation to e = 0.0015 would decrease the dollar price of the bond to $0.0015 \times 500,000 = \$750$. Whether the peso bond has become a bargain depends on expected future peso depreciation.

EXAMPLE 12.6   *FX Rate and Foreign Investment*

> An appreciating dollar means assets in the US become more expensive for foreign investors. Kenneth Froot and Jeremy Stein (1991) find that 10% appreciation of the dollar lowers FDI by a small percentage. Over half of the FDI goes into mergers and acquisitions with no impact on management. The FX rate has no effect on portfolio investment.

Depreciation Discounting

One issue on the mind of an international investor is expected deprecation. What will be the FX rate effect on the 100,000 peso premium of a perpetuity bond? If investors expect the inflation rates to remain at the historical averages of 20% for the peso and 4% for the dollar, the peso is expected to lose 16% every year.

Suppose the exchange rate is e = 0.002 making the 100,000 peso premium worth $200. One year from now the 100,000 pesos are expected to be worth 84% as much or $168. Two years from now, the expectation is $125. The dollar value of the bond is discounted by 16% every year.

The present value of the peso bond is $100,000/(0.20 + 0.16) = 277,778$ pesos. At the exchange rate $/pesos = 0.002, the peso bond would sell for $556. If the peso and the dollar had the same expected inflation rates, the peso bond would sell for $1000. The difference of $444 is the depreciation discount.

Default risk may also be an issue with the peso bond. Suppose peso bonds have a history of defaulting 12% of the time and dollar bonds an average of 4% of the time. An additional 8% risk discount would be placed on the peso bond. The present value of the peso bond would fall to 100,000/0.44 = 227,273 pesos or $454.

International bond prices are discounted by expected depreciation and default risk.

EXAMPLE 12.7   *Country Risk*

Country risk ratings summarize the history of whether loans are repaid. Borrowers in countries with high risk pay higher borrowing rates. LDCs generally have the highest risk and pay the highest interest rates. Investors can earn more but face higher default risk. A few of the top and bottom countries in a recent ranking are Tunisia and the Congo at the median ranking, Germany and the US close to the top, and Switzerland as the least risky.

International Investment and the FX Market

The effects of international financial markets on the FX market are illustrated in the market for Korean won in Figure 12.3. Demand for won is based in part on US investors as potential buyers of Korean financial assets. The demand for

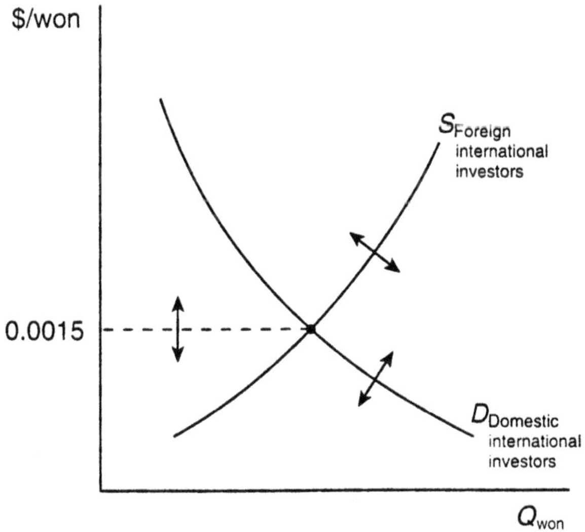

Figure 12.3
International Investment and the FX Rate
Demand for won slopes downward partly because a lower $/won implies a lower price for Korean assets in the US. The supply of won slopes upward partly because a higher $/won exchange rate implies cheaper US assets in Korea. Changes in investment opportunities shift supply and demand in the FX market leading to adjustments in $/won.

won slopes downward. An increase in $/won raises the price of Korean assets in the US, lowering the quantity of assets demanded in the US. The quantity of won demanded in the FX market falls along the demand curve D.

The supply of won comes from Korean investors buying US assets. As $/won rises, the price of US assets in Korea falls, the quantity of US assets demanded in Korea rises, and the quantity of won supplied rises. The supply of won slopes upward.

Suppose the expected return on Korean investments rises because of an announced policy of increased privatization. Investors in the US will want to buy more Korean stocks and bonds because Korean firms are expected to prosper under the new policy. The demand for won rises, causing the won to appreciate.

As a result, the price of Korean assets rises further as the exchange rate reinforces the underlying price change. The FX market works in the same direction as the underlying asset market. Government policy interfering with the exchange market hinders this effect.

International investors try to anticipate government intervention. Erratic behavior in international financial markets has been cited as evidence to increase government regulation. Erratic behavior, however, typically results from market participants trying to anticipate government intervention.

One piece of advice in the FX market is to watch what the central bank is doing and do the opposite. With central banks intervening, market participants turn their attention away from market fundamentals. FX traders, hedgers, and speculators operate more efficiently in a market free from central bank interventions and control.

No scheme of managed exchange rates or regulated financial markets could have handled the financial upheavals since the 1970s. Innovations occur with increased competition that forces banks and financial intermediaries to become more efficient. Competition in banking and financial markets should be the rule.

EXAMPLE 12.8   *News and the FX Market*

FX traders follow the news on trade deficits, investment flows, inflation rates, economic trends, and government policy. Graig Hakkio and Douglas Pearce (1985) examine empirical links between the FX rate and economic news. They find only one type of news has immediate and consistent impacts, namely news about money supply growth. Exchange rates adjust to money supply news after about 20 minutes. If the US money supply increases unexpectedly, traders expect the dollar to depreciate and sell dollars right away. Prior to money supply announcements, there is decreased exchange rate movement as traders wait for the news.

Covered Interest Arbitrage

International asset markets are linked to FX markets through banks and financial intermediaries. An investor in the US with $100 earning the domestic interest rate

$i = 3\%$ will have \$103 at the end of the year. Suppose the Malaysian interest rate is $i^* = 6\%$ and the current spot rate $e = \$/R = 0.26$ where R is the ringgit. The \$100 can be exchanged for $100/0.26 = R385$ that will yield $385 \times 1.06 = R408$ at the end of the year. With an open position, the investor waits until the end of the year to sell the 408 ringgits on the spot exchange market. There is risk of ringgit depreciation during the year.

This foreign exchange risk can be eliminated with a forward exchange contract to sell 408 ringgits at the end of the year. The forward exchange rate is for transactions at a date in the future for a rate set now. The forward rate f will invariably be close to $f = \$/R = \$103$. The reason is that 408 ringgits will convert back to \$103 at that forward rate. If the two returns are not equal, traders could make risk-free arbitrage profit. Covered interest arbitrage (CIA) transactions continuously link international asset and exchange markets.

CIA is the relationship,

$$(1 + i) = (1/e)(1 + i^*)f$$

An investor with \$1 can earn $(1 + i)$ buying a home bond. The alternative is to convert the \$1 to foreign currency at $1/e$, buy a foreign bond with return $1 + i^*$, and cover the earnings back into dollars multiplying by f.

If one side of covered arbitrage is larger than the other, four markets simultaneously restore the equilibrium. Profit makers push the four markets as shown in Figure 12.4 as in the example of the ringgit-dollar arbitrage.

Suppose the Fed increases the supply of credit by selling bonds. The interest rate i falls in the upper left domestic credit market. Investors notice the higher return on covered foreign bonds. To buy a foreign bond the first step is to buy the foreign currency. The demand for ringgits rises, pushing e higher in the lower-left quadrant. The supply of credit in Malaysia rises, pushing the interest rate i^* down in the upper-right quadrant. Investors cover their earnings back into dollars. Ringgits are sold forward, increasing the forward supply and lowering f. These changes of a higher e, lower i^*, and lower f all have the effect of lowering the right side of the no-arbitrage CIA condition.

CIA works through spot exchange markets, international credit markets, and forward exchange markets.

The FX market is very quick and much larger than publicized stock markets. Stock trading involves an exchange of claims to future profit. FX trading supports the entire system of international trade and investment. Unexpected exchange rate movements can result in large profit or loss for international investors. Some large banks have gone bankrupt due to their FX trading.

EXAMPLE 12.9   *Differences in Inflation Rates and Interest Rates*

Recent inflation rates and interest rates compared to the US show that higher inflation leads to higher nominal interest rates. These rates are in the range of

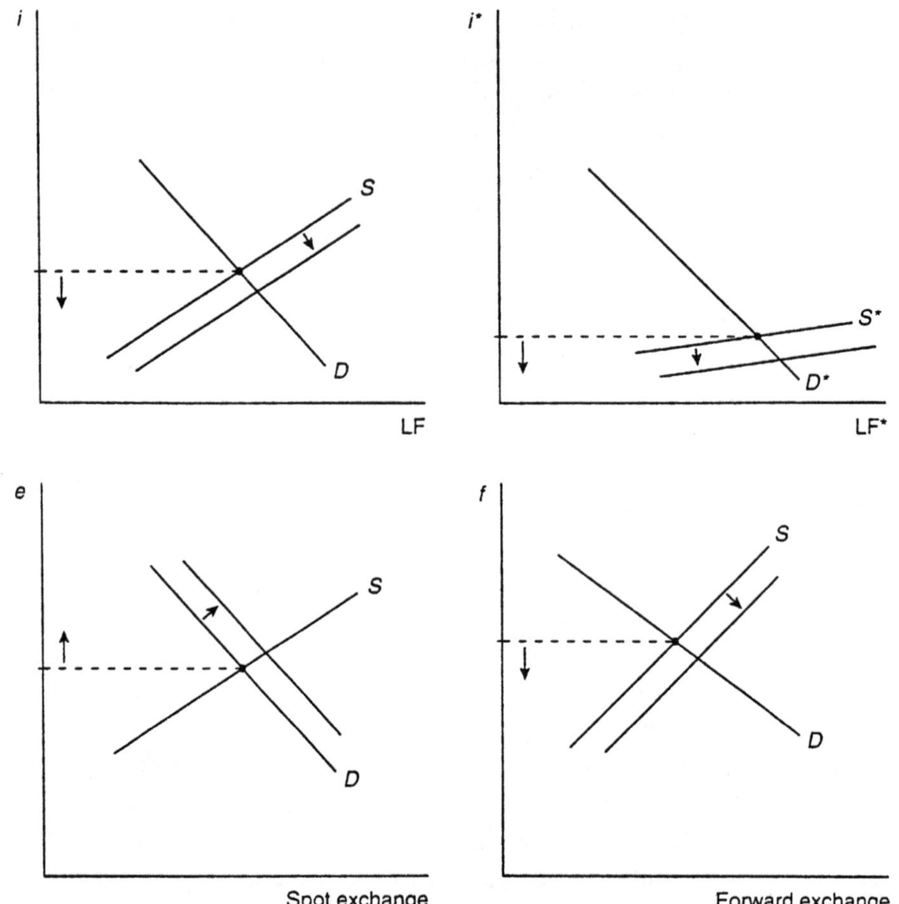

Figure 12.4
Interest Rate and Exchange Rate Markets
CIA equalizes the return to riskless international investments in $1 + i = (f/e)(1 + i^*)$.
If i falls due to a credit expansion, the demand for spot exchange rises, the supply of
foreign loanable funds rises, and the supply of forward exchange falls.

80% for Turkey and for Venezuela 50% above US rates. For Canada and Japan,
the differences are close to zero. Currencies inflating rapidly depreciate. Profitable
CIA ensures the link between exchange rates and interest rates.

Section B Problems

B1. With the example in the text of a perpetuity bond paying 100,000 pesos
per year, suppose the dollar is expected to have inflation of 2%. Find the dollar
value of the peso bond. Do the same if expected inflation is 6%.

B2. Diagram and explain what happens in the FX market in Figure 12.3 when
(a) the domestic interest rate falls, (b) the foreign interest rate rises, (c) faster
growth is expected in the US, and (d) a recession breaks out in Korea.

B3. In the example of CIA, find the profitable position if the forward exchange rate is \$/ringgit = 0.26. Do the same if the forward rate is 0.24.

EXAMPLE 12.10   *Interest Rate Parity*

Interest rate parity holds as investors watch interest rates. These effective real interest rates subtract the rate of depreciation from the nominal interest rate i. While a bond paying over 100% in Turkey may sound attractive, inflation destroys the return. Investors know interest rates but not depreciation ahead of time. Investments are made based on expectations about future exchange rates. High variation in the effective interest rate implies international investment has high risk but high return.

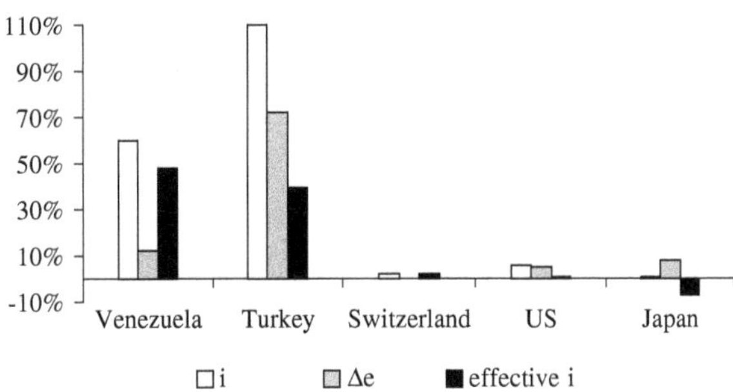

C. INTERNATIONAL MONEY

Inflation is the result of the money supply growing faster than the output. Inflation reduces the purchasing power of money leading to depreciation in the FX market. This section covers the theory and history of fiat currency.

What is Money?

The functions of money are a medium of exchange, store of value, and unit of account. The medium of exchange makes everyday commerce possible replacing barter as the direct trade of products. International commerce involves the exchange of the mediums of exchange in the FX market. Money as a store of value allows saving and delaying spending. Currencies with high inflation rates are a poor store of value depreciating in the FX market. Money also serves as a unit of account to keep books and evaluate income relative to the prices of different goods, services, and assets.

Only certain commodities can perform these functions of money. Gold and silver can be a decent store of value and unit of account but are too heavy as a medium of exchange. Paper currency and coins are handy but cheap to produce leading to oversupply, inflation, and depreciation. Bank cards and electronic currency face even more serious oversupply.

The supply of money is controlled by the central bank through government monetary policy. The banking system is made up of the commercial banks that accept deposits, keep accounts, print checks, provide ATM machines, and make loans. This financial intermediation expands the monetary base supplied by the government to the money supply. The price level and exchange rates provide a gauge of currency performance.

Money Supply and the Price Level

The demand for money is derived from the goods and services it purchases. The price level P is the average price $P = \$/\text{good}$ of all products. Its inverse $1/P = \text{goods}/\$$ represents the purchasing power of money. A higher price level means less purchasing power for each dollar. Money that loses purchasing power with inflation is a poor store of value. Inflation leads to holding less money in favor of more stocks, bonds, gold, jewelry, real estate, or foreign currency.

The money market in Figure 12.5 has the price of money $1/P$ on the vertical axis. Inflation lowers $1/P$ leading to an increase in the quantity of money demanded as a medium of exchange. The purchasing power of money falls with $1/P$. The supply of money is the vertical line at $1 trillion leading to $1/P = 0.8$ and $P = 1.25$. Increasing the money supply to $1.5 trillion would lower $1/P$ to 0.667 with P rising to 1.50. Lowering the money supply to $0.8 trillion would lower the price level to 1 raising the price of money to 1.

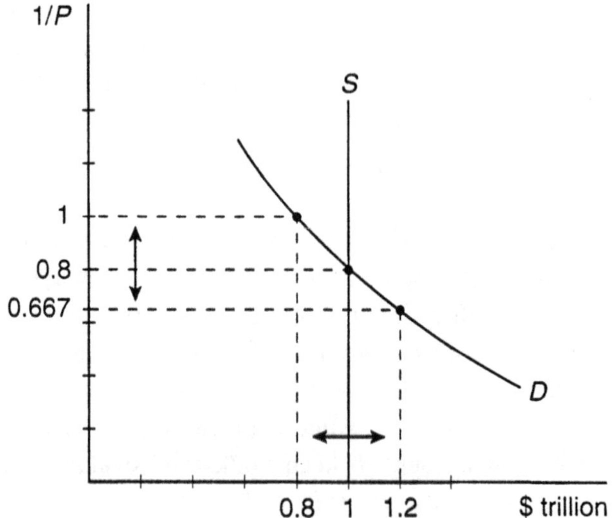

Figure 12.5
The Money Market
The demand for money slopes downward as a higher price level P requires a higher quantity of money demanded for the same transactions. The money market equilibrium price level is $0.8 = 1/1.25$. The price level P is an increasing function of supply S.

Let M_S be the money supply and V the money velocity as the number of times each dollar changes hands during a year. The product $M_S V$ is the value of all transactions in the economy. The price level is P and Q real output. The product PQ is the dollar value of output reported as GDP. The quantity equation $M_S V = PQ$ relates M_S to GDP.

If M_S increases by 20% to \$1.1 trillion in Figure 12.5 and both V and Q are constant, P increases by 20% to 1.50. A higher level of money supply leads to a higher price level given constant money velocity and real output.

Some of the demand for a currency comes from foreign countries. Exports lead to demand for dollars in the FX market. If investors expect the dollar to appreciate more relative to the other currencies, the demand for dollars by foreign wealth holders increases. Increased demand in Figure 12.5 drives the price of the dollar up lowering the price level P. In the FX market, increased demand for dollars appreciates the dollar.

A currency with relatively low inflation appreciates in the FX market.

The US dollar plays an important role as a unit of account with about a quarter of international transactions across the world made in dollars. Government central banks over the world keep FX reserves of dollars. Most countries in the Americas fix their currencies in terms of the dollar. The other two major international currencies are the euro and the yen. Exchange rates for these three currencies are tied together through active triangular arbitrage in the competitive FX market.

The dollar has a record of steady inflation. Goods worth \$100 in 2022 could have been bought for \$58 in 2000 and \$15 in 1970. Inflation has eroded the purchasing powers of the euro and yen at lower rates. Most other currencies are inflating and depreciating at much faster rates.

EXAMPLE 12.11   *Inflation Highs and Lows*

Inflation fueled by faster growth of the money supply than real output, ranges from over 200% in Sudan, Venezuela, and Lebanon to under 2% in Japan, Saudi Arabia, and Switzerland. Each country has its own political process to determine money supply creation. Central banks supply money for the government to spend. The US and EU are in the range of 5% inflation.

Fiat Currencies and Monetary Standards

Governments control their money supplies that affect price levels and exchange rates. Fiat currency is paper money that by law must be accepted as a medium of exchange inside a country. Government central banks physically create money by printing bills and minting coins. Fiat currency is not backed by any commodity such as gold or silver. The US government stopped redeeming dollars for gold in 1933 and stopped defining the dollar in terms of gold in 1971. Instead, its endorsement "This note is legal tender for all debts, public and private" is printed on the dollar.

Under the gold standard of the 1800s, governments exchanged gold for paper money or vice versa. Currency notes were equivalent to a defined amount of gold. The US experimented with a bimetal standard for a period during the late 1890s with the dollar defined in terms of both gold and silver. The Bretton Woods fixed exchange rate system lasted from the end of World War II until the energy crisis of the early 1970s.

The present floating exchange rate system accommodates flat currencies that seek their market exchange rates. Most currencies are fixed or managed by government central banks that routinely intervene in the FX market.

EXAMPLE 12.12   *The Great Contraction*

The Great Depression was the result of poor government policy with a sharp decrease in the money supply and extremely high tariffs. Bennet McCallum (1989) models what would have happened with steady growth in the money supply. Instead of the sharp decline in output, the US economy would have grown steadily. The stock market crash only redistributed unrealized wealth. A fixed money supply growth rule would take away this discretion of the Federal Reserve Bank to control the money supply. The result would be less inflation and more reliable output growth.

Money Standards

The gold standard lasted from the late 1800s until World War I when the English pound as the major world currency. The pound was defined as 0.234 ounces of gold and the dollar as 0.048 ounces, freezing the pound exchange rate at $\$/\pounds = 4.87 = 0.234/0.048$. Other currencies had their own equivalents in gold with all currencies accepted everywhere as they were redeemable into gold. The lack of foreign exchange risk in international commerce created favorable conditions for international commerce. This period stands out with high economic growth.

Under the gold standard, growth in the money supply is limited by the supply of gold. Immigration and output growth in the US outpaced the growth of gold supply leading to deflation. The demand for money grew faster than the supply causing the increase in $1/P$. The pressure to expand the money supply was held back by the scarcity of gold.

The solution was a bimetal standard defining the dollar in terms of silver and gold. The problem with a bimetal standard is the relative price of silver in terms of gold might not stay constant. When the market price of silver fell, traders bought cheap silver to trade with the government for gold. Bad money chased out good money as gold did not circulate.

The principle that bad money circulates is called Gresham's law after a British banker in the 1500s. Coins then contained the metals worth their stamped value. Gresham famously shaved coins and hoarded the shavings. Unshaved coins would be stored or shaved. Only shaved coins as bad money circulated.

EXAMPLE 12.13   *Trade, Cartels, and the Great Depression*

The Great Depression lasted for about 10 years following the stock market crash of 1929. International trade virtually stopped due to the Smoot-Hawley tariffs in the US and similar prohibitive tariffs worldwide. The lost imports of intermediate and capital goods halted economic growth. Harold Cole and Lee Ohanian (1999) point out that the National Industrial Recovery Act (NIRA) of 1933 encouraged cartels that restricted output and raised prices. While NIRA was touted to stimulate the economy, it prolonged the Great Depression.

Collapse of the International Gold Standard

World War I disrupted international commerce and the international money system. Following the war, countries tried to return to the gold standard. Governments increased money supplies to pay back the war debts. As a result, inflation surged in Europe.

The exchange rates from the gold standard era proved unworkable. The British pound was worth more at the government gold exchange window than in goods and services. The British gold supply dwindled as traders cashed in pounds for gold. The overvalued pound made British exports uncompetitive. The UK dropped the gold standard in 1931. The dollar remained redeemable in terms of gold and became the standard international currency. Investors wanted the stability provided by gold. The US gold supply dwindled leading the government to stop redeeming dollars for gold in 1933.

Governments began to devalue their currencies to stimulate exports. Inflation increased worldwide. German hyperinflation created the economic chaos that led to the Nazi party taking control. In misguided efforts to save jobs, high tariffs were imposed worldwide. The US passed the infamous Smoot-Hawley Tariff Act. International investment dwindled due to FX risk. The Great Depression lasted through the 1930s leading to World War II.

EXAMPLE 12.14   *Safe Haven*

The US remains a haven for international investors. The US has political stability with no imminent military threat and prospects for continued economic growth. Relatively high defense spending makes the US appear to be an even safer haven. Robert Ayanian (1988) and Vittrio Grilli and Andrea Beltratti (1989) show that defense spending raises the demand for US assets and dollars on FX market.

The Bretton Woods System

The international monetary system collapsed during World War II. After the war, the desire was a stable monetary system without inflation. An international conference held in Bretton Woods, New Hampshire, to create a monetary system led to a gold exchange standard. Currencies were defined in terms of gold but were not redeemable. The dollar defined as 1/35 ounces of gold became the international standard as the US held more than half the gold stock of the world. Other currencies were defined in terms of the dollar. The English pound was set at $/£ = 2.80, the Japanese yen at $/¥ = 0.0028, and the German mark at $/DM = 0.24.

IMF was created as the bank for central banks to maintain FX reserves at the fixed exchange rates. The Bretton Woods exchange rates were adjustable. A country with a trade deficit could borrow from the IMF to meet the cash shortage. But with a chronic trade deficit, the IMF would allow the currency to depreciate.

During the 1950s, international trade and investment grew slowly but steadily. Money supplies grew at low rates with little or no inflation. Europe and Japan rebuilt from war damage. The balance of trade deficits of the US suggested the dollar should depreciate. If the dollar lost value in terms of gold, anyone holding gold would enjoy a profit. In anticipation, the price of gold went well above the official price of $35 per ounce. The Bretton Woods system managed to hold together even through US inflation during the Vietnam War.

The dollar had not been redeemable for gold since 1933 but the US government continued to redeem gold for foreign governments. The US gold stock steadily declined as other governments, notably the French, accumulated stocks. The credibility of the Bretton Woods system declined with the US stock of gold. In 1971, President Nixon cut the dollar from its stated value in terms of gold leading to collapse of the Bretton Woods fixed exchange rate system.

EXAMPLE 12.15   *Declining Purchasing Power*

Inflation lowers purchasing power of the dollar. During the 1950s and 1960s, there was little decline in purchasing power. Starting in the late 1960s through the early 1980s, purchasing power declined steadily followed by stabilization during the 1980s–1990s and steady declines during the 2000s–2010s. The effects accumulate with purchasing power of the dollar in 2022 at 8% of the 1950 level. Government budget deficits lead to increased money supply diminishing the purchasing power of the dollar.

International Money and Floating Exchange Rates

Differences in inflation rates and growing international trade and investment led to the collapse of Bretton Woods fixed exchange rates. The price of gold was bid up by investors treating gold as a safe haven. The world adopted floating exchange rates by 1973. The only experience with floating rates was a short period during the 1920s and the Canadian dollar float during the 1970s.

With floating exchange rates, each government determines the fate of its currency through its money supply. International banks started FX operations as brokers and traders entered the business. Speculators attempted to outguess the market to make profit. Hedging and speculating in FX increased. The FX market quickly grew into a lively worldwide business.

The floating exchange rate system is not entirely free as governments intervene to influence their exchange rates, impose fixed rates, and require licenses to buy and sell currency. The IMF is a bank for the central banks supplying its own currency, the special drawing right (SDR). The SDR is part of FX reserves and monetary base in each country.

The floating exchange rate system has worked through oil embargoes, debt crises, surpluses, emerging economic powers, banking collapses, government defaults, and rapidly increasing international trade and investment. Any fixed exchange rate system would have collapsed.

Economic theory and history suggest governments should let markets operate. FX markets have shown the capability to handle international trade and finance.

EXAMPLE 12.16   *The FX Rate and Inflation*

Kenneth Kasa (1995) reports that 60% of the trend during the 1970s–1980s in the $/mark rate was due to the difference in inflation rates. The dollar depreciated 5% annually versus the mark with US inflation about 2% higher than German inflation. For the $/yen rate only 20% of the trend was due to the inflation differential. The dollar depreciated an average of 5% per year versus the yen but inflation in the US was only 1% higher. Labor productivity grew 2% higher in Japan.

Section C Problems

C1. Explain how well each of the following would perform each of the functions of money: beaver tails, tobacco, dried buffalo chips, beads, and large boulders. These monies have all been used in history.

C2. Can the supply of money come from private banks? Describe how a private money supply system would operate. Diagram the supply curve. How would the international monetary system operate?

C3. Any commodity standard of money ties the value of money to a certain quantity of some commodity. Explain which of these commodities would function better as money standards: gold, oil, wheat, and a stock market price index.

D. INTERNATIONAL MONEY AND FINANCE

Government deficit spending supported by money supply creation leads to inflation and depreciation. The alternative is for the government to borrow increasing debt through bond sales that raise interest rates and may lead to a twin trade deficit. This section also introduces purchasing power parity and the real exchange rate.

Government Bonds and the Money Supply

Government deficit spending occurs when spending is greater than tax revenue. Governments raise the cash for deficit spending either by creating money or selling government bonds. The bond purchaser has the promise of the future face value of the bond when it matures.

Borrowing by the government increases the demand for loanable funds D_{LF} in Figure 12.1 or excess demand XD_{LF} in Figure 12.2 raising the interest rate. In the bond market, the price of bonds falls. The government creates the new bonds, selling them to acquire the cash to spend.

Central bank purchase of the new bonds with newly created money is accommodating expansion of the money supply. Investors inside the country buying the bonds lowers other investment.

Foreign investors or governments buying the bonds leads to a surplus in the capital account. Such international investment must consider FX risk along with default risk as well as different rates of inflation. Foreign purchase of the bonds appreciates the domestic currency favoring a trade deficit.

The link between the government deficit and the trade deficit is called the twin deficit.

Governments can directly support their deficit spending with new money supply. This monetary expansion is carried out predominantly in open market operations with the central bank purchasing government bonds already in circulation. The money supply increases with the Fed purchase of secondhand bonds in the open market.

Government deficits are financed by new government bonds or by newly created money through open market operations.

EXAMPLE 12.17   *Dollarize*

If the central bank could not buy secondhand bonds on the open market, the government would have to rely on taxes and the sale of new bonds to cover its spending. Panama adopted exactly such money, the US dollar. William Gruben and Sherry Kiser (1999) discuss how dollarization would allow Latin American countries to avoid currency collapses due to money supply increases to cover government deficit spending.

Money Supplies and Price Levels

During the 1700s, David Hume wrote about the links between money supplies, price levels, and international trade. Money supply increases lead to higher price levels that reduce exports as they become more expensive and increase imports due to the lower prices in foreign countries. The trade deficit creates an outflow of cash reducing the money supply leading to falling prices that pull the economy back to balanced trade. Through this influence of prices, currency flows between countries maintain balanced trade.

Hume referred to currency as specie, calling this balancing property the price-specie flow mechanism. This link between the money supply and prices is in the classical quantity equation $M_S V = PQ$. If the government increases M_S while real output Q and velocity V remain constant, the price level P must rise by the same percentage.

Purchasing Power Parity and the Real Exchange Rate

International trade links price levels across countries. Most products are traded or include traded components. Even haircuts in Iowa include a trade with the clippers from Germany and vacuum cleaner from Taiwan. Purchasing power parity (PPP) would hold if all goods and services are traded,

$$P = eP*$$

The price levels $P = \$/\text{good}$ in the home country and $P* = ¥/\text{good}$ in the foreign country represent the average prices of all goods in the two countries. The exchange rate $e = \$/¥$ leads to $eP* = \$/\text{good}$ as the average dollar price of goods in the foreign country.

Arbitrage implies equal product prices across countries as any price difference would generate trade to equalize prices. This ideal situation is called perfect competition. The law of one price relies on arbitrage to equalize the price of the same good across countries. Relative PPP says that percentage changes in P are matched by percentage changes in e and $P*$.

The real exchange rate e_R is derived from PPP as,

$$e_R = P/P*$$

Suppose $P = 1.25$ in the US and $P* = 125$ yen. The real exchange rate would then be $e_R = \$/¥ = 1.25/125 = 0.01$. Competitive trade would result in the real exchange rate. Suppose the market exchange rate is $\$/¥ = 0.02$ making Japanese products overpriced. Competitive trade would mean less exports and more imports for Japan and a trade deficit. Yen depreciation with $\$/¥$ falling would lead toward balanced trade.

Empirical evidence supports PPP accounting for transport costs, tariffs, and nontraded goods. Deviations from PPP diminish over time. Kenneth Froot and Kenneth Rogoff (1995) show half of the deviation from PPP erodes over four years.

EXAMPLE 12.18   *C$ Depreciation and PPP*

> The Canadian dollar declined 25% relative to the US dollar during the 1990s, leaving prices in Canada too low according to PPP. Charles Engel (1999) hypothesizes that firms were pricing to market absorbing exchange rate changes. If Canada has lower or more elastic demand, firms price discriminate and charge lower prices.

EXAMPLE 12.19   *Big Mac PPP*

> *The Economist* tracks relative prices of Big Mac as PPP. Big Macs are produced locally with standardized products including labor and capital along with locally supplied ingredients. The dollar is undervalued against the won, yen, and pound, but overvalued against the Canadian and Singapore dollars. Currencies tend to move as predicted by Big Mac PPP although the timing is difficult to predict.
>
> | Country | Big Mac P^* | P/P^* | e | % |
> |---|---|---|---|---|
> | South Korea | 2400 won | 1188 | 666 | −44% |
> | Japan | 370 yen | 183 | 133 | −27% |
> | Britain | 1.26 pounds | 0.62 | 0.59 | −5% |
> | Canada | 2.15 C$ | 1.06 | 1.19 | 13% |
> | Singapore | 2.80 S$ | 1.39 | 1.96 | 41% |

Relative Money Supplies and the Real Exchange Rate

The relationship between the relative money supply M/M^* and the real exchange rate P/P^* is pictured in Figure 12.6. The numbers are based on $M^* = 76$ billion Swiss francs and $M = \$1,000$ billion leading to $M/M^* = 13.2$ and $P/P^* = 1.12/1.07 = 1.05$. These were the money supplies and consumer price indices in 1989 for Switzerland and the US. If M increases by 10% to $1.1 trillion with outputs and M^* constant, then M/M^* would rise to $1,100/76 = 14.5$ as P increases by 10% to 1.232 leading to the real exchange $e_R = 1.15$.

The positive relation in Figure 12.6 applies over long time periods. Countries with high inflation rates and depreciating exchange rates in recent history include Venezuela, Mexico, Brazil, Israel, and Greece or Italy before the euro. Countries with the lowest rates of inflation and appreciating exchange rates include Germany, Switzerland, and Japan.

Countries with higher money supply growth have inflation and depreciation.

Whether the simple relationship in Figure 12.6 holds depends on the underlying macroeconomic model. If changes in the money supply affect output, the link to the price level in the quantity equation is relaxed. Another point is that PPP may not hold exactly in that not all products are freely traded. The positive relation between M/M^* and P/P^* stands out when there are large differences between money supply growth rates.

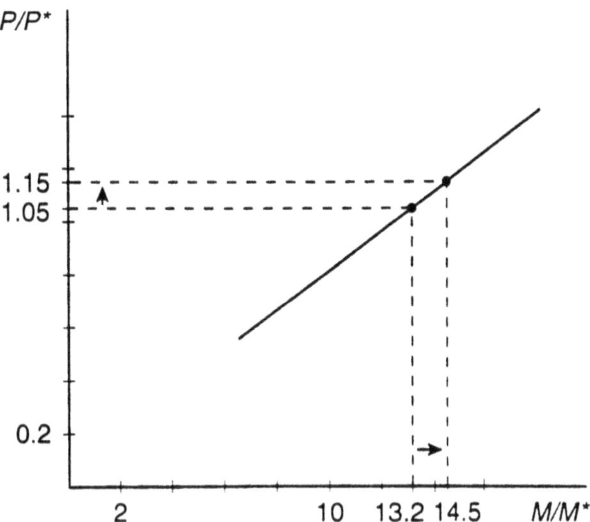

Figure 12.6
Relative Money Supplies and the Real FX Rate
PPP leads to the real exchange rate e_R as the relative price level P/P^*. Increasing M relative to M^* causes an increase in e_R and depreciation.

EXAMPLE 12.20   *One PPP Episode*

In 1931, the UK gave up the gold standard. Speculation turned against the pound leading to depreciation by 30% relative to the dollar. The relative price of US goods rose 10% as described by S.N. Broadway (1987). Two years later PPP became 40% out of line. The US then dropped the gold standard, the dollar depreciated, and P/P^* fell. By 1934, there was a return to PPP.

In credit markets, inflation benefits debtors who are paying off loans but hurts creditors. If lenders and borrowers correctly anticipate inflation, there are no real effects as all economic variables are reduced to real terms.

In trade, businesses in countries with high inflation rates often quote prices in stable currencies for local customers. Inflating currencies ultimately depreciate. Inflation values currencies against products while exchange rates value currencies against each other.

Exchange rates ultimately follow real exchange rates with inflating currencies depreciating.

Monetary Policy Control of the Money Supply

Governments choose their money supply growth rates that determine price levels and exchange rates. Money supply growth is the result of economic processes including central bank control, commercial lending, and spending habits. The primary job of the central bank is to control the money supply.

Monetary policy is a central issue in economics. A competitive banking system with efficient financial intermediation is essential for economic growth. The link between government deficits and money supply growth suggests a government wanting to control inflation should control its budget. When a government spends more that it collects in taxes, the temptation is to create new money to pay for the spending.

Section D Problems

D1. Explain the difference between the Chinese government versus a US citizen buying US bonds to finance a US government budget deficit.

D2. If $P = \$1.25$ and $P^* = 200$ pesos, find the real exchange rate $e_R = \$/peso$. If the market rate is $e = 150$, explain which currency is overvalued and which will appreciate.

D3. Suppose in Figure 12.6 the foreign money supply M^* increases to 79.8 billion Swiss francs with M remaining at \$1 trillion. Find the real exchange rate.

CONCLUSION

International investment continues to develop leading to net gains as countries become increasingly interdependent. The basic lesson of international economics includes the gains from international investment as well as the gains from trade. Chapter 13 turns to open economy macroeconomics focusing on the links among international trade and investment, GDP, unemployment, and inflation.

Terms

Adjustable peg	Hyperinflation
Bimetal standard	Open market operations
Covered interest arbitrage	Price-specie flow mechanism
Fiat currency	Purchasing power parity (PPP)
Forward exchange rate	Real exchange rate
Gold exchange standard	Real interest rate
Gold standard	Special drawing rights (SDR)
Gresham's law	

MAIN POINTS

- Credit markets match lenders and borrowers to determine interest rates and the quantity of loans. International credit markets introduce foreign lenders and borrowers as well as foreign interest rates.

- Exchange rates and international interest rates are tightly related by triangular arbitrage and CIA.
- Money supplies relative to outputs determines price levels across countries. Increased money supply is the underlying cause of inflation and depreciation.
- PPP links price levels across countries and leads to the real exchange rate.

REVIEW PROBLEMS

1. Explain whether borrowers or lenders would favor policy restricting foreign investment inflow. Do the same for foreign investment outflow.
2. Show what happens in Figure 12.2 if home country households increase saving due to tax reductions. Explain the international adjustment.
3. Suppose the home country decides to restrict the inflow of foreign capital in Figure 12.2 to $2 billion. Explain what happens to interest rates.
4. Explain the difference when foreign investors in Figure 12.2 buy private bonds instead of government bonds.
5. The Mexican government historically limits foreign ownership of firms in Mexico to 49%. This restriction was lifted by the North American Free Trade Agreement (NAFTA). Predict the effects on the peso/$ exchange rate.
6. In the example of international inflation and arbitrage, suppose there is a reduction in US credit. Explain the adjustments in other markets.
7. Suppose the supply of loans in the foreign country decreases in the international financial market of Figure 12.4. Explain the effects on the credit market and FX market.
8. Suppose a foreign automaker builds a new plant in the US raising half of the funds through the sale of new stock inside US. Explain how the new plant affects the US capital account and exchange rate. Explain how the US balance of trade will be affected in the future.
9. Starting with the money market in Figure 12.5, show and explain what happens if foreign investors expect the dollar to depreciate.
10. Explain the market adjustments in the following quote:

    News that the US trade deficit fell in November pushed dollar down against the euro. The dollar later recovered in a technical correction for the euro that was overbought in the euphoria over events in Eastern Europe.

11. Suppose the dollar is put on a bimetal standard. The government defines the dollar as 0.0025 ounces of gold and 0.185 ounces of silver standing ready to trade paper dollars for gold or silver. In the market, the price of gold is $393.75 and the price of silver is $5.25/oz. Explain the arbitrage. What will happen to government stocks of gold and silver? Identify the bad money.
12. Describe the link between a government surplus and a trade surplus.
13. Explain three reasons PPP might not hold.
14. Explain whether a country with a relatively young population is more likely or less likely to have an unexpected inflation. Do the same for a country with a relatively wealthy population.

READINGS

Ron Jones and Peter Kenen, eds. (1985) *Handbook of International Economics*, Vol. II, Amsterdam: North-Holland. Surveys of international monetary economics.

Ronald McKinnon (1993) The rules of the game: International money in historical perspective, *The Journal of Economic Literature*. A look at the game played by central banks.

Kenneth Rogoff (1990) Symposia: New institutions for developing country debt, *Journal of Economic Perspectives*. Proposals for dealing with LDC debt.

Gary Smith (1991) *Money, Banking, and Financial Intermediation*, D C Heath & Co. A clear introduction to monetary economics.

MATHEMATICAL APPENDIX

The domestic credit market includes the demand for loanable funds (LF) from borrowers and supply from lenders. The demand D for credit decreases in the interest rate r, and supply S increases. Income Y raises both D and S. Other variables Z affect lenders and borrowers in the credit market equilibrium,

$$\overset{-\ +}{D_{LF}(r,\ Y,\ Z)} = \overset{+\ +}{S_{LF}(r,\ Y,\ Z)}.$$

Both sides of the market include households, firms, and the government. Optimal borrowing and lending are based on intertemporal utility maximization given expectations for related variables in later periods.

The real interest rate $r = i - \pi$ is the nominal rate i less inflation π assuming the market correctly anticipates π. The interest rate r represents the cost of repayment from borrowing and the return to lending of more to liquidity in the future. Income Y has a positive effect on demand as borrowers feel more confident and suppliers have more LF available. Other variables shifting supply and demand include expected income, tax rates, government spending, expected inflation, and expected real interest rates.

Banks borrow from lenders at low rates and lend to borrowers at high rates to generate revenue. In Figure 12.1, banks lend at $r_D = 6\%$ and borrow at $r_S = 4\%$ making net revenue of \$480mil − \$320mil = \$160mil. The size of the margin indicates banking efficiency.

Interest rate controls reduce total surplus generating shortages and surpluses. Increased taxes on interest earnings reduce S_{LF} raising r and lowering Q_{LF} in the market. Increased taxes also lower borrower surplus under D_{LF} and above the higher r.

A small open economy facing the world interest rate r* would be a borrower if r* < r with a capital account surplus $KA = D_{LF} - S_{LF} > 0$. If r* = 4% in Figure 12.1, then KA = \$4bil. Domestic borrowers enjoy benefits paying \$480mil interest expense to borrow \$12bil compared to \$500mil borrowing \$10bil in the closed economy. Domestic lenders suffering a decrease in revenue from \$500mil to \$320mil would favor a tax on foreign loanable funds familiar from import tariff theory. If r* > r, the economy would be a lender with domestic lenders benefiting at the expense of domestic borrowers.

The model of excess supply and demand in Figure 12.2 applies between two large economies. One application is between lending developed countries (DCs) and borrowing less-developed countries (LDCs). The excess demand for credit XD_{LF} in Figure 12.2 is derived from S_{LF} and D_{LF} in Figure 12.1. The world LF market maximizes total surplus although domestic lenders and foreign borrowers would be better off in autarky. The home country in Figure 12.1 has KA = \$4bil, implying future net investment income (NII) = −\$160mil at the world r = 5%. A tax on foreign credit would shift XD_{LF} down lowering r and international credit $KA = -KA^* = Q_{LF}$.

The international credit market interacts with the FX market making the interest rate r and exchange rate e endogenous. Exogenous shifts in either market affect the other market. Shifts in D_{LF} or S_{LF} changing the interest rate r would lead to credit flows between countries shifting D_{FX} or S_{FX}. Another example is expected depreciation raising e increases the price of foreign bonds lowering XD_{LF}.

The interaction between interest and exchange rates is apparent in arbitrage across bond rates i and i*. The nominal return on a \$1 bond in the home country is $1 + i$. The \$1 invested in a foreign bond would return $(1/e)(1 + i^*)$ in foreign currency that could be covered by the forward exchange rate f back into domestic currency. This covered interest arbitrage condition $1 + i = (f/e)(1 + i^*)$ ties the two credit markets to the spot and forward exchange rate market. An exogenous shift in any market leads to adjustments in all markets.

The price index P = \$/good reflects the average price of all goods. The inflation rate $\pi = d\ln P = \%\Delta P$ reflects the changing purchasing power of money. If $\pi > 0$ purchasing power of the dollar falls with the inverse $1/P$ = goods/\$ of the price index. If $\pi > 0$, the decrease in $1/P$ implies a greater quantity of currency is demanded to support the same level of transactions. This downward sloping demand implies an increase in the money supply raises P as in Figure 12.5.

Fiat money has no underlying value except in transactions reflected by $1/P$ and relative to other currencies reflected by $1/e$. A currency losing value with P and e rising is a poor store of value. Increased money supply M_S raises P if real output Q and money velocity V are constant in the classical quantity equation $M_S V = PQ$. Purchasing power parity (PPP) stated as $P = eP^*$ holds given free trade. Increased money supply then depreciates the currency as $e = M_S V/Q$ implies $\partial e/\partial M_S = V/Q$.

Government deficit spending is covered by increasing M_S or by selling bonds increasing the demand for credit D_{LF} and raising the interest rate r. The increase in M_S implies inflation *ceteris paribus*. The increased r lowers investment underlying D_{LF}. Increased r also attracts foreign lenders appreciating the currency e↓ and favoring a trade deficit in the twin deficit effect of government deficit.

The real exchange rate $e_R = P/P^*$ implied by PPP can suggest mispriced currencies in the FX market. If $e = \$/peso > e_R$, the overpriced peso suggests central bank support. The positive relation between M_S/M_S^* and $e_R = P/P^*$ in Figure 12.6 due to the quantity equation is $M_S/M_S^* = (P/P^*)(Q/Q^*)(V^*/V)$. Whether changes in MS/MS* might be able to affect Q/Q^* is a topic for Chapter 13.

CHAPTER 13

Open Economy Macroeconomics

Preview

This chapter covers open economy macroeconomics including:

- Microeconomic foundations of production and optimal saving
- Investment-Saving, Liquidity-Money (ISLM) model
- Inflation in the Aggregate Supply, Aggregate Demand (ASAD) model
- Effectiveness of fiscal and monetary policies, flexible versus fixed exchange rates

---

INTRODUCTION

Open economy macroeconomics focuses on the effectiveness of fiscal and monetary policies depending on the exchange rate regime. The goal of macro policy is to avoid or shorten recessions and diminish unemployment. Expansionary fiscal policy involves short-term increased government spending or decreased taxes. Expansionary monetary policy is a short-term increase in the money supply. The exchange rate is either determined in the foreign exchange (FX) market or fixed by the government central bank.

Expansionary fiscal and monetary policies aim to pull the economy out of a recession when output falls for three or more quarters. There is conflicting theoretical and empirical evidence whether expansionary policy is effective. If successful, expansionary macro policy increases output and lowers the real interest rate. Other effects to consider are a higher price level with inflation, a deficit in the balance of payments (*BOP*), depreciation of the exchange rate. Near-full employment, expansionary policy does not raise output. The views of economists range from policy activists to complete policy skeptics.

Floating exchange rates are relatively new in the world. Until 1973, the US and other countries had fixed exchange rates with money defined by the government in terms of gold or silver. Historical coins contain the metals defining their value when melted. Governments would trade paper money for the metals. Money is now fiat currency simply by legal declaration. Floating exchange rates are determined by transactions in the foreign exchange market, the largest market in the world.

Most countries in the world maintain a fixed exchange rate declared by the government central bank. Fixed exchange rates make monetary expansion totally ineffective. Expansionary fiscal policy is weaker with fixed exchange rates.

The first section presents the microeconomic foundations of production with capital and labor inputs with optimal saving by overlapping generations. The second section introduces the Investment-Saving, Liquidity-Money (ISLM) model. Investment adds to the capital stock relying on saving by households in the loanable funds market. The third section adds balance of payments adjustment to the ISLM model including foreign investment (FI) in the capital account (KA). The final section introduces price level adjustment and inflation in the open economy Aggregate Supply, Aggregate Demand (ASAD) model.

A. THE MICRO FOUNDATIONS OF MACROECONOMICS

Macroeconomics builds on the foundation of production theory and optimal saving behavior. Production theory is based on capital and labor inputs producing aggregate output with diminishing marginal products in competitive markets. Optimal saving is based on the overlapping generations (OLG) model with the young working generation saving for retirement as the retired generation lives off capital income.

The economy produces aggregate output Y with inputs capital K and labor L in the production function,

$$Y = Af(K, L)$$

where K and L have positive diminishing marginal products and positive cross effects. Fixed capital assets in the data imbed technology suggesting A can be considered a constant. The time frame of macroeconomic adjustments is a few quarters up to a few years. Over the decades, A can be considered as a technology shifter.

The Cobb-Douglas production function scaled to the US economy is,

$$Y = AK^{0.3}L^{0.7}$$

Capital and labor are paid marginal products $r = MP_K$ and $w = MP_L$ where r is the return to capital and w the wage. The Cobb-Douglas coefficients are income shares as L receives 70% of gross domestic product (GDP) as wL/Y and capital, and the other 30% as rK/Y. Cobb-Douglas has constant returns to scale with output proportional to the same percentage change in the two inputs.

Figure 13.1 shows the per capita production function,

$$y = \alpha k^3$$

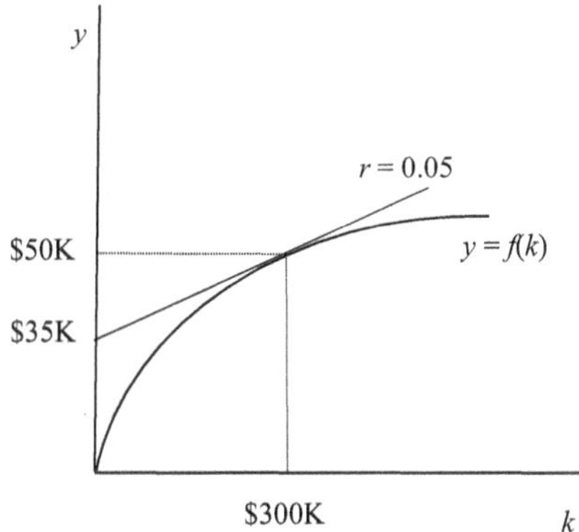

Figure 13.1
Macro Production Function
Income per capita y is an increasing function of the capital labor ratio k. The concave shape is due to diminishing marginal returns.

where $y = Y/L$ is income per capita, $k = K/L$ is the capital/labor ratio, and α is a scalar. Production of $Y = \$10$ trillion of GDP comes from a labor force of $L = 200$ million implying $y = \$50,000$. The labor share of national income is $wL/Y = 70\% = 0.7$ leads to the wage $w = \$35,000$. The return to capital $r = 5\% = 0.05$ and the capital share of income $rK/Y = 0.30$ leads to the capital stock $K = \$60$ trillion and $k = \$300,000$. The production function scales to $y = 1137k^{.3}$. This production function is applied throughout the chapter.

Labor and capital generate national income as the sum of payments to the factors of production in the income statement $Y = wL + rK$. Dividing by L leads to income per capita as the sum of the wage plus capital income per capita, $y = w + rk$.

The slope of the tangent to the production function in Figure 13.1 is the capital return $r = 5\%$. The intercept of the tangent on the y-axis is the wage w. An increase in k implies higher levels of y and w and a lower r. A fundamental property is that per capita income y increases in k.

Income per capita is an increasing concave function of the capital/labor ratio.

EXAMPLE 13.1   *Plots of Production Functions*

Output per capita y is an increasing concave function of the capital labor ratio k as these plots illustrate. The first is the US economy from 1950 to 1990 in thousands, the second a plot of countries in 1990.

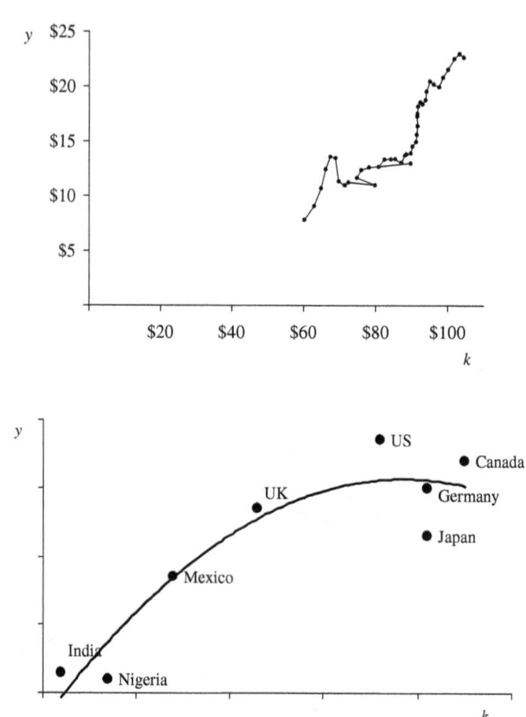

Saving in the Older Generations Model

The decision to save depends on intertemporal preferences between consuming now versus later. The young generation in the OLG model works and saves to retire as the old generation lives off its capital income from past saving. One generation works and saves while the other is retired. The ownership of capital transfers from retired to working in the loanable funds market through saving and investment. Inheritance and capital depreciation make the OLG model more realistic.

Figure 13.2 illustrates the intertemporal optimal saving. Income from labor is the wage w along the horizontal axis. Workers transfer labor income to retirement with saving to earn the interest rate r. The maximum retirement income equal to $(1 + r)w$ cannot be reached as the young must consume to survive. In the example, $w = \$35,000$ and $r = 5\%$ make the maximum potential retirement income $\$36,750$.

Social security systems tax young workers transferring the funds directly to the retired. The tax lowers the budget line leaving workers and retirees worse off. The transfer earns no interest. Motivation for social security transfer that some households could not save enough for retirement occurs with the tax and transfer.

A higher interest rate r would encourage saving with the higher opportunity cost of consumption during youth leading to a higher saving rate $\sigma = S/Y$. Intertemporal preferences differ with the frugal saving more for consumption in retirement. Across countries, more saving translates into higher economic

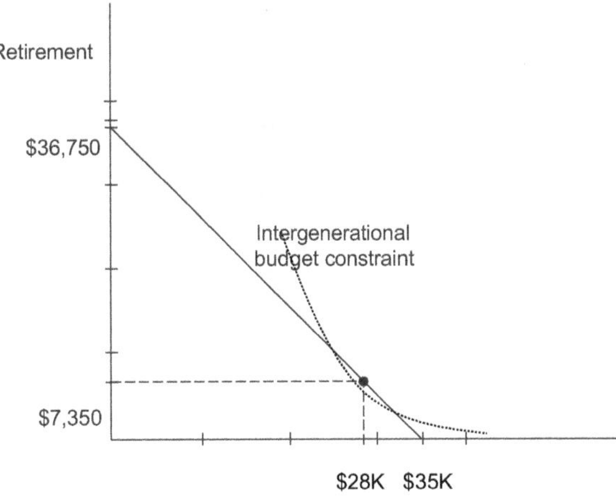

Figure 13.2
Optimal Saving in the OLG Model
Labor income w is saved and transferred to retirement at the interest rate r. With $w =$ $35K and $r = 0.05$, the young consume $28K and the retired $1.05 \times \$7K = \$7.35K$.

growth. Countries with low discount rates for future consumption accumulate capital and become wealthy.

The line connecting w with $(1 + r)w$ is the budget constraint facing the young. Optimization is based on intertemporal indifference curves. In the example, $\sigma = 0.2$ with saving $0.2 \times \$35,000 = \$7,000$, leaving $28,000 for consumption in youth. Saving earns 5% leading to $7,350 income in retirement.

EXAMPLE **13.2**　　*Economic Growth in History*

These growth paths in per capita income y in thousands of dollars from the Maddison Project Database of the University of Groningen show the UK as the leader in the late 1800s. The US and Canada (CN) moved to the front with Japan (JP) and Germany (GE) closing the gap rebuilding after World War II. The growth paths of these developed countries (DCs) are much steeper than in the rest of the world.

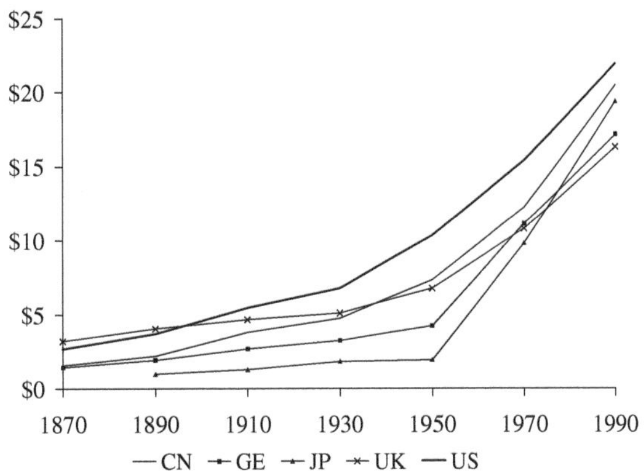

Section A Problems

A1. Find per capita income y and the wage w based on Figure 13.1 if $k =$ \$200,000 and $r = 6.6\%$. Explain the difference in w. Diagram and explain the shift in the production function.

A2. Find the capital labor ratio k if income per capita $y = $ \$60,000 in Figure 13.1. If $r = 3.3\%$, find the wage w. Diagram these two points on the production function.

A3. Suppose workers in the OLG model of Figure 13.2 save 30% of their income. Find their consumption in youth and retirement.

A4. Compare the indifference curve in Problem A4 with one that leads to the optimal consumption in Figure 13.2. Explain the increased saving.

B. INTRODUCTION TO THE INVESTMENT-SAVING, LIQUIDITY-MONEY MODEL

The economy adjusts according to its investment-saving (IS) spending behavior and its liquidity-money (LM) saving behavior. Together IS and LM determine the output and the interest rate. Fiscal policy and monetary policy affect behavior aiming to control output and the interest rate. This section introduces the ISLM model and Section C includes the *BOP* and exchange rate.

Aggregate Production

Output Y produces income spent on consumption by households, investment by firms, and the government,

$$Y = C + I + G$$

Investment spending I adds to the capital stock for future production. Government spending G provides public goods such as streets, ports, national defense, police, and the legal system. Export revenue and import spending are introduced in Section C.

Lending and borrowing are due to some consumers and firms having less cash than they want to spend and others having more. The loanable funds market is based on OLG household saving for retirement and borrowing by firms to invest according to rates of return on capital projects. The government also borrows for deficit spending beyond tax revenue and lends through the central bank creation of money.

Bonds as promises to pay back loans are traded in the loanable funds market. The simplest example is a perpetuity bond paying a fixed income stream forever. The price of a perpetuity bond paying \$1 forever at the interest rate $r = 2\%$ is $p_B = 1/r = $ \$50. Higher interest rates mean lower bond prices.

A firm considering investment projects compares their rates of return to the interest rate. The opportunity cost of spending on an investment project is to buy a bond. Firms short of retained earnings borrow money for projects with higher rates of return. At lower interest rates, more investment projects become attractive and investment spending increases.

Figure 13.3 shows the investment function $I = 4 - 40r$ with a decrease of r by 0.01 raising investment spending I by $0.4 trillion. Firms wanting cash for profitable investment projects can also sell stocks as equity promising stockholders a share of future profit. Stock dividends depend on profits making stocks riskier than bonds. Since the 1800s, stock returns in the US average 6% and bond rates 2% implying a 4% risk premium.

Firms borrow by selling bonds directly or go to commercial banks that aggregate lenders. The other side of the credit market involves saving for future spending. The saving rate $\sigma = S/Y$ implies total saving $S = \sigma Y$. National income less consumption $Y - C = I + G$ is saving S in a closed economy, $S = \sigma Y = I + G$. In the example, $\sigma = 0.2$ implies $S = 0.2 \times \$10$ trillion $= \$2$ trillion.

The IS schedule in Figure 13.4 shows the combinations of r and Y where $S = I + G$. An increase in Y would raise S implying the interest rate r would have to fall to increase I back to equilibrium where $I + G = S$. The IS curve has a negative slope.

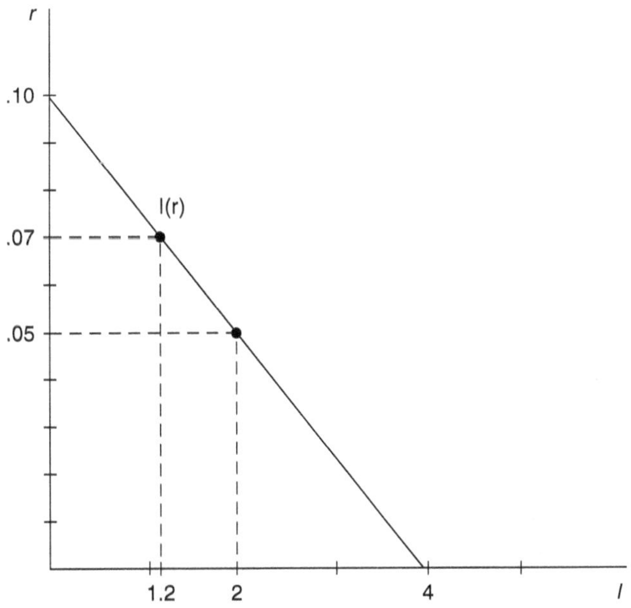

Figure 13.3

Investment Function

The investment function $I = 4 - 40r$ leads to investment spending $I = \$2$ trillion for $r = 5\%$ and to $I = \$1.2$ trillion if $r = 7\%$.

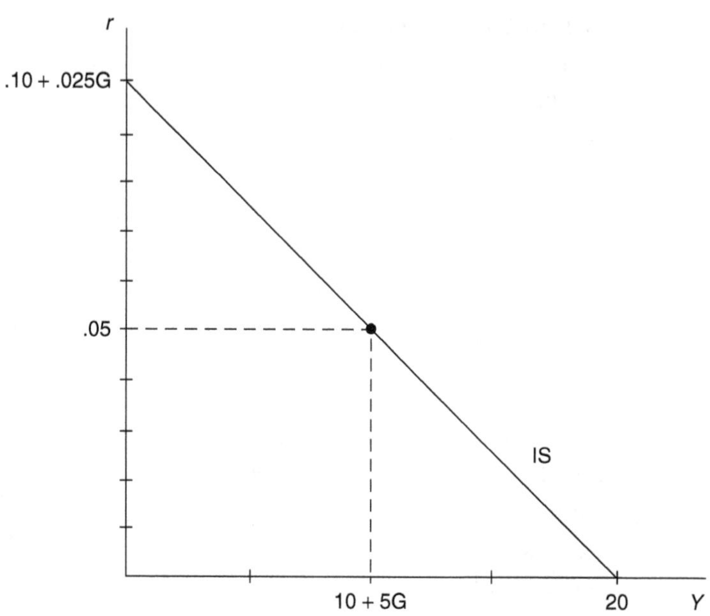

Figure 13.4
IS Curve
If r = 5% then I = \$2 trillion on the investment function in Figure 13.3. The IS curve shows the r and Y where $S = I + G$.

The example with $S = 0.2Y$ and $I = 4 - 40r$ leads to the IS curve in Figure 13.4 with $r = 0.1 + 0.25G - 0.005Y$ implying $Y = 10 + 5G$. On the right side of the IS curve, there is a surplus of loanable funds $S > I$ and on the left a shortage $I > S$. The interest rate adjusts to keep the economy on the IS schedule.

Moving down the IS curve, the lower r moves the economy to a higher capital/labor ratio k along the production function in Figure 13.1. The wage w and per capita income y increase with k. In the short term, capital utilization allows the economy to move down the IS curve.

Capital and Labor Markets

The demand for capital input in Figure 13.5 is its marginal product $MP_K = D_K$ with firms hiring capital according to marginal product in the production function. For the example, production function $y = 1137k^3$ the marginal product of capital is $MP_K = 341k^{-7}$. If r = 5% capital input is K = 60 trillion with k = 300,000 given L = 200 million. If r falls to 4% then K would rise to 84 trillion along the capital demand curve D_K. Firms effectively rent capital from the owners of machinery, equipment, and structures. Moving down the short-term IS curve in Figure 13.3, there is no investment but idle capital is utilized.

Figure 13.6 shows the labor market. The demand for labor D_L is marginal product $MP_L = 796k^3$. Firms hire labor according to marginal product MP_L.

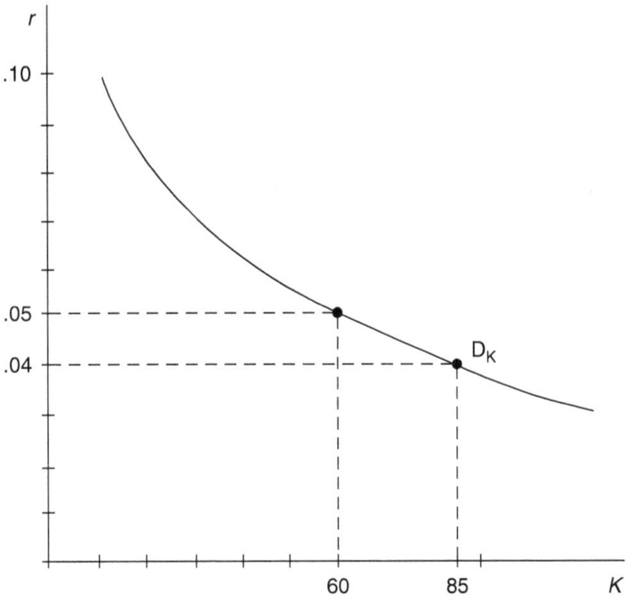

Figure 13.5
Demand for Capital
The marginal product of capital $MP_K = 341k^{-.7}$ comes from the production function $y = 1137K^{.3}$ in Section A. A higher level of r implies K has to fall to increase MP_K.

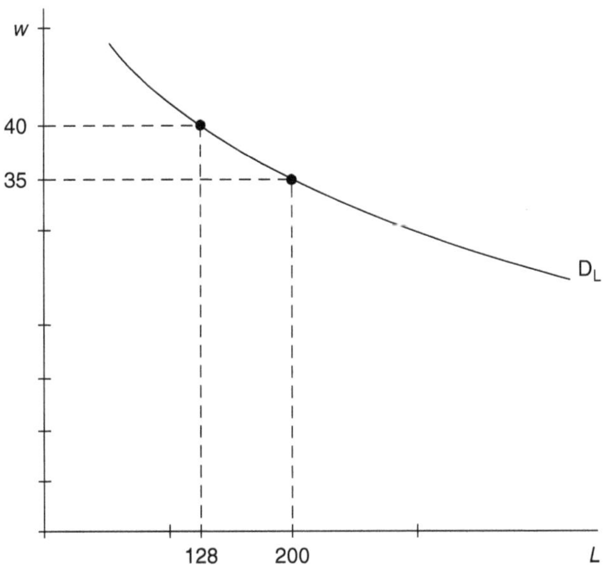

Figure 13.6
Demand for Labor
Labor demand is marginal product derived from the production function. Firms hire labor adjusting marginal product MP_L to the wage w. In the example $MP_L = 796k^{.3} = \$35,000$ and $L = 200$ million.

Given $K = \$60$ trillion, firms employ 200 million at $w = \$35K$. If $w = \$40K$, the quantity of labor demanded falls to 128 million.

Increasing Y along the IS curve K input increases raising MP_L and w. Firms hire more labor due to the increased MP_L. If the total amount of labor available is L_{tot}, the unemployment rate $u = (L_{tot} - L)/L_{tot}$ declines as L increases. Consistent with the declining r along the IS curve k increases.

EXAMPLE 13.3   *Capital Gains From Trade*

When a capital abundant country increases trade, the capital return increases due to capital-intensive exports and the increased price of capital-intensive goods. The higher capital return encourages saving shifting the economy over time toward capital accumulation. Richard Baldwin (1992) finds capital gains range up to 8% across European countries as international trade increases.

The Money/Bond Market

Money is held for transactions with the opportunity cost of not holding bonds to earn interest. Bonds are held as savings accounts or certificates of deposit in banks. The demand for money or liquidity L increases with income and falls with the interest rate, $M_D = L(Y, r)$. Increased spending explains the positive effect of Y. The negative interest rate effect is due to the higher earnings from holding bonds.

The central bank controls the fiat money supply M_S. The central bank lends credit C_{CB} to commercial banks at the federal funds rate i_{FF}. A lower i_{FF} encourages banks to loan more to customers. Buying bonds with newly created money and lending without a profit motive gives the Federal Reserve Bank its discretion over the money supply M_S.

Money market equilibrium occurs along the LM curve where $M_S = L(Y, r)$. The LM curve slopes upward since an increase in Y is offset by a higher r to keep demand L equal to M_S. The interest rate r adjusts to keep the economy on the LM curve.

The money supply M_S is a policy variable. Expansionary monetary policy increases M_S shifting the LM curve to the right. If $M_S = \$1.3$ trillion the ratio of cash to income is $\$1.3/\$10 = 0.13$. An increase of $\$100$ in income raises demand for liquidity by $\$13$. If the elasticity of liquidity demand with respect to the r equals -1 then the marginal effect of r on L would be $-26 = -1.3/0.05$. This money demand function is $L = 1.3 + 0.13Y - 26r$.

Figure 13.7 shows the related LM curve $r = 0.005Y$ given $M_S = 1.3$. Equilibrium in the closed economy ISLM model occurs where the IS and LM curves intersect, $r = 5\%$ and $Y = 10$ assuming $G = 0$ in the example.

The ISLM model determines the interest rate and output clearing the IS and LM sides of the economy.

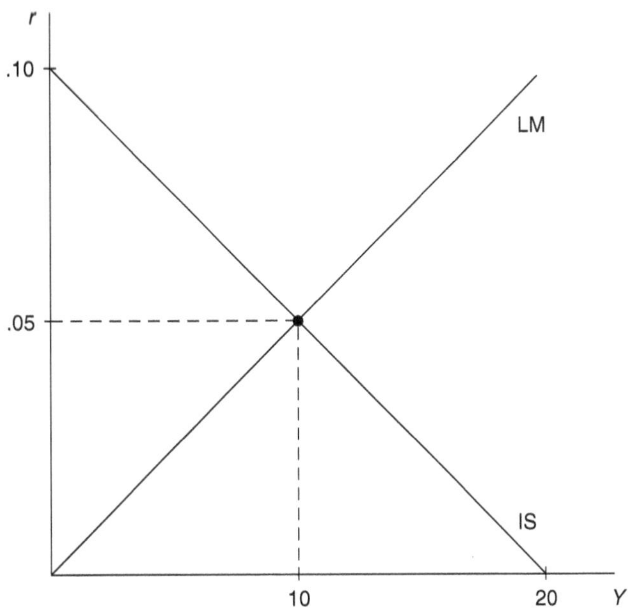

Figure 13.7
ISLM Economy
The LM curve $r = .005Y$ intersects the IS curve $r = 0.1 - 0.005Y$ at the equilibrium
$r = .05$ and $Y = 10$ given $G = 0$.

Monetary Expansion

Monetary policy controls the money supply M_S. Expansionary monetary policy
increases M_S shifting the LM curve right as in Figure 13.8. The increase in M_S
moves the economy down the IS curve raising output Y and lowering the interest
rate r. The 10% increase in M_S from \$1.3 to \$1.43 trillion in the example raises
Y from 10 to 10.5 and lowers r from 5% to 4.75%.

The decreased r implies a higher bond price increasing investment spending
to \$2.1 trillion along $I(r)$ in Figure 13.3. The capital/labor ratio k in Figure 13.1
increases from \$300 to \$327. Output per capita y rises from \$50,000 to \$51,300.
The wage increases from $w = \$35,000$ to \$35,900. The price level P is assumed
to be constant with zero inflation, $\pi = 0$.

Figure 13.8 shows a monetary expansion with no inflation. The primary
political motivation for expansionary monetary policy is to lower the
unemployment rate. Labor market stimulus is possible assuming underutilized
capital. Such a transitory stimulus is possible over a quarter or a year. Continued
expansion of the money supply leads to inflation with no real impact.

Economic growth is a slower process resulting from saving and investment.
Expansionary monetary policy has no effect on economic growth. There is a
predictable political cycle for expansionary monetary policy during the year
before a presidential election. To maintain zero inflation over years, the growth

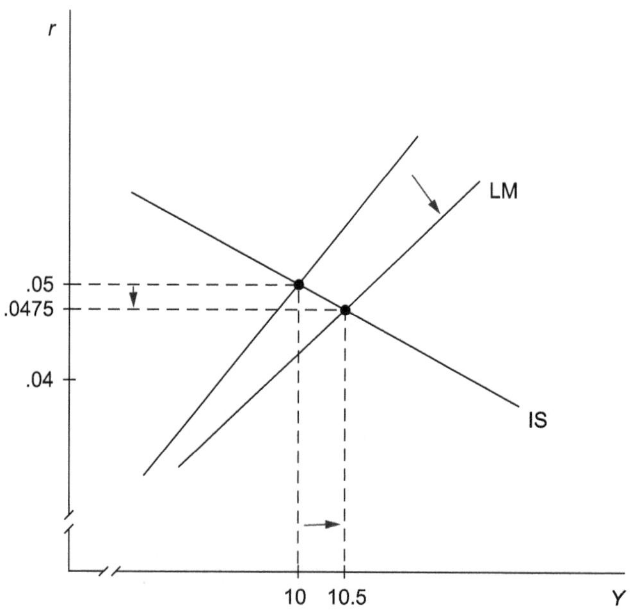

Figure 13.8
Expansionary Monetary Policy
An increase in the money supply shifts the LM curve to the right, lowering the interest rate and raising output. The assumptions are idle capital and labor inputs and no inflation.

rate in the money supply cannot exceed the growth rate of output based on the quantity equation $M_S V = PQ$.

EXAMPLE **13.4**   *Money Supply and Inflation*

Inflation reflects increased money supply. The US inflation rate and real interest rate during the last half of the 20th century are tracked below along with the rate of money supply growth. The Fed has no inflation target. The real interest rate was negative during the 1970s due to the high inflation.

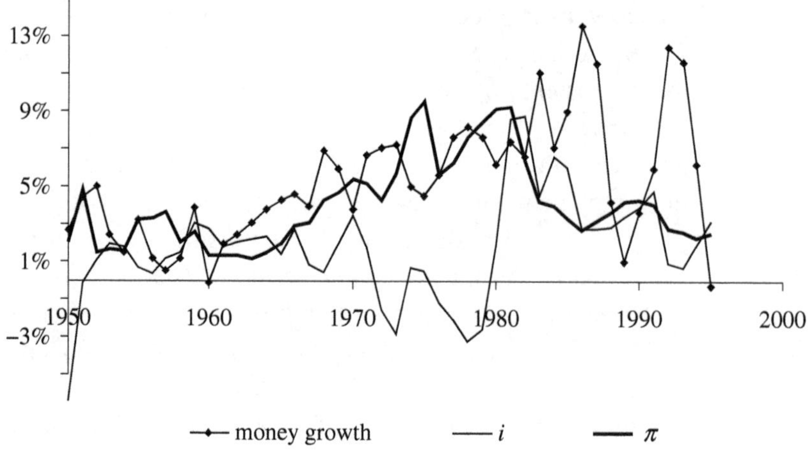

Fiscal Policy

Fiscal policy refers to government spending G and taxes T. Increasing G or lowering T are expansionary fiscal policies with different effects on income distribution. An increase in G shifts the IS curve to the right as saving equals investment plus government spending, $\sigma Y = I + G$.

Figure 13.9 shows the effects of an increase in G equal to 1% of GDP or $100 billion in the example. The IS curve shifts to $r = 0.1025 - 0.005Y$. Output Y increases from $10 to $10.25 trillion as the interest rate r rises from 5% to 5.125% along the LM curve. The higher capital return reduces capital input with k falling along the production function in Figure 13.1.

There is increased employment along the labor demand curve as the wage falls. The unemployment rate u falls as there must be unemployment slack for the increased G to raise Y. At full employment, the LM curve would be vertical with expansionary fiscal policy only raising the interest rate.

Capital owners benefit from the fiscal expansion. Income per capita y falls to $49,600 and w falls to $31,600. In Figure 13.1, the K/L ratio k falls to $293,000. The economy switches toward labor-intensive production. Investment spending is crowded out dropping from $2 to $1.95 trillion along the investment schedule in Figure 13.2 slowing economic growth.

Firms determine employment according to labor demand. There must be available workers willing to work for a lower wage for the increased output in Figure 13.9. Expansionary fiscal policy cannot increase output indefinitely.

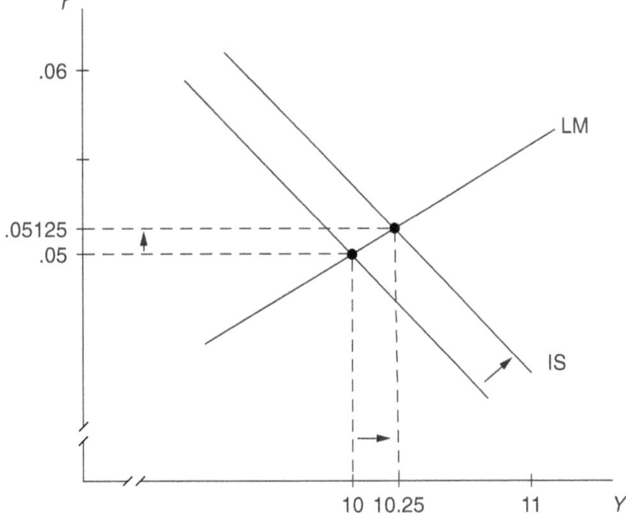

Figure 13.9
Expansionary Fiscal Policy
The IS curve shifts right with increased G or decreased T. Output expands with employment but the wage falls. At full employment, the LM curve would be vertical with no output effect and only an increase in r.

Fiscal policy is inflexible for active management as government programs would have to be expanded or cut. Politics make fiscal policy a weak macroeconomic tool to tune the economy. The declining investment and slower growth due to fiscal expansion suggest unemployment is better addressed with labor market policy.

Another issue is the effect of fiscal policy on government debt. If $G > T$ the government either borrows or increases the money supply. Expanding the money supply amounts to monetary policy that could be pursued without raising G or lowering T. Government borrowing implies future taxes or inflation. Ricardian equivalence is the hypothesis that taxpayers understand this tax liability and increase saving to pay the tax. The increased saving lower the IS curve back to its original position in Figure 13.9.

EXAMPLE **13.5**   *Drachma Supply Increase*

Beginning in the 1970s, the government of Greece increased its money supply to cover popular deficit spending. Inflation rose from nearly zero to over 20%. High tariffs and restrictions on international investment lowered growth. In 1999, the government lost its ability to arbitrarily increase the money supply in the EU leading to default on debt payments and bailout.

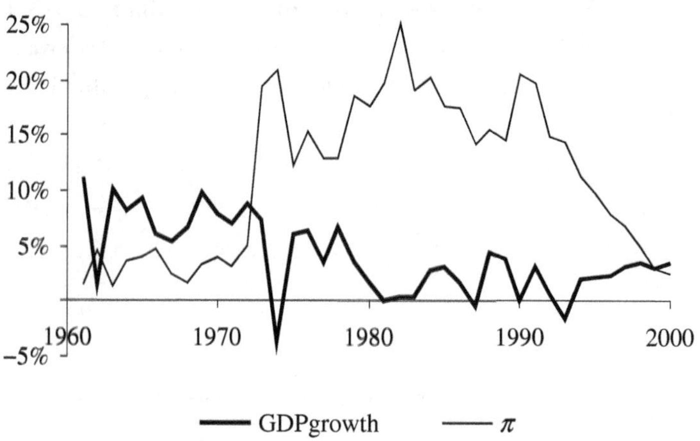

Section B Problems

B1. Show and explain what happens to the capital and labor markets when the interest rate rises along the IS curve.

B2. Use the two input demands to explain how an increase in the interest rate r affects capital utilization and labor employment.

B3. Show and explain the effects of a decrease in the money supply in the ISLM model.

B4. Show and explain the effects of an increase in taxes in the ISLM model.

C. THE OPEN ECONOMY INVESTMENT-SAVING, LIQUIDITY-MONEY MODEL

An economy open to international trade and investment adjusts differently to fiscal and monetary policies due to BOP adjustments depending on its exchange rate regime. FX reserves are part of the money supply. The government determines the exchange rate system as well as *FI* policy in a political process.

Income and the Balance of Payments

The national income equation for the open economy adds the trade balance to the spending side,

$$Y = C + I + G + BGS = A + BGS$$

Absorption $A = C + I + G$ is domestic spending. The balance on goods and services $BGS = X - M$ adds export revenue X that is produced but not consumed and subtracts import spending M that is consumed but not produced.

BGS varies with the exchange rate $e = \$/€$ stated in terms of the euro. Depreciation $e\uparrow$ refers to a decrease in the foreign currency price $1/e = €/\$$ of domestic currency. Depreciation raises the BGS assuming the Marshall-Lerner condition for export and import elasticities.

Higher foreign income Y^* raises X as the foreign country spends more on imports. Higher home income Y raises import spending M. The trade balance becomes part of the IS curve $\sigma Y = I + G + B(e, Y^*, Y)$. Changes in e and Y^* shift the IS curve. A trade deficit $BGS < 0$ would reduce investment spending I.

The balance of payments $BOP = CA + KA$ is the sum of the current account (CA) and the capital account (KA). A deficit in CA is a cash outflow for current goods and services involving a KA surplus.

In the example, $CA = -KA = -\$0.4$ trillion. The country borrows with the promise to repay in the future. The CA deficit lowers domestic investment I as with an increase in government spending G but there an increase in FI. Countries with CA surpluses lend to countries with KA surpluses.

A small country faces the international interest rate r^*. The home country is a lender if $r^* > r$ or a borrower if $r > r^*$. International lending and borrowing between large countries determine the international interest rate. Arbitrage leads toward international interest rate equalization.

EXAMPLE **13.6**   *Trade Beats Fiscal Policy in Portugal*

Portugal is a small open economy that joined the EU in 1992. Unemployment did not respond to expansionary deficit spending or money supply during the 1970s. The unemployment decline from 1985 can be explained by increased trade. Unemployment continued to decline after Portugal entered the EU.

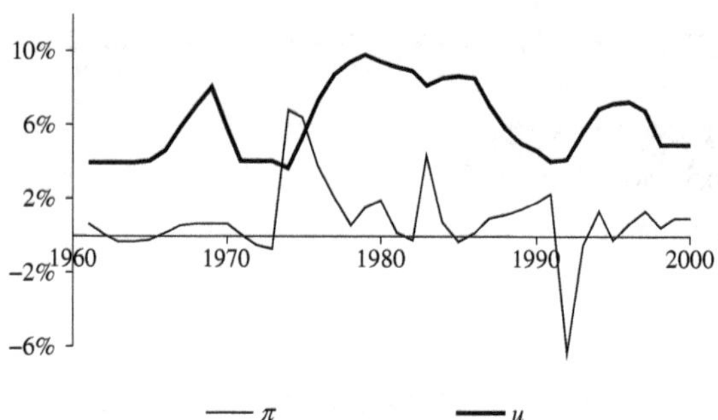

Both r and r^* enter the capital account $KA(r, r^*)$. Increased r creates an inflow of cash to buy home bonds. Increased r^* creates cash outflow to buy foreign bonds. BOP is the sum of the current and capital accounts on the BP curve,

$$BOP = \mathrm{BP}(e, Y^*, Y, r, r^*) = 0$$

Figure 13.10 shows the BP curve that is part of the open economy. An increase in Y lowering BOP is offset by an increase in r along the BP curve. The marginal propensity to import and the interest rate effect determine the BP slope.

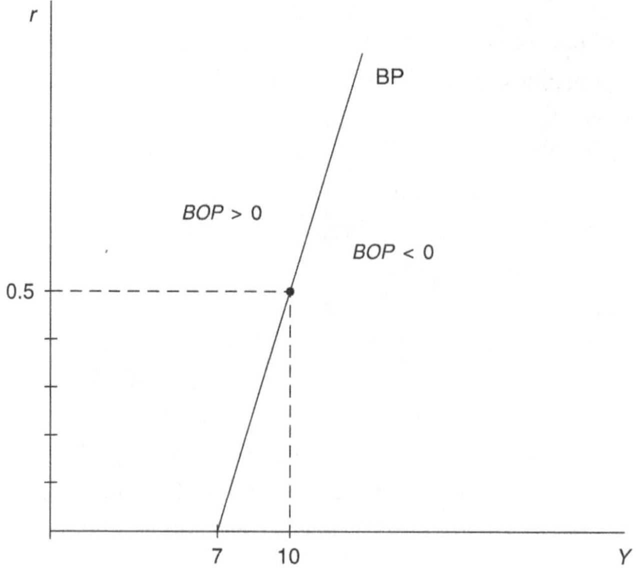

Figure 13.10
BOP Curve
The *BOP* curve shows combinations of Y and r where $BOP = 0$. To the right there is a *BOP* deficit and to the left a surplus.

If the marginal propensity to import is constant at $M/Y = 0.14$ an increase of \$100 in income increases import spending by \$14. If the elasticity of the KA with respect to r equals 1, the marginal effect of r on KA equals 8 when $KA = \$0.4$ trillion and $r = .05$. The derived BP function shown in Figure 13.10 is $r = -0.125 + 0.0175Y$.

The BP curve is combinations of r and Y where $BOP = 0$. To the right of the BP curve there is a BOP deficit and to the left a BOP surplus. A deficit implies a decrease in the money supply M_S as cash flows out of the economy, and a surplus an increase in M_S.

The BP curve shifts right due to depreciation $e\uparrow$, higher foreign income Y^*, or an increase in the foreign interest rate r^*. A flatter BP curve indicates a higher degree of international capital mobility since less of an increase in r is required to offset an increase in Y. Perfect international capital mobility would make the BP curve flat at the international interest rate r^*.

EXAMPLE 13.7   *Components of IS*

The GDP in the US economy is 70% consumption spending C, 18% investment spending I, and 17% government spending G. Trade sums to a negative –5% with 13% export revenue X and –18% import spending M. Services account for about two thirds of GDP and almost all M. The share of services in X has grown to about one third, including finance, intellectual property, business services, engineering, construction, and travel.

EXAMPLE 13.8   *US BOP History*

During the 1800s, the US was a growing debtor country with a KA surplus and CA deficit. FI went into railroads, infrastructure, and agriculture. By the late 1800s, the output had climbed with a CA surplus. Following the Great Depression and two World Wars, a KA deficit arose as the US invested in Europe and Japan. Investment income then led to a CA surplus up to 1980 before increased import spending on oil and consumer goods outpaced exports of resources, high-tech manufactures, and business services. During recent decades, the US has a CA deficit and KA surplus.

EXAMPLE 13.9   *Export and Import Prices in South Korea*

Prices of imports and exports in South Korea rose during the 1970s–1980s with a bump during the energy crisis. The negative balance of trade (BOT) dipped with the higher price of oil. Import prices leveled during the early 1990s with improved terms of trade. BOT fell until 1995 when import prices caught up with export prices.

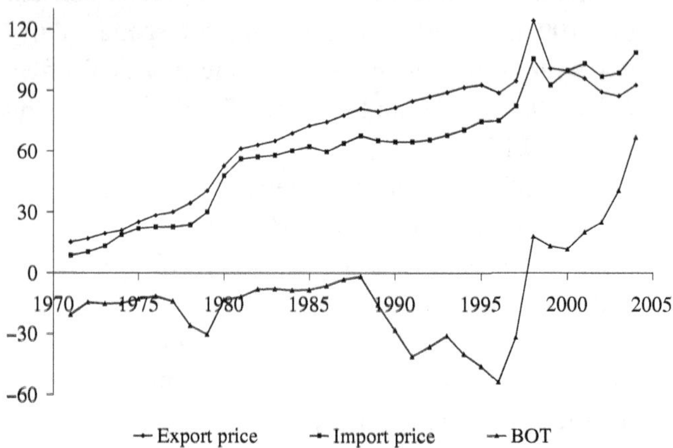

Monetary Policy in the Open Economy

The ISLM model determines the interest rate r and national income Y along with the exchange rate e and *BOP* in an open economy. The equilibrium involves the level of floating exchange rate or changes in the money supply due to the *BOP* with a fixed exchange rate. Figure 13.11 shows the open economy starting at equilibrium at point A where the three curves intersect.

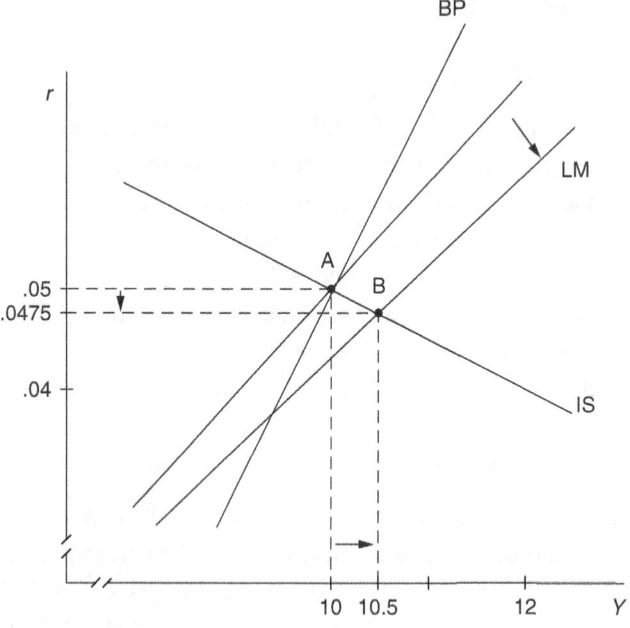

Figure 13.11
Expansionary Monetary Policy
Increased money supply shifts LM right moving the economy from A to B. The *BOP* deficit depreciates the currency shifting the BP curve out to B. A fixed exchange rate implies a decrease in FX reserves and M_S shifting LM back to A.

Expansionary monetary policy shifts the LM curve to the right from point A to B with a *BOP* deficit to the right of the BP curve. A 10% increase in M_S lowers r from 0.05 to 0.0475 and raises Y from 10 to 10.5 in the example. On the BP curve, $BOP = 1 - 0.14Y + 8r = -0.09$ with a *BOP* deficit of $90 billion.

With a market exchange rate, depreciation shifts the BP curve to point B. The effects of the monetary expansion are a lower interest rate and higher output along with increased investment spending, a lower *KA*, depreciation, a higher trade balance, and a decrease in the *KA*. Home investment increases relative to *FI*.

There would be political pressure not to let the currency depreciate. The higher import prices rise with depreciation hurt consumers and firms importing intermediate products. *FI* falls as earnings are discounted when converted back into foreign currency. Exchange market intervention to prop up the currency may follow. This government intervention leads to erratic exchange rate movements as traders focus more on pending government policy than underlying market fundamentals.

EXAMPLE **13.10**   *The Dollar and the BOT for Half a Century*

The dollar exchange rate $1/e$ is shown below with the *BOT*. During the 1950s, the US had *BOT* surplus leading to expansion of FX reserves and gold holdings with the fixed exchange rate. Starting in the late 1950s, the *BOT* deficit grew. The dollar was cut loose from its gold price in 1973 leading to depreciation shrinking the *BOT* deficit with a surplus by 1980. Starting in 1981, the dollar appreciated sharply with the *BOT* falling into deficit. In 1986, these trends reversed with the dollar depreciating and the *BOT* climbing. In the early 1990s, the *BOT* deficit began to grow with increased spending on oil and labor-intensive imports.

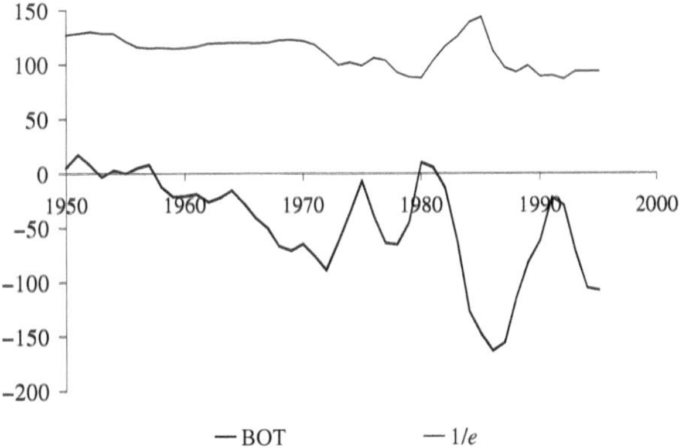

With a fixed exchange rate, the *BOP* deficit at point B in Figure 13.11 leads to a decrease in the money supply. The LM curve shifts back to the left returning the economy back to point A. Monetary expansion is ineffective with a fixed exchange rate.

The government might choose not to "play by the rules" increasing the money supply to offset cash outflow. The money supply M_S is a multiple of central bank credit C_{BC} and FX reserves FX_R, $M_S = \mu \, (C_{BC} + FX_R)$. The *BOP* deficit at point B drains FX_R, lowering M_S. An offsetting increase in C_{BC} is called sterilization of the *BOP* deficit.

Fiscal Policy in the Open Economy

Expansionary fiscal policy increases output but generates a *BOP* deficit with the IS curve shift to the right in Figure 13.12. Starting with $G = T = 0$ in the example, suppose G increase by \$100 billion or 1% of GDP. Output Y increases from \$10 to \$10.5 trillion as the interest rate r rises from 5% to 5.125%. The shift in the IS curve moves the economy from point A to B but with a *BOP* deficit to the right of the BP curve.

The government deficit generated by the increased spending leads to a BOP deficit in the twin deficit effect. Governments fiscal deficits cause *BOP* deficits.

With a flexible exchange rate, the *BOP* deficit causes depreciation and a shift of the BP curve to point B. On the BP curve, $BOP = 1 - 0.14Y + 8r = -\$60$ billion at point B. Depreciation raises the *BGS* from −\$400 billion to −\$340 billion to return the *BOP* to zero.

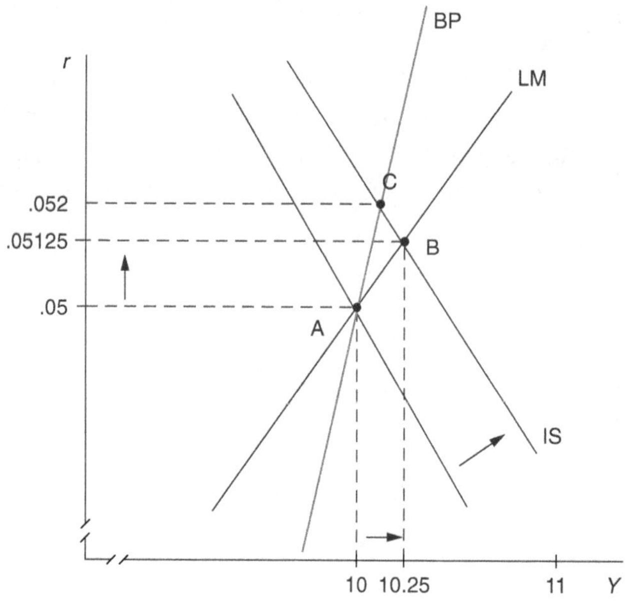

Figure 13.12
Expansionary Fiscal Policy
Increased G or decreased T shifts the IS curve moving the economy from A to B where BOP < 0. A flexible exchange rate depreciates shifting the BP curve to B making fiscal policy effective. With a fixed exchange rate, the money supply falls shifting the LM curve in moving the economy to point C. Fiscal policy has a larger effect on the interest rate but a smaller effect on output relative to a closed economy.

EXAMPLE 13.11   *Money Growth and the Exchange Rate*

Over time, money supply growth depreciates the exchange rate. The chart tracks money supply growth and the dollar exchange rate. The exchange rates was fixed until early 1973. Rising money supply growth led to the depreciation up to 1981. Beginning in 1986, the dollar depreciated until 1990. Erratic monetary policy leads to exchange rate variability.

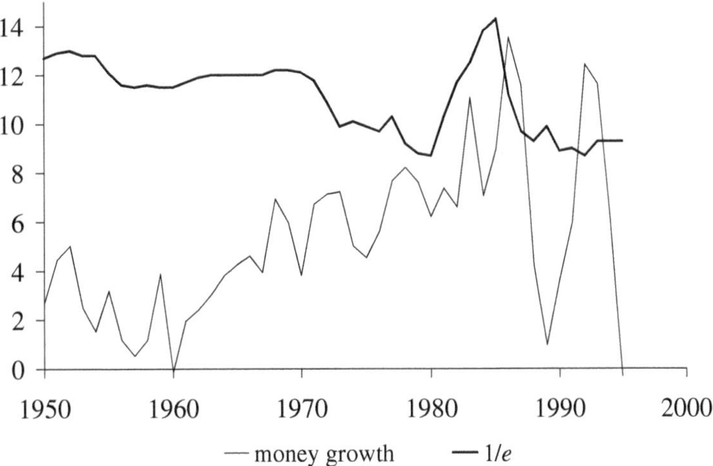

With a fixed exchange rate, the money supply M_S decreases with a *BOP* deficit. This decreased money supply shifts the LM curve left to point C. With a fixed exchange rate, the fiscal expansion leads to an offsetting monetary contraction.

In the example, the BOP deficit of –$60 billion lowers M_S from $1.3 to $1.24 trillion. From point B to C, the interest rate r rises from 5.1% to 5.2% and Y falls from $10.2 to $10.1 trillion along the new IS curve. The *BGS* falls $14 billion due to increased imports.

Fiscal expansion creates less of an increase in output but more of an increase in the interest rate relative to a closed economy. This higher interest rate implies a larger decrease in investment spending. The higher domestic interest rate attracts more *FI*.

Total investment domestic plus foreign falls. At point C with $r = 5.2$, domestic investment falls to $1.92 trillion along the investment schedule. This decrease of $80 billion in domestic investment is partly offset by the $14 billion increase in *FI*. Total investment falls by $66 billion. *FI* only partly replaces domestic investment.

Expansionary fiscal policy may temporarily lower unemployment. The US government tends to increase spending as election time approaches in a political business cycle. Expansionary fiscal policy may increase output but lowers investment and economic growth. Government debt and future tax liabilities make expansionary fiscal policy even less attractive.

EXAMPLE 13.12   *Command and Control Yuan*

China is entering the world economy with trade and investment. One indication of its weight is the higher international price of oil due to increased demand. Incoming *FI* is funding a transition from state command and control. China maintains a fixed undervalued yuan making exports cheaper abroad but hurting consumers and importers of intermediate products. FX reserves led to the Belt and Road program of infrastructure investment around the world.

Competitive Devaluation

Competitive devaluation with a fixed exchange rate generates a *BOP* surplus that increases the money supply. National income increases and the falling interest rate raises investment spending. Devaluation for the home country amounts to revaluation for the foreign country with the opposite effects suggesting retaliation can be expected.

Devaluation shifts the BP in Figure 13.13 to the right. The economy in the domestic equilibrium at point A has a *BOP* surplus. The result is an increase in the money supply shifting the LM curve right and moving the economy to the new equilibrium at point B.

An exchange rate elasticity of the *BGS* equal to 1 implies 10% devaluation of the currency generates a 10% increase in the *BGS* rising from −$400 to −$360

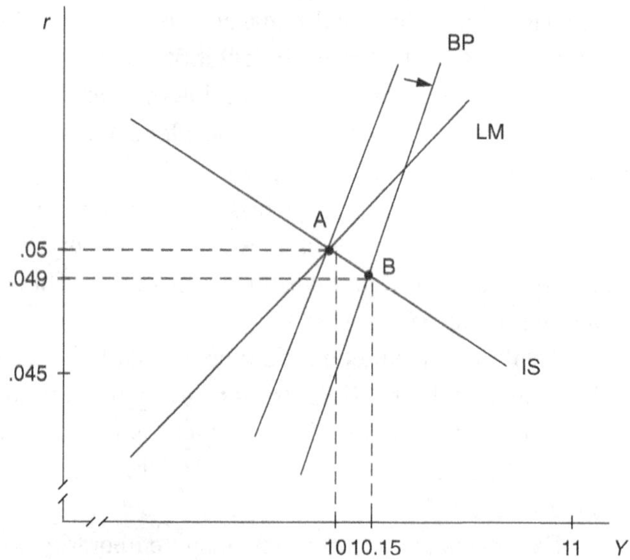

Figure 13.13
Competitive Devaluation
A competitive devaluation shifts the BP curve creating a trade surplus at point A. FX reserves and the money supply increase, shifting the LM curve to point B. The competitive devaluation stimulates output and lowers the interest rate.

billion in the example. The money supply increases from \$1.3 to \$1.34 trillion on the new LM schedule $M_S = 1.3 + 0.13Y - 26r$. At point B, national income Y increases from \$10 to \$10.15 trillion as the interest rate falls from 5% to 4.9% along the IS curve.

The foreign country has a trade deficit decreasing its money supply, lowering national income, and raising the interest rate. Governments are easily entangled in competitive devaluations. Ultimately the confusion discourages trade and investment with little real effects. Negative consequences arise when traders and investors pay more attention to policymakers than market fundamentals.

Another point is that inflation typically occurs with devaluation. The increased output and lower interest rate in Figure 13.13 assume there is no inflation. Inflation on the heels of competitive devaluation lessens any positive effects.

EXAMPLE 13.13   *Asian Exchange Risk and Exports*

Depreciation should raise export revenue but creates exchange rate risk that can discourage trade. WenShwo Fang, YiHao Li, and Henry Thompson (2005) find evidence of negative risk effects in three of eight Asian countries in monthly 1979–2002 data. The currencies depreciated from 1% to 5% on a yearly basis. Risk as standard deviation ranges from 2% to 7%. The small effects of depreciation on export revenue in Singapore, Taiwan, and Japan are outweighed by risk effects. Indonesia, the Philippines, and Thailand gained about 2% export revenue. Risk had no impact in Malaysia, the Philippines, Thailand, and Indonesia. Singapore and Taiwan had the lowest risk but the highest risk effects, almost 8% in Singapore. Traders not familiar with exchange volatility are more vulnerable. Negative risk effects dominate any positive effects of depreciation.

Section C Problems

C1. Suppose investment $I = 2$, government spending $G = 1$, absorption $A = 11$, export revenue $X = 6$, and national income $Y = 15$. Find consumption spending C, import spending M, and the BGS. Find the real exchange rate, given the home price level $P = 1.1$ and foreign $P* = 1.5$.

C2. Derive the open economy IS equation $\sigma Y = A - C + BGS$ from the national income equation in Problem C1.

C3. Show and explain the effect on the BP curve of

(a) an increase in foreign income $Y*$
(b) an increase in the foreign interest rate $r*$
(c) a revaluation of the domestic currency.

C4. Show and explain the effects of a decrease in the money supply in the open economy ISLM model with a flexible exchange rate and a fixed exchange rate.

EXAMPLE **13.14**   *The Dollar and US Tourism*

> The depreciating US dollar during the 1990s–2000s made travel to the US
> relatively cheaper. Nevertheless, the US share of international travelers declined
> from 8% in 1994 to 6% in 2004. One reason was the increased competition from
> new destinations including Dubai, Budapest, and China. Another problem was
> that US foreign policy and tight security discourages travelers. This declining
> export demand causes the BP curve to shift left leading to a *BOP* deficit and
> depreciation.

D. INFLATION IN THE MACRO MODEL

Inflation as the percentage increase in the price level occurs when the money
supply grows faster than output. This section includes the price level in the open
economy ASAD model.

Macroeconomics in Real Terms

The price level P is relevant for data covering years. The inflation rate is
the percentage increase in the price level $\pi = dP/P = \%\Delta P$. Real output Y is
distinguished from nominal output Y_N according to $Y = Y_N/P$. The real money
supply $M_S = M_S^N/P$ is the basis of the LM side of the economy. In the IS
condition, the fiscal variables $G = G_N/P$ and $T = T_N/P$ are deflated. The ISLM
model operates on real variables.

Inflation also affects *BOP* and exchange rate. Real export revenue is $X =
X_N/P$ and real import spending $M = M_N/P$. Purchasing power parity (PPP) $P =
eP^*$ suggests the real exchange rate $e_R = P/P^*$ as the relative domestic price
level. Relative inflation $\pi > \pi^*$ implies real depreciation with a rising e_R. The
market exchange rate e tends to follow e_R over time.

EXAMPLE **13.15**   *Long-Term PPP*

> PPP would hold if countries produced and consumed the same products traded
> freely with exchange rates determined in a competitive market. These conditions
> do not hold perfectly making PPP an empirical issue. William Crowder (1996)
> presents evidence of PPP between US dollars and UK pounds during the 20th
> century. A weaker relationship holds between Canadian and US dollars.

Aggregate Supply and Demand

The ASAD model introduces an endogenous price level P in the macro model.
The aggregate demand curve in Figure 13.14 shows combinations of the price
level P and real output Y consistent with the ISLM equilibrium. Fiscal and

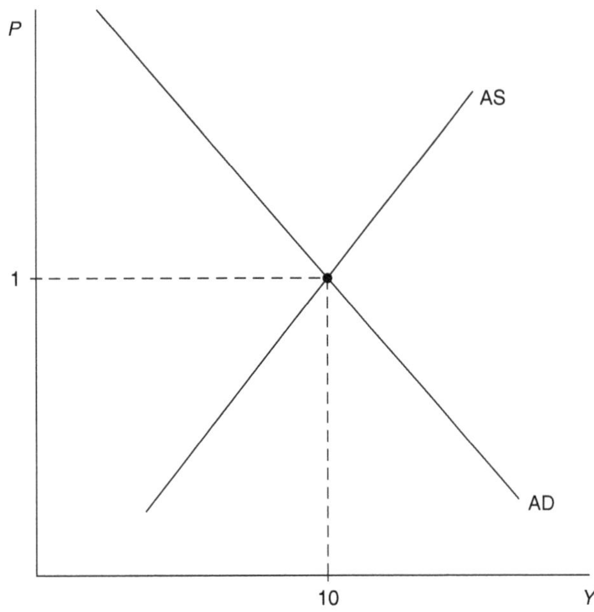

Figure 13.14
Closed ASAD Economy
Aggregate supply AS and demand AD determine P and Q. The AS curve slopes upward assuming firms respond to rising prices with increased output.

monetary expansion shift AD right. Increasing G or decreasing T with P constant shifts the IS curve right and raises real output Y. An increase in M_S with P constant shifts the LM curve right also raising Y.

The upward sloping aggregate supply AS curve in Figure 13.14 relies on firms reacting to price changes. Firms interpret a rising price of their product as a signal to increase output. Over time, input prices and wages rise due to inflation suggesting the increased Y will not be permanent. The AS relation holds over a short time horizon of a year or two. At full employment, the AS schedule is vertical.

The ASAD equilibrium at the intersection of AS and AD determines the price level P and output Y. Expansionary fiscal and monetary policy shifts the AD schedule right raising Y but also P. If the economy is at full employment, the AS curve would be vertical implying the only effect of expansionary policy is inflation.

An open economy introduces adjustments in the *BOP*. A higher P raises the relative price of home exports, lowering X and raising M. Higher income with increased Y raises import spending M lowering the *BGS*. The FF curve in Figure 13.15 shows the combinations of P and Y where $BOP = 0$.

To the right of FF there is a *BOP* deficit implying depreciation $e\uparrow$ with a market exchange rate e_{float} or a decrease in the money supply $M_S\downarrow$ with a fixed

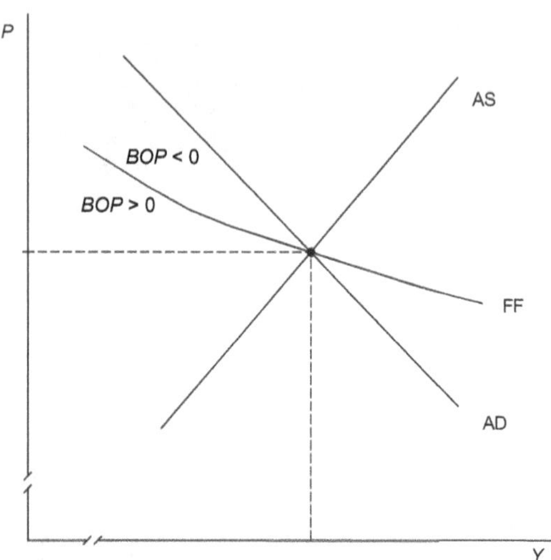

Figure 13.15
ASADFF Model
The FF curve shows a higher P is offset by a lower Q to maintain $BOP = 0$. The open economy equilibrium P and Y are determined where AS-AD-FF intersect.

exchange rate e_{fix}. To the left of the FF curve, the BOP surplus implies the opposite.

To consider the effects of expansionary macro policy, in Figure 13.15 start at the equilibrium where AS-AD-FF intersect. Expansionary fiscal or monetary policy shifts AD to the right. Output and the price level increase with a *BOP* deficit that requires depreciation with e_{float} or a decrease in the money supply with e_{fix}.

Depreciation with e_{float} would shift FF out to point B with the expansionary policy raising output but creating inflation. With e_{fix} the *BOP* deficit decreases M_S lowering AD back to its original position making the expansionary policy ineffective.

Macro Policy With Inflation in the Open Economy

Table 13.1 summarizes the effects of monetary and fiscal policies in the open economy. The positive output effects assume the aggregate supply curve slopes upward below full employment. Near full employment, the output effects approach zero. Fiscal expansion raises the real interest rate r lowering investment spending and economic growth.

The reasons governments should shy away from active fiscal and monetary policies include:

- Fiscal expansion raises the interest rate and lowers investment
- Inflation can distort economic decisions

Table 13.1   Macro Policy in the Open Economy

Monetary expansion	e	Q	r	π	i
Floating e	↑	↑*	↓	↑	?
Fixed e	0	0	0	0	0
Fiscal expansion					
Floating e	↑	↑*	↑	↑	↑
Fixed e	0	↑*	↑**	↑	↑**

*Approaches 0 near full employment
**Larger than with floating e

- Financial markets become preoccupied with the policy process
- Any successful policy would lead to retaliation by other countries
- Positive output effects require slack below full employment
- Near full employment the only effect is on the interest rate

Fiscal policy should be based cost/benefit analysis and a balanced budget. Monetary policy should target zero inflation.

Section D Problems

D1. Explain how an increase in the foreign money supply affects the exchange rate.

D2. Show the effects of expansionary policy on real output and the price level in a closed economy with full employment.

D3. Show what happens in the ASAD economy with currency devaluation.

D4. Show the effects of money supply contraction on output, the price level, and interest rates with a floating exchange rate versus a fixed exchange rate.

CONCLUSION

Active fiscal and monetary policies are ineffective to actively manage the economy on a quarter-to-quarter basis. In practice, government spending, taxes, and central banking cater to special interests in a distorting political process. The government should aim to provide public goods with a balanced budget and zero inflation.

Terms

Absorption	ISLM open economy
Appreciation	Liquidity demand

ASAD	Monetary policy
ASAD open economy	Monetary model of the exchange rate
BOP function	National income
Crowding out	Neoclassical production
Depreciation	Overlapping generations (OLG) model
Competitive devaluation	Perpetuity bond
Economic growth	Political business cycle
Fiscal policy	Real exchange rate
Fixed exchange rates	Ricardian equivalence
Floating exchange rates	Saving rate
Inflation	Sterilization
Investment function	Twin deficits

MAIN POINTS

- The microeconomic foundations of macroeconomics are the neoclassical production function, optimal saving in the overlapping generations model, and investment spending based on rates of return.
- The ISLM model includes the IS and LM sides of the economy to determine the interest rate and output. The model analyzes adjustments to fiscal and monetary policies assuming a constant price level with zero inflation.
- The open economy ISLM model *BOP* with adjustments in a floating exchange rate. With a fixed exchange rate, the government loses control of the money supply.
- The ASAD model introduces the price level. Any positive outcome of expansionary monetary or fiscal policy are dampened or eliminated by inflation.

REVIEW PROBLEMS

1. Similar to Figure 13.1, diagram the production function $y = 10k^{.4}$ with $k = \$1000$. Indicate income per capita y and the wage w when $r = 6.3\% = .063$. Sketch the production function.

2. In Problem 1, suppose the growth rate of labor is 1% and the saving rate $\sigma = 20\%$. What more information is required to determine whether the economy is growing?

3. The economy of Problem 1 grows until the capital labor ratio k is constant at the steady state $k^* = 2188$. Find the steady-state income per capita y^s. Given the steady-state interest rate $r^s = 4\%$, find w^s.

4. Explain the labor and capital market changes in Problem 3. Use changes in supply and demand to illustrate what happens in the two markets as the economy grows.

5. Explain the changes in y, w, and r due to:

   (a) a decrease in the saving rate
   (b) improved technology
   (c) foreign investment
   (d) immigration

6. In the overlapping generations (OLG) model, suppose the wage is $\$50,000$ and the interest rate $r = 10\%$. Diagram the intertemporal budget

line. Find consumption in retirement if \$40,000 is consumed while working.

7. If the interest rate in Problem 6 falls to $r = 5\%$, explain what will happen to the saving rate and consumption in both periods.

8. Find the level of saving that would equate consumption for both generations in Problem 5 when $r = 10\%$.

9. Explain what happens in the capital and labor markets when the interest rate rises moving the economy down the IS curve.

10. Suppose there is a decrease in the money supply M_S in the ISLM model. Explain the adjustments in the capital and labor markets.

11. Explain the labor and capital market effects of an increase in taxes T. Show the adjustment in the ISLM model along the production function and the IS curve.

12. Show and explain the effects of an increase in taxes in an open ISLM economy with

    (a) a flexible exchange rate

    (b) a fixed exchange rate

13. Show and explain the effects of a decrease in the money supply in an open ISLM economy with

    (a) a flexible exchange rate

    (b) a fixed exchange rate

14. Show how an increase in foreign income Y^* affects output and the price level in the ASAD model. What happens to real and nominal interest rates?

15. Contrast the effects of a decrease in the money supply on output in the ISLM and ASAD models.

16. Show the effects of expansionary policy on output and the price level in an open economy with full employment.

17. Explain adjustment due to a sharp devaluation in the ASAD model.

18. Explain why depreciation and inflation occur together in the ASAD economy.

READINGS

Gustav Cassel (1921) *The World's Monetary Problems*, Constable. A classic on money.

Robert Hall and David Papell (2005) *Macroeconomics: Economic Growth, Fluctuations, and Policy*, Norton. Macro text with an international slant.

Nelson Mark (2001) *International Macroeconomics and Finance*, Blackwell. A concise advanced text on theory and application.

Maurice Obsfeld and Kenneth Rogoff (1997) *Foundations of International Macroeconomics*, MIT Press. A thorough advanced text.

Francisco Rivera-Batiz and Luis Rivera Batiz (1994) *International Finance and Open Economy Macroeconomics*, Prentice-Hall. The complete source for the ISLM model.

MATHEMATICAL APPENDIX

Macroeconomics rests on constant returns production of aggregate output $Y = F(K, L)$ with positive diminishing marginal products $f_i > 0$, $f_{ii} < 0$ and a positive cross effect $f_{ij} > 0$. Factor incomes exhaust output due to Euler's theorem $Y = rK + wL$ with competitive markets implying the capital return $r = f_K$ and wage $w = f_L$. In per capita terms, the production function $y = f(k)$ with $y = Y/L$ and $dk = K/L$ leads to the concave function $y = w + rk$. An increase in k lowers r and raises w and y.

Saving is motivated in the overlapping generations (OLG) model with the young saving $S = \sigma wL$ to consume $(1 + r)S$ when retired. A competitive loanable funds market implies investment $I(r)$ at $r = f_K$.

The macro equilibrium for r and Y starts with the national income statement,

$$Y = C + I + G + X - M,$$

where output is Y = GDP accounted for by C = household consumption, I = investment, G = government spending, X = exports produced but not consumed, and M = imports consumed but not produced. Introducing absorption $A = C + I + G$ simplifies the income statement to $Y = A + BGS$.

The IS schedule derives saving as $S = Y - C$ leading to,

$$\overset{+}{Y} - \overset{+\ -}{C(Y - T)} = \overset{-}{S(Y, T)} = \overset{+}{I(r)} + \overset{+}{G} + \overset{-\ +}{X(e, Y^*)} - M(e, Y).$$

The IS schedule has negative slope in (r, Y) space as an increase in Y requires a decrease in r to keep the two sides equal. Exogenous variables are G and T as taxes. The exchange rate e can be fixed e_{fix} or flexible e_{flex}.

Fiscal expansion as an increase in G or a decrease in T shifts the IS curve right. Higher foreign income Y^* raises export revenue X. Depreciation $e{\uparrow}$ raises export revenue X and lowers import spending M given elastic imports.

The other side of the economy is the liquidity-money equilibrium,

$$M_S = \overset{+\ -}{L(Y, r)}.$$

Money supply M_S must equal demand for liquidity L given the option to hold bonds paying interest rate r. Income Y raises liquidity demand L for transactions in the positive effect. The interest rate r has a negative effect on L as the opportunity cost of holding cash. The government controls the exogenous money supply M_S. The LM curve slopes upward in (r, Y) space. Monetary expansion as an increase in M_S shifts LM right.

Fiscal expansion $G{\uparrow}$ or $T{\downarrow}$ shifts IS right, raising Y and r. The increased r lowers $I(r) = dK$ and future Y and w. Monetary expansion $M_S{\uparrow}$ shifts LM right, raising Y and lowering r. The falling r and increased $I(r)$ are an advantage of monetary over fiscal expansion.

Introducing the balance of payments,

$$BOP = CA + KA = X(e, Y^*) - M(e, Y) + KA(r, r^*) = 0.$$

This BP schedule slopes upward in (r, Y) space. Sufficient capital mobility makes BP steeper than LM.

Fiscal expansion raising Y and r causes a BOP deficit to the right of the BP curve. A fixed exchange rate e_{fix} implies cash outflow $M_S{\downarrow}$ shifting LM left to raise r further and eroding the increase in Y. A floating exchange rate depreciates $e_{float}{\uparrow}$ shifting BP right raising X and lowering M to maintain the higher Y and r.

Monetary expansion $M_S\uparrow$ shifts LM right with $Y\uparrow$ and $r\downarrow$ but $BOP < 0$. With e_{fix} the monetary expansion is ineffective as M_S leaves the country. With e_{float} the BOP deficit depreciates the currency shifting BP right to maintain the new equilibrium Y and r.

A competitive devaluation shifts the BP schedule right, leading to $BOP > 0$ at Y and r. Due to e_{fix}, the money supply increases shifting LM right leading to $Y\uparrow$ and $r\downarrow$. If trading partners retaliate, there is a race to the bottom.

Fiscal and monetary policies are more effective with e_{float}. Approaching full employment, the IS and LM schedules become vertical implying fiscal and monetary policies only affect r.

The aggregate supply, aggregate demand (ASAD) model introduces an endogenous price level P. The inflation rate is $\pi = dP/P$. Nominal figures are deflated to real terms. The real money supply is M_S/P. The purchasing power parity (PPP) relation $P = eP^*$ suggests the real exchange rage $e_R = P/P^*$.

Aggregate demand AD is downward sloping in (P, Y) space as output decreases with an increased price level in the Investment-Saving, Liquidity-Money (ISLM) equilibrium. Fiscal or monetary expansion shifts AD right.

Aggregate supply AS is upward sloping assuming firms respond to a higher price by increasing output. At full employment AS is vertical. Over time, wages and input prices increase with inflation making AS vertical. Assuming upward sloping AS expansionary fiscal or monetary policy shifting AD right raises Y and P.

The increased P lowers exports and increases imports due to depreciation of the real exchange rate $e_R = P/P^*\uparrow$. The downward sloping FF schedule shows combinations of P and Y where $BOP = 0$.

Expansionary fiscal or monetary policy shifting AD right leads to a BOP deficit to the right of FF. The expansionary policy is offset by falling AD as e_{fix} leads to a decrease in M_S and e_{float} implies depreciation $e\uparrow$.

Hints and Partial Answers

Chapter 1

A2. Domestic supply rises.
A4. With identical supplies, the country with lower demand exports.
C2. XS increases.
D2. In the US, $S/M = 3/2$.

Review

2. Japanese XD rises.
4. Russian XD rises.
6. XD^* from ROW rises.
8. XD from US falls.
10. Venezuelan steel costs \$450.
12. Avoid mercantilist arguments.
14. Consider resource availability, technology, and climate.

Chapter 2

A2. 105 on the M axis, 135 on the S axis, $MRT = 105/135 = 0.78$.
B2. The economy specializes in M.
C2. Producing S has higher opportunity cost with growth biased toward M.
D2. The cost of living is lower inside an FEZ.

Review

2. The 1986 PPF has the point $(M,S) = (625,2200)$.
4. See Figure 3.2.
6. $tt = M/S = 1.2$ and the gains from trade are 21%.
8. Growth biased toward exports means more trade and higher income.
10. Differences are created by local customs, laws, and input costs.
12. Agricultural output and exports drop.

Chapter 3

A2. Which industry can better influence politicians?
B2. Domestic quantity supplied is greater with a quota.

C2. There is no incentive to trade if prices are equal.
D2. Consider the increasing geographical areas.

Review

2. P rises to $1.5 \times \$30 = \$45$.
4. $D = 100 - P = S = -10 + P$ and $P = \$55$.
6. Price is \$50 and total loss is \$500.
8. Imports are $D - S = 30$ and $P = \$40$.
10. The economy specializes in M but the tariff reduces M output.
12. Less local interests imply less protectionism.

Chapter 4

A2. Offer curves do not cross.
A4. Foreign offer curve falls toward its import axis.
B2. Similar to A2.
C2. H 4%, F 6%, H 5%, ...
D2. At 6%, the P series runs \$20, \$21.20, \$22.47, ... , \$35.82.

Review

2 and 4. Foreign offer curve falls toward import axis.
6. Tariff expands domestic production.
8. Foreign reaction function is horizontal at 4%.
10. Reaction functions lie along the axes.
12. A tariff on M pulls OPEC offer curve in toward its import axis.

Chapter 5

A2. The PPF is $220 = 4S + 5M$, $M/S = 4/5$ and output of S is 27.5.
B2. $M/S = 5/4$ at home.
C2. Upper limit to tt is $.01 > tt$.
C4. 114 on the A axis.
D2. Labor became less productive.
D4. Total M expands to $52 = 260/5$.

Review

2. Delta is the intermediate country and might produce both goods.
4. F specializes, producing 60 S and exports half.
6. Consumption with trade at home is worth 72.5 M and H gains more.
8. $ew^* = \$8.80$. $tt = 0.7$ and $w = \$12.32$.
10. $(3/5)(w/w^*) > e > \ldots$
12. $L^*/L = 5$ for good 2, and H exports it.
14. The lower limit is $e > 0.0053$.

Chapter 6

A2. *MR* for M is \$150. For the 5th unit of L, *MRP* = \$2.25.
B2. S_L should be higher.
C2. $k = 1$.
C4. F exports M.
D2. Unemployed L implies less labor intensive production.

Review

2. Demand rises in the market for M capital.
4. r should be less than r^*.
6. K input rises to 0.3.
8. $K/L = 0.28$.
10. H is labor abundant.
12. The endowment point lies between M^* and S expansion paths.
14. If $L^* = 100$, $(K,L) = (200,50)$
16. $(M,S) = (400,500)$ in H and $(300,600)$ in F, $tt = 1$

Chapter 7

A2. Temporary losses can be offset by future profit.
A4. Foreign P would be lower than home P.
B2. Aggregation simplifies theory but hides information.
C2. Unspent income is loaned to others.
D2. Protection is not productive.

Review

2. P rises to \$800.
4. Foreign revenue is \$192.
6. US: $wL/rK = \$209/\$134 = 1.56$ and $w/r = 1.4$.
8. *DF* runs from \$10 to \$3 on the demand curve.
10. Equilibrium high output for both, SA could pay Russia to remain.
12. PPF expands with bias toward M.

Chapter 8

A2. Find emigration from F.
B2. Incoming L raises K productivity.
C2. A 5% increase in skilled labor raises unskilled wage to \$8060.
D2. Production of high tech goods & business services fall in DC.

Review

2. Consider other influences on supply and demand.
4. Immigration impacts labor intensive production.

6. US has comparative advantage in these activities.
8. Investment in US raises US wage.
10. The specific factor model can predict the effects.
12. Mexico is abundant in unskilled labor and scarce in capital.
14. FTZs are free from protectionism.

Chapter 9

A2. Consider standard techniques and specific inputs.
B2. Consider the pollution tax revenue.
C2. North PPF is biased toward S. Trade raises wages in South.
D2. Do the countries oppose free trade and free factor mobility?

Review

2. Each plant produces the same output.
4. Less TV output and higher prices.
6. Domestic firms would ask for the same favor.
8. North exports services in exchange for manufactures.
10. CU would be tough with free migration.
12. Some states would have government budget deficits and inflation.

Chapter 10

A2. Import elasticity is $15/17 = 0.88$.
B2. The *BOT*, *DI*, and *KA* increase. *NII* falls in the future.
C2. Which country is growing, which stable and wealthy?
D2. *PI* and *KA* increase now.

Review

2. XD, P, q_{imp}, and M all move in the same direction.
4. $S/M = 5/12.50 = 0.4$.
6. $BOT = -\$744$, ...
8. Investment flows are US debits.
10. Some countries are in recessions while others are in expansions.
12. There is no necessary links.
14. Export taxes would decrease exports.

Chapter 11

A2. Demand for euros is affected now.
A4. *BGS* is positive during the contract period, negative during pass through.
B2. Limit exchange of foreign currency.
C2. Work through excess supply and demand.
D2. Real return drops to $97.

Review

2. Yen prices are 495 and 562.5.
4. Supply of euro falls.
6. Change in export revenue is 2%. BOT rises.
8. Central bank is selling assets that should rise in value.
10. Central banks were buying marks, yen, and pounds.
12. Profit is $320.51.

Chapter 12

A2. Interest payments are $160 million.
A4. *NII* is −$0.94 billion. A3 and A4 are *NII* of the US in 1990.
B2. Shift S_{won} or D_{won}.
C2. Banks want to maintain value of their notes. Supply slopes upward.
D2. $P/P^* = 0.000625$, $/peso = 1/1500$.

Review

2. XD for loans falls.
4. Explain which is riskier.
6. Consider forward exchange market.
8. KA rises by $5 million. BOT will rise.
10. Demand for dollars falls.
12. Work through the credit market.
14. Wealth prefers stability.

Chapter 13

A2. Use production function $y = 1137k^{.3}$ to find k.
A4. Consumer optimization requires tangent optimal indifference curve.
B2. Consider the change in the quantity of capital demanded.
B4. Higher taxes shift the IS curve.
C2. Saving is the key.
C4. The decreased M_s shifts LM curve left.
D2. AS cannot pass full employment output Y_{full}.
D4. AD shifts with the money contraction.

Review

2. In the closed economy, capital growth equals total saving.
4. Remember the labor force L grows.
6. Start with total income in retirement.
8. What is not saved in youth is consumed.

10. The decrease in the money supply shifts LM.
12. The increase in T shifts IS.
14. The higher Y^* shifts the FF curve.
16. Separate fiscal and monetary policies.
18. Consider changes in AD.

Acronyms

ASEAN	Association of Southeast Asian Nations
APEC	Asia-Pacific Economic Cooperation
BOP	Balance of payments
BOT	Balance of trade
BGS	Balance on goods and services
CA	Current account
CIA	Covered interest arbitrage
DI	Direct investment in the BOP
DC	Developed country
EU	European Union
FDI	Foreign direct investment
FTAA	Free Trade Area of the Americas
FX	Foreign exchange
GATT	General Agreement on Tariffs and Trade
GDP	Gross domestic product
GSP	Generalized System of Preferences
IMF	International Monetary Fund
IRP	Interest rate parity
ITC	International Trade Commission
KA	Capital account
LDC	Less developed country
MNF	Multinational firm
NII	Net investment income
NBER	National Bureau of Economic Research
NIC	Newly industrialized country
NTB	Nontariff barrier
OECD	Organization for Economic Cooperation and Development
PI	Portfolio investment in the BOP
PPP	Purchasing power parity
SDR	Special Drawing Rights
TS	Trade in services in the BOP
VER	Voluntary export restraint
WTO	World Trade Organization

References

Aizenman, Joshua & Eileen Brooks (2005) Globalization and task convergence: The cases of wine and beer, *NBER Working Paper*

Alavi, Jafar & Henry Thompson (1988) Toward a theory of free trade zones, *International Trade Journal*

Amaya, Naohiro (1988) The Japanese economy in transition: Optimistic about the short term, pessimistic about the long term, *Japan and the World Economy*

Amuedo-Dorantes, Catalina, Cynthia Bansak, & Susan Pozo (2005) On the remitting patterns of immigrants: Evidence from Mexican survey data, *Federal Reserve Bank of Atlanta Economic Review*

Anderson, Kym & Hege Norheim (1993) Is world trade becoming more regionalized? *Review of International Economics*

Arndt, Channing & Thomas Hertel (1997) Revisiting 'The fallacy of free trade', *Review of International Economics*

Aw, Bee Yan & Mark Roberts (1986) Estimating quality change in quota-constrained import markets: The case of US footwear, *Journal of International Economics*

Ayanian, Robert (1988) Political risk, national defense and the dollar, *Economic Inquiry*

Bailey, Jessica & James Sood (1987) An export strategy for banana producing countries, *The International Trade Journal*

Baldwin, Robert (1971) Determinants of the commodity structure of US trade, *American Economic Review*

Baldwin, Richard (1992) Measurable dynamic gains from trade, *Journal of Political Economy*

Baldwin, Robert & Glen Cain (2000) Shifts in relative US wages: The role of trade, technology, and factor endowments, *Review of Economics and Statistics*

Ballie, Richard & William Osterberg (1997) Central bank intervention and risk in the forward market, *Journal of International Economics*

Batra, Ravi (1992) The fallacy of free trade, *Review of International Economics*

Batra, Ravi & Daniel Slotje (1994) Trade policy and poverty in the United States: Theory and evidence, 1947–1990, *Review of International Economics*

Beard, T. Randolph & Henry Thompson (2003) Duopoly quotas and relative import quality, *International Review of Economics and Finance*

Beeson, Patricia & Michael Bryan (1986) Emerging service economy, *Economic Commentary*, FRB Cleveland

Ben-David, David (1993) Equalizing exchange: Trade liberalization and income convergence, *Quarterly Journal of Economics*

Ben-David, David & Alok Bohara (1997) Evidence on the contribution of trade reform towards international income equalization, *Review of International Economics*

Berman, Eli, John Bound, & Stephen Machin (1998) Implications of skill-biased technological change: International evidence, *Quarterly Journal of Economics*

Bernard, Andrew & Bradford Jensen (1998) Exceptional exporter performance: Cause, effect, or both? *Journal of International Economics*

Bernhofen, Daniel M. & John C. Brown (2005) Comparative advantage gains from trade: Evidence from Japan, *American Economic Review*

Bohara, Alok, Kishore Gawande, & William Kaempfer (1998) The dynamics of tariff retaliation between the United States and Canada: Theory and Evidence, *Review of International Economics*

Bougheas, Spiros, Panicos Demitriades, & Edgar Morgenroth (1999) Infrastructure, transport costs and trade, *Journal of International Economics*

Branson, William & Nikolaos Monoyios (1977) Factor inputs in US trade, *Journal of International Economics*

Broadberry, S.N. (1987) Purchasing power parity and the pound-dollar rate in the 1930s, *Economica*

Brook, Douglas A. (2005) "Meta-Strategic Lobbying: The 1998 Steel Imports Case", Business and Politics, Article 4. *http://www.bepress.com/bap/vol7/iss1/art4*

Brown, Lynn (1986) Taking in each other's laundry: The service economy, *New England Economic Review*, FRB Boston

Bryan, Michael & Susan Byrne (1990) Don't worry: We'll grow out of it, *Economic Commentary*, FRB Cleveland

Burluwar, Murli, Henry Thompson, and Kamal Upadhyaya (1996) Devaluation and the trade balance in India: Stationarity and cointegration, *Applied Economics*

Caprio, Gerard & Patrick Honohan (1999) Restoring banking stability: Beyond supervised capital requirements, *Journal of Economic Perspectives*

Card, David (1990) The impact of the Mariel boatlift on the Miami labor market, *Industrial and Labor Relations Review*

Casas, Francisco & Kwan Choi (1985) The Leontief paradox: Continued or resolved? *Journal of Political Economy*

Cha, Baekin & Daniel Himarios (1995) The internationalization of the US wage process, *Review of International Economics*

Childs, Nathan & Michael Hammig (1987) An examination of the impact of real exchange rates on US exports of agricultural commodities, *The International Trade Journal*

Clerides, Sofronis (2005) Gains from trade in used goods: Evidence from the global market for automobiles, *CEPR Discussion Paper # 4859*

Cline, William (1997) *Trade and Income Distribution*, Washington: Institute for International Economics

Cole, Harold & Lee Ohanian (1999) The Great Depression in the United States from a neoclassical perspective, *Quarterly Review*, FRB of Minneapolis

Crowder, William (1996) A reexamination of long run PPP: The case of Canada, the UK, and the US, *Review of International Economics*

Davis, Donald & David Weinstein (1995) Intra-industry trade: A Heckscher-Ohlin Ricardo Approach, *Journal of International Economics*

Davis, Donald & David Weinstein (1998) Economic geography and regional production structure: An empirical investigation, *Federal Reserve Bank of New York Staff Reports, #40*

Deardorff, Alan & Robert Stern (1984) The economic effect of complete elimination of post-Tokyo Round tariffs. In *Trade Policy for the 1980s*, William Cline, ed., Washington: Institute for International Economics

DeLong, Bradford & Larry Summers (1990) Equipment, investment and economic growth, *NBER Working Paper #3513*

Dinopoulos, Elias & Mordechai Kreinin (1988) Effects of the US-Japan auto VER on European prices and on US welfare, *The Review of Economics and Statistics*

Dollar, David & Edward Wolff (1988) Convergence of industry labor productivity among advanced economies, 1963–1982, *The Review of Economics and Statistics*

Dollar, David & Edward Wolff (1993) *Competitiveness, Convergence, and International Specialization*, Cambridge: MIT Press

Eckels, Alfred (1998) Smoot-Hawley and the stock market crash, 1929–1930, *The International Trade Journal*

Edwards, Sebastian (1999) How effective are capital controls? *Journal of Economic Perspectives*

Eichengreen, Barry (1991) Historical research on international lending and debt, *Journal of Economic Perspectives*

Eichengreen, Barry (1999) *Toward a New International Financial Architecture: A Practical Post-Asia Agenda*, Washington: Institute for International Economics

Engel, Charles (1999) Are we globalized yet? *Economic Letter*, FRB San Francisco

Engel, Charles & John Rogers (1994) How wide is the US border? *NBER Working Paper #4829*

Falzoni, Anna, Giovanni Brunno, & Rosario Crino (2004) Foreign Direct Investment, Wage Inequality, and Skilled Labor Demand in EU Accession Countries, *Centro Studi Luca d'Agliano Development Studies Working Paper #188*

Fang, Wenshwo, Yihao Lai, & Henry Thompson (2005) Exchange rates, exchange risk, and Asian export revenue, *International Review of Economics & Finance*

Feenstra, Robert (1988) Quality change under trade restrictions in Japanese autos, *The Quarterly Journal of Economic*

Feenstra, Robert & Gordon Hanson (1997) Direct foreign investment and relative wages: Evidence from Mexico's Maquiladoras, *Journal of International Economics*

Feenstra, Robert & Gordon Hanson (1999) The Impact of outsourcing and high-technology capital on wages: Estimates for the United States, 1979–1990, *Quarterly Journal of Economics*

Fischer, Stanley (1999) On the need for an international lender of last resort, *Journal of Economic Perspectives*

Ford, Jon & Henry Thompson (1997) Global sensitivity of neoclassical and factor proportions models to production technology, *International Economic Journal*

Francis, John & Henry Thompson (2009) Tariff elimination and the wage gap in an industrial specific factors model, *Review of International Economics*

Frenkel, Jeffrey & Kenneth Froot (1990) Exchange rate forecasting techniques, survey data, and implications for the foreign exchange market, *NBER Working Paper #3470*

Froot, Kenneth & Jeremy Stein (1991) Exchange rates and foreign direct investment: An imperfect capital markets approach, *Quarterly Journal of Economics*

Froot, Kenneth & Kenneth Rogoff (1995) Perspectives on PPP and long-run real exchange rates, Chapter 32 in *Handbook of International Economics*

Garten, Jeffrey (1998) In this economic chaos, a global central bank can help, *International Herald Tribune*, 25 September

Gartner, Bruce (1987) Causes of US farm commodity programs, *Journal of Political Economy*

Glesjer, Herbert, K. Goosens, & J. vanden Eede (1982) Inter-industry versus intra-industry specialization in exports and imports, *Journal of International Economics*

Goldberg, Linda & Keith Crockett (1998) The dollar and US manufacturing, *Current Issues in Economics and Finance*, FRB of New York

Goldberg, Linda & Michael Klein (1999) International trade and factor mobility: An empirical investigation, *Staff Reports*, #81, FRB New York

Golub, Stephen (1995) Comparative and absolute advantage in the Asia Pacific region, Working paper, FRB San Francisco

Griffen, James & David Teece (1982) *OPEC Behavior and World Oil Prices*, London: Allen & Unwin

Grilli, Vittrio & Andrea Beltratti (1989) US military expenditure and the dollar, *Economic Inquiry*

Grossman, Gene & Jim Levinshon (1989) Import competition and the stock market return to capital, *American Economic Review*

Grubel, Herbert & Peter Lloyd (1975) *Intraindustry Trade*, London: MacMillan

Gruben, William & Sherry Kiser (1999) Hey, Mr. Greenspan, can you spare a dollar? *Southwest Economy*, Dallas Federal Reserve Bank

Gylfason, Thorvaldur (2004) Natural resources and economic growth: From dependence to diversification, *CEPR Discussion Paper*

Hakkio, Graig & Douglas Pearce (1985) The reaction of exchange rates to economic news, *Economic Inquiry*

Hanson, Gordon (1998) Regional adjustment to trade liberalization, *Regional Science and Urban Economics*, 419-44

Hansen, Wendy & Thomas Prusa (1997) The economics and politics of trade policy: An empirical analysis of ITC decision making, *Review of International Economics*

Harris, James & Michael Todaro (1970) Migration, unemployment and development: A two-sector analysis, *American Economic Review*

Haskel, Jonathan & Matthew Slaughter (2002) Does the sector bias of skill-biased technical change explain changing skill premia? *European Economic Review*

Hickok, Susan (1985) The consumer cost of US trade restraints, *Quarterly Review*, FRB New York

Hickok, Susan & James Orr (1989) Shifting patterns of US trade with selected developing Asian economies, *Quarterly Review*, FRB New York

Himarios, Daniel (1987) Devaluation, devaluation expectations and price dynamics, *Economica*

Huber, Richard (1971) Effect on prices of Japan's entry into world commerce after 1858, *Journal of Political Economy*

Hufbauer, Gary, Diane Berliner, & Kimberly Elliott (1986) *Trade Protection in the United States: 31 Case Studies*, Washington: Institute for International Economics

Hunter, Linda (1990) US trade protection: Effects on the regional composition of employment, *Economic Review*, FRB Dallas

Hunter, Linda & James Markusen (1988) Per-capita income as a determinant of trade, Robert Feenstra ed., *Empirical Methods for International Economics*, Cambridge: MIT Press

Irwin, Douglas (1988) Did late nineteenth century US tariffs promote infant industries? Evidence from the tinplate industry, *NBER Working Paper #6835*

Jevons, Stanley (1865) *The Coal Question*, London: Macmillian

Karrenbrock, Jeffrey (1990) The internationalization of the beer brewing industry, *Review*, FRB St Louis

Kasa, Kenneth (1997) Understanding trends in foreign exchange rates, *Weekly Letter*, FRB San Francisco

Kaufman, Henry (1998) Preventing the next global financial crisis, *Washington Post*, 28 January

Kelly, Kenneth & Morris Morker (1998) Do unfairly traded imports injure domestic industries? *Review of International Economics*

Knetter, Michael (1989) Price discrimination by US and German exporters, *American Economic Review*

Kouparitsas, Michael (1997) A dynamic macroeconomic analysis of NAFTA, *Economic Perspectives*, FRB of Chicago

Kreinin, Mordechai (1984) Wage competitiveness in steel and motor vehicles, *Economic Inquiry*

Kreinin, Mordechai (1985) United States trade and possible restrictions in high-technology products, *Journal of Policy Modelling*

Krugman, Paul (1987) Is free trade passé? *Economic Perspectives*

Krugman, Paul (1998) Saving Asia: It's time to get radical, *Fortune*, 7 September

Leamer, Ed (1980) The Leontief paradox reconsidered, *Journal of Political Economy*

Leamer, Ed (1984) *Sources of International Comparative Advantage: Theory and Evidence*, Cambridge: MIT Press

Lee, Jong Wha (1994) Capital goods imports and long run growth, *NBER Working Paper #4725*

Lee, Jong Wha & Phillip Swagel (1994) Trade barriers and trade flows across countries and industries, *NBER Working Paper #4799*

Leontief, Wassily (1953) Domestic production and foreign trade: The American capital position re-examined, *Proceedings of the American Philosophical Society*

Lewis, Ethan (2004) How did the Miami labor market absorb the Mariel immigrants? *FRB Philadelphia Working Paper 04-3*

Lipsey, Robert (2000) The role of foreign direct investment in international capital flows, *NBER Working Paper #7094*

Lucas, Robert (2004) Lectures on Economic Growth, Harvard University Press

MacDougall, Donald (1952) British and American exports: A study suggested by the theory of comparative costs, *Economic Journal 62*

Maneschi, Andrea (1992) Ricardo's international trade theory: Beyond the comparative cost example, *Cambridge Journal of Economics*

Marjit, Sugata (1994) The fallacy of free trade: Comment, *Review of International Economics*

Markusen, James & Randall Wigle (1989) Nash equilibrium tariffs for the United States and Canada: The roles of country size, scale economies, and capital mobility, *The Journal of Political Economy*

Marshall, Alfred (1926) *The Official Papers of Alfred Marshall*, London: McMillan

Marston, Richard (1998) Pricing to market in Japanese manufacturing, *Journal of International Economics*

Maskus, Keith (1985) A test of the Heckscher-Ohlin-Vanek theorem: The Leontief commonplace, *Journal of International Economics*

Maskus, Keith & Mohan Penubati (1995) How trade-related are intellectual property rights? *Journal of International Economics*

McCallum, Bennet (1989) Targets, indicators, and instruments of monetary policy, *NBER Working Paper #3234*

Mishkin, Frederic (1999) Global financial instability: Framework, events, issues, *Journal of Economic Perspectives*

Moran, Theodore, Edward Graham, & Magnus Blomström (2005) *Foreign Direct Investment Promote Development?* Washington: Institute for International Economics

Panagariya, Arvind, Shekhar Shah, & Deepak Mishra (2001) Demand elasticities in international trade: Are they really low? *Journal of Development Economics*

Polachek, Solomon (1997) Why democracies cooperated more and fight less: The relationship between international trade and cooperation, *Review of International Economics*

Rassekh, Farhad (1992) The role of international trade in the convergence of per capita GDP in the OECD: 1950–1985, *International Economic Journal*

Rassekh, Farhad (1994) An evaluation of Batra's "Fallacy of free trade" *Review of International Economics*

Rassekh, Farhad & Henry Thompson (1993) Factor price equalization: Theory and evidence, *Journal of Economic Integration*

Rassekh, Farhad & Henry Thompson (1997) Adjustment in general equilibrium: Some industrial evidence, *Review of International Economics*

Rassekh, Farhad & Henry Thompson (1998) Micro convergence and macro convergence: Factor price equalization and per capita income, *Pacific Economic Review*

Ray, Ed (1991) Foreign takeovers and new investments in the US, *Contemporary Policy Issues*

Reinert, Kenneth & David Roland-Holst (1998) North-south trade and occupational wages: Some evidence from North America, *Review of International Economics*

Revenga, Ana (1992) Exporting jobs? The impact of import competition on employment and wages in US manufacturing, *The Quarterly Journal of Economics*, 255-84

Reynolds, Clark and Robert McLeery (1988) The political economy of immigration law: Impact of Simpson-Rodino on the United States and Mexico, *Journal of Economic Perspectives*

Richardson, David & Chi Zhang (1999) Revealing comparative advantage: Chaotic or coherent patterns across time and sector and U.S. trading partner? *NBER Working Paper #7212*

Rogoff, Kenneth (1999) International institutions for reducing global financial instability, *Journal of Economic Perspectives*

Romer, Paul (1994) New goods, old theory, and the welfare costs of trade restrictions, *Journal of Development Economics*

Rousslang, Donald & Theodore To (1993) Domestic trade and transport costs as barriers to international trade, *Canadian Journal of Economics*

Ruffin, Roy (1988) The missing link: The Ricardian approach to the factor endowments theory of trade, *American Economic Review*

Ruffin, Roy & Farhad Rassekh (1987) The role of foreign direct investment in US capital outflows, *American Economic Review*

Sachs, Jeffrey (1995) Do we need an international lender of last resort? Princeton University, Frank Graham Memorial Lecture

Schott, Peter (2004) Across-product versus within-product specialization in international trade, *Quarterly Journal of Economics*

Seshan, Ganesh (2005) The impact of trade liberalization on household qelfare in Vietnam, *World Bank Policy Research Working Paper # 3541*

Shapiro, Matthew (1987) Are cyclical fluctuations in productivity due more to supply shocks or demand shocks? *NBER Working Paper #2147*

Smith, Alasdair & Anthony Venables (1988) Completing the internal market in the European community, *European Economic Review*

Stern, Robert & Keith Maskus (1981) Determinants of the structure of US foreign trade, *Journal of International Economics*

Stiglitz, Joseph (1997) Dumping on free trade: The US import trade laws, *Southern Economic Journal*

Sweeney, George, T. Randolph Beard, & Henry Thompson (1997) Quotas and quality in international trade, *Journal of Economic Integration*

Tarr, David & Morris Morkre (1987) Aggregate costs to the United States of tariffs and quotas on imports, in *The New Protectionist Threat to World Welfare*, Dominick Salvatore ed., Amsterdam: North-Holland

Thompson, Henry (1986) Free trade and factor price polarization, *European Economic Review*

Thompson, Henry (1987) Do tariffs protect specific factors? *Canadian Journal of Economics*

Thompson, Henry (1991) Simulating a multifactor general equilibrium model of production and trade, *International Economic Journal*

Thompson, Henry (1994a) An investigation of the quantitative properties of the specific factors model of production and trade, *Japan and the World Economy*

Thompson, Henry (1994b) NAFTA and industrial adjustment: A specific factors model of production in Alabama, *Growth and Change*

Thompson, Henry (1995a) Factor intensity versus factor substitution in a specified general equilibrium model, *Journal of Economic Integration*

Thompson, Henry (1995b) Free trade and income redistribution in some developing and newly industrialized countries, *Open Economies Review*

Thompson, Henry (2001) International trade with three factors, goods, or countries, *Keio Economic Studies*

Thompson, Henry & Kamal Upadhyaya (1998) The impact of the exchange rate on local industry, *Economia Internazionale*

Toledo, Hugo (2005) Coca substitution and free trade in Bolivia: The pending crisis, *Review of Economic Development*

Toledo, Hugo & Henry Thompson (2001) Bolivia and South American free trade, *The International Trade Journal*

Trela, Irene & John Whalley (1995) Internal quota-allocation schemes and the costs of the MFA, *Review of International Economics*

Wacziarg, Romain & Jessica Wallack (2004) Trade liberalization and intersectoral labor movements, *Journal of International Economics*, 411-39

Wall, Howard (1999) Using the gravity model to estimate the costs of protection, *Review*, FRB St. Louis

Walter, Ingo (1983) Structural adjustment and trade policy in the international steel industry, in *Trade Policy in the 1980s*, William Cline ed., Washington: Institute for International Economics

Weidenbaum, Murray & Tracy Munger (1983) Protection at any price? *Regulation*, July

Wickham, Elizabeth & Henry Thompson (1989) An empirical analysis of intraindustry trade and multinational firms, in *Intraindustry Trade: Theory, Evidence, and Extensions, ed. Peter Tharakan*

Williamson, Jeffrey (1996) Globalization, convergence, and history, *Journal of Economic History*

Wong, Kar-yiu (1995) *International Trade in Goods and Factor Mobility*, MIT Press

Xu, Zhenhui (1996) On the causality between export growth and GDP growth: An empirical reinvestigation, *Review of International Economics*

Xu, Zhenhui (2000) Effects of primary exports on industrial exports and GDP: Empirical evidence, *Review of Development Economics*, 307-25

Index

Printed in the USA
CPSIA information can be obtained
at www.ICGtesting.com
JSHW050850190324
59341JS00002B/3